Guardians of the Revolution

The Council on Foreign Relations (CFR) is an independent, nonpartisan membership organization, think tank, and publisher dedicated to being a resource for its members, government officials, business executives, journalists, educators and students, civic and religious leaders, and other interested citizens in order to help them better understand the world and the foreign policy choices facing the United States and other countries. Founded in 1921, CFR carries out its mission by maintaining a diverse membership, with special programs to promote interest and develop expertise in the next generation of foreign policy leaders; convening meetings at its headquarters in New York and in Washington, DC, and other cities where senior government officials, members of Congress, global leaders, and prominent thinkers come together with CFR members to discuss and debate major international issues; supporting a Studies Program that fosters independent research, enabling CFR scholars to produce articles, reports, and books and hold roundtables that analyze foreign policy issues and make concrete policy recommendations; publishing *Foreign Affairs*, the preeminent journal on international affairs and U.S. foreign policy; sponsoring Independent Task Forces that produce reports with both findings and policy prescriptions on the most important foreign policy topics; and providing up-to-date information and analysis about world events and American foreign policy on its website, www.cfr.org.

Guardians
of the Revolution

Iran and the World in the Age
of the Ayatollahs

RAY TAKEYH

A Council on Foreign Relations Book

OXFORD
UNIVERSITY PRESS

OXFORD

UNIVERSITY PRESS

Oxford University Press, Inc., publishes works that further
Oxford University's objective of excellence
in research, scholarship, and education.

Oxford New York
Auckland Cape Town Dar es Salaam Hong Kong Karachi
Kuala Lumpur Madrid Melbourne Mexico City Nairobi
New Delhi Shanghai Taipei Toronto

With offices in
Argentina Austria Brazil Chile Czech Republic France Greece
Guatemala Hungary Italy Japan Poland Portugal Singapore
South Korea Switzerland Thailand Turkey Ukraine Vietnam

Published by Oxford University Press, Inc.
198 Madison Avenue, New York, New York 10016

www.oup.com

First published as an Oxford University Press paperback in 2011

Oxford is a registered trademark of Oxford University Press

Library of Congress Cataloging-in-Publication Data
Takeyh, Ray, 1966–
Guardians of the revolution : Iran and the world
in the age of the Ayatollahs / Ray Takeyh.
p. cm.
Includes bibliographical references and index.
ISBN 978-0-19-532784-7 (Hbk); 978-0-19-975410-6 (Pbk)
1. Iran—Foreign relations—1979–1997. 2. Iran—Foreign relations—1997–
3. Iran—Politics and government—1979–1997. 4. Iran—Politics and government—1997–
I. Title.
DS318.83.T36 2009
327.55—dc22 2008045035

1 3 5 7 9 8 6 4 2
Printed in the United States of America
on acid-free paper

To Nick

Contents

PART III. THE AGE OF REFORM

PART IV. HEGEMONY AT LAST?

Acknowledgments

WRITING A BOOK CAN BE A DIFFICULT AND TAXING PROCESS. As such, I am grateful to the Council on Foreign Relations for providing me with a remarkable place in which to work. The Council's president, Richard Haass, and the director of studies, Gary Samore, have been a source of support and countless constructive suggestions about how to improve this book.

A number of colleagues and friends read through the manuscript with care and offered important comments. Ruhollah Ramazani, the dean of Iran's foreign policy study, was an early and enthusiastic supporter of this project and proved generous with both his time and patience. As always, Ervand Abrahamian bravely went through the entire manuscript and kindly entertained my numerous queries of requests. Farideh Farhi and Vali Nasr similarly shared with me their many useful suggestions that did much to improve this book. I am grateful to Houchang Chehabi for providing me some rare Persian sources from his own collection that would be nearly impossible to track down in the United States.

Through researching this book I spent some time at the Library of Congress and its meticulously maintained Persian language collection. It is to the credit of the entire staff, particularly Hirad Dinavari, that the Library is such an impressive depository. Hirad went beyond the call of duty and assisted me with the process of transliteration, whose complexities I have never been able to properly master.

This book could not have been completed without the generous support of the Carnegie Corporation of New York. Under the imaginative leadership of Vartan Gregorian and Stephen Del Rosso, the Carnegie Corporation has done much to advance the study of international relations.

A number of my friends at the Council on Foreign relations deserve special mention. Steven Simon, Charles Kupchan, Steven Cook, Peter Beinart, Charles Ferguson, and James Goldgeier have proven generous with both their time and ideas. All of them cheerfully tolerated the fact that I routinely spent many hours in their offices. My time at the Council has been much richer and vibrant due to the presence of these individuals.

My agent Larry Weissman reposed his role as advisor and counselor as he good-naturedly worked with me to conceptualize and develop this project. David McBride proved a remarkable editor. With his easygoing manner and careful eye for detail, he frequently rescued this book from traps and pitfalls that too easily eluded me.

As always, I owe much to Suzanne and Alex as well as our most recent arrival, Nick.

Guardians of the Revolution

Introduction

Through the Looking Glass: Iran's Approach to the World

"THE LATE IMAM WAS THE GREATEST POLITICAL AND MILITARY analyst and a great politician. Imam Khomeini was the best possible pattern for all people in all ages and eras," declared President Mahmoud Ahmadinejad in 2008.[1] It is rare for a revolutionary leader to exercise such influence over the imagination of his successors two decades after his passing. However, Ayatollah Ruhollah Khomeini was no ordinary leader, as his vision and words continue to resonate with generations of Iranian politicians. All of this raises the following questions: What kind of a state is the Islamic Republic of Iran? Is it still a revolutionary regime bent on upending the prevailing order, or is it prepared to accommodate the mandates of the international community? The truth lies somewhere in between. More than any other Middle Eastern country, Iran defies easy characterization. The best way of understanding the Islamic Republic's priorities is to expand the canvass and assess its foreign policy over the entire duration of its existence. Only through such an exercise can we come to terms with the complexities and contradictions that have shaped Iran's approach to the world.

Iran is an intact, ancient nation that has sought for centuries to define its place in the Middle East. Successive dynasties perceived that by virtue of its advanced civilization, location, and demography Iran had the right to dominate the region. The notion that Iran's hegemonic claims began with the revolution is a misreading of history. The shahs were just as adamant about pursuing Iran's national aspirations as the mullahs who displaced the monarchy. To the hubris of preeminence one must add the insecurity of isolation. As a Persian, Shiite nation struggling in an Arab, Sunni Middle

East, Iran has always lived with the fear of being surrounded by foes. A country that has been the subject of numerous invasions and whose boundaries have shrunk over the centuries is legitimately suspicious of both its neighbors and the Western empires that have coveted its land and resources. Paradoxically, Iran's international orientation has historically been shaped by a presumption of greatness, an undiminished sense of superiority over its neighbors, and an acute concern about foreigners' intentions.

It is this national character that the clerical rulers inherited. To this sense of nationalism and historical grievances, the mullahs added an Islamist dimension. Ayatollah Khomeini bequeathed his country an ideology that divided the world between the oppressed and the oppressors. The Islamic Republic was to be a vanguard state leading the subjugated masses toward freedom and justice. Such views stemmed from Shiite political traditions that enshrined the principle of resisting tyranny. In clerical cosmology, Iran was no ordinary state seeking to maximize its advantages though a subtle projection of its power. The Islamic Republic had a transnational mission of redeeming the Middle East for the forces of righteousness. Despite its costs and burdens, Iran would have to struggle against a range of iniquitous forces, particularly the United States and its proxies.

No country can persist on ideology alone. Iran had to operate its economy, deal with regional exigencies, and meet the demand of its growing constituency. The task of governance saps revolutionary energies as it requires routine concessions to an often unpalatable reality. Pragmatism and a careful calibration of national interests would thus enter Iran's foreign policy calculus. The clerical rulers would transact agreements with their rivals, compromise with their enemies, and occasionally seek to diminish the hard edges of their creed. However, the Islamic Republic would not follow the model of a typical revolutionary state and gradually discard its ideological legacy. The genius of Khomeini was his ability to weave his dogma into the theocracy's governing fabric. Through the constitutional arrangements that he crafted and a dedicated cadre that he molded, Khomeini ensured the survival of his vision. In this sense, Khomeini remains one of the most successful revolutionary leaders of the twentieth century. The uneasy balance between ideological compunctions and pragmatic designs would come to define Iran's international perspective. This would often yield a contradictory policy as Iran sought to realize its objectives in a regional order that it pledged to overthrow.

The 1980s would be the apogee of revolutionary activism. Khomeini had assumed power not to focus on the mundane tasks of economic development and diplomatic outreach but to assert his dogmatic philosophy. This was to be a "revolution without borders," as Iran flailed around the Middle East seeking to impose its Islamist template on an unwilling Arab world. The Gulf princely class with its ostentatious lifestyle, false piety, and close ties to the United States greatly offended the clerical rulers. Iran would plot their ouster through assassination campaigns, thereby provoking Shiite secessionism and subsidizing opposition forces and terrorists with little or no political agenda. Nor did Iran's ideological crusade stop at the edges of the Persian Gulf, because the incumbent Sunni regimes of the Arab east and North Africa proved as unacceptable to the mullahs as their Gulf counterparts. Islamist militants in places as varied as Algeria and Lebanon would now become beneficiaries of Iranian largesse. Perhaps no country felt the ire of the theocracy more than Israel. The Islamic Republic not only embraced the Palestinian cause but openly called for the annihilation of the Jewish state. This was a time when Iran's internal convulsions defined its international relations.

Despite Iran's revolutionary excesses, it was Saddam Husayn's opportunism that launched one of the most devastating conflicts in the modern Middle East. Far from dislodging the theocracy or diminishing its zeal, the war that began a year after the revolution only reinforced Iran's radical tendencies. For Khomeini, the war was not a mere interstate conflict but an epic battle between infidels and the forces of virtue. Iran seldom defined its war aims in conventional terms of regaining lost territory or securing reparations. In its propaganda and proclamations, the theocratic regime stressed that the war was an opportunity for Iran to demonstrate its religious devotion. Long after a crestfallen Saddam was prepared to acquiesce to an armistice, Khomeini prolonged the conflict that was to reclaim the Middle East for the path of God.

The pragmatic impulses of Iranian foreign policy were seldom in evidence during the turbulent first decade of the revolution. By the end of his tenure, Khomeini had created a beleaguered state at odds with much of the international community. The goal of exporting the revolution eluded Khomeini inasmuch as the region rejected his theocratic model of governance. Despite his determination to dominate the Middle East, Khomeini left Iran an isolated pariah.

It would not be until the end of the war and the passing of Khomeini in 1989 that his successors took stock of the revolution. Importantly, the clerical leaders did not revisit the assumption that Iran had a right to dominate the region. The critical debate was whether Iran should export the revolution or try to realize its objectives within the existing state system.

Would the Islamic Republic remain a revolutionary state or become just another imperial power?

It was at that juncture that factionalism emerged as a real source of division within the theocracy. On the one side, a more pragmatic bloc led by President Ali Akbar Hashemi Rafsanjani appreciated the fact that, in the absence of Khomeini's charismatic authority and the unifying symbol of the war, the Islamic Republic had to offer a practical justification for the continuation of its rule. Moreover, the requirements of economic reconstruction and national rehabilitation demanded a more normal relationship with the international community. The new supreme leader, Ali Khamenei, would lead the hard-line elements who maintained their devotion to the essential pillars of Khomeini's vision. The tensions and compromises between these two factions eventually produced a contradictory foreign policy that, while recognizing the importance of moderation, could not entirely divest itself of the revolutionary imperatives of its founder.

The divided clerical regime had to chart its foreign policy at a time of sweeping global changes. The collapse of the Soviet Union and Saddam's invasion of Kuwait perplexed Tehran. America now entered Iran's neighborhood largely unencumbered by the restraints of the cold war. The issue of how to deal with the United States would provoke the greatest disagreement within Iran. While Rafsanjani and his allies appreciated the need for a more constructive approach to the world's sole superpower, for the conservatives, America remained not just a strategic threat but also a cultural challenge that could erode the foundations of theocratic rule. Given their institutional power, the hard-liners easily thwarted any opening to the United States that Rafsanjani may have contemplated.

All of this is not to suggest that Iran's policy remained static; indeed, the theocracy's contending factions were capable of coming to an agreement on certain critical issues. Iran did behave responsibly during the Gulf War, and Tehran did seek to mend fences with the both the European Community and the emirates. Despite such rational calculations, the pull of ideology continued to obstruct Tehran's path toward realism. Iran continued to challenge the legitimacy of the Gulf sheikdoms and yielded too easily to terrorism as an expression of its policy. The assassination of dissidents in Europe and continued support for radical forces throughout the Middle East undercut Iran's promise of moderation.

In the end, Rafsanjani's term proved to be an era of uncertain pragmatism. Beyond the obstructionism of the Right, it was Rafsanjani's own tentativeness that precluded a fundamental departure from the past. Despite his promises, Rafsanjani recoiled from challenging the hard-liners and pressing ahead with his program of change. Confronted with a conservative backlash, he quickly retreated and abandoned both his principles and his allies along the way. Rafsanjani may have pledged a new dawn, but by the time he left office his country was isolated in its neighborhood, estranged from its European commercial partners, and at loggerheads with the United States.

No aspect of the Islamic Republic's history is in need of a greater revision than the presidency of Muhammad Khatami, which lasted from 1997 to 2005. Although it is customary to deride Khatami as lacking any successes, in the realm of international relations his achievements proved momentous. The essence of the reform movement was that democratic accountability at home mandated a foreign policy that respected prevailing conventions. The "Dialogue among Civilizations" was not a mere slogan but a sincere belief that détente and cooperation were the best means of advancing Iran's practical interests. Khatami would also launch his "Good Neighbor" policy, which sought to repair relations with the Gulf states by acknowledging the legitimacy of their rule. Furthermore, during this time Iran finally achieved a rapprochement with Saudi Arabia and reclaimed its ties with the European Union. For a brief moment, it appeared that Iran was finally willing to relinquish its revolutionary past and join the community of nations.

The impressive aspect of Khatami's presidency was that his accomplishments came despite conservative resistance and American hostility. The hard-liners, devoted to their ideological verities and in command of key agencies of the state, did much to subvert Khatami's moderation. In the meantime, unaccustomed to real change in Iran, a flat-footed Washington failed to comprehend the scope of Khatami's promise and sustained its policy of sanctions and isolation long after it proved counterproductive. A more imaginative U.S. policy might have tipped the internal balance of power in favor of the reformers.

The 9/11 tragedies and the nuclear crisis did much to resurrect the fortunes of the hard-liners. The Bush administration's unrelenting hostility toward Iran allowed the conservatives to denigrate the reformers for allegedly enabling U.S. plots. In the meantime, once the international community chose to deal with Iran's nuclear infractions through sanctions and pressure, it further empowered the conservatives, who thrived on confrontation. An exhausted reform movement, besieged by its domestic detractors and American animus, would cede to a hard-line government.

As the face of Iran changed and the elders of the revolution receded from the scene, a new international orientation gradually surfaced. A combustible mixture of Islamist ideology, strident nationalism, and a deep suspicion of the West compose the global perspective of President Mahmoud Ahmadinejad and the younger conservatives. As uncompromising nationalists, they are unusually sensitive to Iran's prerogatives and sovereign rights. As committed Islamists, they continued to see the Middle East as a battleground between forces of secularism and Islamic authenticity. As suspicious rulers, they perceive Western conspiracies where none may in fact exist.

The rise of the New Right in Iran coincided with important changes in the Middle East. As the Iraq war drains America's power and confidence, and as Islamist parties in Lebanon and the Palestinian territories claim the mantle of leadership, Iran has emerged as a pivotal power within the region. The goal of dominance and hegemony that eluded previous Persian rulers seems fortuitously within grasp. Tehran's determination to sustain its nuclear program, its quest to evict U.S. forces from Iraq, and its holding aloft the banner of resistance against Israel are all means of asserting its regional influence. The old balance between ideology and pragmatism has yielded to one defined by power politics and religious fervor. In the early twenty-first century, Iran finally has a government that Khomeini could be proud of.

Although the primary focus of this book is on Iran's foreign policy, no such study can exempt itself from an assessment of its domestic politics and rivalries. This book is divided into four broad sections that conform to a timeline. The first segment assesses the tumultuous 1980s and the imprint that early debates made on Iran's international orientation. The rise of a theocratic state, its momentous war with Iraq, and its enduring enmity toward the United States and Israel are dealt with in detail. The 1980s remain the Islamic Republic's most important decade, as the ideology that was molded during this period and the experiences of the war continue to have an immeasurable impact on Iran's global perspective.

The second section of this book explores the reasons Rafsanjani failed to usher in a pragmatic international policy. The theocratic regime understood that the demands of postwar reconstruction and the mandates of its restive citizenry required a different approach to the world. Yet such recognition did not translate into constructive policies across the board. The irony is that a cagey president who sensed the need for change ended up overseeing an isolated country.

The reform movement remains one of the most intellectually ambitious forces for social and political change in modern Iran. The unnecessarily maligned President Khatami and his allies sought to achieve a new form of government—an Islamic democracy. A state that balanced plural-istic demands with its religious ideals may have eluded the reformers, but the discourse and deliberations of that period are bound to condition sim-ilar efforts in both Iran and the greater Middle East in the future. In this segment of the book, the notion that the reformist government was with-out accomplishments is challenged, and its foreign policy achievements are more carefully assessed.

The task of the next section of the book is to move beyond rhetoric and examine the ways in which Iran's foreign policy has actually changed during the tenure of Mahmoud Ahmadinejad. Iran has been offered unprecedented opportunities as its principal American nemesis finds itself unsure how to proceed in the Middle East, while its oil wealth has provided it with sufficient revenues to offset Western financial pressures. Iran's Shiite allies are poised to assume political power in the key states of Iraq and Lebanon, while much of the region is seeking to accommodate rather than confront Iranian power. The question then becomes, how have Ahmadinejad and the hard-liners used these advantages to enhance Iran's national interests?

In the concluding chapter, we look ahead. Iran has entered the twenty-first century with a strong, centralized state, ample natural resources, and capable armed forces. Given the changes that the region has undergone since 9/11, it is poised to assume a commanding role in the Middle East. The key challenge for the United States is to ascertain how to deal with a state that is too powerful to ignore and whose influence cannot be easily contained. The strategies and decisions that Washington makes will deter-mine whether this dangerous neighborhood can find a modicum of stability.

This book conforms to the prevailing standards of transliteration. However, at times, popular usage of names and places has been retained given their familiarity to the general reader.

PART I

The Revolutionary Years

1

Khomeini's Ideology and Iran's Grand Strategy

O N JUNE 6, 1989, THE FOUNDER OF THE ISLAMIC REPUBLIC, Ayatollah Ruhollah Khomeini, passed away. The announcement of his death was greeted with mass demonstrations and a remarkable display of grief and passion throughout the country. However, nearly two decades after his death, Khomeini remains one of the central figures in Iran's political narrative. By creating a web of institutions and nurturing a dedicated corps of disciples, the enterprising cleric has managed to implant his vision in Iran's social fabric. The remarkable aspect of Khomeini's tenure was not just his novel reinterpretation of Shiite political theory or his ushering in of a populist revolution but also conceiving an organizational structure that would perpetuate his ideas long after his death. In essence, of all the twentieth-century revolutionaries, Khomeini would emerge as the most successful, as the Islamic Republic sustains its allegiance to his core principles and all of its contending factions continue to justify their conduct by appealing to his message and legacy.

An assessment of the Islamic Republic's foreign policy cannot be done without an appreciation of Khomeini's ideological improvisations and the changes that he induced in Iran's international orientation. The most suitable way to begin the study of Iran's foreign policy is to examine Khomeini's ideals, aspirations, and perceptions of the world beyond the seminary.

Khomeini the Avenger

Ruhollah Khomeini was born in 1902, and during his lifetime he achieved momentous changes in the history of Iran and the greater Middle East. The rebellious cleric would displace a powerful monarchy, challenge the prevailing regional order, and confront the United States with one of its most acute strategic quandaries. Khomeini's success stemmed not just from his determination but also from his clever attempt to weave his revolutionary message into Iran's national identity. The notion that religion and traditional values should play a greater role in Iran's political and social order was a proposition acceptable to a vast majority of Iranians. This does not mean tolerating a theocratic regime with stringent Islamic strictures, but Khomeini nonetheless managed to craft his message as consistent with popular claims. The idea that Iran should emerge as the preeminent power of the Middle East was a priority of successive monarchs and empires that reigned over Persia for centuries. Once more, Khomeini succeeded in presenting his quest to export his Islamist revolution as in line with the nationalistic aspirations of both his predecessors and his subjects. To be sure, the Iranian masses would not be willing to pay the price of the revolution's excesses, yet in the initial stages, they found Khomeini's message of defiance and independence attractive.[1]

Although the common perception of Khomeini is of a stern, forbidding cleric whose imagination was frozen in time, he was a man of remarkable intellect and tactical dexterity.[2] He borrowed ideas from leftist ideologues, employed modern technologies to spread his message, and remained vague about his objectives when such ambiguity served his purpose.[3] In pursuit of his ideas, Khomeini was capable of extraordinary cruelty inasmuch as he remained largely indifferent to the sufferings of his people when it came to imposing his ideological template on an unwilling Middle East. The process of his political maturity, his uncanny ability to develop a revolutionary coalition, and his consolidation of power are critical if one is to understand the essence of the Islamic Republic and its perception of the international system.

Khomeini arrived in Qum in 1921 to find a clerical community so preoccupied with its rarified theological disquisitions that it paid scant attention to public affairs.[4] The insular nature of the clerical estate belied a country in political ferment. The rise of Reza Shah, the founder of the Pahlavi dynasty, and the continued interference of the great powers in Iran's internal affairs had provoked a nationalistic backlash. From early on Khomeini was intent on fusing religion and politics and quickly sought out the one seminary teacher, Mirza Muhammad Ali Shahabadi, who had spoken out against the misdeeds of Reza Shah. To further distinguish himself from his cohort, Khomeini undertook the study of philosophy and even mysticism, topics long abjured by a clerical class devoted to religious jurisprudence and Quranic commentary.[5]

Upon assuming his own lectureship, Khomeini turned his classes on ethics into a commentary on public affairs and criticisms of the regime's misbehaviors. The lectures given at the prestigious Madrasah-i Fayziyah-i Qum proved popular beyond the seminarians and attracted a wide-ranging audience. It was at this juncture that Khomeini developed a core of devoted disciples such as Murtaza Mutahhari and Ali Husayn Muntaziri, who would prove his loyal collaborators during his long political struggle.[6] However, even more significant was Khomeini's attempt to reach beyond the class of mullahs and appeal to a larger audience agitating against monarchical absolutism.

Despite his interest in politics, throughout the 1930s Khomeini found that his junior standing within the hierarchical clerical community and the overarching authority of Ayatollah Muhammad Husayn Burujirdi, who objected to mingling in temporal affairs, precluded sustained political engagement.[7] Only in the 1940s would Khomeini take a more assertive stance, demonstrating his lifelong focus on monarchical tyranny and foreign exploitation of Iran. In his first major publication, *Kashf-i Asrar,* he sought to refute various secular intellectuals who were claiming that Shiism had to reform and discard some of its rituals. However, in a subtle turn, Khomeini claimed that such an assault on tradition was made possible by Reza Shah's own attacks on religion as a source of backwardness. Nonetheless, at this stage Khomeini was not calling for the elimination of the monarchy but was merely claiming that the leading ayatollahs should choose a "monarch who will not violate God's laws and shun oppression and wrongdoing."[8] Still, the young Khomeini emphasized the primacy of Islamic jurisprudence and was dismissive of alternative forms of government. He was quick to stress that "other than their deceiving appearances, there is no fundamental distinction among constitutional, despotic, dictatorial, democratic and Communistic regimes."[9] Although far from his later call for direct assumption of power by clerics, he did imply that the monarchy should behave as an agent of the religious sector and that Islam should condition the political order and cultural norms.[10]

Khomeini's political commitment came more fully to the surface in the 1960s, as the passing of Grand Ayatollah Burjuridi and his own elevation as one of the leading figures of the religious establishment freed him from his previous constraints. Khomeini's turn to political affairs coincided with the emergence of anticolonial and nationalist movements that were sweeping the developing world. The traditional institutions' neglect of progressive causes and their frequent association with established authorities was alienating them from the younger generation of activists.

Khomeini lamented that "the irrational person has taken it for granted that religious people have trampled upon the rule of reason and have no regard for it. Is it not the religious people who have written all the books on philosophy and the principles of jurisprudence?"[11] He seemed anguished about the possibility that Islam might be displaced by fashionable ideologies of the West and the frequent irrelevance of the mosque in the emerging nationalist struggle.

The 1963–1964 crises offered Khomeini the perfect opportunity to claim the leadership of the anti-shah forces.[12] During the 1960s, the shah sought the concomitant secular modernization of Iran and a close alliance with the United States—two tendencies that Khomeini condemned. The measure that finally sparked the crisis was the shah's proposed legislation exempting the burgeoning U.S. military presence from Iranian law. Unlike his clerical brethren, Khomeini sensed that the vast majority of Iranians abhorred the legislation as a reenactment of the infamous "capitulation laws" frequently imposed by the Western powers on Iran. He appealed to the masses by claiming that the document attested that "the nation of Muslims is barbarous."[13] However, Khomeini quickly moved beyond Muslim sensibilities and stressed the notions of foreign exploitation at the hands of a pliant shah and a greedy capitalist class. The resulting massive demonstrations in 1964 were to presage the 1979 revolution as seminarians, the urban middle class, the bazaar, and leftist students agitated under the banner of Islam held aloft by an uncompromising Khomeini. The themes of religious grievance, nationalistic affront, and even class struggle now laced Khomeini's pronouncements as he attempted to reach a larger audience in a changing Iran.

The crisis of "capitulation laws" not only propelled Khomeini to the forefront of oppositional politics but also marked his departure from clerical norms and their propensity to compromise with the ruling monarchy. In an unmistakable rebuke to his fellow clerics, Khomeini declared, "I am not one of those who put on their turbans and are satisfied through worship only."[14] His evolving ideology with its denunciation of clerical passivity, the illegitimacy of imported ideologies, and the exploitive nature of the West had a limited audience within the clerical community. Ironically, it would be among a radical cadre of intellectuals such as Jalal Al Ahmad and Ali Shari'ati that Khomeini would find kindred spirits.[15] Many Western-trained Iranian intellectuals had grown weary of Marxism and socialism and were seeing Islam as an authentic, indigenous ideology of dissent. However, their Islam had a distinct political content. In their view, Prophet Muhammad was not just a spiritual leader but also a revolutionary who challenged vested interests, a reformer who rearranged the existing socio-economic order, and a man of faith who constructed a progressive society based on religion and reason. While greatly disparaged by elder clerics, the new intellectuals were reconceptualizing Islam as an ideology focused on class cleavages and division of the international system between capitalist powers and the larger developing bloc. To such thinkers, the traditional clergy with their indifference to social change were ossified agents of reaction.[16]

More than any of his counterparts, Khomeini sensed the popularity of these intellectuals among the youth and the modern middle class and realized that for the clerical estate to remain relevant it had to appropriate the discourse and ideas of the radicals.[17] Khomeini's speeches eschewed the predictable themes of sermons with their arcane religious imagery. The notions of Western exploitation of the Third World and the shah's tyranny, which was at the service of the predatory capitalist class, became the mainstay of his language. For both ideological and practical reasons, Khomeini was drawn to the musings of the new generation of political activists and their call for Islam as a symbol of resistance.

In invoking such leftist concepts, Khomeini incorporated new ideas into his ideological lexicon, adopting a critique of the prevailing order common among Marxists. The notion of *Mustaz'afin* (the downtrodden) as an oppressed economic class became one of his typical references. Yet despite his appreciation of the popularity of such intellectuals and the inclusion of their language in his presentations, Khomeini did not alter the essence of his vision. Islam as Khomeini interpreted it would have to remain the basis of any governing order. And although he was often at odds with many senior ayatollahs, he still perceived that clerics were the only ones capable of ushering in a new political system. By this time, Khomeini had developed a dedicated and growing number of young clerical followers who not only shared his views but would also remain his most intimate allies throughout the remainder of his career.

All of this did not save Khomeini. In fact, his role in the 1963–1964 uprisings led to his expulsion from Iran and his prolonged exile, which would take him to Turkey, Iraq, and France. Khomeini may have lost the initial battle with his monarchical nemesis, but he had established his message of defiance with its marriage of Islam and nationalism and conceived a nascent coalition of opposition that cut across class boundaries.

During his exile Khomeini finally completed his blueprint for Islamic governance. In Iraq, Khomeini's radicalism was further honed by the influences of the powerful and dynamic Shiite religious community. Under the charismatic leadership of Ayatollah Muhammad Baqir Sadr, the clerical order had become the epicenter of Shiite revivalism, with its quest to merge religious ardor with political militancy.[18] Moreover, Sadr's message of faith and his model of practical activism were gaining adherents in Shiite strongholds from Lebanon to the Persian Gulf. Khomeini stepped into this contested terrain with his own contribution and delivered a series of lectures that were published as a book, titled *Hukumat-i Islami* (Islamic Government). In this seminal work, Khomeini outlined his concept of *vilayat-i faqih* (guardianship of the jurist), which called for direct assumption of power by the clergy.

Since Islamic government is a government of law, those acquainted with the law (or more precisely, with religion)—the clergy—must oversee its functioning inasmuch as they supervise all of the country's executive and administrative affairs, as well as all of the planning.[19] The normative Shiite doctrine had stressed that power lies with the imams, the descendents of the Prophet. However, once the twelfth Imam went into occultation in 941, all temporal power was deemed illegitimate until his return, which would usher in the end of time. Although the need for order during the period of occultation made government a necessity, the clergy's proper role was nevertheless to divest themselves of political power with its temptations and corruption. This is not to suggest that national affairs should not be informed by religion but that the clergy must maintain a suitable distance from the ruling elite.[20] In a pronounced revision of Shiite canons and customs, Khomeini stressed that, given their superior knowledge of Islamic jurisprudence, the clergy were the only suitable rulers during the period of occultation. In a sense, the lectures were the predictable trajectory of his evolving thought process since the 1940s, which had come to see the clerics as natural leaders in a society undergoing continuous change.[21]

The publication of *Hukumat-i Islami*, with its call for direct rule by the clerics, was not only a revision of Shiite thought but also a denunciation of alternative political organizations, whether monarchical or republican forms of government. For all his flirtations with radical philosophies and appropriation of modern discourse, Khomeini firmly believed that Islam was the proper ideology and the clergy, appropriately radicalized, the only viable rulers. There would be limited room in Khomeini's conception of government for democratic accountability, checks and balances, and individual sovereignty. Islamic law and traditions may have required interpretation by an informed priestly class, but they did not need the mediation of representative bodies. The purpose of government would be the realization of God's will on earth, and any deviation from that constituted not just dissent but sin as well.

In one of the paradoxes of Khomeini's ideological revisions, his concept of rule by a jurist actually presented an attack on the prevailing clerical estate. Historically, the Shiite clerical class was marked by pluralism and diversity of views.[22] The grand ayatollahs sustained their own seminaries and pupils and preserved their autonomy in a decentralized order. Khomeini's idea of *vilayat-i faqih* vested political authority in a narrow circle of clerics, thereby mandating compliance by the entire community of mullahs.[23] Such compulsion would be enforced with discipline as the prosecution of disobedient clerics, even the unprecedented defrocking of grand ayatollahs, became an acceptable practice. It ultimately proved a futile struggle, however, as the ancient Shiite clerical establishment did not acquiesce easily to the dictates of a revolutionary mullah. In due time, Iran's religious sector would be divided between learned clerics who isolated themselves in shrine cities and activist mullahs who commanded bureaucracies and ministries. Nonetheless, the irony of Khomeini's Islamic Republic, which routinely criticized its monarchical predecessors for transgressing the sanctuary of the mosque, is that it is responsible for its own share of clerical persecutions.

During his exile, Khomeini not only undertook a radical reinterpretation of Shiite doctrines but also managed to forge a national opposition movement to the shah.[24] The oil wealth, massive corruption, close association with the United States, and his own megalomania caused the shah to behave in an erratic and dictatorial manner that gradually alienated much of his constituency. Although distant from Iran, Khomeini refused to remain a forgotten mullah preaching his sermons and contemplating theological tracts. He forged ties with student groups in Europe and America, maintained close connections to Iran through his clerical supporters, who disseminated his messages, and reached out to opposition figures from a wide variety of backgrounds. A stream of speeches denouncing the shah's excesses, protesting the inequalities of his economic modernization plans, and deprecating Iran's alliance with the United States made the imam, as his followers increasingly called him, the central figure in his country's political drama. Through his undisputed charisma, incorruptible nature, and adroit use of leftist and religious slogans, he appealed to the Iranian people's Islamic and nationalistic identities. As the revolution unfolded, all eyes were fixed on Khomeini as he became the acknowledged leader of a vast coalition of disaffected Iranians.

Given Khomeini's overarching ambition, it would be too facile to suggest that he ushered in the revolution only to displace the monarchy.

His Islamist musings had a distinct internationalist claim, as the aging mullah sought to change not just Iran but the entire Muslim world as well.

The Imam's Foreign Devils

Iran's Islamic Revolution and its inscrutable philosopher-king offered a unique challenge to the concept of nation-state and the prevailing norms of the international system. The essence of Khomeini's message was that the vitality of his Islamist mission was contingent on its relentless export. Moreover, because God's vision was not to be confined to a single nation, Iran's foreign policy would be an extension of its domestic revolutionary turmoil. "We have no choice but to destroy those systems that are corrupt and to overthrow all oppressive and criminal regimes," declared Khomeini.[25] For the grand ayatollah, the global order was divided between states whose priorities were defined by Western conventions and Iran, whose ostensible purpose was to redeem a divine mandate. All local regimes had a choice— they could sustain their allegiance to the West or conform to the new Islamic epoch launched by Iran.

For Khomeini the notion of nationalism and territorial demarcation were relics of a discredited past. Iran would now be the epicenter of a new Islamic order, seeking allies wherever Muslims existed, irrespective of sectarian division or ethnic differences. "We don't recognize Iran as ours, as all Muslim countries are a part of us," declared Khomeini.[26] This was to be a "revolution without borders," whose appeal would not be limited by boundaries, cultural differences, and national sensibilities. The common religious bonds would unit a diverse people under the leadership of a newly empowered theocratic state.[27]

In a perverse manner, Khomeini's universalism and his denunciations of nationalism as a Western conceit were initially embraced by a highly nationalistic population that favored the projection of Iran's influence. Persian monarchs had historically aspired to emerge as the leading regional actors, and the Iranian masses were long accustomed to seeing their nation as a model for the benighted Arabs. Khomeini's call for Iran to emerge as the nucleus of a new Middle East resonated with a populace imbued with images of Persian greatness. Instead of military conquest and claims of civilizational greatness, Khomeini employed religion to justify Iran's expansionist designs. However, the Muslim rage that Khomeini typified was different from monarchical assertions. For the shahs, what mattered was how the local states behaved toward Iran, while for the Islamic Republic the central issue was who ruled these countries. Given Khomeini's Islamist ambitions, the best means of ensuring that the Middle Eastern regimes pursued a righteous foreign policy was to make certain that they were ruled by like-minded ideologues.

Khomeini's internationalist vision had to have an antagonist, a foil to define itself against. A caricatured concept of the West soon became the central pillar of his Islamist imagination. The Western powers were rapacious imperialists determined to exploit Iran's wealth for their self-aggrandizement. The Islamic themes were not far behind, as the West was also seeking to subjugate Muslims and impose its cultural template in the name of modernity. In a sense, for Khomeini the shah was a mere tool of a larger Western conspiracy to plunder and abuse the Muslim world. One of the principal purposes of the Islamic Revolution was to expose the manner in which the West sustained its exploitive presence through local proxies. Khomeini stressed this point when claiming, "The sacred Islamic movement leads to the cutting off [of] the hands of instruments of foreigners, those who advocated colonialism and Westernization."[28] Disunity among Muslims, the autocracies populating the region, the failure of the clerical class to assume the mantle of opposition, and the young people's attraction to alien ideologies were all somehow byproducts of a Western plot to sustain its dominance over Islam's realm.

To some extent, Khomeini's animus toward the West was validated by his own experiences. During the course of his life, the ayatollah witnessed the occupation of Iran by allied forces, an American-sponsored coup that ended Iran's quest to reclaim its national oil wealth, the crushing of the religious uprisings of 1963–1964, and finally his own expulsion from Iran. All along, the United States sustained and assisted an unaccountable monarch who served its strategic purposes. As such, his well-honed animosities toward the West were reinforced by personal knowledge that often saw the United States and Britain plotting against Iran's independence.

Given Khomeini's delineation of the temporal order as a continuous struggle between the oppressed and the oppressors, it was easy for him to view the relations between America and the Middle East as a battle between good and evil. In this context, the oppressed were victims of Western imperial aggression, which was sustained by local proxies like the Pahlavi dynasty. In such a conception, there were no independent states inasmuch as all nations were in some way an adjunct of the superpowers. The international order with its norms and standards had no real value because it was merely designed to sustain Western hegemony. Nonetheless, the oppressed had an obligation to resist and should not merely acquiesce in their predicament. The path for their awakening and mobilization was Iran's revolution and leadership. Its revolt was never a national event but an occasion to usher in a larger transformation of the Middle East. Iran's purpose was "to liberate the discontented masses of Muslims, whether they live in the independent states of Egypt, Saudi Arabia, and Morocco or under non-Islamic government," declared Khomeini.[29]

On the surface, a degree of commonality existed between Khomeini's vision and the previous Iranian opposition leaders, who advocated a policy of nonalignment. Prime Minister Muhammad Musaddiq, who nationalized Iran's oil industry and was toppled by a CIA-sponsored coup in 1953, had, after all, enunciated the concept of "negative equilibrium," claiming that Iran could best protect its interests by exempting itself from the superpower conflict.[30] Suspicion of the West and the cold war rivalry was a hallmark of the Iranian intelligentsia, who saw no reason why its country should expend its wealth and act as a subsidiary of America's containment network in the Middle East. However, once more Khomeini and his slogan of "neither East nor West" must be differentiated from the typical Iranian reaction against the superpower struggle. His ideal governing order, his third way, called for a militant strategy of exporting the revolution. Thus, Iran's Islamist message would contest both American capitalism and Soviet communism. On the surface, such grandiose pretensions for a leader of a medium-sized country may seem absurd if not delusional, but Khomeini genuinely perceived himself as deputized by God to achieve his divine will. A pristine Islamic order blessed by God would now challenge the colonial exploitation of the West and the senseless materialism of the East.

Khomeini's postulations necessarily identified Israel as an enemy of Islam. Indeed, among the crimes of the West none was greater than its creation of the Zionist state, which transgressed on Islam's sacred domain. Khomeini's hostility to Israel was not a cynical strategy of appealing to the larger Arab society but an essential and enduring pillar of his ideology. During his years in seminary and exile, Khomeini persistently called for an embargo of Israel and stressed that "Any connection with Israel and its agents whether commercial or political is forbidden."[31] Decades before the Islamic Republic's subsidization of Hezbollah and Palestinian terrorist organizations, Khomeini implored his followers to donate a portion of their religious taxes to the Palestinian cause. "It is absolutely worthy that some portions of such religious alms be allocated to Palestinian fighters in the path of God," he insisted.[32] Financial boycotts and in due course violence would be the hallmarks of his immutable hostility toward the Jewish state.

In a sense, Khomeini's ideology was similar to that of Islamic reformers who stressed that the Muslim realm could reclaim its genuine independence only through greater unity. Important figures such as Jamal al-Din Afghani and Muhammad Abduh had already emphasized the themes of pan-Islamism as a means of escaping the tentacles of Western colonialism.[33] Indeed, one of the most important organizations pioneering Islamic activism was Egypt's Muslim Brotherhood, which developed branches throughout the Middle East.[34] Such movements may have been the mainstay of Arab activists battling against incumbent regimes throughout the twentieth century, but their embrace by a Persian, Shiite cleric was unusual. By the 1970s, Khomeini was seeking to transcend two propositions that had historically denied Iran a leading role in the Middle East: Persian ethnicity and the Sunni-Shiite divide. The Arabs' suspicion of Persians and the sectarian cleavages had prevented successive Iranian monarchs from escaping their insularity and dominating the region. For Khomeini, however, the revolution was "for an Islamic goal, not for Iran alone. Iran has only been the starting point."[35] Given all the talk of a "Shiite crescent," which is so fashionable today, it is important to appreciate that, for Khomeini, his revolt was always an Islamic one free of confessional restraint. It would be Saddam's Iraq and the House of Saud who would denounce the Islamic Republic as a Shiite, Persian enclave as a means of limiting its appeal.

Khomeini's meanderings may not have been relevant except that they came at a time when the region was searching for an alternative path. By the 1970s, it had become evident that the vanguards of modernity in the form of the military officers who had assumed power in the aftermath of decolonization had failed to usher in the pledged era of economic justice and autonomy from the West.[36] To compound the problems of the incumbent regimes, their continual defeat at the hands of the Israeli army had further eroded their legitimacy, and the Palestinian plight was a glaring reminder of the region's failures. Islamism was initially offering a sanctuary for a disillusioned population searching for guidance and solace. Throughout the Middle East, the intellectual class was abandoning the secular ideologies of pan-Arabism, socialism, and Marxism, which had once held great promise. Religious resurgence was proving to be alluring to a populace that had grown weary of economic dislocation, political autocracy, foreign policy humiliation, and institutional decay. A fiery mullah who was defying the West and its monarchical surrogate and offering a path to salvation appealed to a large cross-section of the public despite his Shiite faith and Persian ancestry.

In the path of his revolutionary exertion, the grand ayatollah was prepared to offer up his nation's blood and treasure. Martyrdom has always been a central symbolic tenet of Shiite Islam; indeed, the murder of Imam Husayn at the hands of the iniquitous Yazid bin Muawiyah offered a paradigm of suffering in the service of faith. For Khomeini, that historic event was not a mere ritual displayed at the annual commemoration ceremonies but an act of continuous defiance. In his reinterpretation of that event, Iran was to displace Husayn, and the great evil was to be the United States and its proxies. The Iranian populace had to bear the unimaginable burden of a permanent revolution. The nation that Khomeini commanded would suffer much through a devastating war, international ostracism, and economic sanctions. Yet despite the Islamic Republic's ritualistic celebrations of its martyrs, the founder of the world's first modern theocracy was largely unconcerned about the calamitous loss of life that his policies had caused. Like all ideologues, Khomeini was prepared to sacrifice a nation in the service of his ideals.

On the eve of Iran's triumphant revolution, none of this was obvious to a nation enthralled by the return of its clerical redeemer. The intriguing aspect of Iran's revolutionary coalition was that all of its contending blocs perceived that Khomeini would retreat to scholastic preoccupation and leave the task of governance to the modern elements.[37] In this sense, like many before them, Iran's revolutionaries underestimated the determination and skill of Khomeini and his clerical cohort. The imam had finally returned to fulfill his mission of realizing God's mandate. By exploiting factional divisions, the ruthless employment of terror, and the adroit use of foreign crises, Khomeini not only displaced his rivals but also created an Islamic Republic that could not easily escape the burden of his legacy.

God's Way

On a crisp morning in February 1979 Khomeini made his triumphant return to Iran. Approximately three million people were on hand to greet the imam and celebrate his momentous achievement. However, Khomeini and his clerical disciples understood that the success of their mission was by no means inevitable since the revolution had featured a powerful and diverse coalition of forces with their own claims and constituents. The liberal elements of the middle class, led by parties such as the National Front and the Liberation Movement of Iran, pressed for a parliamentary system of government and even a return to secularism and the rule of law. The radical Left, led by organizations such as the Mujahidin-i Khalq (MEK), with its discursive mixture of Marxism and Islam, commanded substantial support among the students.[38] Its call for nationalization, redistribution of wealth, and an anti-American foreign policy found a receptive audience among many progressive circles. The Chirik'ha-yi Fada'i-i Khalq-i Iran, another guerrilla organization that had evolved during the shah's reign, could still mobilize vast demonstrations, and its publications enjoyed a wide readership.[39] Despite ample repression at the shah's hands, the Communist Party—Tudah—had not just survived but also established an important base in the universities and within the labor force. Even the clerical class had its divisions, as senior ayatollahs such as Kazim Shari'atmadari, Muhammad Reza Gulpaygani, and Hasan Tabatabai Qummi were prepared to relinquish power and return to the quiet ways of the seminary.[40]

During its three decades of rule, the Islamic Republic has undergone remarkable changes. The revolutionary regime has endured one of the most prolonged interstate wars in the annuals of modern history, witnessed the rise of an extraordinary reform movement that sought to reconcile religion and democracy, and experienced its share of domestic turmoil and international crises. Yet the period between 1979 and 1981 stands as one of the most significant in this tumultuous history. At this juncture a new order, one that ensured clerical hegemony, came into existence. On the eve of the revolution, it was still unclear whether Iran would become the theocratic regime that Khomeini envisioned or a state commanded by moderate forces. Subsequent to the events of this period, it would have been difficult for any Iranian government to fully transcend its ideological inheritance.

The vast and varied nature of the revolutionary coalition that overthrew the monarchy meant that the calculating Khomeini had to proceed with caution and eliminate his rivals by exploiting their differences and generating external crises to galvanize the population.[41] In the maelstrom of the revolution stood the seventy-three-year-old Mahdi Bazargan, the provisional government's first prime minister. Born into a prominent religious family, Bazargan was a nationalist with impeccable credentials as an opposition leader often jailed by the shah. An engineer by training, he had spent decades trying to reconcile his scientific background with his sincere devotion to Islam. Given his fears that many of Iran's youth were being drawn to Marxist ideas, in the 1960s he joined forces with the progressive cleric Ayatollah Mahmud Taliqani in organizing the Liberation Movement of Iran. The purpose of the party would be to bridge the gap between modern intellectuals and the religious society. Finding himself suddenly in the midst of revolutionary chaos, Bazargan sought to create a government of competence, institute a rule of law, and establish international responsibility. In accepting his office, Bazargan noted, "All of you know that I am a man of democracy, consultation, tolerance of other viewpoints, thus avoiding radicalism and haste, looking for prudence and gradualism."[42] Such sentiments were on display when his spokesman, Abbas Amir-Intizam, declared in July 1979 that "the revolution is over. The era of reconstruction has begun."[43] Along the way, Bazargan's judicious path was subverted by both Khomeini, who was determined to impose his model of governance, and the Left, which felt confident that its ideological appeal and organizational strength would ensure its power once Bazargan was out of the way.

While the contending revolutionary factions were battling each other, Khomeini quickly created a parallel government whose purpose was not just to destroy the vestiges of the old order but also to consolidate his vision. The shadowy Revolutionary Council was manned by Khomeini loyalists such as Muhammad Bihishti, Ali Akbar Hashemi Rafsanjani, Ali Khamenei, and Ali Husayn Muntaziri. Although Bazargan was ostensibly a member, the council's essential decision-making powers rested with the clerics. The Revolutionary Council continued to exist alongside the provisional government; the Revolutionary Guards coexisted with the military; the local committees, with the police; and a network of Friday prayer leaders, with the municipal governments. The parallel government not only had more authority and resources but was also adept at manipulating popular passions to undermine its rivals.[44] As Bazargan complained, "In theory, the government is in charge; but in reality, it is Khomeini who is in charge—he with his Revolutionary Council, his revolutionary Komitehs, and his relationship with the masses."[45] Given Khomeini's stature, all of the factions sought to appeal to his authority for the advancement of their agenda. Thus, Khomeini was in a position to arbitrate all of the disputes and manipulate the situation by turning one faction against another.[46]

The institutional power of the clergy unfolded gradually through the political arrangements they created and the governing documents they largely crafted. The original 1979 referendum calling for an Islamic Republic and the debates on what constituted Islamic rule reflected the eclectic nature of the revolutionary coalition. The draft of the constitution had all of the relevant democratic trappings, with separation of power, an independent judiciary, a strong presidency, and an elected parliament.[47] Nonetheless, a series of institutions was also conceived that would exercise power beyond the scope of public scrutiny. The office of the supreme leader, with its authority over the entire system, was secured for Khomeini while a council would serve as a watchdog during elections and have veto power over parliamentary legislation.[48] Moreover, the essential religious identity of the state would assume predominance over social and economic considerations.

The early constitutional debates demonstrated an important difference between Khomeini and some of his disciples. Given the absolutist nature of Khomeini's ideology and his insistence that sovereignty rest with his clerical designates, the role of the parliament and the presidency became a source of controversy. Throughout the revolution, the leftist and secular forces that needed Khomeini's charismatic appeal chose to ignore his contempt for democratic rule. However, for those who were attentive, Khomeini was open about his ideas. The imam often deprecated democratic norms by stressing that the elected institutions were to address "matters beneath the dignity of Islam to concern itself with."[49] Throughout his writings and speeches, Khomeini rarely made references to a republic, as he firmly believed that laws should be derived from scriptural sources as interpreted by the clerical elite. Thus, traditional democratic institutions and practices such as assemblies, the right to vote, and referendums were not to infringe on the prerogatives of an unaccountable clerical class. To placate the progressive elements, the façade of republicanism was sustained while in practice the collective will was effectively obstructed by religious fiat. Throughout the 1980s, the Islamic Republic may have been an Islamic state, but it certainly was not a republican one.

In contrast to Khomeini, some of his younger followers such as Rafsanjani and Mutahhari did not oppose the creation of representative institutions. For this cohort there was no contradiction between a narrowly defined clerical cadre assuming power and the expansion of the democratic infrastructure. Elections were seen as a means of mobilizing poor people and the lower classes for political purposes. Thus, both the legitimacy of the system and the street power of the clerical forces would be enhanced by the democratic process. Khomeini's callow followers did not seek to undermine the elected bodies but perceived that, through suitable mobilization, they could use the ballot box to further consolidate their rule. Paradoxically, in the initial postrevolutionary phase, the elections and plebiscites worked against the liberals, who had far more concern for representative rule than the reactionary mullahs. However, history has vindicated Khomeini's suspicion that clerical absolutism could not coexist with representative order. In due course, the constitution's democratic provisions and its inclusion of the citizenry in the process of governance would do much to bedevil the theocratic order. The birth of the reform movement in the 1990s and the persistence of popular agitation for change would present Khomeini's successors with an explosive political challenge.

Beyond the struggle to define the parameters of the Islamic Republic, the other debate gripping Tehran was the question of exporting the revolution. The Bazargan government sought to pursue a conventional non-aligned policy within the existing order.[50] To be sure, it quickly renounced Iran's membership in America's containment network and cancelled a series of mutual defense treaties with the United States. However, Bazargan sought to improve ties with the regional states and seemed open to a new relationship with Washington. Iran would not serve as an agent of American power in the Persian Gulf but would pursue ties based on respect and equality. In essence, Bazargan acknowledged the legitimacy of the international system and viewed the United States not as a source of imperial transgression but as a superpower that had to be dealt with cautiously.

Bazargan's position was buttressed by the support of the most esteemed ayatollahs. The senior clerics, led by Shari'atmadari, eschewed a forceful export of the revolution and stressed that the development of an ideal religious state in Iran would serve as a model for all Muslims. An Islamic city on the hill would inspire Muslims around the world and lead them to reclaim their societies. The more temperate mullahs seemed to comprehend the daunting task of managing a large country in a complicated regional environment and were reluctant to alienate Iran's neighbors and the larger international community.

In the heady days of the revolution, the proponents of aggressive expansion proved more vociferous, better organized, and more in tune with Khomeini's ideals. As we have seen, for the aging cleric, the entire international system, with its territorial divisions and ideas of nationalism, was inauthentic.[51] Khomeini always perceived that Iran's revolution was merely a first step in a larger struggle against the forces of inequity and oppression. "We should set aside the thought that we do not export the revolution because Islam does not regard various countries as different," declared Khomeini.[52] Muntaziri similarly noted the universalistic character of the revolution: "Our revolution is an Islamic Revolution and not an Iranian one."[53] In an equally grandiose claim, Bihishti stressed that "Islam recognizes no borders."[54] Soon associations such as the Revolutionary Organization of the Masses began to dispatch men and supplies to places as varied as Lebanon, the Gulf states, and Palestinian territories.[55] Terrorism, subversion, and the use of local surrogates became part of the exalted mission of exporting the revolution.

By fall of 1979 the ongoing disputes with Bazargan and the need to ratify the constitution had made a confrontation between the mullahs and the engineer inevitable.[56] The Khomeini loyalists in the provisional government had already been busy appropriating power, negating the determinations of the official government, and amassing the wealth of the defunct regime in the new religious foundations—the *bunyads*—that subsidized their foot soldiers.[57] However, in order to displace Bazargan, a crisis was needed that could further radicalize the populace and discredit the moderate center.

On November 4, 1979, a group of Iranian students breached the walls of the U.S. embassy and took sixty-six American diplomats hostage for 444 days. Although the next chapter addresses this episode in more detail, at this point suffice it to say that it provided Khomeini with the crisis he needed to inflame popular sentiment and claim that external enemies with the aid of domestic accomplices were plotting against the revolution. The fact that the shah had recently been admitted to the United States for medical treatment offered Iran's rash revolutionaries sufficient evidence to buttress their case. To a frenzied populace, the notion that the United States, which had used its embassy to restore the Pahlavi dynasty to power in 1953, was up to similar mischief seemed plausible. As the Iranian public rushed to the defense of the revolution, the demise of Bazargan's premiership and the passage of the constitution along the lines envisioned by Khomeini seemed inevitable.[58]

Given his inability to obtain the release of the hostages and facing an erosion of his domestic standing, Bazargan tendered his resignation. In the end, Mahdi Bazargan was a man of moderation in the midst of revolutionary disorder; he was an advocate of gradualism at a time of radical change; and he was a tolerant liberal during a clerical power grab. The insidious aspect of his downfall was not so much the result of clerical plotting but that the leftist forces, such as the MEK and the Tudah Party, chose to side with the clerics in the misguided hope that, once the provisional government was removed, they could easily reclaim the revolution from the mullahs.

On December 2, 1979, the Iranian constitution, which granted essential power to the unelected branches of government, was duly submitted to the public.[59] The imam warned the nation that failure to support the constitution at such a critical juncture would demonstrate signs of disunity and provoke an attack by the United States. The regime's propaganda machine insisted that only secular intellectuals tied to U.S. imperialism were averse to the governing document. The plot worked: A full 99 percent of the population voted for the constitution.

In the aftermath of their triumph, the clerical rulers had no compunction about defending their governing arrangement. Khomeini acclaimed the nondemocratic nature of the new constitution by claiming that "It is right that the supreme religious authority should oversee the work of the president and other state officials, to make sure that they don't make mistakes or go against the law and the Quran."[60] As for the export of the revolution, the new constitution pledged that Iran would "exert continuous effort until political, economic and cultural unity is realized in the Islamic world."[61] In order to achieve this goal, the Islamic Republic's founding document pledged to "strive in concert with other Islamic and popular movements to prepare the way for the formation of a single world community."[62] In the atmosphere of conflict with the United States and domestic political tensions, the Iranian masses turned to the father of the revolution for guidance and direction. Iran's national narrative was unfolding as Khomeini had intended. As Muhammad Musavi-Khu'ini'ha, the students' spiritual leader and confidant of Khomeini recalled, "We reaped all the fruit of our undertaking—we defeated attempts by liberals to take control of the machinery of state. We forced Bazargan's government to resign. The tree of the revolution has grown and garnered strength."[63] However, the revolution had not yet been fully consolidated: The leftist parties and the traditional clergy still had to be dealt with.

At this point, Iran still had an elected president, Abu al Hasan Bani-Sadr, whose ideas diverged from those of the clerical powerbrokers. As was typical of the new Iranian elite, Bani-Sadr was born into a prominent religious family from the provincial city of Hamadan. After completing his education at Tehran University, he obtained advanced degrees from the University of Paris. From the outset the relations between the modernist president and the clerical oligarchs was tenuous. In his quest to achieve supreme power, Khomeini had initially focused on capturing the parliament, the Assembly of Experts, and the judiciary. As Khomeini informed his close aid, Ayatollah Muhammad Reza Mahdavi-Kani, these institutions were the most critical for the establishment of the Islamic Republic.[64] However, in the midst of this power grab, it was important to be cautious and at least offer the appearance of pluralism and diversity of views within the state. Having just disposed of the Bazargan government, the office of the presidency had to be occupied by a noncleric. Nonetheless, Khomeini assured his clerical disciples that "I am not afraid. And if I must, I will remove him with one finger."[65] In due time, Bani-Sadr's preference for a more tolerant Islamist regime with a limited clerical representation would cause irreparable damage between the president and the mullahs.

The latent disagreements between Bani-Sadr and the clerical leaders were coming to the surface at a time of a deepening crisis in the revolutionary coalition. The MEK, student organizations, and elements of the middle class that had far more affinity for Bani-Sadr's vision than the mullahs were still capable of mobilizing support against theocratic rule. The path of clerical consolidation of power needed another crisis. On September 22, 1980, in yet another one of his miscalculations, Saddam Husayn invaded Iran. Iraq's invasion, which was designed to destroy the nascent Islamic revolution, further assisted the clerical firebrands in their consolidation of power. Once more, a bewildered populace looked to Khomeini to lead the nation out of its latest predicament.

Saddam's invasion completely transformed Iran's internal political landscape, as the debates were no longer between despotism and freedom but loyalty to the revolution and resistance to external invaders. The cynicism of the clerical elite was on full display, as Rafsanjani quickly exploited the national emergency by defaming the critics of the Islamic Republic. "I am certain that there exists a relationship between Saddam, America, and the internal opposition," stressed the newly elected speaker of the Majlis.[66] In a convenient manner, the documents from the captured U.S. embassy were selectively used to discredit political opponents. Suddenly, records were unveiled to demonstrate that Bani-Sadr had met with an American businessman who was actually a CIA agent. Such evidence further fueled the mullahs' sense of paranoia, as the main clerical political organization, the Islamic Republican Party, now agitated for the displacement of Bani-Sadr on the grounds that he was proving a poor commander of the armed forces while the mullah-dominated parliament pressed for his impeachment. Finally relenting, Khomeini withdrew his support from the beleaguered president, warning him to "go back to Europe, to the United States or wherever else you want."[67] Quickly escaping to exile in France, Bani-Sadr had become the latest victim of the clerical consolidation of power.

At this juncture the dormant animosities between Khomeini and the senior clerics surfaced. As we have seen, Khomeini's theological innovations had long been deprecated by the esteemed men of religion. The notion of *vilayat-i faqih* was seen by many traditionalists as a superficial religious warrant for the establishment of a dictatorship. Ayatollah Fazl-Allah Zanjani now warned against "despotic rule," while Ayatollah Abu al-Hasan Khan Shirazi stressed that "circumstances have slowly become worse than before."[68] The most strenuous challenge to Khomeini's rule, however, came from Grand Ayatollah Shari'atmadari, who commanded strong support in the restive Azerbaijan area. Shari'atmadari favored a greater degree of freedom and consistently invoked terms such as "nationalism" and "democratic sovereignty," which were anathema to Khomeini. For Shari'-atmadari, the existence of the presidency, the parliament, and local assemblies negated the need for institutions that were unaccountable to the popular will.

In an unmistakable rebuke to his clerical detractors, Khomeini warned that they should "understand that the country has been aware of your conduct. Your writings are doing more damage to Islam than the democrats."[69] The imam's disciples soon came to his defense, with Bihishti insisting that "Khomeini has been accepted and recognized by the majority of the people and therefore his leadership is not an imposition on the people."[70] Khamenei also dismissed the claims of the new institutions' arbitrariness: "One who acts on God's behalf is not a dictator."[71] Nonetheless, the Islamic Republic soon established special tribunals for the prosecution of the clergy, and hundreds of the most accomplished and learned men of religion would be harassed and even imprisoned. In an unprecedented move in the history of Shiism, the regime defrocked a grand ayatollah and confined Shari'atmadari to house arrest for the remainder of his life. Khomeini and his allies would never gain the allegiance of the traditional clerical establishment, but through intimidation and pressure they managed to silence their most important critics.

At this point the Republic of Virtue unleashed its reign of terror against the remaining leftist opposition. On June 28, 1981, a massive bomb destroyed the headquarters of the Islamic Republican Party, killing more than 100 individuals, including Bihishti, four cabinet members, six deputy ministers, and twenty-seven members of the parliament. The episode sparked an internal war that destroyed the last remnants of the left-wing opposition. Pitched battles in the streets, the summary execution of MEK guerrillas, and the closure of all critical press became the order of the day. Longstanding nationalist politicians, secular intellectuals, writers, journalists, and artists all became targets of suspicion and persecution. Before the year was over, the regime had executed approximately six thousand of its opponents. In one of its most gruesome displays, the pictures of those executed were exhibited on the front pages of the newspapers. The brutality of this period was best noted by then minister of interior, Ali Akbar Natiq-Nuri, who pledged that "I am not like the cancer-ridden shah; I will not retreat."[72] In the end, the Islamic Republic's superior firepower and sheer brutality allowed it to triumph and effectively end popular dissent.

The violence of this period gave rise to a Second Republic, a regime that was manned by Khomeini's clerical loyalists in the name of Islamic militancy. As with most revolutionary governments seeking to usher in a utopian epoch, a cultural revolution was soon unleashed. Through purges of university personnel and curriculum revisions, the new educational system was to inculcate revolutionary and Islamic values. As Khomeini noted, "We are not afraid of military attacks, we are afraid of colonial universities."[73] The purpose of the new educational structure was to produce students who were devoted to Islam's sacred values and the pan-Islamic mission of the state.

Beyond the universities, mass communications, newspapers, and the arts came under a similar degree of scrutiny and censorship. Various agencies such as the Ministry of Islamic Guidance and the Islamic Propaganda Organization were to ensure that revolutionary images, defiance of the West, and Islamic mores became the prevailing social messages. A spirit of oppression had descended on Iran, where students were advised to inform on their teachers, children on their parents, and employees on employers. The terror and repression of this period produced a government that not only displaced its monarchical foe and secular rivals but also sought a thorough ideological and political transformation of Iran. An entirely new structure of government and a new, dedicated, religious cadre came into existence with a determination to ensure the perpetuation of Khomeini's vision.

In a perverse manner, Khomeini's totalitarian aspirations would be undermined by the structure and norms of the very religion in whose name he professed to rule. Unlike the Roman Catholic Church, with its strict hierarchy and notions of papal infallibility, Shiite ulema—Muslim scholars—were always loosely organized. The fact that most of the traditional clergy were dismissive of Khomeini's theological improvisations ensured that a body of ayatollahs remained in a state of perpetual dissent. Even within Khomeini's circle of adherents, contrasting ideas and disagreements would prevent the Islamic Republic from becoming a pure totalitarian state or even developing consistent policies on important issues.[74]

Unlike many of its regional counterparts, the theocracy developed institutions with their own mindset and sense of autonomy. The factionalism of the state would find an organizational expression as the ministries, Revolutionary Guards, seminaries, and elected bodies spoke in diverse voices—and often at cross-purposes with each other. Hovering over the system was Khomeini, who sought to provide a balance among his revolutionary followers. In due course, various mediating bodies were created to settle disputes whose irresolution threatened the government's functionality. In the end, Khomeini may have succeeded in creating an Islamic Republic, but one with distinct fault lines and ample divisions.

Such diversity of views within the elite structure was acceptable to Khomeini. The imam's management style now became much more aloof as he worked to establish broad national guidelines and serve as the authority of last resort but rarely intervene in the daily conduct of the state. The one area where Khomeini was more directly involved was the Ministry of Intelligence. Its first minister, Muhammad Muhammadi Ray'shahri, even compiled a "bulletin of differences" for the imam, which chronicled the disagreements and tensions within the regime.[75] Given his portfolio, it is not unreasonable to assume that clandestine methods such as eavesdropping and espionage were used to garner that information. Although Ray'shahri was prepared to use that knowledge against state officials, Khomeini admonished him that "differences are necessary."[76] The grand ayatollah may have been wary of his disciples, but he still preferred their inclusion in the system. This would be a stark contrast to his successor, Ali Khamenei.

Once in power, all revolutionary regimes deviate from their declared precepts, moderate their objectives, and even adjust to the prevailing order. In many ways, Iran's theocratic state was no different, as it could not sustain its hostility to both superpowers and its commitment to the overthrow of its neighbors. Khomeini's ideological contentions still had to exist in an international arena dominated by the United States and a political economy that made Iran vulnerable to economic pressure. The Islamic Republic's enforced pragmatism would come partly through a prolonged and devastating war with Iraq that compelled the regime toward certain adjustments of its core objectives. However, even in the absence of war with Iraq, it is unlikely that the aging ayatollah would have realized his Islamist dreams. In due course, internal dissent, economic hardship, and divisions among the governing elite would crystallize the impracticalities of his vision.[77]

From the outset, the notion that Iran's revolution could have been exported seemed far-fetched. Iran's rhetoric was certainly ferocious, and its commitment to impose its model was indeed sincere. However, the limits of its power and its place in the region militated against a significant projection of its influence. In terms of possessing a strong military or reliable alliances, Iran was after all not the Soviet Union or even China. The underreported story of Iran as a menace or hegemon is its isolation. A Shiite power struggling in a Middle East dominated by Sunnis and a Persian nation seeking to lead the Arab realm would always encounter natural barriers. Moreover, Khomeini was certainly a trendsetter and made important adjustments to normative Shiite political philosophy with its historical emphasis on clerical disengagement from daily politics. However, the notion of pan-Islamic unity and the resistance of the West were not particularly novel. Such ideological assertions had permeated the Middle East since the demise of the Ottoman Empire, yielding important thinkers and transnational associations such as the Muslim Brotherhood. In the end, the region's revolutionaries and activists have always had to contend with the durability of state power and the inability of their Islamic claims to alter the regional order.

However, it is too facile to suggest that Iran has gone the way of a typical revolutionary state, namely, relinquishing its ideological patrimony for more mundane considerations. Khomeini was too much of an innovator in terms of the institutions he created and the elite that he molded to see the passing of his vision. On a range of issues from its antagonism to the United States and Israel to its attempts to undermine the Gulf states' princely class, Iran sustained its animus long after such hostilities proved disadvantageous and self-defeating. The theocratic regime would remain a state perennially divided against itself—with pragmatists and radicals battling one another; with a foreign policy struggling to define coherent objectives; and with revolutionary pretensions pitted against national-interest imperatives. The Islamic Republic would alter its course, limit its horizons, and make unsavory compromises but would not completely temper its raging fires. In the end, Khomeini may not have been able to impose the totality of his views on Iran, much less the Islamic world, but neither would he become another faded revolutionary commemorated on occasion and disregarded most of the time.

2

Relations with the "Great Satan"

SINCE THE INCEPTION OF THE ISLAMIC REPUBLIC, NO DECADE HAS left a greater mark on U.S.-Iranian relations than the 1980s. During this period, Iran held fifty-two American diplomats hostage for 444 days, engaged in a proxy war with the United States in Lebanon, and even indulged in skirmishes with the U.S. Navy in the Persian Gulf. However, the decade was not a story of unrelenting animosity, as the two powers managed to come together in a peculiar exchange of arms for hostages, culminating in the Iran-Contra scandal. Tehran and Washington seemed not only to relish their confrontation but also sporadically to appreciate its strategic impracticality. Although influential actors in both nations would at times acknowledge their common interests, domestic politics, ideological rigidity, and fear of failure would prevent both sides from taking measurable steps to defuse the conflict.

During the 1980s a series of events took place that would cast a long shadow on U.S.-Iranian relations. The hostage crisis convinced a significant portion of the American public that Iran was an unsavory, irrational actor imbued by an unusual hatred of the United States. Such impressions have hardly been dispelled, as popular distrust of Iran restrains any U.S. administration from seeking renewed ties with the Islamic Republic. In its own way, the Iran-Contra affair cast a similar pall over the relationship, as its exposure went on to deter a generation of bureaucrats from creatively approaching the clerical regime. In the meantime, confrontation in Lebanon, America's tilt toward Iraq in its war with Iran, and the destruction of an Iranian civilian aircraft by an errant U.S. naval vessel provided

Tehran with its own narrative of victimization and antagonism. In many ways, the wall of mistrust that was erected in this decade continues to condition U.S.-Iranian relations in the twenty-first century.

America Held Hostage

The hostage crisis, which proved to be one of the most important episodes in Iran's political history, can be understood only in the context of a series of developments that took place in the immediate postrevolutionary period. The internal power struggles, suspicion of American plots, and clerical opportunism made the capture of the U.S. diplomats inevitable. Seldom has an event proved so instrumental in defining the American public's impression of a distant and ill-understood state.

All revolutionary regimes are born out of paranoia, sensing conspiracies and plots where none exist. Years of clandestine struggle, political betrayals leading to stiff prison sentences, and tactical bargains designed to be renounced at an opportune time produce a distorted mental framework. Iran's revolutionaries were no different, as years of underground activity had honed their fears. Indeed, Iran's new rulers had even more of a justification for caution since the revolutionary coalition had little in common other than enmity toward the shah. Each faction within the alliance was plotting its own strategy of ascendance, which often involved the elimination of its rivals. Moreover, Iran's revolution had no external patrons, allies, or supporters. The superpowers were uneasy about its radical pretensions, while the neighboring states were alarmed about its quest to transform the region. Khomeini and his narrow band of clerical disciples stood alone, confronting forces they did not always comprehend and concocting their strategy in an era dominated by conflict and deceit.[1]

As we have seen, one of the first issues that caused a rupture between the clerical radicals and the provisional government was the latter's approach toward the United States. Bazargan did not seek to break ties with the United States but hoped to reformulate them on basis of respect and equality. Although Tehran would not be a pawn in the U.S.–Soviet conflict, it was eager to open normal diplomatic and economic relations with Washington. As part of this strategy, plenty of meetings were held between the provisional government ministers and embassy officials. After the seizure of the U.S. compound and the capture of its records, such innocuous activities would be seen as part of a counterrevolutionary plot, and selective documents were released to defame and undermine the moderate forces.[2] The Islamic Republic, however, was careful not to reveal the record of meetings between U.S. officials and clerical oligarchs such as Muntaziri and Bihishti.[3] At any rate, the activities of the U.S. embassy seemed to have been closely monitored by a suspicious regime sensing imaginary plots.

For Khomeini, the Islamic revolution had taken place not just to depose an autocratic monarch but also to strike a blow against the United States. The provisional government's lax attitude toward the United States and its willingness to contemplate resumed ties was an affront to the clerical militants. Once more, the revolutionaries seemed to have misapprehended the nature of the U.S. embassy's outreach to Bazargan and his cabinet. For the clerical hard-liners, such contacts were an indication of a collusion to undermine the Islamist regime. Yet, there is nothing unwarranted or unusual about an embassy reaching out to a new government. Ironically, the purpose of such contacts was to secure an understanding with the Islamic Republic and rebuild the bridges between the two states.

By the spring of 1979, the atmosphere of tension between the two governments was worsening. On May 17, 1979, the U.S. Senate passed a resolution that condemned the summary executions that were taking place with regularity in Iran.[4] The fact that the resolution was sponsored by Senator Jacob Javits, a close friend of the shah's, further inflamed Iranians' suspicions. In a pattern that would often repeat itself, Iran viewed such comments as not only an intervention in its internal affairs but also an attempt by Washington to establish a justification for the overthrow of the regime. However, there was nothing inappropriate about the Senate's condemnation of Iran's arbitrary judicial system, which executed defendants without the benefit of a real trial or access to defense attorneys. The head of the Revolutionary Court, Hujjat al-Islam Sadiq Khalkhali (soon to be nicknamed the hanging judge), relished such executions and even filled his memoirs with before-and-after pictures of those whose execution he presided over.[5] It would be unfortunate for the foremost legislative body of the world's leading democracy to remain silent with regard to such flagrant perversions of justice. Moreover, Iran's clerics did not object to criticisms of human rights when it pertained to the shah's government. In his memoirs, Muntaziri goes to great length in extolling the virtues of Carter's human rights declarations: "At the time that we were in jail, prisoners would say that dear Jimmy will arrive and solve our problems and we will be set free."[6] The notion that any criticism constitutes a violation of Iran's sovereignty is a privilege that the regime arrogates only to itself.

On October 22, 1979, another humanitarian gesture by Washington further contributed to the paranoid mindset of the clerical estate. After considerable consultation with Tehran, the Carter administration finally agreed to admit the ailing shah to the United States for medical treatment. Given the gravity of the shah's cancer and the type of advanced care that was available only in New York, Carter finally relented to the persistent demands by the deposed monarch and his many well-connected friends in the United States, such as former secretary of state Henry Kissinger and financier David Rockefeller. To further hone the clerics' suspicions, during the annual celebration of Algeria's independence, the visiting Iranian delegation, headed by Bazargan, Foreign Minister Ibrahim Yazdi, and Defense Minister Mustafa Chamran, held a meeting with national security advisor Zbigniew Brzezinski.[7] The confluence of these events seemingly persuaded many within the theocratic regime that the United States was plotting the restoration of the monarchy. In a sense, Iran's revolutionaries simply could not believe that Washington would acquiesce to the demise of its valuable ally without any reaction. The fact that the U.S. embassy had been the locus of counterrevolutionary activities in 1953 only validated such fears.

The broader context of U.S.-Iranian relations and the qualms of the revolutionary regime should not obscure the domestic power struggles that contributed to the hostage crisis. Determined to consolidate their power, Khomeini and his clerical allies increasingly saw the Bazargan government as an impediment to the realization of their larger objectives. The task of redrafting the constitution along radical lines and electing a clerically dominated Parliament and Assembly of Experts mandated displacing the provisional government. In the end, a combination of concerns regarding nonexistent American plots and a determination to monopolize political power pressed the radicals to provoke a crisis that would galvanize the populace behind the cause of the Islamic Republic.

Although Khomeini and his clerical allies often laced their pronouncements with anti-American invective, they soon focused more directly on the U.S. embassy. A few days before the actual takeover of the embassy, Khomeini called for massive demonstrations outside the compound. During the marches, Khomeini's office released a statement calling on the protestors to "expand the attacks against the United States and Israel so that they may force the United States to return the deposed and criminal shah."[8] For his part, Rafsanjani stressed, "America anticipated conspiring with the shah, and they created their base of conspiracy at the embassy."[9] In an unsubtle manner, Khomeini and his allies were urging their followers to see the embassy as the foundation of nefarious American conspiracies.

On November 8, the scene outside the U.S. embassy did not seem all that different from that on any other day. Demonstrations denouncing the shah and protestors chanting "Death to America" were not unusual occurrences. However, this time a number of students successfully breached the walls of the embassy and found startled diplomats unsure about how to proceed. At first, even the occupation of the embassy did not seem all that untypical. After all, on February 14, 1979, a contingent of leftist students briefly had taken over the compound and held 109 Americans hostage. At that time, the provisional government, with Khomeini's backing, condemned the assailants and dispatched its forces to reclaim the embassy. Not only did the crisis pass easily, but, through an intermediary, Khomeini even issued an apology to Ambassador William Sullivan, who was still in Tehran.[10] An enhanced security arrangement and assurances of safety from the regime ended the first embassy crisis in short order.

However, despite the appearance of business as usual, something was different about the November occupation, as the students were now a pawn in a larger game whose full scope was beyond their purview. To the extent that the group had a motivation it was a sincere but misguided belief that the United States was plotting the overthrow of the regime. In their view a bold stroke of resistance might just save the sacred revolution. Ma'sumah Ibtikar, the group's spokesperson and one of the student leaders, claimed, "We believed then that action was essential. We were determined to take a stand against past and possible future humiliation by the U.S."[11] And with that declaration began 444 days of captivity for the American diplomats.

The notion that Khomeini did not have foreknowledge of the embassy takeover has become conventional wisdom, widely accepted by the leading scholars of Iran. The evidence that supports this claim is not inconsiderable, as the students have asserted that, although they hoped Khomeini would approve of their action, the imam did not provide them with an explicit green light. Nearly three decades after the event, a cogent, circumstantial case can be made that Khomeini did approve of the plot in advance.

In his recently published memoirs, Ayatollah Muhammad Reza Mahdavi-Kani, a member of the Revolutionary Council and the head of the revolutionary committees, offers an intriguing insight into the events surrounding the hostage crisis. Soon after the occupation of the embassy, in his role as head of the revolutionary committees, which were largely responsible for internal security, he contacted Khomeini's son, Ahmad, who acted as his father's chief of staff and intermediary between the imam and his advisors, to inquire about the developments surrounding the embassy. His comments are of sufficient importance to be quoted at length: "The night of the embassy's occupation I contacted Ahmad and asked him what is happening? Initially he just laughed and would not answer. I asked him did you know about this? He laughed. Finally, after I insisted, he said, the Imam is satisfied with this and you should not get involved."[12] Mahdavi-Kani's pointed questions to Ahmad about his knowledge of the event only elicited bemused laughter, suggesting a prior understanding. Moreover, it is hard to believe that Ayatollah Muhammad Musavi Khu'ini'ha, the students' spiritual leader, did not consult with Khomeini. Musavi Khu'ini'ha was a former student and disciple of Khomeini and was known to be in close touch with Ahmad. Indeed, shortly after the embassy take-over, the younger Khomeini arrived at the compound and acknowledged the students' contributions to the cause of the revolution.[13]

In the end, the hostage crisis cannot be properly understood without taking into consideration Iran's domestic political context and the clerical radicals' obsession with subverting the provisional government. Even after Bazargan submitted his resignation, many within Khomeini's inner circle perceived that the resignation was a ploy to press them into pledges of power sharing. Rafsanjani speculated that the "resignation was perhaps designed to increase pressure on the imam and the Revolutionary Council."[14] In his own account, Ahmad Khomeini goes even further:

> I was sure that his resignation was tactical, designed to put pressure on the students. At that time within the Revolutionary Committees and the state they were many who did not believe in the imam's path and given an opportunity they would agitate and exert pressure. I contacted the head of the National Radio and Television Network and ask them to broadcast the news of the resignation. At any rate, the opposition of the provisional government was broadcasted.[15]

All of this suggests that the demise of the Bazargan government was so critical to the clerical oligarchs that even its resignation was viewed as a trick to prolong its life at the expense of the revolution. A crisis that would ensure its collapse could only have been welcomed by Khomeini.

Domestic political rivalries and fears of a potential U.S.-sponsored coup have often been seen as the most likely culprits for the hostage crisis. However, two other factors must also be taken into consideration, namely, the clerics' quest to usher in a militant foreign policy and a desire to strike a psychological blow against the United States. As we have seen, Bazargan's approach to international relations was strict nonalignment but with a willingness to have normal relations with the United States. Such modest objectives found no audience among the newly empowered militants, however. The long-time commander of the Revolutionary Guards, Yahya Rahim Safavi, recalls, "The policy of the provisional government was not acceptable to the revolutionary forces and the line of the imam. They were afraid of America."[16] The hostage crisis was designed not just to disrupt a nonexistent American coup but also to provoke a different international orientation. As such, Iran's foreign policy would not merely be an exemption from the superpower conflict but assertion of radical Islamism as the foundation of its approach to the world as well. Through a symbolic attack on the U.S. embassy, the new revolutionaries demonstrated not only their antagonism toward the United States but also their contempt for the prevailing international norms. Iran would now inveigh against the United States, assist belligerent actors throughout the Middle East, and plot against the state of Israel.

In addition, the psychological dimension of the crisis was hardly unimportant, as Khomeini relished the opportunity to humiliate America. Throughout their long struggle, Iran's revolutionaries often complained that the United States denied Iran its sovereign rights and manipulated its internal affairs to its advantage. The 1953 coup and, even more important for the clerical cohort, the 1963–1964 uprisings reflected America's sense of superiority over Iran. In 1953 the United States arrogated to itself the right to directly interfere in Iranian politics and depose an elected prime minister because he was insufficiently deferential to its own anti-Communist agenda. Furthermore, in the early 1960s Washington demanded the exemption of its personnel from Iranian law, thereby humiliating a country with a rich history and a well-developed system of justice. The hostage crisis was designed to avenge both of these episodes. By capturing and parading the diplomats for 444 days, Tehran injected itself in America's domestic politics the way Washington had intervened in Iran's affairs in 1953. In a sense, the mullahs pulled off their own coup, as the turmoil in Iran torpedoed the reelection of the Carter administration. In addition to humiliating the United States, the hostage crisis was analogous to the sense of degradation that Iranians had felt in 1963, when Washington deemed Iran's laws as too primitive to judge its personnel. As with nearly every aspect of U.S.-Iranian relations, the hostage crisis played itself out in an emotional context.

Given Khomeini's determination to consolidate power and displace Bazargan, derail a potential American plot, and humiliate the United States, it is hard to believe that he would not have instigated a crisis that would achieve all of these objectives. It is entirely possible that both leading members of the government and the students were unaware of Khomeini's complicity. In fact, by working through his son and Musavi Khu'ini'ha, the imam could have orchestrated the entire affair. The hostage trauma galvanized the populace behind the cause of anti-Americanism and subverted the provisional government. In Khomeini's view, the path of amassing power and ushering in a radical foreign policy necessitated a crisis that could even endanger Iran's practical and long-term interests.

Whatever his foreknowledge may have been, Khomeini was quick to bless the students' rash conduct. Iran's supreme leader sanctified the capture of the embassy as a second revolution that in many ways was more important than the first. As Iran entered one of its most acute crises, Khomeini and his followers were content to exploit the situation to their advantage, while their student followers felt elated that their imam had sublimated their impetuous conduct. The notion that they had violated international law, antagonized a superpower, and created a lasting image of Iran as an irrational actor in the minds of the Americans was largely lost on the theocratic elite.

The hostage crisis became the first international event to fully capture the attention of the American public. Even before the advent of twenty-four-hour cable news channels, the drama played itself out in living rooms throughout the United States. The venerable anchorman Walter Cronkite signed off every night by counting down the days that the diplomats had so far been held in captivity, while a new program called *Nightline*, hosted by Ted Koppel, garnered a large audience by focusing nearly exclusively on the crisis. The images of bearded mullahs, blindfolded Americans, and crowds chanting "death to America" were displayed daily on television screens across the United States. In many ways, the hostages were a reflection of America's powerlessness, as the United States seemed incapable of releasing its official representatives from their harsh ordeal. The hostages seemed to reinforce the malaise of the 1970s inasmuch as defeat in Vietnam, the Watergate scandal, and the retrenchment of American power finally culminated in a radical theocracy that defied the United States and egregiously held its diplomats against their will. The more America was humiliated, the more the implacable mullahs relished their vengeance against the "Great Satan."

A week after the seizure of the embassy, the Iranian government finally offered its fantastical terms for the release of the captives. The agreement called for the return of the shah and his assets, an apology by the United States for its crimes against the Iranian people, and a pledge of noninterference in Iran's internal affairs. It is inconceivable that any U.S.

administration would have conceded to such absurd provisions. Moreover, given that the primary motive for the embassy takeover was domestic politics, it is unclear that even acceptance of the totality of Iran's claims would have ended the crisis. As the clerical militants were busy exploiting the events to the detriment of their moderate rivals, they needed to perpetuate the conflict.

During the 444 days of the hostage crisis, Jimmy Carter was often vilified for his handling of the issue, and the Republican outcry at his purported weakness did much to undermine his presidency.[17] However, in retrospect, Carter has to be credited for his deft and astute management of the situation. The much-criticized president imposed economic sanctions on Iran, including the freezing of its considerable assets in the United States, built an international consensus against the Islamic Republic, patiently guided the various diplomatic moves, and more important, did not yield to popular passions that could have led the country on an ill-advised course of action. A less-principled politician might have been tempted to exploit the confrontation with an indisputably unsavory adversary for personal advantage, but Carter chose to place the hostages' welfare above his own political viability. To be sure, the United States had limited options: A military attack would have endangered the hostages' lives, and measures such as embargos and mining of the harbors would have inflicted damage on Iran without necessarily ending the conflict. For all of these reasons, the administration opted for diplomacy, economic sanctions, and international pressure, which succeeded in isolating Iran among the community of nations.[18]

In the meantime, the clerical state was taking full advantage of the hostage crisis to inflame the domestic situation and discredit its rivals. It selectively released the embassy's records in order to purge and intimidate its political opponents. The students' first communiqué out of the embassy ominously warned that "the CIA has substantial influence in Iran's government."[19] Rafsanjani soon followed suit: "Inside the embassy documents were discovered demonstrating that the provisional government was working against the line of the imam and the revolution."[20] In the midst of the turmoil and tension, Iran was to hold elections on the powers of the clerical state. Khomeini set the tone of the elections by stressing, "We are facing a satanic power today, and it wants to destroy our country. Don't let the foundations of the Islamic Republic be weakened or the enemies of Islam fulfill their dreams."[21] In December, 1979, Iran held a referendum on a new constitution, whose provisions granted extensive authority to the office of the supreme religious leader.[22] Not long after the passage of the constitution,

Iran held elections for the parliament, which the Islamic Republican Party dominated. The exclusion, dismissal, and purging of independent political actors was now fully accomplished under the banner of resisting foreign agents. The institutional encroachment of the religious extremists was moving forward as the result of the prevailing crisis.

At a time when the political dividends of the hostage crisis precluded an Iranian compromise, the Carter administration was facing some stark choices. The economic sanctions imposed on Iran were casually dismissed by Khomeini, who proclaimed, "We will go hungry, but we will not submit."[23] The continued Iranian intransigence and the inefficacy of the political and economic pressures made the idea of a rescue mission an appealing option. The military plan, codenamed Operation Eagle Claw, was logistically complicated, as it involved flying a contingent of U.S. Special Forces into a desert location. Once situated there, they would switch aircrafts and proceed toward a location in Tehran. From there, using prepositioned vehicles, they would assault the compound and free the hostages. Even under the best of circumstances, this would be a difficult operation to execute without casualties. The night of April 25 was hardly a propitious time for launching a military action as desert storms caused one of the helicopters to crash with a refueling aircraft, causing the death of eight American servicemen. Even before the succeeding stages unfolded, the operation was deemed too risky to proceed, and the entire enterprise was aborted.[24]

The failure of the rescue operation was widely celebrated in Iran as an indication of God's approbation. Khomeini typically took the lead, claiming that the sandstorms "were divinely commissioned."[25] The Iranian National Television repeatedly broadcast the macabre scene of crashed aircraft and dead soldiers. In the meantime, the students were strengthened in their resolution and embraced Khomeini's peculiar rationale that God was on their side. Although the rescue mission was a legitimate expression of a frustrated administration concerned about its lack of diplomatic success, it probably prolonged the crisis. An emboldened Iranian regime witnessing yet another American humiliation was seemingly reinforced in its determination.

The same combination of internal political considerations and external exigencies that initially provoked the seizure of the embassy contributed to its conclusion. By 1980, the clerical militants' control over key institutions of the state was largely complete. Bani-Sadr was still the president, but his authority had been so circumscribed that he was largely irrelevant. On the international level, Iraq's invasion of Iran and the election of a hawkish Reagan administration meant that the continuation of the crisis was ill serving Tehran's interests. As Bihzad Nabavi, one of the regime's leading figures, claimed, "The hostages were like a fruit from which all the juice had been squeezed out."[26] Upon the inauguration of Ronald Reagan as president, the hostages were finally released, ending their 444-day ordeal.

For the Iranian people, the hostage crisis is a faded memory, annually commemorated by the regime to little public notice. To the extent that average Iranians focus on the crisis, it is seen as a consequence of America's prolonged intervention in Iran's affairs. Iran's reaction to the hostage crisis has been marked by a lack of concern for and sensitivity to the plight of the captured Americans. The reality remains that the United States has been far more generous in its treatment of Iran's emotive 1953 crisis (former secretary of state Madeline Albright even issued an apology for America's complicity in the coup). No official apology has ever been issued by the Islamic Republic. The closest expression of contrition came from the reformist president Muhammad Khatami, who expressed regret for the incident. At the core, Iranians view the hostages not as victims but as the agents of an exploitive power unfortunately caught up in the maelstrom of the early revolutionary period.

The conceptual divide between the United States and Iran is nowhere more visible than in their different assessments of the legacy of the hostage crisis. For many Americans, the hostage drama continues to define their impressions of the Islamic Republic. In essence, a certain image is frozen in time, and all of the arguments that stress that a unique combination of legitimate fears, unwarranted suspicions, and clerical opportunism led to the crisis are often dismissed by a skeptical public. Iran held fifty-two Americans hostage not because of any concerns it may have had but because of the type of regime that it is. The Islamic Republic has certainly changed, and it has modified its international outlook in important ways. Yet none of these seem sufficient to placate an American public that was humiliated and distressed. Conversely, in the decades that have passed since the seizure of the embassy, the Iranians have come to see the hostage crisis as resulting from a revolutionary spasm that should not preclude the resumption of relations with the United States. Such arguments may be factually valid, but they cannot ameliorate the grievances of a nation that was subjected to such gross maltreatment.

The hostage crisis undeniably assisted the clerical estate in the consolidation of its power, as it exploited the frenzied atmosphere to eliminate its rivals. However, in the long run, the crisis proved detrimental to Iran's interests and stature. A legacy of suspicion would plague U.S.-Iranian relations and thereby create a wall of mistrust that successive administrations in both countries could not breach. In a sense, the relations between the two states were clouded by emotion, and neither the passage of time nor the emergence of common interests could fully heal the rift. Once more, Khomeini's conduct had generated a narrative that would haunt and damage Iran for decades to come.

The Iran-Contra Scandal

In an interview on July 2007, the former head of the Revolutionary Guards, Mohsen Reza'i, mused that "I have always said that Americans are not prepared for negotiations. The only person of courage that spoke of dialogue and relations with Iran was Reagan."[27] The former guardsman was speaking of the Iran-Contra affair, which ultimately involved the disastrous trading of arms for hostages. However, the centrality of that episode lies not in its sordid details but in its continued impact on the bureaucracy. After the damage that it inflicted on the Reagan administration, few in the national security establishment have been prone to use daring and creative approaches with the Islamic Republic. Although flawed in both its conception and assumptions, the secret opening to Iran constituted the last time that senior U.S. officials were inclined to think outside the box. More than two decades after its revelation, the Iran-Contra affair still haunts the bureaucracy, and the trail of scandal and terminated careers has had a stultifying impact on American deliberations, making caution the currency of the debate.

The cast of characters involved in the plot could not have been more bizarre. The Middle East has a long tradition of amoral politics with competing political actors amenable to dealing with the enemy of their enemy. However, even in that context, the Iran-Contra affair ranks as one of the strangest episodes. The opportunistic mullahs mingling with Israeli officials in European capitals, mendacious arms dealers, and naïve Americans in search of moderates somehow came together to produce a comic drama. All of the actors played their part, concealed their real motives, and downplayed their true ambitions. The Iranians deftly dangled the hostages, the Israelis crafted a long tale of struggling moderates determined to accommodate the United States, and the arms merchants lied to all of the parties involved.

In the aftermath of the earlier hostage crisis, the relations between the United States and Iran remained tense. The Islamic Republic's revolutionary zeal and its commitment to the export of its vision clashed with the America's objectives throughout the Middle East. However, the most serious conflict between the two parties would take place in Lebanon. That was where the United States would suffer its worst terrorist attack prior to 9/11 and where it began the policy of trading arms for hostages as well.

The tale of the Iran-Contra affair goes back to the tribulations of Lebanon in the early 1980s. In June 1982 Israel invaded Lebanon in the hope of evicting the Palestinian Liberation Organization (PLO) from its latest sanctuary and installing a more docile, Christian-dominated government in Beirut. The first goal was achieved with ease, whereas the task of stabilizing war-torn Lebanon under a friendly regime would largely elude Jerusalem. The arrival of multinational forces to supervise the PLO's departure coincided with the advent of Iran's Revolutionary Guards. Given their longstanding connection to the radical Shiite forces in southern Lebanon, Iran began amalgamating these disparate groups into a cohesive force in the form of Hezbollah. Rafsanjani expressed the Islamic Republic's commitment to the Shiites:

> The resistance in Lebanon is under pressure. However, all this takes place at a time when the Islamic Republic has arrived in the world. At a time when 40 million Muslims are willing to be martyrs; at a time when an eastern front is formed against Israel, and at a time when the ocean of Iranian oil has been added to the strength of the Muslim people, we shall prevail.[28]

Iran would remain Hezbollah's main organizational, financial, and spiritual backer, nurturing a protégé that succeeded as a paramilitary group, political party, and purveyor of social services to the impoverished masses.

In the midst of Lebanon's turmoil, Israel, with the blessing of the United States, sought a formal peace treaty with the Christian-minority government that it had installed in power. The opposition to such an opportunistic move pervaded Lebanon's complex, multiconfessional society. On April 18, 1983, a truck bomb exploded outside the U.S. embassy in Beirut, killing sixty-three people, including seventeen Americans. The Israelis proved undaunted, however, as they signed the second peace treaty with an Arab country since the Camp David Accords. Whatever the historical dimensions of the agreement might have been, it soon unraveled amid the reverberations of Lebanese politics.

As Washington became further embroiled in Lebanese affairs to the point of deploying its own contingent of U.S. Marines as peacekeepers, it soon became a target of revenge. On October 23 of the same year, one of the first spectacular uses of suicide bombings in the Middle East killed 241 American soldiers. Hezbollah, with strong operational assistance from Iran, made its presence powerfully clear. The subsequent withdrawal of U.S. forces constituted an important lesson for Iran and the region, namely the notion that asymmetrical warfare and the use of terrorism could negate America's superior firepower. The implausible Israeli scheme for remaking Lebanon's political landscape and the hasty U.S. intervention had brought Iran fully into Lebanon's mix, and hostage taking became the next point of contention.

In Lebanon's tit-for-tat politics, the abduction of ordinary citizens was the norm among factions pressuring their rivals. Soon American academics, clergymen, journalists, and even intelligence officials were caught up in the whirlwind. Once more, Washington looked impotent as its citizens were falling victim to enforced captivity while it seemed unable to either retaliate or resolve the situation. The plight of the hostages arrived at a time when Iran and Israel were coming together in a peculiar relationship that would soon involve the United States.

By the mid-1980s the stalemated war with Iraq was causing considerable problems for the theocratic regime. The inability of the state to deliver its pledged military victory and the economic burdens of the war were causing a popular backlash. As the war dragged on, the U.S.-equipped Iranian army desperately needed spare parts. The Reagan administration's Operation Staunch had successfully closed off many avenues for Iran to obtain either American or European arms. Despite the Islamic Republic's frequent castigations of the United States, Tehran had respect for American technology. The ruling mullahs often derided the French and Russian arms that Iraq was purchasing as inconsequential to the course of the war and claimed that only U.S. munitions could have a meaningful impact.

The notion that the Iranian moderates required arms from the United States to tip the internal balance of power in their favor became the core logic of the arrangements between the United States and Iran. To be sure, even after the purges of the early revolutionary period, the Islamic Republic continued to feature a diversity of views. The more radical faction led by Prime Minister Mir Husayn Musavi and Ayatollah Muntaziri pressed for the creation of a pristine Islamic order and continued defiance of the superpowers. Through state control of the economy, rigid enforcement of religious strictures, and a revolutionary foreign policy, Islamic unity would be maintained. The war with Iraq was seen as just one episode of a larger struggle against the West and its regional proxies. The more pragmatic faction led by Rafsanjani and Khamenei did not dispute such revolutionary

commitments but called for balancing them with national-interest calculations. The need to prosecute the war made the management of the economy and the task of procuring weapons urgent priorities. These objectives
mandated some adjustments and even a reexamination of the country's
ties with the "Great Satan." Isolation and needless provocations of the
United States would only endanger the revolution.

However, at this point the arbiter of all of these debates and disputes
remained Khomeini, whose entire career was dedicated to his ideological
enterprise. Khomeini was not an ordinary politician prone to abandon
declared principles at the altar of expediency. The grand ayatollah was
intensely devoted to his Islamist mission, which always identified the
United States as a source of imperial transgression and cultural contamination. He was not blind to the exigencies of Iran's predicament and thus
the need to obtain weapons for a war he would not abandon. The dealings
with the United States certainly contravened Iran's political assertions and
the regime's ideological pillars. However, they were not an indication of a
return to realism or a propensity to reach out to America but a necessary
prioritization of enemies. For Khomeini, the United States remained the
"Great Satan" and Israel a moral abomination, but the greater task of
defeating Saddam mandated tactical bargains with reprehensible entities.
Khomeini would go along with Rafsanjani's schemes and even withhold
information of such dealings from the more radical elements of the state.
Once the entire affair was revealed, he went to great lengths to protect
Rafsanjani from any retribution. However, to imply that such arrangements constituted a fundamental reorientation of Khomeini's long-held
views is misplaced and fanciful.

The developments in Lebanon and Iran's quest for American military
equipment might not have developed into a full-blown arms-for-hostages
deal had it not been for Israel and its own set of calculations. Given its
precarious location and its constant conflict with surrounding Arab countries, there has always been a strain in Israel's international orientation that
has pressed for improvement of relations with non-Arab Middle Eastern
states. The proponents of the so-called periphery doctrine called for Israel
to develop ties with Turkey and Iran as a means not only of escaping its
isolation but also of pressuring the Arab governments into ceasing their
belligerence. The periphery doctrine has had important successes, such as
the forging of close diplomatic and commercial ties between Israel and
Iran during the shah's tenure. In yet another of the Middle East's many
paradoxes, even the advent of a stridently anti-Zionist revolution in Iran
failed to disabuse the Israelis of the value of the periphery doctrine.

Perceiving the Khomeini interlude as an anomalous period in Iran's history, many within Israel sensed that in due course the aging mullah would pass from the scene and Persian nationalism would reassert itself. Thus, through arms sales, Israel would maintain contact with Iran's military and its moderate politicians, who were bound to succeed Khomeini.[29]

Israel's inclination to develop links with Iran was reinforced by its identification of Iraq as its greatest enemy. By the early 1980s, Israel's strategic position in the Middle East had vastly improved. In its immediate neighborhood, Egypt's embrace of the Camp David Accords removed a perennial source of concern for the Jewish state. The Palestinians had been evicted from Lebanon, while the tacit understanding with Jordan was intact. Syria could sustain its antagonism, but, deprived of measurable support from other neighboring Arab states, it had a limited impact on Israel's practical security. The one factor that loomed large in Jerusalem's calculations was Saddam Husayn; his desire to forge a new Arab coalition against Israel; his large, Soviet-armed military; and his nuclear aspirations.[30]

The Iran-Iraq war provided Israel with a great opportunity to weaken Baghdad while developing relations with Tehran. As part of this scheme, Israel began selling arms to Iran shortly after the commencement of hostilities. The problem was that, increasingly, Israel could not transfer the type of arms that Iran needed without violating U.S. laws that prohibited such exchanges without American approbation. To continue with its conduct, Israel needed not just Washington's consent but active participation as well. The idea of freeing American hostages held in Lebanon and reaching out to Iranian moderates was a convenient manner for Israel to bring the United States into its ongoing plot. The Israelis' calculations fortuitously coincided with the Reagan administration's own reconsideration of its Iran policy.

By the mid-1980s, the U.S. bureaucracy was growing more concerned that Iran's isolation could only benefit the Soviet Union in the Middle East.[31] A beleaguered Iran in search of allies might just reach out to Russia and gradually come under the Soviet orbit. For many officials within the Central Intelligence Agency and the National Security Council, it was time for an opening to Tehran. Moreover, in Iran's persistent factionalism, they saw hope for a policy that could strengthen the more temperate elements. As part of such an outreach effort, some within the CIA even recommended arms sales.[32] In essence, the United States was seen as insufficiently engaged with Iran, which thereby deprived Washington of an ability to influence important trends within the theocratic regime.[33]

The Soviet-centric view found a hospitable home in the White House, which saw most regional issues within a cold-war context. Donald Regan, the White House chief of staff, claimed that Reagan told him emphatically that "We cannot allow Iran to fall into the Soviet camp."[34] William Casey, director of the CIA and a close presidential advisor, similarly stressed that "The U.S. could not turn its back and allow it [Iran] to fall under Soviet influence."[35] The Russian occupation of Afghanistan, which both Washington and Tehran opposed, was seen as an example of geopolitical commonalities that could be enhanced through dialogue and cooperation.

Beyond the strategic arguments, the plight of the American hostages held in Lebanon weighed heavily on Reagan. As with his predecessor, Reagan found himself preoccupied with the fate of the hostages, whose release continued to elude his administration. The humanitarian claims were particularly acute in the case of one hostage, William Buckley, the CIA station chief in Beirut, whose condition was considered worrisome given the torture and other maltreatment that he was subjected to. The ordeal of the captured Americans led Reagan to press his intelligence services and the State Department to produce results. As Secretary of State George Schultz recalled, "the pressure mounting on the White House and from the White House was to do something."[36] In a strange twist of events, the Americans, the Israelis, and the Iranians were all eyeing each other at the same time and searching for a means of establishing contact.

The genesis of the Iran-Contra affair was a series of meetings between Israeli officials and Manuchehr Ghorbanifar, an Iranian arms merchant of dubious credibility. Ghorbanifar offered a rationale that was bound to prove tantalizing to his prospective American interlocutors and provided the sordid affair with a veneer of strategic justification. The arms merchant noted that moderate elements within the theocracy were battling the radicals and seeking to establish better relations with the United States. The contours of the deal began taking shape. Israel wanted to sustain its periphery doctrine, Iran needed arms, and the unsavory weapons dealers were looking for profits.

As the transaction unfolded, many within the U.S. bureaucracy were left in the dark since the National Security Council (led initially by Robert "Bud" McFarlane and the deceitful Colonel Oliver North) was largely in charge. McFarlane seems to have genuinely anticipated an opening to Iran, while North was nurturing his obsession with assisting the Nicaraguan rebels, the Contras, who were battling the Communist government in Managua. Indeed, the attempt to resist and roll back Communist gains in Latin America had become one of the central pillars of the so-called Reagan

Doctrine, which pledged a more aggressive stance against leftist forces throughout the developing world. The struggle to sustain the anti-Communist government of El Salvador and topple the Marxist regime of Nicaragua were among the most important objectives of the Reagan administration. Soon the American military equipment began flowing into Iran, while a number of hostages were occasionally released. In an even more bizarre development, the proceeds from the arms sales were diverted to the Contras—in contravention of congressional mandates.

On May 25, 1986, McFarlane, North, and four other officials were finally presented with an opportunity to embark on a historic journey of reconciliation. The American emissaries had come bearing gifts, including a Bible signed by Reagan and a chocolate cake. The former national security advisor and his entourage landed in Tehran, hoping to meet President Khamenei, Prime Minster Musavi, and, of course, Rafsanjani. McFarlane came prepared to discuss the means of ending the Iran-Iraq war, restoring the severed ties between the United States and Iran, and securing the freedom of the American hostages held in Lebanon.

Once in Tehran, McFarlane was relegated to meeting second-tier officials, particularly Muhammad Ali Hadi Najafabadi, chairman of the parliament's Foreign Affairs Committee. In the course of discussions, the two exchanged expansive but inconclusive views on how to mend relations between Iran and the United States and stabilize the Middle East. The promised meeting with senior officials never materialized. Even Najafabadi finally informed McFarlane that, although discussions could continue, the notion of a rapprochement was premature. In essence, the trip was a means of placating the exasperated Americans while dangling the possibility of future talks so long as additional weapons were received. Moreover, even the few hostages that were released were soon replaced by other hapless Americans in Beirut: Captives had proved to be a lucrative commodity.

As with the Reagan administration, many influential Iranian officials were also left out of the deliberations between Washington and Tehran. Upon discovering the secret meetings, the radical faction of the theocracy wasted little time in scuttling the whole affair. Mahdi Hashemi, son-in-law of Ayatollah Muntaziri, soon leaked the entire episode to a Lebanese newspaper, *al-Shirra*. The public revelation that Americans were trading arms for hostages effectively ended one of Washington's few attempts to reexamine its relationship with the Islamic Republic.

The Iran-Contra affair inflicted significant damage on the credibility and standing of the Reagan administration.[37] The final congressional report issued a scathing indictment of the whole affair: "The Iran initiative succeeded only in replacing three American hostages with another three, arming Iran with 2004 TOW missiles (Tube-launched Optical-tracking Wire-guided) and more than 200 vital spare parts for Hawk missile batteries, improperly generating funds for the Contras and other covert activities."[38] Indeed, the diversion of funds to the Contra rebels transformed the entire affair from an embarrassment into a scandal.

Less well known was the impact of the arms deal on the theocracy's internal balance of power. The radicals criticized any idea of a rapprochement with the United States and viewed the occasion as a suitable time to marginalize their moderate rivals. Muntaziri denounced the entire affair by claiming that "All the difficulties in the Islamic world have their roots in America and Zionist enemies of Islam."[39] Premier Musavi similarly stressed that "Relations between America and Iran are like those between a wolf and a sheep, and its [sic] only purpose is to commit crimes."[40] In the meantime, the parliament threatened an investigation and called on the Foreign Ministry to explain who had met with the Americans and for what purpose. The conservative newspapers, led by Kayhan and Risalat, also began agitating against Rafsanjani and his allies.

For his part, Rafsanjani quickly retreated, covering himself in a barrage of anti-American rhetoric and false claims to justify his role. In his initial comments, the speaker of the parliament stressed that "America has taken many risks and without our agreement and in violation of law entered our territory. This demonstrates the value of the Islamic Republic and the extent that they will go to [to] get close to us."[41] However, the notion that the series of meetings between the two sides, McFarlane's secret trip to Iran, and the purchase of arms were somehow an illegal American ploy failed to impress his militant critics.

The clamor against Rafsanjani finally subsided, but only when Khomeini stepped in and quelled all of the investigations and attempts at score settling.[42] After all, Khomeini himself had approved the enterprising designs of his more pragmatic disciples and understood the desperate need for arms that had motivated the entire affair. "You should not create schism. This is contrary to Islam," Khomeini admonished the parliamentarians and the radical newspapers.[43] In his unsubtle spin, Khomeini, who always relished humiliating the United States, tried to present the affair as a great triumph for the Islamic Republic. The imam stated that "The Iranian nation must be proud for the large explosion that it has inflicted on the Black House [Khomeini's typical reference to the White House] and the infamy that it has brought on the heads of the American state."[44] Sensing the direction in which Khomeini was going, Rafsanjani also took up the theme of celebrating America's embarrassment. The speaker of the parliament now rebuked the Americans: "You have been defeated and you must accept and admit the victory of the Islamic Republic."[45]

The Iran-Contra affair, including its comical sideshows and opportunistic cast of characters, has always been presented as an illustration of how difficult it would be to craft a diplomatic approach toward the Islamic Republic. Despite its ultimate failure, the core argument of the Reagan administration—that Iran's isolation was ill serving U.S. interests in the Middle East—was understandable. However, a number of factors would bedevil the initiative. The administration's poor understanding of Iranian politics and Khomeini's overarching animosity toward the United States made a significant breakthrough nearly impossible. Moreover, somehow the means of establishing contact between the two nations became trading arms for hostages. For Washington the release of the hostages became a barometer of Iran's seriousness, while, for Tehran, the continued dispatch of arms was seen as an indication of America's goodwill. Once the transaction of arms for hostages became the foundation of the new relationship, its failure was certain, as its inevitable exposure would subject the administration to untenable political pressure.

By far the most glaring misconception of the initiative was the notion that moderate elements would use the arms deal to displace the radical faction. The theocratic regime did indeed include pragmatic actors such as Rafsanjani, who were prepared to reexamine the country's ties with the United States. However, given the fact that the radical cohort included Khomeini himself, a dramatic diplomatic breakthrough was precluded. For the Iranians, the entire affair was not a grand gesture of reconciliation with the United States but a commercial arrangement designed to secure much-needed military equipment. Tehran would likely have played the game of trading hostages for arms much longer had it been in better control of its internal factions. Nonetheless, the scandal that enveloped Washington terminated otherwise favorable dealings for the Islamic Republic.

As with the hostage crisis, the Iran-Contra affair is not a passing episode. The sad trail of broken careers, congressional investigations, and criminal indictments continues to have an impact on U.S.-Iran relations. Although it is easy to deride McFarlane and the CIA analysts who were pressing for a reconceptualization of U.S.-Iran relations, they in fact acted in a bold and imaginative manner. If a thaw in U.S.-Iranian relations is ever to occur, then officials and bureaucracies must think creatively and assume great risks. After the scandalous failure of the Iran-Contra affair, few functionaries would favor such dramatic gestures. Yet another casualty of the incident was the discrediting of the entire concept of Iranian moderates in Washington. Even after Khomeini's passing and the ascendance of pragmatists and eventually reformers, the United States remained mired in stalled images of the past. Bureaucratic caution and onerous preconditions to any series of talks would come to characterize America's approach to Iran.

A Tragedy and a Fatwa

In the aftermath of the Iran-Contra affair, America's credibility reached its nadir in the Middle East. After imploring the Arab states to confront Iran and launching a concerted international effort to deny weapons to the Islamic Republic, Washington was caught selling arms to Iran and speaking the language of reconciliation. Given the need to bolster its disillusioned allies and avenge its humiliation at the hands of the mullahs, the Reagan administration was determined to contain Iran. A further tilt toward Iraq and a more assertive American presence in the Persian Gulf were to remind Tehran of U.S. power. For its part, the theocratic regime also seemed unwilling to revisit its relationship with the United States and focused more on its draining conflict with Iraq. At a time when the United States was seeking to reassure the Gulf states monarchies of its reliability and Iran was equally determined to punish those very same states for their support of Iraq, a clash between the two seemed inevitable.

The occasion that finally triggered the conflict was the American reflagging of Kuwaiti oil tankers. As part of its war strategy, Iran was increasingly targeting neutral shipping, particularly the vessels of the Gulf sheikdoms, who were generously subsidizing Iraq's war effort. For the Islamic Republic, such complicity in the war made the Gulf commerce a legitimate target of retribution. Although the Reagan administration initially demurred, once Kuwait appealed to a willing Soviet Union for help, the die was cast, and the U.S. Navy entered the contested waters of the Persian Gulf on the sheikdoms' behalf.

The arrival of the U.S. Navy did not necessarily deter Iran from its course of action. The Revolutionary Guards actually seemed to relish the opportunity to take on the "Great Satan." Iran continued to mine the Gulf and harass ships with its small-boat operations and hit-and-run tactics. Although both sides were leery of escalating the conflict, the presence of so many navy vessels in the Gulf, the ongoing discord between Iran and the

United States, and both parties' determination to demonstrate their resolve led to skirmishes and exchanges of fire. A pattern of Iranian provocation and American retaliation became the order of the day.

July 2 was a particularly troublesome day in the Gulf, with U.S. helicopters coming under fire from Iranian gunboats. Retaliation by the United States was swift, as one of the navy's more sophisticated cruisers, the USS Vincennes, had sunk two of the attacking vessels and was in search of further Iranian mischief. As the confrontation on the high seas was taking place, an Iranian passenger plane, Iran Air flight 655, took off from Bandar Abbas on its route to Dubai. The Bandar Abbas airport was known to house both civilian and military aircraft, and in recent weeks the Iranians had been busy constructing a launching path for their new antiship Chinese missiles in the area. As the aircraft appeared on the Vincennes' radar screen, the ship's captain assumed that it was a hostile carrier and fired two missiles. At least one of the missiles hit its target, killing all 290 passengers on board, including sixty-six children. The bluster and conflict of the past months had finally produced a tragedy.[46]

Despite days of mourning and incendiary speeches, Iran's reaction was basically subdued, as Tehran comprehended that the asymmetry of power and pervasive war weariness militated against escalation of the conflict. Rafsanjani declared that "we will not do anything wrong, not do as the United States did."[47] Such gestures of restraint and magnanimity concealed Iran's impotence, as the war with Iraq was draining its national resources without producing tangible military gains. In its determination to prosecute the war, the theocratic state had compromised many of its declared values. Whether purchasing arms from its archenemy, Israel, or now accepting without retaliation the downing of its civilian airliner, the revolution that had pledged defiance and dignity appeared enervated.

The shooting down of the passenger jet was yet another critical event in the formation of the legacy of mistrust between the two powers. The attack on the civilian airliner was an accident and a byproduct of the escalating tensions between Tehran and Washington, which were playing themselves out in the Gulf. However, for the Islamic Republic, there was nothing accidental about the strike. It was a premeditated U.S. attempt to intervene in the war on behalf of Iraq with the purpose of overthrowing the Islamic Republic. Once again, the mullahs and the populace concluded that the United States was implacably hostile to the theocratic order and, in its antagonism, would even target defenseless civilians. The fact that the Reagan administration had leaned toward Iraq and was providing Baghdad with intelligence and credits had already set the stage for Iran's suspicions.

The U.S. naval escort of Kuwaiti vessels and the downing of the airbus were viewed as deliberate escalations whose purpose was the demise of Iran.

The one dramatic consequence of the downing of the passenger plane was that it finally convinced the clerical elite that it was time to abandon the war.[48] Indeed, the conclusion of the Iran-Iraq conflict generated a new spirit of independence among the Iranian people. After long years of struggle and sacrifice, the public began defying the cultural restrictions and demanding a greater say in political affairs. The monumental task of reconstruction meant that many in the regime now sought to focus on internal challenges as opposed to radical crusades.

As the imam approached the end of his life, he grew apprehensive about the vitality of his revolution. Suddenly there was a risk that the vanguard Islamic Republic would become a temperate and cautious state. It was at this point that Khomeini undertook two specific acts to ensure that his disciples would sustain his revolutionary radicalism and guard against temptations of moderation. In 1988, shortly after the ceasefire with Iraq, the imam ordered one of his last acts of bloodletting. In less than a month, contrived tribunals executed approximately twenty-eight hundred leftist prisoners who were languishing in Iran's jails.[49] Apostasy and the denigration of Islam were the typical charges hurled at the victims. The mass executions were designed to test Khomeini's supporters and make certain that they were sufficiently committed to sustain the revolution. Those who yielded to humane compunctions would be seen as half-hearted and dismissed from the corridors of power. Indeed, when Muntaziri objected, he was forced into early retirement. The imam was confident that the government he left behind had the courage to inflict massive and arbitrary terror to maintain its power. However, he still had to ensure against possible backsliding on the issue of the United States.

These concerns led Khomeini to manufacture another external crisis and once more to stroke the revolutionary fires. The publication of Salman Rushdie's *Satanic Verses,* which depict the Prophet Muhammad in an unflattering light, offered the grand ayatollah the perfect opportunity. In February 1989 Khomeini issued a statement that was bound to inflame:

> I would like to inform all intrepid Muslims in the world that the author of the book entitled *The Satanic Verses,* which has been compiled, printed and published in opposition to Islam, the Prophet and the Quran, as well as those publishers who were aware of its contents, have been sentenced to death. I call on all zealous Muslims to execute them quickly, wherever they find them, so that

no one will dare to insult the Islamic sanctions. Whoever is killed
on this path will be regarded as a martyr, God willing.[50]

Soon Tehran added that the reward would not just be the celestial privilege
of martyrdom but the bounty of $2.6 million for an Iranian assassin and $1
million for a non-Iranian killer.

The imam's fatwa was clearly designed to radicalize the masses in sup-
port of the regime's ideology of wrath. In the midst of the ensuing contro-
versy, no one mentioned that Rushdie had previously won a literary prize
from Iran. Khomeini took advantage of the uproar that his order incited:
"As long as I am alive, I will not let the state fall into the hands of liberals."[51]
Prime Minister Musavi echoed this theme, claiming that the clash with the
West "will drive home the fact to Iranians that they should not rely on
Europe."[52] As with the hostage crisis, in Iran all politics remained local.
While the international community saw the imam's egregious act as an
indication of his intolerance and militancy, for Khomeini, domestic politi-
cal calculations were paramount. Iran was once more ostracized, a devel-
opment entirely acceptable to Khomeini.

As Iran stood alone and beleaguered, the imam celebrated its new status. "We must become isolated in order to become independent," implored
the aging ayatollah.[53] As a callous ruler who placed ideological purity above
the sufferings of his people, the imam was indifferent to the deprivations
his nation endured. Khomeini pointedly rebuffed any criticism: "What you
wanted was Islam, what you wanted was an Islamic Republic, what
you wanted was neither West nor East. All these objectives have been
achieved."[54] The revolution had once more managed to reassert itself,
denying pragmatism and progress as the basis of its legitimacy.

During the tumultuous 1980s, Iran's policy toward the United States
was defined by an ideological antagonism that largely defied practical considerations. More so than at any other time, a series of events would take
place that would make it hard for either party to develop trust and confidence in its adversary. The hostage crisis, the failed Iran-Contra gambit,
and the shooting down of a civilian aircraft all buttressed a legacy of suspicion that successive U.S. and Iranian administrations would find difficult
to overcome. The order to assassinate an author for publishing a book further reinforced popular images of the Islamic Republic as an irrational
state prone to extreme and destructive conduct. Iran's policy during this
time was conditioned by Khomeini's antagonism toward the West and the
exigencies of the Iran-Iraq war. At times these competing demands would
lead Iran in opposite directions. The need to prosecute the war with Iraq

led Iran to deal with the United States and trade hostages for arms. Yet the imam's all-consuming hatred for the United States brought about confrontations with the "Great Satan" in both Lebanon and the Persian Gulf. As he approached the end, Khomeini feared that the conclusion of the war with Iraq would dissipate the spirit of revolutionary solidarity and even lead some of his more moderate disciples to a settlement with the West. The death sentence pronounced against Rushdie was a parting shot, yet another attempt by Khomeini to cement his anti-American ideology as a pillar of the Islamic Republic.

Historians and observers of Iran have correctly noted that during the three decades since the inception of the Islamic Republic, the United States has missed various opportunities to reconcile with the clerical regime. To be sure, U.S. policy has often displayed an ignorance of Iran and a lack of appreciation for the subtleties and intricacies of its political order. Still, during the 1980s no serious occasion for the normalization of relations between the two states ever presented itself. Khomeini's animosity toward the United States and his determination to export his radical vision precluded an improvement of ties. The tragedy of Iran is that the imam created a system of governance and an ideological framework that would go on to restrict the initiatives of even the most enterprising of his successors.

3

Turmoil in the Levant

Iran, Israel, and the Politics of the Arab East

A CURSORY EXAMINATION OF IRAN'S APPROACH TO ISRAEL MAY lead some to dismiss its incendiary rhetoric and its periodic calls for the eradication of the Jewish state as symbolic gestures without practical relevance. After all, the mullahs did secretly mingle with Israeli officials and purchase large quantities of Israeli arms at exorbitant prices. Moreover, despite persistent mutual denunciations, the two powers never went to war against one another. Beneath the cynical arms deals and furtive cooperation, however, lies a durable animosity that is predicated on both strategic designs and ideological values.

For a generation of Iranian leaders, Israel would remain an illegitimate state whose existence fractured the unity of Islam's realm and provided a foundation for America's imperial intervention in the Middle East. Iran's antagonism toward Israel defined its policy in the Levant and led it to make common cause with radical states such as Syria and militant actors ranging from Hezbollah to Palestinian rejectionist groups. The Islamic Republic's anti-Israeli stance was not devoid of strategic calculations, as its links to groups such as Hezbollah offered it a pathway to a region beyond its military reach. Over the years, Iran's foreign policy would modify itself along pragmatic lines. Still, in the midst of all of the changes, its animus toward Israel remained largely intact.

Battling the "Little Satan"

The Islamic Republic's enduring hostility toward Israel is an anomaly that can be explained only by an assessment of its Islamist ideology. Iran has no shared border with Israel, no Palestinian refugee problem, and no history of armed conflict with the Jewish state. Indeed, as a Persian, Shiite nation, Iran has often been at odds with the very same Arab states that oppose Israel. The theocratic regime's strident opposition to Israel is a new development inasmuch as Iran and Israel established close economic and security ties during the monarchical years. After the revolution, slogans denouncing Israel and calls for its extinction became a hallmark of Iran's rhetoric. Tehran went beyond demanding the establishment of a Palestinian state and essentially challenged the entire legitimacy of the Zionist enterprise.

Although the shah would go on to establish constructive, if tacit, relations with Israel, the Shiite seminaries were always a hotbed of anti-Zionist resistance. During the 1940s the clerical class was led by figures such as Ayatollah Abdulqasem Kashani, who called for political rallies against Jewish immigration and even organized volunteers to fight alongside the Palestinian forces. In the intervening decades, the clerical community often agitated against the Israeli state, urging a boycott of its goods and denouncing the emerging diplomatic relations between the two powers. The clerical tradition of staying out of politics that pervaded Qum at this point seemed to have shattered over the issue of Israel.[1]

During Khomeini's prolonged political struggle, a consistent anti-Israeli theme emerged in his many speeches, writings, and declarations.[2] Khomeini continuously propounded the notion that Israel was an enemy of the Muslims and was behaving as a sinister agent of U.S. imperialism in the Middle East. The imam insisted, "This source of corruption which has settled in the hearts of the Islamic countries under the protection of foreign powers should be uprooted through the efforts of Islamic countries."[3] Israel's very existence was attributed not just to superpower intrigue but also to the disunity of the Arab states and the propensity of the regional rulers to subordinate themselves to dictates from the United States. As such, Khomeini stressed, "Selfishness, servitude, and the surrender of some Arab governments to direct foreign influence has prevented tens of millions of Arabs from freeing Palestine from the yoke of Israeli occupation and usurpation."[4] Increasingly, the overthrow of the prevailing ruling caste was seen as a necessary prelude to the eradication of Israel.

Once he began his political activities in the 1950s, Khomeini vociferously opposed the shah's association with Israel. In his predictably militant manner, Khomeini went beyond condemning the nascent alliance between the two states and sensed Zionist conspiracies everywhere. "The independence of the court and the economy have fallen into the hands of the

Zionist," emphasized the imam.[5] In yet another inflammatory declaration, Khomeini claimed that the Jews were purposely publishing thousands of distorted Qurans in order to sow disbelief among Muslims and diminish their religious observance. A steady pattern soon emerged linking Israel and the shah in a nexus of opposition to Iran's national interests and religious identity.[6]

Although the Islamic Republic would go to great lengths to differentiate its opposition to Zionism from hostility toward Jews, a distinct strand of anti-Semitism characterized Khomeini's perspective. His writings reflected anti-Semitic themes, as he distorted Jewish history and the tenets of its beliefs. In his seminal book, *Hukumat-i Islami,* which became the blueprint of the theocratic state, the imam stressed, "Since its inception, the Islamic movement has been afflicted with Jews, for it was they who first established anti-Islamic propaganda."[7] Khomeini depicted Jews as surrogates of Western imperialism who had even distorted Islam's scriptural texts. As such, it was the responsibility of the clerical class to make "people aware that the Jews and their foreign masters are opposed to the very foundation of Islam and wish to establish Jewish dominance throughout the world."[8] One of Khomeini's most-often-repeated accusations was that the shah had allowed the Jews to infiltrate key sectors of society and that they in essence controlled Iran's economy. The Jewish penetration had been so thorough that the shah was reduced to a pliant proxy of their interests. The continuous caricaturing of Jewish power, noxious conspiracy theories, and denunciations of Jewish perfidy laced the public pronouncements of both Khomeini and his clerical followers. Moreover, Khomeini's indisputable anti-Semitism was not a passing phenomenon. Indeed, it has become a pillar of Iran's Islamist ideology.

It is important to note that Khomeini's frequent anti-Israeli invocations were not tactical ploys to gain popular acclaim in the Arab street but stemmed from a genuine belief that Israel was an artificial Western construct whose aim was to oppress Muslims. The imam did not suddenly discover the Israeli issue upon assuming political power but spent decades denouncing the Jewish state and admonishing the Arab leaders for their alleged passivity in the face of Zionist encroachment. For Khomeini, the most important sin was the original one, namely, the creation of Israel. On the eve of his triumphant revolution, Khomeini returned to his favorite theme: "We must rise up, destroy Israel, and replace it with the heroic nation of Palestine."[9] Also in this vein the imam was quick to condemn Arab leaders for their submissiveness: "We see that at a time when the enemy of Islam is occupying another land, other than Syria and the Islamic

Republic, no other Muslim country is doing anything serious."[10] In one key respect, then, the Islamic Republic's antagonism toward Israel exceeded even its anti-Americanism. After all, the theocratic regime may view the United States as a rapacious, imperial power that seeks to exploit and dominate the Middle East, but it has not denied its right to exist. Such deference, however, has always been withheld from Israel.

Khomeini's uncompromising position toward Israel came to differ from the calculations of the Arab states. In the ensuing decades after Israel's creation, the Arab regimes routinely denounced its legitimacy and even waged a series of wars against it. However, for the most part this was a nation-state conflict, and Palestine was seen as the heart of a dismembered Arab world. In due time, the Arab struggle confined itself to the territorial dimensions of the Jewish state as opposed to it actual existence. Iran sublimated the disputed territory and injected religious values and symbols into the conflict. This was not a mere territorial dispute but a conflict between the forces of Islamic righteousness and a profane, alien entity. The Palestinians may be the most direct victims of Israel, but the continued existence of the Zionist state constituted an infringement on the rights of all Muslims. Given its stridency, Iran would have more in common with the radical Islamist movements and would largely be excluded from the councils of Arab states as they plotted their strategy toward Israel.

Khomeini was hardly alone in his opposition to the Jewish state. His most intimate disciples echoed his claims of Israel's inauthenticity. Ali Akbar Hashemi Rafsanjani's *Isra'il va Quds-i Aziz* maintains that the anti-Zionist struggle was a "sacred Muslim duty."[11] The long-time foreign minister Ali Akbar Vilayati has also published a flawed book, *Iran va mas'alah-i Filastin: Bar asas-i asnad-i Vizarat-i Umur-i Kharijah,* which claims that Palestine was the essence of the Muslim world and that its restoration was necessary for Islamic cohesion.[12] The current supreme leader, Ali Khamenei, has also chimed in, wondering how it was that Palestine was "wiped from the world's map and replaced with a fabricated and fake state by the name of Israel."[13] Ali Akbar Muhtashami'pur, one of the most influential voices in the formulation of Iran's Israeli policy, similarly noted, "Israel is like a cancer in the region and this region can never be at peace with this tumor."[14] The notion of Israeli illegitimacy, the necessity of its demise, and the imperative of Muslim unity behind the cause of anti-Zionism became standard rhetoric in the Islamic Republic.

Upon their triumphant return to Iran in 1979, the one issue that all of the revolutionaries seemed to agree on was opposition to Israel. As we have seen, Prime Minister Bazargan differed from the clerical militants on a range of issues, including ties with the United States. However, one of the first acts of the newly inaugurated provisional government was to sever all connections with Israel. Bazargan explained that his decision was "in keeping with the policy announced before we came to power."[15]

The onset of the revolution brought a series of symbolic yet significant moves toward Israel. The first foreign visitor to rush to Iran and have an audience with Khomeini was Yasir Arafat, who arrived in Tehran and effusively proclaimed, "No one can believe that we are in Iran. Can anyone believe that the Palestinian revolution is in Iran? We now believe that new days have begun."[16] Clearly imbibing the revolutionary spirit of the Islamic Republic, Arafat exclaimed, "Israel will be destroyed and Palestine will triumph."[17] The trip was not without its moments, however, as the keys of the Israeli embassy were presented to the PLO emissary and the street where the compound was located was renamed Palestine Street.[18]

However, the lofty rhetoric and pledges of solidarity concealed an underlying tension between the two parties. The clerical rulers deprecated the PLO's secular nationalism and pressed Islamism as the suitable ideology of resistance. The PLO's most important supporter, the left-leaning Ayatollah Mahmud Taliqani, was being obscured by clerical firebrands who demanded fundamentalism as the basis of Iran's international relationships. To further compound the difficulties, the PLO's presence in southern Lebanon was provoking tensions with the Shiite populace and antagonizing a core base of support for the Islamic Republic. In a contest between the PLO and the Lebanese Shiites, Iran was bound to side with its coreligionists. For Tehran, the struggle to reclaim Palestine would assume a high priority, but the PLO would not always be its preferred instrument.

Further contradictions and paradoxes appeared in Iran's strident opposition to Israel, as mandates of governance and the quixotic struggle against Israel contradicted each other. Iran's only suggestion for resolving the Arab-Israeli impasse was combat. However, Iran would largely exempt itself from participation in a direct military confrontation with a state of such superior force. Instead, Rafsanjani implored Arab states "to go and take the place by force and say our government will be established here."[19] Vilayati similarly suggested that "Arabs in general and Palestinians specifically should take action based on armed struggle."[20] In an interesting formulation, Iran's calls for hostilities and the eradication of Israel did not entail a commitment of its own military. All of this is not to suggest, however, that the Islamic Republic remained passive, for it soon emerged as the benefactor of an entire range of terrorist organizations, particularly the lethal Hezbollah. Despite its incendiary rhetoric, Iran always preferred to work through surrogates as a means of shielding itself from Israeli retribution.

The use of indiscriminate violence would seemingly raise troubling quandaries for a theocracy devoted to spiritual pursuits. For example, how can a religious state justify terrorist attacks on civilians? Once more, the imam stepped in with his own contrived justifications. Khomeini declared, "The Jews in other countries differ from the Jews in the occupied Palestine. All the Jews who have settled in the occupied Palestine are part of the tyrannical regime and attacking them is equivalent to attacking Israeli soldiers."[21] In essence, Khomeini insisted that there was no difference between civilians and combatants and that the entire Israeli population was a legitimate target of retribution.

Given the intense antagonism between the two states, how does one explain the arms deals that began in 1981 and culminated in the notorious Iran-Contra affair? Although the unseemly arrangement is dealt with in the previous chapter, it is important to understand how a combination of geopolitical calculations and humanitarian concerns pressed Israel to sell arms to its archenemy. At the time of the revolution, Israel was concerned about the fate of the approximately ninety thousand Jews who were still living in Iran. During his exile, Khomeini had met with Jewish leaders and assured them that his opposition to Zionism did not translate to hostility toward the local Jewish citizenry. The disingenuousness of this pledge was soon evident as most of the religious minorities were relegated to second-class citizenship. For the Jewish population the situation seemed even more ominous; in fact, soon after the revolution, the elderly president of the Jewish community, Habiballah Ilqanian, and a number of other prominent Jews were executed. Given the mullahs' continued assertions of Jewish conspiracies and their reliance on crude anti-Semitic propaganda, the Israeli state had to be concerned about the welfare of Jews living under such conditions. Israel faced an unenviable dilemma, as a policy of pressure would not necessarily alleviate the condition of Iran's Jews. However, an opening to Iran could offer a potential avenue for extracting the increasingly desperate Jews from their predicament. Jerusalem began entertaining the possibility of a new bargain, namely exchanging military spare parts for Jewish emigration.

The other facet of Israel's arms sales was the notion that the Islamic revolution was an aberration and that, in due time, Persian nationalism would reassert itself and even lead to the displacement of the mullah regime. As we have noted, a core element of Israel's strategic conception was the notion of the periphery doctrine, the idea that Israel could forge favorable relations with non-Arab states of the Middle East as a means of escaping its isolation. The advent of the theocratic regime did not disabuse influential Israelis of the utility of that doctrine. Through arms sales, Israel could not only bring about the release of the local Jews but also maintain links with the armed forces, which would likely succeed the theocracy. A leading Israeli voice on these issues was Israel's former chief representative in Iran, Uri Lubrani, who claimed that "Israel should relate to Khomeini's frightening revolution as if it were a passing phenomenon."[22] In a similar vein, David Kimche, a senior Israeli Foreign Ministry official, recalled, "There was a feeling that if we in Israel could somehow maintain relations with the [Iranian] army, there [sic] could bring about an improvement of relations between Iran and Israel."[23] Through arms transactions, Israel would maintain connections not only to the "true Iran" but also to the one institution that had the power and credibility to effect regime change.

The advent of the Iran-Iraq war was the final trigger that brought these two unlikely actors into an arrangement of tacit cooperation. Once Saddam launched his devastating attack, a purged and demoralized Iranian army appeared in full retreat. Given the hostage crisis and American animosity, it was difficult for Iran to obtain the U.S. military equipment that its armed forces desperately needed. For the Israeli leaders the collapse of Iran was a real fear since they still identified Iraq as their greatest strategic challenge. An Iran capable of repelling Saddam could not only deflate his regional ambitions but also devastate his menacing military might. After all, as an Israeli official conceded, "One of the major reasons for the cooperation between the two countries is the likely access of Iraq to atomic bombs and its unconditioned support for the PLO."[24] For Jerusalem, the proposition of aiding an enemy to defeat a more immediate foe justified the transactions. Yitzak Rabin, Israel's defense minister, similarly sanctioned the deals: "What is good for Israel is a no-win situation in the Iran-Iraq war. This is in Israel's strategic interest and the political mileage that Israel has gotten out of it has been incalculable."[25] A prolonged war would allow Israel sufficient time to cultivate elements within Iran's armed forces, weaken the Khomeini regime to the point that its overthrow could be contemplated, and diminish Iraq's power. These mutually reinforcing advantages necessitated dealing with an ardently hostile theocratic state.

The remarkable aspect of this relationship was its flexibility and the propensity of the two parties to compartmentalize their disagreements. By 1982 Iran and Israel were involved in a proxy war in Lebanon, with Jerusalem seeking to impose a Christian-dominated government, while Tehran was actively organizing the Shiite resistance. Yet the cooperation forged ahead, and Israel provided Iran not just arms but also intelligence data and even reliable third parties that could supply additional sophisticated weapons. However, these arrangements were hardly concealed from the Reagan administration, as Washington tacitly acquiesced to Israel's schemes. The hawkish Ariel Sharon openly admitted to the sales: "We told the American officials that we know the ayatollahs are dictators, but we have no choice except to keep a window open toward Iran for the day the war would be over and somebody else would take over in Iran."[26] In due time, the Israeli-Iranian arrangement would encompass the United States and produce a full-fledged scandal that nearly toppled the Reagan presidency.

It is at times suggested that the Israeli-Iranian arms deal reveals the hollow nature of Tehran's ideological assertions and the essentially pragmatic nature of its foreign policy. Such perceptions miss the point, however, that it was Iraq, not pragmatism or moderation, that brought the two states together. Moreover, the Iranians never denied their cynical motivations and the tentative nature of the deal. During the first meeting between the two sides, Ayatollah Hasan Karubi, Iran's point man on this issue, plainly noted that "any cooperation between Israel and Iran on Iraq should not be taken as a sign that the Islamic government would recognize Israel, but should be seen as a matter of expediency."[27] The fact that nations under duress make adjustments to their ideological stance is neither exceptional nor without precedent in international affairs. The exigencies of the conflict and Iran's acute isolation mandated a tacit arrangement with Israel. Such dealings implied neither an abandonment of Iran's ideological aversion to the Zionist state nor a propensity to cease opposing it throughout the Middle East.

During its first decade in power, the Islamic Republic evinced considerable hostility toward Israel, and its indictment involved an entire range of issues. At one level, Khomeini and many of his clerical allies saw the Jews as always plotting against Islam, and the creation of Israel as the mere continuation of that historical pattern. The foundation of Israel added to the indictment. It had not just displaced Palestinians and fractured Islam's domain but also provided a base for Western intervention in the Middle East. Israel was to be a surrogate for America's power by policing the region on behalf of its superpower patron. The fact that Israel maintained close relations with the shah and did much to buttress his power further estranged the revolutionaries. A combination of anti-Semitic caricatures, historic grievances, and Islamist perceptions propelled Iran toward an enmity that has remained largely intact despite substantial changes in its international relations during the intervening three decades.

The ideological antipathy toward Israel still required a tangible expression other than calls for Islamic unity and steadfastness. It is here that Iran was more subtle in that it utilized proxies and agents. Given the asymmetry of power, Iran had to live with Israel without acknowledging that reality. Tehran's opposition to Jerusalem would prove enduring yet without remarkable impact, as Israel continued to flourish and succeed. In a curious manner, the Islamic Republic itself stood to benefit from such a low-intensity conflict. So long as Iran could avoid a direct and costly confrontation with Israel, then its antagonism served both its strategic interests and its ideological values. On the strategic front, such moves granted Iran access to the Arab east. In the meantime, Iran's strident opposition to the Jewish state and its subsidization of Islamist rejectionist forces and terrorist organizations garnered it the acclaim of the Arab world. It is to Iran's allies and enablers that we must now turn.

Islamizing Lebanon

As with all revolutionary regimes rebelling against the established authority, the Islamic Republic sought to support a wide variety of liberation movements, Islamist forces, and terrorist organizations. Once in power, the clerical state gradually lost its appetite for an alignment with radical Western groups such as the Irish Republican Army and focused more or less exclusively on the Islamic nations. However, even within this narrower context, the Sunnis, who were initially enthusiastic about Khomeini's defiance, grew wary of the Shiite revolutionaries. The war with Iraq, Saddam's largely successful depiction of that conflict as a struggle between Shiites and Sunnis, and Khomeini's own rigid fundamentalism estranged moderate Sunni opinion, leaving Iran with its hard-pressed coreligionists. The coincidence of interests between the Shiites and the Islamic Republic was most evident in Lebanon.

The Shiite Muslims constituted a minority sect throughout much of the Middle East, and where they constituted a majority, they were usually ruled by Sunni tyrants. In Lebanon, the Shiite community suffered from the twin forces of a raging civil war and the Israeli invasion. By 1975, the delicate confessional order that had balanced the various ethnic and religious sects had broken down into a vicious civil war. In addition, Lebanon's problems were compounded by the PLO's decision to use its territory as a sanctuary for attacking Israel. A virtual Palestinian state was created in southern Lebanon, leading to persistent Israeli incursions.[28] The Shiite community, which was frequently left out of power and omitted from the distribution of economic wealth, suffered most as Lebanon's political order collapsed and Israel extracted its revenge against the unfortunate state.[29]

It was not the Iranian revolution that triggered the political awakening of Lebanon's Shiites. In the preceding decades important clerical forces had been discarding the tradition of quietism for one of militancy and activism.[30] Musa Sadr was the first renowned cleric to step into Lebanon's contested terrain and mobilize the Shiite forces.[31] In due course, however, the main Shiite political party, Afwaj al-Muqawmat al-Lubnaniyya (AMAL), was transformed into a largely secular force that accepted even the Christian parties' political prominence. Such developments worried the more austere clerics such as Shaykh Muhammad Husayn Fadlallah, who had grown alarmed about the spread of secular ideologies and the young people's attraction to Western political imports. As with the Iranian mullahs during the 1960s, he bemoaned the irrelevance of the clerical estate to Lebanon's emerging struggle and advocated the formation of religious parties and even militias. The demands of this newly empowered community were simple and direct: Lebanese Shiites should enjoy political and economic power commensurate with their demographic plurality.

Into this combustible mix arrived Iran's revolution. Suddenly it appeared that through simple belief and bold resistance the downtrodden could reclaim their society. A populace battling for its share of political power and seeking relief from its constant dislocation was moved by Iran's improbable revolution. The Islamic Republic was happy to reciprocate, as its financial assistance made a real difference in the everyday lives of the Shiites. Schools, clinics, hospitals, sanitation facilities, and cheap housing were all provided by Iran. The clerical regime viewed its presence in Lebanon as an effective means of attacking American and Israeli interests while propagating its Islamist message. Before the overthrow of Saddam by the United States, Lebanon was the central arena of Iranian activism and one of the few places where the revolution appeared to make inroads.[32]

Iran's commitment to Lebanon was strengthened by the fact that a number of key officials—Defense Minister Mustafa Chamran, Ali Akbar Muhtashami'pur (Iranian ambassador to Syria and later interior minister), and Muhammad Muntaziri (a leading figure in many revolutionary groups)—had their formative political experiences there.[33] The fact that a core group of the Revolutionary Guard commanders had trained in Lebanon in the 1970s before returning to take on the shah's regime meant that the more extreme elements of the state had practical knowledge of Lebanon and its factions. The Israeli invasion of 1982 led to a more direct

Iranian involvement, as a contingent of the Revolutionary Guards took up the task of organizing the Shiite militias while Muhtashemi'pur mediated the differences among the widely varying Shiite political parties and associations. Despite the war with Iraq, Iran was still prepared to be involved in Lebanon's war. Foreign Minister Vilayiti claimed, "We see no difference between Saddam and Zionist aggression and we are prepared to fight on both fronts."[34] The seamless connection between these two battlefronts was also noted by Ayatollah Ali Mashkini, the influential Friday prayer leader of Qum: "I am hopeful that soon we will go through Karbala and hand-in-hand with Shiites of southern Lebanon liberate Jerusalem."[35] Eventually, under Iranian supervision, a number of armed Shiite groups and political organizations were amalgamated into Hezbollah.

The exact nature of Iran's financial assistance to Hezbollah remains an area of conjecture and speculation. The principal group overseeing these operations was the Section for Movement of Islamic Liberation, which did not declare the scope of its activities. However, Western sources have claimed that, between 1982 and 1986, Iran's monthly donations totaled $3–$10 million.[36] In an important article, Abbas William Samii demonstrates that the Imam Khomeini Relief Committee donated more than $96 million to Hezbollah from 1988 to 2002.[37] The Islamic Republic also offered its share of military hardware, as Khomeini claimed that it was impractical to dispatch a large number of Iran's own forces and that the best thing to do was to "prepare and equip them to defend their own country against Israel and retrieve what is the right of the people of Palestine and Lebanon."[38] Furthermore, Iran's financial assistance was designed not just for paramilitary and terrorist activities but also for social services, which did much to enhance Hezbollah's standing and stature in Lebanese society.[39]

Although Iran is routinely credited with creating Hezbollah, the critical role that Syria played should not be discounted. The Syrian regime may not have shared Iran's ideological enthusiasm for the emergence of the Shiite bloc, but it still saw certain advantages to the ascendance of this community. The ties to Hezbollah allowed Iran and Syria to buttress their alliance, as Damascus became an indispensable geographical bridge between Tehran and its Shiite ally. For Syria, Hezbollah presented a means of indirectly striking Israel and the United States, and, properly unleashed, the Shiite force could keep various other Lebanese factions in line. All of this is not to suggest that Syria was excited about the triumph of an armed Islamic group since it sporadically confronted its own fundamentalism problem. However, for the brutal and Machiavellian Hafiz al-Asad, a connection to Hezbollah, however convenient, was a means of keeping all options open.[40]

At a very essential level, the endurance of Iran's relationship with Hezbollah stems from the fact that it conforms to the Islamic Republic's ideological values, as well as its strategic objectives. At a time when Iran's revolutionary message was finding only a limited audience in the Middle East, Hezbollah proved a loyal protégé. In its founding document, Hezbollah made its allegiance unmistakably clear: "We address all Arab and Islamic peoples to declare to them that the Muslim experience in Islamic Iran leaves no one any excuses for it proved beyond all doubt that bare chests motivated by faith are capable, with God's help, of breaking the iron and oppression of tyrannical regimes."[41] The document clearly reflected Iran's influence. Its Islamist imagery and depiction of the global struggle between the oppressed and the oppressors were standard fare in Tehran's discourse.[42]

Hezbollah's founding charter was also a challenge and a rebuke to the regional rulers. As with Khomeini, Hezbollah insisted that disunity among the Muslim states was the reason Israel flourished and the United States dominated the Middle East. Such fragmentation was the deliberate design of Western imperialism. By investing power in a pliant and corrupt ruling class, the United States sustained its presence. The use of violence was therefore important in order to achieve "the departure of America, France and their allies from Lebanon and the termination of the influence of any imperialist power in the country."[43]

Along the Iranian model, Hezbollah also departed from the Arab consensus on the need for negotiations to extract territorial concessions from Israel. Such talks were derided as legitimizing the Zionist state and sanctioning its hold on Islamic lands. Hezbollah's solution was not that dissimilar to Khomeini's, as it pledged that "Israel's final departure from Lebanon is a prelude to its final obliteration and the liberation of Jerusalem from occupation."[44] Again, at a time when the Arab states were moving away from such absolutist positions, Hezbollah firmly took its place next to the Islamic Republic and decried the existence of the Jewish state.

Despite its religious pretensions, Hezbollah followed Iran's theocratic paradigm by defying normative Shiite political tradition with its insistence on clerical quietism. The notion of an Islamic Republic and a direct assumption of power by an esteemed ayatollah finally found a receptive audience among the Shiite clerical order in Lebanon. Fadlallah hinted at this when he claimed, "Lebanon is an Islamic country and is comprised of [a] majority of Muslims. The objective of the struggle of Lebanese Muslims will be toward an Islamic system."[45] The religious class's active engagement in politics and even its organization of armed struggle were seen as imperatives. After all, the ulema, with their superior knowledge of Islamic jurisprudence, could best decipher the divine will and lead the society along the path of righteousness and solidarity. This was the vanguard argument preferred by Iran's revolutionary militants, whereby an elite group would lead the masses. There would be more fluidity in Hezbollah's leadership, but its organizational claims seem to have derived from the experiences of the Islamic Republic. As Hezbollah pursued its struggle, the mosque became the party headquarters, social service organization, and even a center for military indoctrination. In this formulation, the mosque was not just a place of worship but also a venue for political and social mobilization.

On the strategic plane, Hezbollah soon emerged as an instrument of Iranian foreign policy, and its terrorist mastermind, Imad Mughniyya, conducted many operations at the behest of the Islamic Republic. As we have seen, the most spectacular of such actions was the bombing of the U.S. Marine barracks in 1983, which provoked America's withdrawal from Lebanon. The collaboration between the two parties would not end there, however, as Hezbollah undertook the assassination of many Iranian dissidents, abducted Western hostages, who were duly traded for U.S. arms, and continuously pressured Israel. Hezbollah's violent campaign was also critical in scuttling the 1983 Israeli-Lebanese accord, which both Washington and Jerusalem had hoped would be the second important peace compact between an Arab state and Israel. The mere presence of Hezbollah offered Iran a reach into the Arab east, as the power of its protégé meant that Tehran could not realistically be excluded from the political deliberations of the local states.

Although in recent years the international community has grown accustomed to the Islamic Republic's ritualistic denials of its ties to terrorist organizations, in this earlier period, it readily acknowledged its assistance to Hezbollah. Shortly after the 1983 bombing, the head of Iran's judiciary, Ayatollah Abdul Karim Musavi Ardabili, noted that the Lebanese have learned the "lessons of the revolution from Iran." The Iranian Foreign Ministry offered its own justification: "The United States and the multinational force have entered Lebanon, supported by the Zionist regime with the objective of usurpation of Lebanese nation."[46] For his part, Mohsen Rafiqdust, minister for the Revolutionary Guards, recalled the importance of Iranian activism: "We infused Lebanese Shiites with the spirit of resistance, and if the U.S. intervenes it will be taught the lessons of Vietnam."[47] Although Tehran did not explicitly admit its role, it did suggest that the attack was appropriate and a necessary lesson for the foreign forces. So long as Hezbollah was willing to inflict damage on Iran's foes, the

Islamic Republic could maintain its distance and target its nemeses with impunity.

The fact that Iran's revolution found a hospitable home in Lebanon is ironic since the Mediterranean nation has long been known for its cosmopolitan nature and its rich literary tradition. However, the ravages of the civil war, external intervention, and the plight of the Shiite community offered Iran an opening to project its power. The inability of the central government to mediate the local rivalries and the virtual autonomy of the Shiite clerical community led to a type of connection between Iran and Hezbollah that would prove difficult to sever. In the intervening decades, both Lebanon and Hezbollah would change, yet Iran's influence has remained largely intact. The survival and triumph of Hezbollah is one of the most important achievements of Iran's quest to export its revolution.

An Improbable Alliance: The Iran-Syria Axis

Among the most enduring yet anomalous alliances in the Middle East is the Syrian-Iranian relationship. On the surface it may seem improbable for a Shiite regime determined to redeem the region for the forces of religious virtue and a secular state devoted to pan-Arabism to come together. Yet a series of shared antagonisms led both sides to overlook the incongruity of their alliance and collaborate on a range of critical issues. The expressions of friendship, frequent high-level visits, and numerous commercial contracts, however, failed to conceal the fact that on topics such as the Arab-Israeli conflict and the disposition of Lebanon, the two powers have had substantive disagreements. In the end, a strategically opportunistic Hafiz al-Asad would find the fundamentalist Ayatollah Khomeini an uneasy partner.

The 1979 Iranian Revolution came at an opportune time for the Syrian regime, which had grown isolated and increasingly marginalized in regional affairs. The Camp David Accords had led to Egypt's defection from the struggle against Israel and left Syria to face a strengthened Jewish state on its periphery. In Damascus the fear was that the Reagan administration was hoping to facilitate additional peace treaties and was particularly targeting Jordan and Lebanon, two other states that border Syria. In the meantime, the perennially bad relations between the two Ba'athist parties governing Syria and Iraq had only worsened amid charges of interference in each other's internal politics. Through its willingness to oppose Syria's Israeli and Iraqi nemeses, Iran's revolution altered the Middle East's political configuration. The Islamic Republic's embrace of anti-Americanism as a core element of its foreign policy distanced Tehran not only from the United States but also from the conservative Arab states, which were wary of Syria. In one fell swoop, the Middle East's balance of power changed, leading Damascus to escape its insularity and become a more critical player in Arab politics.[48]

For an Islamic Republic determined to both wage war against Iraq and pursue a harsher policy toward Israel, the alliance with Syria proved particularly valuable. The Asad regime's willingness to supply arms to Tehran came at a time when the American-led embargo was depleting Iran's arsenal. Moreover, an alignment with an Arab state fractured the wall of Arab solidarity and diminished Saddam's ability to portray his war as a contest between Arabs and Persians. The alliance also offered Iran a reach beyond its borders, as Tehran suddenly had access to Lebanon and could more vigorously pursue its anti-Israeli campaign. In a perverse manner, in order for Iran to wage its Islamist crusade against Israel and displace Saddam's regime, it had to forge a relationship with a state whose internal composition must have been anathema to the mullahs.[49]

The ensuing association with Syria reflected the Islamic Republic's propensity to prioritize its ideological antagonisms. The contradictions between an Islamist regime predicating its policy on pristine religious values and a secular, Ba'athist state became starkly evident during the 1982 rebellion in the city of Hamah, when Asad viciously decimated his fundamentalist opposition. The carnage and brutality of that campaign stand as unique even in the context of the blood-soaked politics of the Middle East. Iran's response to the massacre was to denounce the Muslim Brotherhood "as a gang carrying out the Camp David conspiracy against Syria."[50] A theocratic state ostensibly devoted to propagating its divine message not only stood by as fellow fundamentalists were annihilated but offered words of support to the offending regime as well. As with the Israeli arms deal, this was a question of priority. Waging war against Iraq and weakening Israel ranked higher than the fate of Syria's beleaguered Islamists.

The strategic tensions underlying the Syria-Iran alliance became evident in Iraq.[51] For Iran, the alliance proved nothing but beneficial. Beyond gaining an important source of weaponry, Syria's closure of Iraq's oil pipeline, which traversed its territory, inflicted an economic penalty on Baghdad. The support of a major Arab nationalist state allowed some of the Persian Gulf sheikdoms to hedge and not sever their ties to Tehran. Despite the ample assistance that Iraq obtained from Saudi Arabia, some other members of the Gulf Cooperation Council such as Oman and the

United Arab Emirates used the Syrian fig leaf to sustain their formal relations with Iran. It is arguable that, without the Arab cover provided by Damascus, these sheikdoms could not have disregarded the nearly uniform Arab consensus for isolating Tehran. As Rafsanjani recalled with gratitude, Asad did not disassociate "himself from a country that advocated Islam because this country is not an Arab country."[52]

As the war dragged on, the Syrian regime found it had to reconsider its approach to its problematic ally. In Damascus, the initial justification for supporting Iran was that Saddam's invasion had diverted the resources of an important Arab country from the main struggle against Israel. Thus, Baghdad's opportunistic designs were actually damaging the Arabs and constituted yet another defection from the main anti-Israeli cause. Saddam's invasion was even more egregious given that the state he targeted was willing to devote its national power to battling Israel. It was Saddam who had destroyed the "eastern front" and prevented both Iran and Iraq from concentrating their resources on Jerusalem. Beyond such assertions, Syria sought to further rationalize its alliance by suggesting that its close ties to the Islamic Republic gave it sufficient credibility to mediate the conflict and even impose restraint on the theocracy.

Syria's claims became more difficult to justify as Iran appeared dogmatic in its pursuit of the war and seemed prone to expand the conflict into the Persian Gulf. As a champion of Arab nationalism, Damascus could ill afford a prolonged alliance with a country that disregarded Arab sensibilities and was determined to dispatch its armies into Iraq and disrupt the Gulf commerce. The specter of Persian armies capturing important seats of Arab civilization such as Basra could not enhance Syria's position among the regional states and the larger Arab public. Moreover, Asad's reliance on aid from Saudi Arabia and Kuwait meant that he could not always ignore the estrangement of the oil-rich sheikdoms. The claim that his alliance had helped resolve the conflict proved fallacious since Khomeini did not seem open to a peace settlement. The tensions between supporting Iran and sustaining a place in the Arab system led Damascus to oppose certain Iranian measures. After 1982, when Iran successfully evicted Iraq from its territory and took the offensive, Syria disapproved of extending the war to the Gulf states and went so far as to promise to support Kuwait against Iranian aggression.[53] By the mid-1980s, Syria had come to oppose Iran's appropriation of Arab lands, a policy that was articulated in a variety of Arab summits and emphasized to Iranian emissaries. Had the war continued beyond 1988 or had Iran triumphed in the conflict, Asad might have been forced to make some fundamental choices and reassess his ties to the Islamic Republic.

Lebanon was another arena of contentious cooperation between the two powers. After the Israeli invasion, the coordination of policy between Tehran and Damascus demonstrated the utility of the alliance. For Syria, the potential absorption of Lebanon into an American-Israeli sphere of influence threatened its basic security. Coming on the heels of Egypt's peace treaty with Israel and Jordan's tentativeness, Syria could ill afford yet another setback. For Iran, the invasion offered an opportunity to directly intervene in Lebanon's internal affairs and establish its own footprint in that besieged nation. Iran's mobilization of Islamist forces increased the cost of Israel's invasion and helped scuttle Jerusalem's attempt to install a friendly Christian government in Beirut. Despite the Arab clamor against Israel's attack, Iran was the only state to dispatch troops to the front line of the conflict. Moreover, irrespective of its ongoing war with Iraq, the Islamic Republic was prepared to deploy forces to Syria should it be invaded by Israel.[54] At a time when Asad desperately needed help to fend off Israeli designs, such assistance proved invaluable.[55]

Although the two sides could collaborate against an external actor in times of war, their divergent perceptions of Lebanon ensured a degree of tension. For the imam, Lebanon was an arena for the export of his revolution and a base for the pursuit of his anti-Zionist campaign. Asad understood the strategic nature of the conflict and sought to use Lebanon as a means of extracting concessions from the Jewish state. Syria dismissed the impractical notion of obliterating Israel in favor of a more realpolitik approach. As such, Syria could potentially concede to a peace compact, while the Islamic Republic remained devoted to obstructing all diplomatic efforts to resolve the conflict between Israel and its neighbors. Given Iran's geographic distance, it could afford to be less cautious in its policies and more absolutist in its pretensions. As a frontline state, Syria did not have the luxury of abiding by Iran's determinations. The injection of Iran's radical ideology into the Arab east threatened to widen the conflict and provoke a war that Syria simply did not want. In this regard, Iran's ideological zeal and Syria's calculated strategic designs did not mesh well.

The other problem for Damascus was Iran's close ties with Hezbollah. For decades Syria had sought to dominate Lebanese politics by crafting a balance of power among its bewildering factions and militias. The ascendance of Hezbollah, with its call for an Islamic state and its close ties to Iran, gave the Shiite militia a degree of autonomy from Syrian control. The fact that Hezbollah was militarily more capable than Syria's preferred AMAL and that it was more efficient in the distribution of social services to its constituents further concerned Asad.[56] In the late 1980s, there would be sporadic clashes between Syrian forces and Hezbollah, as Damascus sought to clip the wings of the insurgent militia. Such moves did not sit well in Tehran, which had come to identify Hezbollah as its most successful client.

Yet another area of contention between the two parties was the rampant hostage taking that was engulfing Lebanon in the 1980s. Initially Asad approved of the abductions because it put pressure on the Western power to leave and made Syria's military presence a useful counterweight to Hezbollah. However, by the mid-1980s, as Asad was seeking to improve his image in the West, the hostages were proving an obstacle. Their release might have been in Damascus's immediate interest, but Tehran was in no mood to compromise. As we have seen, the hostages were proving a lucrative commodity for the mullahs, who were busy exchanging them for arms from the United States. Ultimately, it was the vicissitudes of Iran's internal politics that led to the exposure of the affair and ended the capture of innocent Americans in Lebanon. The hostage drama indicated not only that the national objectives of the two states were not always consistent but also that Syria could not easily impose its will on either Iran or Hezbollah. The reality remains that the emergence of Iran as a power player in Lebanon infringed on Syria's prerogatives.

Although the Islamic Republic was an intensely ideological state, its relationship with Syria reflected its propensity to come to terms with a secular government that was assisting it in its prosecution of the war with Iraq and shared its animus toward Israel. This was not the only such compromise that Iran made during this period, as it even purchased arms from Israel in order to wage a war against Saddam. In the context of the Levant, for Iran to be able to implant its fundamentalist vision in Lebanon and pressure the Jewish state, it had to deal with a Syrian regime that was both secular in outlook and forcefully suppressing Muslim activists. The alliance's great advantage was also its weakness. Given that the relationship between Iran and Syria was predicated on common enmities and crass opportunism instead of shared values, it would always be plagued by tension and mutual suspicion. Nonetheless, the fact that the alliance has persisted for so long should not surprise us. Indeed, it reflects the Middle East's basic inability to resolve its conflicts, the continuance of which often serves Iran's larger strategic ends. A successful mediation of the differences between Israel and Syria and a more concerted attempt to stabilize Lebanon might have deprived Tehran of its indispensable Syrian alliance.

During the first decade of the revolution, the Islamic Republic took a series of steps that established its policy toward the Levant. Despite decades of war, conflict, and even peacemaking between Israel and its neighbors, Iran's hostility toward the Jewish state guided its policy in the Levant. A combination of ideological antipathy and strategic interests consolidated the theocratic state's antagonism toward Israel. In its mischievous path, Iran would find an enduring ally in the hapless state of Lebanon. As Hezbollah garnered acclaim and support across the Middle East, Iran stood to benefit from the triumph of its protégé. In an improbable move, the theocratic regime also managed to forge a relationship with Syria, which, regardless of its tensions and incongruities, has survived and flourished. The "revolution without borders" managed to score impressive gains in the Arab world, which only made it more difficult for the clerical elite to envision a policy change.

4

Iran-Iraq War

THE IRAN-IRAQ WAR REMAINS ONE OF THE LONGEST CONFLICTS in the history of the modern Middle East. The war would define Iran's foreign policy orientation, as the exigencies of the conflict conditioned its approach to the United States, the Arab world, and even Israel. Iran fought the war with remarkable disadvantages in view of the fact that it lacked reliable allies, a dependable supply of arms, and the goodwill of the superpowers. The regime's ability to sustain an eight-year conflict reflects its resilience and ability to mobilize the society and consolidate its power under duress. The state, which was often viewed as a transient phenomenon, proved that it could deal with domestic challenges and international isolation while waging total war.

Iran's conduct in the war reflected its militancy and revolutionary fervor. This was not an interstate conflict fought for territorial adjustment or limited political objectives. What was at stake was a contest of ideologies and a competition for power. The clerics, whose revolution had succeeded against great odds, assumed that spiritual valor would compensate for Iraq's technological edge. Military planning and issues of strategy and tactics were cast aside for the sake of martyrdom and sacrifice. The war and the revolution had somehow fused in the clerics' imagination. To wage war was a way of demonstrating one's commitment to the divine mission launched by Khomeini in 1979.

The war that Khomeini hoped would realize his ideological values ended up undermining the transnational mission of the state. After an inconclusive but costly struggle, Iran failed to defeat Iraq, transform the

Middle East, and even project its Islamist template beyond its boundaries. The Islamic Republic would now have to rest its legitimacy on factors other than its religious imperatives or revolutionary aspirations. A state that had so long resisted mundane considerations uneasily became another government preoccupied with providing services to its constituents and achieving its objectives within the prevailing international system.

Provocations

The triumph of Iran's revolution, with its denial of the legitimacy of the prevailing order, and its calls for reformulation of the state structure along religious precepts portended conflict. Revolutions are frequently followed by war, as the newly empowered militants often look abroad for redemption of their cause. International relations are a means of affirming the vitality of the larger mission as opposed to realizing national interests. Revolutions, with their perception that their claims are universally applicable and their blurring of the distinction between domestic and foreign affairs, are inherently unpredictable. Not only did Iran's theocratic revolt share these impulses, but, given its religious characteristics, it also cast all of the issues in a distinct binary context with the forces of piety battling a profane order. For Khomeini, the success of his revolution at home mandated its wider regional relevance.

The onset of the revolution did not immediately change the uneasy truce that had characterized relations between Tehran and Baghdad since the 1975 Algiers Accord had settled the dispute over the Shatt al-Arab waterway. The Ba'athist regime even welcomed the demise of the shah, whose great pretensions to power and close ties to the United States led to frequent clashes with Iraq. The moderate and judicious Bazargan government, with its neutralist foreign policy and a determination to improve relations with Iran's neighbors, did not overtly concern the masters of Iraq. Indeed, Bazargan was even invited to Baghdad in July 1979 with an eye toward improving relations between the two erstwhile nemeses.

The demise of the provisional government and the consolidation of power by radical clerics dramatically altered Iran's approach to the region. During the heady days of the revolution, Iran's frenzied leaders sought to aggressively export the revolution. The speedy collapse of the shah's regime convinced them of the brittle nature of the Persian Gulf dynasties and the Arab secular republics. Iran did not limit itself to denouncing the authenticity of these regimes but also established an entire array of unofficial institutions to aid the opposition forces. For the local states, Iran's conduct constituted a gross interference in their internal affairs, not to mention a violation of their territorial integrity.

A disturbing pattern then emerged, with Iran mixing aggressive propaganda, subversion, and terrorism to advance its cause. As always, Khomeini and his clerical cohort would begin by denying the legitimacy of the existing ruling class and castigating the sheikdoms for their close ties to the United States. Terrorism and violence were not far behind, as such measures were a necessary response to iniquitous regimes. Whether it was plotting a coup in Bahrain, bombings in Kuwait, or instigating riots during the annual Hajj pilgrimages, Iran quickly estranged its neighbors. In a retrospective gaze, Ayatollah Muntaziri, who has grown moderate since being ousted from power, noted Iran's complicity in its fate: "Our harsh slogans against them and talk of exporting the revolution provoked them to act against us and these slogans became the basis for provoking Iraq and causing eight years of war."[1] To be sure, the Gulf states had vulnerabilities. All of these nations contained sizeable Shiite populations, which had historically been left out of the spoils of power. The blatant discrimination of the Sunni rulers had confined the Shiites to second-class status, in which they were deprived of both political standing and an important share in the national economy. By providing sanctuary to the opposition forces, working through the network of mosques, and misusing its diplomatic missions for political agitation, Tehran made itself a source of animosity.

Perhaps nowhere was Iran's message of Shiite empowerment received with greater acclaim than in Iraq. A defiant and resolute Ayatollah Muhammad Baqir Sadr shattered the conventions of political passivity by openly embracing Iran's revolution and its clerical patron. In a 1979 fatwa, Sadr declared his "total support for the imam" and even suggested that it was dishonorable for Muslims to join the Ba'ath Party.[2] These were not idle claims of an errant cleric, as Sadr's stature, close connections to the leading Shiite political party, al- Da'wa, and his street power made him an important opponent of the state. Sadr's frequent arrests not only led to his further radicalization but also sparked riots in the shrine cities of Karbala and Najaf. In the meantime, a number of Iraqi Shiite parties united under the banner of the "Islamic Liberation Movement," which was devoted to armed struggle against the Ba'athist rule.[3] The culmination of all of this was an assassination attempt against Tariq Aziz, the deputy prime minister, by Shiite forces during his speech at the University of Baghdad. Saddam's reaction featured all of the brutality and excess that characterized his tenure. In light of the Iranian revolution, whereby a rebellious cleric led a national revolt by force of personality and his religious pedigree, Saddam brooked no disobedience and executed the esteemed man of religion. Sadr's death was followed by random arrests, summary executions, and the expulsion of countless Shiites of Iranian origin. Saddam seemed to have genuinely feared the spread of Khomeini's Islamist revolt and blamed his Shiite problem on Iranian manipulation.[4]

The rise of dogmatic clerics in Iran placed the conflict between the two powers not just in practical but also ideological terms. The religiosity of Khomeini's revolution and his unique appeal to the hard-pressed Shiite masses threatened to undermine a secular regime that was governing a restive majority. For Khomeini, the Arab socialist republics were as much of an anathema as the monarchical states that he had always disparaged. On the strategic front, Khomeini's assertion of predominance over the Persian Gulf unnerved an Iraqi state that had its own hegemonic aspirations. Moreover, as a leading pan-Arab state, Iraq saw an opportunity to rebuff a Persian nation that had grown comparatively weaker due to the ravages of the revolution.[5]

However, Iran's provocations cannot alone account for the war, as opportunism and greed also pressed Saddam toward conflict.[6] Saddam's ambition to emerge as the leading actor in the Middle East was reinforced by Iraq's changing regional position. By 1979, the Iraqi regime was at its most stable, as it had largely silenced the Kurdish insurgency while its oil wealth stood second only to Saudi Arabia's. Within the Middle East, Egypt's expulsion from the councils of Arab states because of its peace treaty with Israel made Iraq the focal point of Arab order. The size of its army, its rising oil revenues, and its geopolitical centrality enhanced its predominance as well. Saddam seemed to have perceived that his move against Iran was a necessary step toward consolidating his regional position. The opportunity to tame Khomeini and emerge as the Arab hegemon coincided with internal convulsions in Iran that made that task seemingly much easier.

In the midst of these changes, Saddam must have noticed how his antagonist was dismantling its armed forces. The confusion of Iran's policy at this point was nowhere more evident that in its conduct just before the war. On the one hand, Iran was providing material and moral sanctuary to Saddam's opponents and engaging in similarly inflammatory acts throughout the Gulf region. Yet the revolutionaries' distrust of the military and their perception that the armed forces were an instrument of oppression led them to systematically downgrade the shah's impressive strength. Iran was canceling military purchase orders, reducing the size of its armed forces by a third, and delaying conscription calls. In a sense, the revolutionaries, who had come to power rebelling against the prevailing order, disdained conventional military preparations in favor of people's militias. In the initial frenzied stages of the war, the Iranian mullahs perceived themselves as the vanguards of a new epoch immune from the constraints of politics and history. Iran indulged in its rhetorical assaults and mischievous practices while at the same time making itself vulnerable to the retribution that such conduct often provokes.

Sensing great opportunities within his grasp, Saddam convinced himself that this would be a quick war. History has shown over and over again that, as a political leadership contemplates war, it overstates its own military capabilities and undervalues its foe's ability to wage war. Overconfidence accompanied fear and opportunity, as Saddam sought to gain strategic advantage while dispelling a grave threat. This was a preventive campaign: a war of ambition and a war to punish a strident regional rival. Saddam sensed that a quick thrust could either cause the collapse of the theocratic regime or force it to quickly petition for peace, leaving him with the sizeable and valuable Khuzistan territory in southwestern Iran. The seeming imbalance of military power between the two states and a suitable international environment whereby Iran was distrusted and isolated made the invasion inevitable.

In the summer of 1980, Iraq began to establish the antecedents of an invasion of Iran. Saddam's rhetoric underwent a subtle transformation, directly indicting Tehran for Iraq's internal disturbances. In a pointed measure, Saddam called on the Iranian masses to overthrow the "mummy Khomeini" and stressed his hope that the "Iranian people would find someone else other than this rotten Khomeini."[7] In an even more belligerent tone, Saddam virtually promised war: "It is not a bad thing to avoid a clash with Iran, unless a clash is a patriotic and national duty."[8]

Iraq's incendiary rhetoric was accompanied by a series of actions that exacerbated tensions. Although Iran can be blamed for its provocations, it is important to note that Iraq was hardly a blameless actor. Baghdad not only launched its own virulent propaganda campaign that denounced the Islamic Republic in harsh terms but also took concrete measures to buttress its antagonism. Iraq offered its own aid to Kurdish, Baluchis, and Arab guerrillas operating in the border areas. In the meantime, Saddam augmented Iraq's military capabilities by signing arms deals with France and even seeking naval control of the Gulf. Iraq, in its new role as the standard-bearer of Arab nationalism, was also demanding that Iran return the offshore islands initially captured by the shah and concede the autonomy of the Khuzistan province, which Saddam labeled "Arabistan." A vicious cycle of charges and countercharges, invectives, and insults now characterized relations between the two powers.

All of the discussion of ideological antagonisms and treaty violations cannot by itself explain the cause of the war since the personalities of the two leaders involved were also critical in triggering the conflict. One can argue that, had Khomeini and Saddam not emerged as leaders of their respective states, war could have been averted. As we have seen, Khomeini was a relentless ideologue willing to sacrifice his nation for the sake of his religious speculations. Even more ominously, the imam deeply resented Saddam and the Ba'athist state, where he had spent more than a decade in exile. During the early 1970s, when Iran and Iraq were locked in a territorial dispute, both sides aided each other's opponents. The shah was providing support for the Kurdish rebels while the Ba'athist regime took a benign view of Khomeini's agitation.[9] The relations between the Shiite ayatollah and the radical Ba'ath government were never intimate, but both sides saw some utility in tacit cooperation. After the 1975 treaty, which ended the conflict between the two parties, Baghdad tried to clamp down on Khomeini's activities by warning him that continued defiance would cause his expulsion. In due course, the grand ayatollah would be forced to leave the familiar confines of a Shiite city for alien France. As a vengeful leader with a long memory, Khomeini was already ill disposed toward the Ba'athist regime, giving him even more cause to plot Saddam's ouster.

For his part, Saddam also nursed grievances against Iran. The Iraqi strongman, who had been forced to retreat and sign the 1975 agreement, awaited his turn for retribution. Given Saddam's brutality and tendency toward self-aggrandizement, it is easy to forget that he was an Arab nationalist who felt that Iraq, as the ancient seat of Arab civilization, had an obligation to resist Persian encroachment. In his role as representative of the Sunni Arab order, Saddam saw himself as an avenger of a great cause: standing up to the Persian, Shiite menace. Saddam, the Iraqi nationalist, the Arab crusader, and the champion of secular modernity, had to vanquish the fundamentalist hordes led by a retrogressive mullah. As a risk-prone leader who had already failed to adequately consider the consequences of his invasion, Saddam possessed a personality that was critical to Iraq's persistent aggression.

The ostensible territorial source of the conflict was the division of the Shatt al-Arab, a 120-mile waterway that abuts Iraq's main oil terminals around Basra, as well as important Iranian ports and installations in Abadan. Since 1937, the waterway had been governed by an agreement that conceded essential control to Iraq. It was this arrangement that the shah forcibly revised in 1975, producing an accord whereby the deepest waterline was recognized as the new frontier. At that time, facing a militarily powerful Iran, which was actively sustaining the Kurdish insurgency, Baghdad felt it had no real option other than to acquiesce. All of this obviously changed with the Islamic revolution.

As the border clashes between the two states intensified, Saddam simply renounced the 1975 treaty, which had provided a means for operating the waterway. In his impetuous style, he claimed that "since the rulers of Iran have violated this agreement from the beginning of their reign as the shah before them, I announce before you that we consider the March 1975 agreement abrogated."[10] Finally, on September 22, 1980, the Iraqi dictator made the predictable, yet catastrophic, decision to launch an invasion of Iran, thereby provoking one of the most devastating wars in the annals of modern Middle Eastern history.

From Resistance to Aggression

Iraq's invasion initially scored impressive gains, as the city of Khurramshahr fell and the important industrial cities of Abadan and Ahvaz were besieged and isolated. Saddam flamboyantly proclaimed his desire to fight "until every inch of usurped land was restored to Arab control," an unsubtle claim on the oil-rich Khuzistan province.[11] Nonetheless, Saddam's ambitions outstripped his military acumen, and his forces soon encountered logistical difficulties that were the result of poor planning and unexpectedly stiff Iranian resistance. Even in the early stages of the conflict, Saddam's misjudgments were becoming obvious. For instance, the notion that Iraq's battlefield successes would lead to a mass uprising grossly misunderstood the mood of the Iranian people. Moreover, the belief that a revolutionary regime claiming to be in command of a new epoch would quickly cede vast portions of its territory and resettle itself in a truncated terrain was a misperception of how militant leaders behave during times of national crisis.

The Iran-Iraq war remains one of the most peculiar conflicts in history. For the clerical state, the progress of the war was seldom measured in territory lost or gained, boundary demarcations, or offers of reparation. The Islamic Republic's conceptualization of the war sought to merge its religious pedigree with its nationalistic claims. For the theocratic regime, the war was an assault on Islam and the Prophet's legacy by profane forces of disbelief. In his first declaration after the beginning of the conflict, Khomeini stressed, "You are fighting to protect Islam and he is fighting to destroy it."[12] This was not just a tool for the mobilization of a populace by a government that sublimated all of its struggles and sacrifices. The clerical estate genuinely identified itself with the Prophet's mission and saw Saddam's secular reign as yet another manifestation of inauthenticity and corruption. Iran had not been attacked because of its provocations or lingering territorial disputes but because it embodied Islam and sought to achieve the Prophet's injunctions. Thus, it was the moral obligation of the citizenry to defend Iran as if it were safeguarding religion itself.

In its propaganda, the Islamic Republic presented the war as a gift to its Muslim constituents and an opportunity to confirm their faith through deed. The Friday prayer leaders routinely used their sermons to suggest that God had offered Iranians such an unsavory foe to vanquish in order for them to claim a special place in his kingdom. From early on, Iran's war aims involved the maximalist objective of overthrowing not just Saddam but his entire Ba'athist state as well.[13] Armed with faith, Iran was bound to prevail because God would not allow the forces of righteousness to be defeated. Although the most obvious triumph was the demise of Saddam's tyrannical rule, the war offered another important reward, namely martyrdom. Not only would God ensure victory, but, on the path to success, all sacrifices would be recompensed by eternal reward.

Despite the catastrophic invasion of its territory and the burdens of war, the Islamic Republic welcomed the conflict as a means of consolidating its power, displacing its rivals, and transforming Iran's political culture. The onset of the war was celebrated as the "third revolution," whose purpose was not just to repel the invaders but also to cleanse Iran of all secular tendencies. In order to politically exploit the war, the state had to present the conflict in distinct religious terms. A revolutionary order that sought to usher in a new era could not wage a limited war designed to achieve carefully calibrated objectives. Rather, the war had to be a crusade—a rebellion against the forces of iniquity and impiety. Through collective sacrifice and spiritual attainment, the theocratic regime would fend off the invaders, change Iran, and project its power throughout the region.

In its quest to defend the war, the clerical state did not neglect Persian nationalism but fused it with the larger Islamic task. As a vanguard revolutionary state, Iran was the first nation to inaugurate an Islamic Republic and dedicate itself to the awakening of humankind. This task may have placed Iran in an ideal leadership position, but it also made it the target of retribution and revenge. Thus, to serve the nation and Islam were the same, as Iran was no ordinary country but an exalted entity devoted to a divine duty. The imam proclaimed, "The Islamic Republic is a trust given by the

Almighty to the Iranian nation. And all of us, young and old, man and woman, are responsible for guarding this trust."[14]

In the clerical cosmology, the defense of the nation and the propagation of the revolution were seen as part of the same continuum. Again, Iran in this conception was transformed from a mere country into an agent of revolutionary zeal. The Islamic Republic War Organization felt no compunction in advising the nation's youth "to perform your historical mission and your responsibility toward human society as the architects of this lasting phase of history."[15] By enduring the hardships of war, the Iranian people were demonstrating not just nationalistic ardor but also religious devotion.

The focus on Saddam and his moral decadence did not deflect Khomeini from blaming the United States and its allies. The Iranian narrative of the war clearly identifies Saddam as an aggressor, but his aggression was on behalf of a larger imperial conspiracy. As we have seen, for Khomeini the most important task was the spread of the Islamic revolution, and he saw the shah's downfall as the first step in a longer journey. The alarm and consternation of the Western powers and regional states naturally led them to try to stifle Iran's Islamist message. The war that Saddam launched was thus seen as a larger plot concocted by Washington and reactionary Arab leaders. The imam took the lead in urging his compatriots to "cut off the hands of America, which has emerged from Saddam's sleeve."[16] For his part, Rafsanjani noted, "We see this war as an American war. Thus, it is natural for Saudi Arabia, Jordan, and others to support Iraq."[17] The notion of presenting the conflict as a vast international effort to stymie Iran's Islamist revolt reflected the centrality of that transnational cause to Khomeini. To wage war until Saddam was overthrown may have been impractical, but for a leadership dedicated to spreading God's word, it was the only valid reason for fighting.

If Iran embodied and represented Islamic virtue, then its adversaries were naturally the forces of disbelief. However, Tehran's definition of who belonged in this unsavory category was elastic and not limited to Saddam's Ba'athist rule. An entire range of actors and nations that assisted Iraq's war effort were identified with apostasy and vice. This category in due course came to include the Gulf sheikdoms, the United States, the European nations, and all those who buttressed Iraq's war machine. The advantage of such a stark and convenient demarcation was that it drew a clear line between Iran and its enemies.

Whatever promises and perils the war held out, in its initial stages it had a surprisingly limited impact on the country's political stalemates and even on its focus on the raging Kurdish insurgency in the north. The clerical oligarchs continued their efforts to subvert Bani-Sadr's presidency, while the leftist opposition and regime loyalists persisted in their street battles. To be sure, the surge in revolutionary fervor did allow the government to castigate its opponents as a fifth column, but dissent and division remained a fact of life in the Islamic Republic. Even more intriguing was that the military leadership's determination to suppress the Kurdish rebellion remained largely intact because some of the more capable units were not quickly relocated to the south to obstruct Iraq's advance.

In January 1981 Iran finally began its counterattack and quickly scored impressive gains. The siege of Abadan (along the Persian Gulf) ended in the spring, and Iran then moved to expel the remaining Iraqi forces from its territory. Despite battlefield success, however, Iran's military establishment was plagued by tensions: The task of coordinating the Revolutionary Guards, the regular armed forces, and the Basij militias was not always easy. The commander of the ground forces, Sayyid Ali Shirazi, who had established a good relationship with the clerical leadership, noted these challenges:

> In these circumstances we did not have just one or two problems. It was not just a shortage of supplies, but the leadership of the forces. During such sensitive times, this was difficult as on the one hand were elements with a revolutionary spirit and on the other those whose long years during the reign of decadence gave them a different culture. This was very difficult.[18]

The ostensible Iranian strategy was to have the Basij and the Revolutionary Guard units carry out human-wave assaults that would overwhelm the ill-prepared Iraqi defenses. Once such an opening was achieved, the regular military contingents would finish the attack. Because they conserved munitions while achieving victories, these unrelenting offensive operations proved successful.

Along its revolutionary path, Iran dismissed conventional war planning and instituted a strategy that relied on religion and valor. "We depend on ourselves, our faith, and the strength of our people," explained Rafsanjani.[19] Prime Minister Musavi similarly stressed that "the power of faith can outmaneuver a complicated war machine."[20] Curiously, Iran perceived that its lack of reliable suppliers, sufficient hardware, and an experienced officer corps was not a disadvantage but an opportunity to prove that revolutionary idealism can overcome stark reality. The clerical leadership insisted that it had found a new Islamic warfare strategy that was not wedded to conventional tactics. In practice, this involved costly improvisation, poor coordination between different branches of the armed forces, and human-wave assaults, which were basically large-scale suicide missions. From the regime's perspective, though, this type of warfare demonstrated the vibrancy of the revolution.[21]

In the ensuing battle over tactics and strategy, Bani-Sadr often sided with the regular military rather than the zealous, yet largely incompetent, Revolutionary Guard leaders. As president, Bani-Sadr was initially the commander of all of the armed forces, including the Revolutionary Guards. However, that prerogative was soon encroached upon by the establishment of the Supreme Defense Council, which was dominated by the clerical firebrands. The mullahs used their institutional standing to intervene in war decisions, countermand Bani-Sadr's orders, and even appoint their own favorite officers. The imam's militant disciples equated caution and planning with lack of revolutionary commitment. Bani-Sadr's inevitable demise left unabridged the differences between the military and the Revolutionary Guards for the duration of the war.

The war was not without its share of mediation and diplomacy seeking to resolve the conflict. The foreign ministers of the Islamic Conference launched their own fact-finding tours, while Yasir Arafat made unsuccessful visits to both Tehran and Baghdad. Rafsanjani rebuffed all of these efforts by simply asserting, "As we are sure of victory and do not want to reward aggression, we refuse to negotiate."[22] The UN Security Council also issued a call for the termination of the war and the restoration of the borders. Moreover, the United Nations went beyond mere declarations and took a more activist posture with the appointment of former Swedish prime minister Olof Palme as its emissary. However, Palme's mission was frustrated by both parties. Iran continued to insist on designating Iraq as an aggressor and on the removal of all Iraqi troops from its territory before any discussion could even begin. For its part, Baghdad balked at any withdrawal of its forces and claimed that such a move could be considered only as part of negotiations. Both sides appeared willing to continue the war and engaged in laborious discussions over technicalities in the hope of impeding an actual settlement. The war would be decided on the battlefields, not around conference tables.

Because they distrusted both Iran's Islamist aspirations and Iraq's pan-Arab pretensions, the Persian Gulf emirates found themselves in a precarious position. The pull of Arabism and their disdain for an Iranian regime that was openly calling for their overthrow seemingly made supporting Saddam an easy choice. Yet the inter-Arab relations were not always harmonious, as the legitimacy of the monarchical states had long been challenged by the radical Arab socialist republics. As the war dragged on and Iran grew determined to export its revolution, the sheikdoms sided with the Iraqi strongman. Along this path, they augmented Iraq's military capabilities, came together in an unprecedented anti-Iranian alliance in the form of the Gulf Cooperation Council (GCC), and sporadically tried their hands at diplomacy, which they hoped would somehow end the conflict. In the end, in terms of political sympathies and financial assistance, the Gulf states made the faithful decision to stand with Saddam.[23]

Furthermore, the war confronted the United States with its own share of quandaries and dilemmas. As we have seen, the theocratic regime came to blame the conflict on America's machinations and continued to hold Washington responsible long after the war had ended. The United States did side with Iraq and eventually provided Baghdad with intelligence data and commercial credits. Iraq's European allies also proved generous arms merchants. The Reagan administration may have fully grasped the unsavory nature of Saddam's cruel dictatorship, but that did not prevent it from embracing the notorious despot. In the aftermath of the hostage crisis and Iran's relentless hostility toward the United States, Washington decided that it could not allow Saddam's Iraq to fall to a radical clerical regime. In hindsight, it is clear that this decision compromised America's values and moral standing.

By June 1982 Iran had essentially evicted Iraq from its territory and was focusing on whether it should cross into Iraq. Given the economic costs and the human toll that it ultimately extracted, the decision to attack Iraq remains one of the most contentious in Iran's modern history. In today's Islamic Republic one can rarely find a politician who does not claim that he had qualms about the invasion and even opposed it. In a grotesque act of historical revisionism, it is even suggested at times that Khomeini himself was against the move and wanted to end the war.[24] The theocratic state's attempt to whitewash its history does not change the fact that, besides Bazargan and his Liberation Movement and various commanders of the regular military, the regime had formed a consensus on the need to continue the conflict. As Rafsanjani conceded nearly two decades after the war, "During that time in Iran no one was prepared to accept a ceasefire. At that time we convened a meeting regarding the direction of the war, and the imam commanded that no one should speak of a ceasefire and that the war must achieve its goals."[25] Thus, a combination of ideological convictions, the misperception that the war would be brief, and the fear that Saddam would not remain contained pressed Iran toward the disastrous decision to prolong the conflict.

For the clerical rulers, the war was not just about territorial restoration but also about defending Islam and spreading the revolution. Thus, the ideal outcome was an extension of Iran's Islamist template to Iraq. As early as March 1982, there were discussions within the Islamic Republic about the need to pursue the war and overthrow the Ba'athist government.[26] The imam was vociferous in his insistence that "If we indulge Iraq's aggression, then we have indulged a certain idea, meaning we have encouraged perpetrators of oppression."[27] Ali Khamenei, who had succeeded Bani-Sadr as president, similarly claimed, "After the enemy has returned within his own border, then it is our duty and obligation to exert ourselves until the nation of Iraq is delivered from the evil of oppressive powers and an Islamic government and republic have been founded."[28] Rafsanjani echoed these sentiments: "It is not enough for us to say we were not defeated. We have to strengthen the revolution, and the interest of the revolution is to win the war and spread its ideas."[29] The goal of exporting the revolution by prolonging the war became a consensus position within the Islamic Republic.

The decision to invade Iraq took place at the time of Israel's attack on Lebanon. The anti-Israeli dimension of Iran's policy and its attachment to Lebanon's Shiites, however, did not deter it from pursuing the war. At the time of the Israeli incursion, an Iranian military delegation led by Shirazi visited Damascus and pledged to dispatch some of Iran's more seasoned forces to the new war front. This promise, however, was countermanded by Khomeini, who insisted that the "path to Jerusalem was through Karbala." A confused Shirazi readily conceded to the imam's perspicacity: "Once the forces of Islam reach Iraq and the Iraqi revolution takes place it will be evident that this revolution will spread through the region, connecting to the borders of Jordan, Saudi Arabia, Syria and elsewhere. At that time Israel will be in danger."[30] As we have seen, for the Islamic Republic, the war was not a mere interstate conflict but a means of achieving larger ideological aspirations. In that context, there was little room for diplomatic solutions or a compromise armistice.

The other motivation for prolonging the war was the notion that Saddam could not be trusted and that he would soon regroup his forces and once more invade Iran. Khamenei captured this point: "Given the slightest opportunity Saddam will continue his aggression."[31] Ali Akbar Natiq-Nuri, minister of interior, reflected Iran's distrust of Saddam: "If we give an excuse to the enemy and end the war in the hope of not increasing fatalities, then we will be merely preparing ourselves for a longer war with more damages. We have to continue the war until complete victory."[32] In an even more pointed exchange, Kamal Kharrazi, head of the War Propaganda

Office, asked, "Who can assure us that the regime of apostate Saddam, after ending the war, will not regain its strength and attack us once more?"[33] Nearly two decades after the war was over, Bihzad Nabavi, who served as the minister of heavy industry, also recalled that "the military commanders were gradually of the view that a stable peace cannot come about so long as Saddam remained in power."[34]

Not unlike Saddam, the theocratic regime indulged in its own misperceptions by exaggerating the opportunities available to it while underestimating the costs of a military surge into Iraq. To begin with, Tehran perceived that its military victories might in fact provoke Saddam's overthrow. In March 1982, when Iran was assuming the initiative in the war, the commander of the Revolutionary Guards, Moshen Reza'i, given the recent battlefield victories, suggested the "smell of a military coup in Iraq is in the air and we have to prepare ourselves for that."[35] Recalling a conversation with Muntazeri at that time, Rafsanjani stated that Muntazeri had implored him to quickly dispatch forces into Iraq, given the imminence of a coup. "Mr. Muntazeri spent half the night calling me, asking me what are our forces waiting for? Why are we not entering Iraq? Iraq is in chaos and we can go to Baghdad and finish this whole thing. There are some waiting to implement a coup as soon as we enter Iraq," Muntaziri stressed to the speaker of the parliament.[36] Should Iran's armies cross over into Iraq, the clerical rulers firmly believed they would have the Iraqi peoples' support. As Muntazeri noted, "We are certain that the Muslim nation of Iraq will assist us."[37]

To the extent that Iran had a plan for post-Saddam Iraq, it was that, once the liberated Iraqis had a chance to choose their own government, they would opt for an Islamic one. Khomeini went even further and stated that the hard-pressed Iraqi populace would select a government that would not only realize their "Islamic hope" but also establish intimate ties with Iran.[38] Given the clerics' belief that all of the inhabitants of the Middle East desired an Islamic government and that they were foiled in that aspiration by tyrannical rulers installed by the United States, they had no doubt that a free choice for Iraqis would yield an Islamic polity. Somehow Tehran convinced itself that the incursion into Iraq would quickly achieve the desired results without either a prolonged war or a cumbersome occupation and that the Iraqi people would welcome the invading armies as liberators. More than two decades later, the Bush administration would make many similar arguments in its own reckless path of invasion.

When the outcome of the conflict appeared to be changing, the panicked Gulf states undertook another diplomatic gambit in the hope that a generous offer of reparations would entice Iran to stop the war. The Saudis now stepped forward and offered to mediate the conflict and provide a $70-billion reconstruction package to Iran. Saddam, eager to put the war behind him, accepted a potential cessation of hostilities, only to be rebuffed by the triumphant and vengeful mullahs. Indeed, as Iran scored battlefield successes, its attitudes toward the Gulf emirates hardened. Khomeini, in his expanded declaration of war aims, not only called for close ties with a "liberated Iraq" but also hinted at the outright control of the Persian Gulf. "If Iran and Iraq can merge and be amalgamated, all the diminutive nations of the region will join them," exclaimed the imam.[39] All of this solidified the Gulf states' support for Saddam, not to mention the international community, which did not want to cede this crucial area to a radical theocracy.

On July 13 the die was finally cast. Operation Ramadan witnessed the mobilization of approximately one hundred thousand troops, whose initial target was Basra. The crossing into Iraq quickly petered out, however, as Iran did not have sufficient tactical dexterity, adequate air cover, or sophisticated arms to carry out a concerted attack. The character of the war now came into focus, and limited territorial gains were acquired at a huge cost. The war resembled the carnage of World War I, with trenches, fixed movement of forces, and, in due time, ample use of chemical weapons. Finally it was Iran's turn to miscalculate, as it transformed itself from victim to aggressor.

A War of Attrition

Subsequent to the 1982 invasion, the roles of the two antagonists underwent an important change. During the initial phase of the war, Iraq was the belligerent, launching wide-scale offensive military operations. Once Iran crossed into its territory, Iraq largely retreated into a defensive formation and rebuffed the persistent Iranian attacks in the hope that Tehran would grow weary of the war. As the conflict dragged on, both sides modified their tactics, experimented with new weapons, and cultivated opposition forces. However, in the end, all of the altered strategies failed to adjust the war's essential parameters. The Iran-Iraq war had turned into a classic stalemate that neither party could win or quit.

The theocratic regime's depiction of the conflict as a battle between forces of Islamic purity and agents of the devil gravely limited its choices. The legitimacy and authority of the Islamic Republic became intertwined with victory on the battlefield, and all social and economic problems were subordinated to the task of vanquishing Saddam. Indeed, it was even suggested at times that winning the war would somehow resolve all of Iran's mounting problems. Khomeini was very clear about this: "Ending the war victoriously is key to solving all difficulties."[40] "War, war until victory" became the slogan of a regime that had come to justify its rule through a people's war.

Despite its commitment to the fighting, the clerical state was concerned with the unease that the conflict was provoking among its constituents. As the costs of the conflict increased and the projected victory still seemed remote, the regime began to change its propaganda. Suddenly the official proclamations and Friday prayer sermons emphasized the Quranic injunctions that advise patience and perseverance in times of crisis. Among the values that traditional Shiism treats as an indication of superior faith is the endurance of oppression. The clerical leaders transformed this concept by noting that tolerating prolonged material and personal sacrifice was also a sign of religious devotion. It was therefore insufficient to merely volunteer for the war or passively concede to its hardships. The sign of true faith was a willingness to accept the burdens of the conflict for an undetermined period of time with aplomb and steadfastness.[41]

The impetuous Iraqi leader whose miscalculations had led to the stalemated conflict sought a way out of his predicament. Unable to compel Iran's acceptance of any ceasefire proposals, Saddam sought to change the dimensions of the war by targeting cities and damaging Iran's oil infrastructure. In 1984 Baghdad warned Tehran that its continued defiance would lead to a more concerted attack on its cities. Undaunted and seemingly unconcerned, however, Iran forged ahead. The result was Iraqi retaliation against the city of Dizful. This was the beginning of the "war of the cities," in which the two powers assaulted each other's civilian population centers. During the latter stages of the war, as Iraq enhanced its missile capacity and was able to attack Tehran and other distant cities, the war on urban areas contributed to the demoralization of the Iranian populace and ultimately to the cessation of the conflict.

As part of its pattern of escalating the war costs, Iraq began attacking Iran's oil facilities. The purchase of French Super Étendard aircraft in 1983 allowed Iraq a greater range and brought Iran's main oil installations on Khark Island within Iraq's striking capability. Baghdad's gambit did have an economic impact, but it failed to diminish the clerical regime's determination. The Islamic Republic did not confine itself to merely complaining about Iraq's latest infraction. When it retaliated, it ended up interfering with Gulf commerce more generally. Given the fact that Iraq's oil was being exported largely overland, Iran found few Iraqi vessels that it could target. Consequently, Tehran chose to retaliate against the shipping activities of the Gulf emirates who were financially sustaining Saddam's war machine. Despite later recriminations, it was Iraq that initially disturbed the Persian Gulf and made oil shipping a legitimate target of military reprisal. Iran had a limited interest in extending the war to the Gulf since its main focus was on ground operations. As Rafsanjani noted, "Saddam's policy is to bring the Persian Gulf states into the war, but we don't want to destabilize the region."[42] Iraq wanted to internationalize the war and perceived that, by threatening the critical waterways, it could induce the great powers to impose a settlement on Iran. As with many facets of the conflict, Iraq expanded the hostilities—in this case, the "tanker war"—but the clerical regime took the blame.

Despite its unsavory reputation, Iran was subject to further Arab machinations, as the Middle East had largely coalesced around Saddam. As the conflict went on without an end in sight, oil policy became another area of tension between Iran and its neighbors. The Islamic Republic's contention that Saudi oil production was partly designed to retard Iran's war efforts has some justification in fact. After its battlefield successes in the mid-1980s, Iran had to content itself with the Saudi-led Gulf community, which increased its oil output to depress prices and damage Iran's financial prospects. Tehran began denouncing the "oil conspiracy," and Khomeini warned that the "price of the war is no less important to us than the price of oil."[43] Rafsanjani similarly complained about plots by "enemies to reduce the price of oil." The Saudi ploy did succeed, as in 1986 oil prices plummeted to nearly $10 per barrel. However, as always with economic pressure exerted on Iran, the Islamic Republic absorbed the costs and persisted in its policies.[44]

The problem with Iran's regional diplomacy was that it simply could not sustain a coherent approach toward the Gulf sheikdoms. At times Tehran would sense the need to decouple Iraq from the emirates and dispatch various Foreign Ministry delegations with offers of better ties. In 1984, when the Saudis shot down an Iranian aircraft, Iran's reaction was muted if not conciliatory. Yet the longer the Gulf states supported Saddam, the more difficult it was for the clerics to maintain a policy of reconciliation. In the end, Iran's determination to prosecute the war, its frequent denunciation of these states' legitimacy, and its support of local opposition groups obscured its hesitant and modest efforts to reach out. The fact that the Gulf states remained a steady source of support for Saddam had much to do with Iran's self-defeating and contradictory practices.

Among the most egregious developments of the war was Iraq's employment of chemical weapons against Iranian combatants. As early as 1983, Iraq began using chemical agents as an integral component of its war strategy. The purpose of the gas was not just to blunt Iran's human-wave assaults but also to terrorize the enemy and sap his morale.[45] Although the use of such weapons initially failed to achieve its objective, in due time it gave Iraq a great advantage in the war. Once more, Saddam's brutal behavior was largely ignored. The international community's focus was on the Persian menace, not the Iraqi dictator's gross violations of the laws of war.

Baghdad's proclamations on its use of chemical weapons were usually couched in ambiguity and stressed the need to employ "all measures" to defend the country. However, at times such tentative denials gave way to open acknowledgement, if not outright boasting. Major General Maher Abd-al Rashid captured the essence of Iraq's position: "The invaders should know that for every harmful insect there is an insecticide capable of destroying it whatever their numbers and that Iraq possess this annihilation insecticide."[46] The theme of using a pesticide to exterminate the "swarms of mosquitoes" became a frequent reference in statements by the Iraqi leadership.[47] At times even such subtleties gave way to open confession. In a heated exchange with Les Aspin, chairman of the House Armed Services Committee, Tariq Aziz exclaimed, "Yes, of course, we use chemical weapons. These are savages and we need to defend ourselves. We would use nuclear weapons if we had them."[48] Not since World War I had a nation relied so heavily on chemical agents to achieve its strategic objectives.

Despite Iraq's continued employment of gas, there is no indication of comparable use by the Iranians. Neither the many United Nations investigations at the time nor the testimonials of Iraqi officers nor captured documents since the American invasion suggest Iran's utilization of such weapons. It appears that Iran did begin research on chemical munitions but never developed sufficient capacity for battlefield use. The inability of many in the West and the Arab world to acknowledge this reality does not change the fact that Iran was a victim rather than a perpetrator of chemical warfare.[49]

Iraq's use of gas confronted its American ally with the difficult choice of either upholding its values or sustaining its support of an unsavory despot who was proving strategically useful. Not unlike many other episodes in its history, the United States opted for expedience over principle. The Reagan administration's tilt toward Iraq was neither intermittent nor tentative, and the war solidified Washington's embrace of Baghdad. By 1983, the United States had already begun providing Iraq with aid in the form of

Commodity Credit Corporation guarantees for the purchase of agricultural products. This assistance amounted to $652 million in 1987. The agricultural credits allowed Iraq to divert funds to military appropriations that it would otherwise have spent on foodstuffs. In the late 1980s, the annual trade between the two nations reached $3.7 billion and included the sale of trucks, transport vehicles, and helicopters.[50] Even more disconcerting was the decision by the United States to begin a "limited intelligence sharing program with Iraq."[51] This "limited" program provided Saddam with information on Iran's battlefield positions and critical data for bombing runs. The Reagan administration was not without its rationalizations, however. Secretary of State George Shultz stated that "Our support for Iraq increased in rough proportion to Iran's military success. The United States could not stand idle and watch the Khomeini revolution sweep forward. In this situation, a tilt toward Iraq was warranted to prevent Iranian dominance of the Persian Gulf and the countries around it."[52] To be sure, it was the concern with Iran rather than devotion to Saddam that was conditioning America's policy. The Iraqi strongman was seen as an indispensable barrier to Iranian expansionism, and thus his violations of international law were reluctantly tolerated. Nonetheless, inordinate fear and loathing of Khomeini's revolution propelled Washington toward embracing one of the most odious dictators in the history of a region replete with morally repugnant autocrats.

The remarkable aspect of U.S. policy was that it remained undisturbed by well-documented revelations of Iraq's use of chemical weapons. This was not a position born out of ignorance, however; indeed, the United States quickly became aware of Iraq's reliance on gas. On occasion, the State Department would ritualistically condemn Iraq's use of chemical weapons as a violation of international conventions. However, such formalistic criticisms did not diminish its desire to buttress Iraq's war effort. On one of his trips to Baghdad, presidential emissary Donald Rumsfeld informed the Iraqis that "Our chemical weapons condemnation was made strictly out of our strong opposition to the use of lethal and incapacitating chemical weapons, wherever it occurs." However, Rumsfeld also emphasized that "Our interests in 1) Preventing an Iranian victory and 2) Continuing to improve bilateral relations with Iraq, at a pace of Iraqi choosing, remain undiminished."[53] For the United States to even reluctantly accept such behavior and condone the use of weapons of mass destruction remains one of the more shameful episodes in its history.

The ebbs and flows of the stalemated conflict appeared to be challenged by one of Iran's most enterprising and successful operations. In

February 1986 Iran launched an operation that involved two attacks, one aimed at Basra, which was largely diversionary, and the other at Faw Peninsula, nearly forty miles south of Basra. The real aim of the operation was to capture Faw, which would cut off Iraq from the Persian Gulf and its essential communication links with Kuwait. The occupation of Faw would thus allow Iran to move against Basra with the real hope of capturing an important city. The success of the Iranian operation (particularly the tactical skill displayed under poor weather conditions) surprised the Iraqis.[54] However, after the initial surge, Iran was incapable of sustaining its attack. Iraq's heavy use of chemical weapons and the disarray within Iran's command structure greatly undermined the operation. The perennial conflict between the Revolutionary Guards, with their amateurish war planning, and the regular military, with its deliberate tactics, led to yet another purge of the army officers. Iran followed up its operation with a series of inconclusive attacks that yielded few gains. The war soon returned to a deadlock, with neither side achieving a fundamental breakthrough.

As Iran entered its sixth year of the war, the internal divisions that had developed over the course of the conflict began to manifest themselves more clearly. Although it is still difficult to decipher the internal deliberations of the theocratic regime, it appears that an important government faction began to sense that the war was endangering the Islamic Republic. Speaker of the parliament Rafsanjani and President Khamenei were among those who were advising caution and even probing for a diplomatic solution. Saddam's international support and his capacity to wage chemical warfare with impunity were ruefully noted by Rafsanjani, who warned, "They will do all they can to rescue Saddam and will not cease efforts to prevent our victory. We also have to think about defense against those dangerous weapons."[55] Yet they were confronted by a Revolutionary Guard leadership and important clerical firebrands who still insisted that the cause of the revolution had to be redeemed in the deserts of Iraq. Ironically, the divisions within the regime initially led to a more aggressive prosecution of the war. From 1982 to 1987 Iran had largely limited itself to a strategy of attrition, with periodic offensives designed to exhaust its adversary into submission. As the population's patience with the war diminished, the Revolutionary Guards called for a mass mobilization to achieve the final victory. As Reza'i noted in 1986, "The war today should be completely transformed into a people's war, in accordance with a scheme in which all industrial schools will begin manufacturing military hardware."[56] It was hoped that a massive offensive could defeat Saddam's armies before the Iranian populace completely gave up on the war.

Whatever the internal debates may have been, Khomeini still supported the radicals. Even after all of the devastation, the imam was not prepared to abandon the conflict or his quest to export the revolution through the force of arms. Khomeini seemingly accepted the arguments of the Revolutionary Guard leaders that, through a more forceful effort, Saddam would fall. Echoing those sentiments, the imam warned the regional states, "Those who inhabit the Gulf should not devote themselves to Saddam, for he will soon be gone."[57] The supreme leader's decision not only prolonged the war but also led to one of its most hazardous periods.

Internationalization of the War

The final years of the war were difficult ones for the Islamic Republic of Iran, which had made the demise of Saddam's regime the centerpiece of its strategy. Iran had managed to sustain the war despite its acute isolation, economic difficulties, and popular disenchantment. However, as the war on the ground appeared stalemated and the tensions in the Persian Gulf drew in the United States, the theocracy had to revisit its most fundamental national decision. Given the intense factionalism and ideological divides, it was difficult for Tehran to act quickly or decisively. As events unfolded, the more pragmatic faction managed to gain the upper hand and eventually convince the imam to end the war.

By 1987, Iran was inexplicably moving toward an expanded conflict on the high seas. Iran's relations with Kuwait had never been harmonious; in fact, the Islamic Republic had previously plotted the ouster of its leadership. Not only was Kuwait one of Iraq's generous benefactors, but its geographic proximity to Iran and its weak military capabilities made its commercial activities a tempting target. However, Kuwait now effectively manipulated cold-war rivalries by insisting that, unless the United States provided protection for its oil vessels, it would turn to the Soviet Union. The fear that Moscow might reach into the Persian Gulf and the need to demonstrate its resolve to the Arab allies in light of the Iran-Contra scandal pressed the Reagan administration toward the reflagging of Kuwaiti ships.[58] As Reagan confessed, "If we don't do the job, the Soviets will. And that will jeopardize our national security as well as our allies."[59] The theme of credibility was stressed more directly by Assistant Secretary for Near Eastern Affairs Richard Murphy: "Frankly, in the light of the Iran-Contra revelations, we had found that the leaders of the Gulf states were questioning the coherence and seriousness of U.S. policy in the Gulf along with our reliability and staying power."[60] At any rate, Washington's decision brought it into direct confrontation with the Islamic Republic.

The U.S. convoys and naval deployments provoked another heated internal debate within the theocracy. For the more moderate elements, the prospect of provoking the American armada was not a promising development. Rafsanjani took the lead in emphasizing to the Gulf states and the United States that "We do not want anything from you except that you stay neutral."[61] However, for the regime's firebrands the prospect of clashing with the "Great Satan" was another means of proving Iran's revolutionary mettle. Mohsen Rafiqdust, head of the Revolutionary Guard's ministry, flamboyantly proclaimed, "We are ready to go to war against America to resist any threat against the Islamic Republic's interests."[62] Reza'i, the disastrous commander of the Revolutionary Guards, whose countless miscalculations inflicted serious damage on his country, once more displayed his lack of judgment: "Americans should be assured that so long as they are in the Persian Gulf they are at war with us."[63] These were hardly idle threats since Iran's speedboat attacks and mining of the Gulf escalated hostilities with the U.S Navy. This was another self-defeating move, however; while its position was weakening, Iran invited additional belligerents into the conflict.

The setbacks in the Persian Gulf were mirrored by Iran's difficulties on the ground. Since 1982, Iraq had been largely reacting to Iran's myriad of offensives in the hope of exhausting its enemy. In the spring of 1988, Iraq finally moved beyond its static defenses and recaptured the Faw Peninsula, thereby handing Iran a demoralizing defeat. Faw had become a symbol of Iran's success, a single tangible conquest after years of inconclusive fighting. The rapid collapse of Iran's fortifications concerned its military leadership, which was accustomed to believing that the Iraqis lacked sufficient courage and daring to resume offensive operations. To be sure, Iraq's victory was partly facilitated by its heavy use of chemical weapons and the intelligence data that the United States provided. Nonetheless, Iraq not only evicted Iran from its territory but, for the first time since 1982, reentered Iranian lands.

Baghdad's more effective prosecution of the war did not stop at the border but intensified by attacking Iran's urban centers.[64] The importance of the "war of the cities" was not so much the damage that it inflicted (only about two thousand Iranians lost their lives in the missile attacks). The significance of the assaults was their psychological impact, as they provoked a panic among the urban dwellers, leading to a mass exodus from cities such as Tehran. The regime simply had lost control of events and could neither offer assurances to a frightened public nor meaningfully retaliate against Iraq's latest act of aggression.

By 1988 Iran was exhausted from having waged an eight-year war without any measurable international support. Iraqi counterattacks, American assaults in the Persian Gulf, and the "war of the cities" undermined the arguments for continuing the war. The difficulties of the conflict were compounded by a smaller pool of volunteers, which undercut Iran's strategy of utilizing manpower to overcome technological superiority. Iran's inability to muster sufficient volunteers meant it had to embark on a more rigorous conscription effort, which further estranged the population. Even then, the draft calls failed to generate enough troops; as a result, Iran simply could not provide adequate forces to relaunch its typical offensives with their human-wave attacks.

Throughout the war, a variety of people and institutions had initiated numerous feelers and suggested peace proposals. Given its depiction of the war as a conflict between Islam and disbelief, Iran had abjured all such entreaties. However, the United States now sought to pressure Iran by drafting UN Resolution 598, which outlined an eight-stage plan for terminating hostilities. The resolution stressed that whichever power rejected the proposal would be subject to mandatory sanctions. Baghdad's acceptance of the resolution placed Iran in a bind. Should the Islamic Republic dismiss the offer, it would face more debilitating sanctions. In a gesture of uncharacteristic restraint, Iran did not summarily reject the proposal but raised questions and asked for various clarifications. It would be wrong, however, to suggest that Tehran's more tempered approach was motivated strictly by a desire to avoid sanctions; in fact, the regime seemed genuinely divided about how to proceed.

As we have seen, by 1987 a pragmatic coalition featuring Rafsanjani, Khamenei, members of the regular military, and moderate clerical politicians had come together to press for ending the war. Initially, the moderates failed to achieve their objectives, as the imam conceded to the Revolutionary Guard's desire to break the stalemate through more attacks. However, the battlefield failures and the increasing internationalization of the war offered the moderates another chance to reclaim the initiative. Khamenei stressed that, although Iran viewed Saddam's removal from power as desirable, it no longer insisted upon it as a precondition for ending the war.[65] Typically, Rafsanjani went even further: "There are two ways to end the war. The first is that the Ba'athist regime of Saddam falls through military force. Naturally, the war would then end. The other way is to end the war politically. If the Security Council does its duty then we believe that the war will end by political means."[66]

These calls for the termination of the war were also being echoed by critical clerical associations. The Friday prayer sermons, always an important barometer of the sentiments of the official clergy, were once more relying on Islamic imagery to discuss the war. However, this time the Prophet's various armistice agreements with his implacable foes were offered as models of emulation. In one of his main addresses, Khamenei, who at times acted as Tehran's Friday prayer leader, stressed that Iran's endurance, sacrifices, and national solidarity throughout the long war meant that it had already fulfilled its divine mission irrespective of final victory. It is clear that, by 1988, important elements within the theocratic regime were looking for a means of settling the conflict.

The one faction that wanted to persist with the war regardless of its tribulations and traumas was the Revolutionary Guards. It is often suggested that, at some point, the guards recognized the futility of the conflict and agreed to the cessation of the war. The evidence does not bear this out, however. In actuality, the guards did not end their objections; they were merely overruled by higher authorities. Irrespective of their inability to recruit enough volunteers or procure the necessary armaments, the guards were determined to resist. In June 1988 Majid Ali Reza, the guards' spokesman, dismissed the rumors of truce: "The war will be decided on the battlefield and not on the conference table."[67] In the imam, the guards had found an important patron, one who appreciated their commitment to his revolutionary message. Khomeini's indispensable support not only shielded the guard's leadership from criticism but also allowed them to triumph in the internal debates.

It is hard to determine exactly when Iran decided to accept Resolution 598. The accidental shooting down of an Iranian airliner in July 1988 by a U.S. naval vessel appears to have been the catalyst that convinced Khomeini that it was time to end the war. The destruction of the aircraft seemingly persuaded the imam and the leading members of the state that a sinister American conspiracy was unfolding. To be sure, Iran had long feared the internationalization of the conflict, but now it sensed that, given Saddam's inability to conquer Iran, the United States had decided to finish the job itself. Rafsanjani warned, "It is obvious the Global Arrogance has decided to prevent our victory."[68] An influential newspaper stressed the conspiracy theme: "This was in no way an accident, and in our view, it is a notification."[69] Coming on the heels of the ongoing clashes with the United States in the Persian Gulf, the airliner incident was viewed as the beginning of a new and more robust American military campaign against Iran.

The other factor that facilitated the end of the war was Iraq's persistent use of chemical weapons. The indiscriminate use of chemical agents against the Kurdish population in the city of Halabja caused considerable consternation in Tehran. There was widespread fear within the ruling elite that similar measures could be used against Iran's urban centers. Rafsanjani recalled, "Iraqis constantly used chemical weapons, and an example of that was Halabja, where people fell like autumn leaves. We thought that it would be a huge event if similar crimes took place against our cities such as Tabriz and Kermanshah."[70] The Iraqis' chemical weapons attacks, which had successfully blunted various Iranian offensives, proved instrumental in the decision to conclude the conflict.

Despite overwhelming pressures on the state, debates still raged with regard to ending the war. In his final appeal for the continuation of the war, Reza'i listed his requirements for achieving victory. In a letter to Khomeini, he acknowledged that the war would probably last another five years and its prosecution would need an additional "350 infantry brigades, 2,500 tanks, 300 fighter planes, and 300 helicopters, as well as an ability to make a substantial number of laser and atomic weapons."[71] Despite this daunting list, the commander of the Revolutionary Guards recommended that the war continue. Prime Minister Musavi, who oversaw the management of the economy, further tipped the scales against the guards by claiming that the country simply could not meet their demands.[72] Musavi seems to have been the pivotal figure in ending the war, as he reportedly warned that the "government does not have the capacity for an appropriation of a single dollar."[73] In his own private response to his disciples, the imam finally acquiesced to the termination of hostilities. Khomeini noted that, given that the "commanders, who are specialists, openly confess that the Islamic military will not be victorious for some time and in light of the recent defeats and the enemy's extensive use of chemical weapons and our lack of equipment to neutralize them, I give my consent to a ceasefire."[74] It was only after Khomeini's decision that the Revolutionary Guards reluctantly accepted the armistice.

The imam now had to confront his compatriots with his momentous decision. A more humbled Khomeini proclaimed, "Today, this decision was more deadly than drinking hemlock. I submitted myself to God's will and drank this drink to His satisfaction. To me, it would have been more bearable to accept death and martyrdom. Today's decision is based only on the interests of the Islamic Republic."[75] Khomeini's statement was followed by more elaborate explanations by the clerical leaders, particularly Rafsanjani and Khamenei. In its latest narrative, the Islamic Republic emphasized that prolonging the war would only distract Iran from the more important goal of spreading its divine message. This was an ironic confession, given that the state had long maintained that the war would define the success of the revolution. In the end, the conflict that was to transform the Middle East ended up threatening the survival of the Islamic Republic and forcing it to sue for peace.[76]

The Iran-Iraq war is no passing event, as its legacy continues to haunt the Islamic Republic and shape nearly all of its deliberations. The regime has been adroit in cultivating a culture of martyrdom that paints the visages of the combatants throughout urban areas and celebrates their memory in countless ceremonies. An entire genre of filmmaking dedicated to producing movies that commemorate the "lost generation" who fought the war continues to flourish twenty years after the fighting ended. Moreover, the prominent conservative newspaper *Jumhuri-i Islami* still carries the testimonials of martyrs in every issue. The politicians who made critical choices at the time are routinely asked to account for them, while conferences and seminars debate the merits of the regime's diplomatic decisions and strategies of war. Far from being a forgotten episode, the war remains alive in the public's consciousness and the government's calculations.

The war has also left its imprint on Iran's international orientation. The notions of self-sufficiency and self-reliance are hallmarks of the Islamic Republic's foreign policy, and the guardians of the revolution recognize that the survival of their regime depends entirely on their own efforts. International organizations, global opinion, and prevailing conventions did not protect Iran from Iraq's chemical-weapons assaults. Saddam's aggression, his targeting of civilians, persistent interference with Persian Gulf commerce, and use of weapons of mass destruction were all condoned by the great powers. Any suggestion that Iran should forego its national prerogatives for the sake of treaty obligations or Western sensibilities has a limited audience among the aggrieved clerics.

As is not unusual for a prolonged conflict, the war is beginning to change the face of Iran's politics. As with the United States in the aftermath of the Second World War, many returning veterans are gradually dominating Iran's national affairs. Service in the war is seen as an important prerequisite for business connections and political prominence. Yet, in one sense, the country has not fully come to terms with the consequences and implications of the war. So long as Khomeini and his contentious tenure remain beyond reproach or question, Iran cannot have a true grasp of one of the most crucial turning points in its long history.

One of the ironic legacies of the war is that it has obscured the export of the revolution as the primary function of the Islamic Republic. A country that fought a devastating eight-year war for the sake of imposing its ideals on a reluctant foe finally sought a more careful balance between its practical interests and its revolutionary mandates. An aging Khomeini attempted to sustain the revolutionary fires by condemning to death British writer Salman Rushdie for writing a book that allegedly disparages the Prophet. However, even the imam's escalating radicalism could not save his revolution from the ravages of war. The Islamic Republic simply had to find another basis for its legitimacy than the transformation of the Middle East along Islamist lines. That task would be left to Khomeini's cantankerous and divided successors.

PART II

The Rise of Pragmatism and the New Priorities

5

Pragmatic Restraint

Iranian Politics during the Rafsanjani Era

NINETEEN EIGHTY-NINE STANDS AS ONE OF THE MOST PIVOTAL years in modern Iranian history. The end of the Iran-Iraq war and the passing of Grand Ayatollah Khomeini suddenly removed both the unifying national cause and the symbol of the revolution. On a tumultuous June day the guardians of the revolution gathered to bid farewell to their departed leader, and uneasy days lay ahead. The imam's disciples would soon lapse into an intense factional struggle, as personal rivalries and differing ideological tendencies ruptured the unity of the Islamist regime. The simmering conflicts within the corridors of power that had been held in check by Khomeini's authority now became all too evident. In essence, the tension between the regime's revolutionary ideals and its practical requirements now surfaced, bedeviling Iran's new rulers. Khomeini's absence made all of the disputes seem irresolvable, as stalemate and deadlock became the new currency of Iranian politics.[1]

More so than that of other Middle Eastern countries, Iran's international orientation has been shaped by its internal evolutions. The need to rehabilitate its war-shattered economy now pressed the Islamic Republic toward a pragmatic redefinition of its national interests. The domestic imperatives were reinforced by the changes taking place in the region. This became all too evident when Saddam went from protector of the Arab order to rash ruler intent on breaking all Arab conventions with his invasion of Kuwait.

The Middle East was not the only world region undergoing unpredictable change. The demise of the Soviet Union altered the international balance of power by removing the cold-war shackles that had inhibited America's power. The Islamic Republic had no choice but to accommodate itself to the sweeping changes all around it. All of this is not to suggest, however, that the regime completely abandoned its ideological compunctions and transcended its historical animosity toward the United States. The imam's legacy was too entrenched to easily dissipate. Amid internal convulsions and external transformations, the theocratic regime found it difficult to cobble together a consensus. The need for pragmatism and the pull of ideology would continuously press Iran in different directions.

Given the importance of domestic debates in conditioning Iran's approach to the world, the proper place to begin an assessment of the Rafsanjani years is the internal situation. Rafsanjani's tenure would be characterized by his attempt to transcend revolutionary dogma and inject a measure of pragmatism into state deliberations. From economic planning to cultural impositions, Rafsanjani sought to mold a more efficient and tolerant theocracy. In this task, he confronted a new supreme leader and a conservative faction, whose attachment to Islamist ideology militated against his enterprising moves. The template of ideology and pragmatism that evolved out of Iran's domestic squabbles would become the basis of its approach to world affairs.

The Islamic Republic and the Politics of Factionalism

The 1990s belonged to two men who did much to guide Iran's ship of state. Shortly after the imam's passing, Ali Khamenei was elevated to the position of supreme leader, while Rafsanjani assumed the office of president. However, beneath the veneer of a smooth transition, the Islamic Republic quickly splintered into competing blocs of conservative, pragmatist, and radical factions. All of the contending clerics appealed to the imam's legacy and presented themselves as his true heirs. However, despite the disagreement that gripped the regime, all of the factions involved in the debates were loyal soldiers of the revolution and accepted the essential mandates of the theocratic state.[2]

The pragmatic wing of the clerical elite was led by one of Iran's most intriguing politicians. Rafsanjani was one of the founders of the republic, and his ability to traverse the treacherous waters of the Islamist regime reflected his unparalleled political acumen. As his memoirs reveal, Rafsanjani spent his years as speaker of the parliament settling disputes, dispensing favors, and cultivating close ties with a vast array of national and provincial officials. However, despite his uncanny ability to sense the mood of the country and his fundamental dedication to change, Rafsanjani proved a reluctant reformer. His crass opportunism and inordinate caution limited his ability to effect fundamental change.

Rafsanjani assumed the office of president at a time when its powers were augmented by its absorption of the prime minister's functions, which made him one of the country's most significant politicians. More than any of his counterparts, Rafsanjani sensed that, given the passing of the imam and the end of the war, the regime had to reestablish its legitimacy and once more connect with its constituency. Khomeini's stature and the solidarity of the war years had held the country together, but for the Islamic Republic to survive, it had to craft a new national compact. Iran had to reconstruct its economy and provide for at least the practical needs of its youthful and growing population. In one of his first declarations, Rafsanjani outlined his course of action and subtly admonished the clerical proponents of the status quo: "There are some people who still believe that Islam and other holy religions do not concern themselves with the material life of the people, that they have plans for heaven and not the earth. We who are in the position of managing the society must wipe away such misgivings."[3] To realize his vision of economic innovation, Rafsanjani devoted his presidency to creating a strong state with a capable bureaucracy. This was to be the "era of reconstruction," during which Iran would focus on rebuilding its war-torn society and healing the wounds of the bitter eight-year conflict.

Rafsanjani's economic policies were reflected in his choice of cabinet members, who largely had technocratic backgrounds.[4] Because he emphasized graduate degrees and professional training, Rafsanjani appointed only four clerics to his government during his two presidential terms. In defense of his selections, he stressed that his commitment to rejuvenating the economy mandated turning to those with "modern training." The challenges that faced the republic could not be addressed by relying on individuals with clerical or military backgrounds. The outcome of this approach was remarkable: The theocratic regime that had just waged a prolonged and religiously inflected war now featured a cabinet that included very few ranking military personnel or clerics.[5]

Rafsanjani's economic modernization found political expression in the party known as Karguzaran-i Sazandagi (Servants of Construction), which had been formed by his allies in 1996.[6] The essence of their message was that a strong state was necessary for the creation of a modern, industrial economy capable of generating exports, distributing wealth and services, and providing full employment. This was not just an activist but indeed an intrusive government that needed tax revenues and regulatory power to pull Iran out of the doldrums. For Rafsanjani and the technocratic faction, the success and survival of the regime were contingent on its economic efficiency as opposed to any assertion of its ideological history. The emphasis was now less on religion than on state performance. In this context, the president and the governing institutions had to be dynamic, spearheading efforts to eradicate poverty, control pollution, and rein in population growth. The locus of power was to be the presidency, aided by a competent bureaucracy whose pioneering efforts would be sanctioned by a compliant clerical establishment.[7]

The economic policies were not without effect, as Iran did indeed invest in its infrastructure—building dams, airports, oil refineries, and irrigation systems.[8] The regime ended the practice of rationing, reintroduced the national stock market, and initiated various free-trade zones. Heavy industries such as steel production and petrochemicals also came in for their own share of expenditures. The first five-year plan was effective in reducing the size of the government inherited from the war years and loosening state controls. The level of economic growth between 1988 and 1993 was an impressive 8 percent per year, while oil production went from 2.6 to 3.9 million barrels per day. During this period Iran's growth was still being facilitated by rising oil prices as opposed to domestic industrial capability.

Despite all of the talk of privatization, this was state-mandated development in which still-bloated bureaucracies determined the pace of change. Moreover, borrowing from abroad led Iran into an international debt crisis that further burdened an already beleaguered nation. Rafsanjani's government accumulated a debt of approximately $28 billion, a startling figure for a country that went through the war without incurring substantial arrears. In due course, the twin forces of inflation and unemployment would inflict their own damage on Rafsanjani's designs.

The focus on economic reform should not obscure the emergence of corruption as a serious threat to the legitimacy of an Islamic government. As with most developing countries, Iran has had its share of financial malfeasance. Yet throughout the war years, the need to mobilize national resources limited the depletion of the treasury for personal gain. It was during the Rafsanjani presidency that corruption became endemic. The new president's penchant for self-enrichment, the granting of privileged access to a select few, and increasing class stratification undermined the Islamic Republic's claim of virtuous governance. Just as during the shah's era, tales of the "thousand families" dominating the economic realm became the order of the day. As a politician deeply immersed in corrupt dealings, Rafsanjani not only undermined his own stature but also did much to enhance the authority of the more austere Ali Khamenei, who resisted the temptations of power.

At a certain level, Rafsanjani understood the difficulty of promoting economic development without political reform. As an astute student of history, he knew that such an imbalance had undermined the shah's rule and provoked an upheaval that he could neither contain nor mediate. However, Rafsanjani's centralizing ambitions and his timidity when facing the conservatives' resistance obstructed true political change. At the core, Rafsanjani wanted power in his own hands and had only a limited desire to truly open up the system. The success of East Asian autocracies, which still managed to foster economic growth, comforted the Iranian president into believing that his desire for power was in the nation's interest.

Rafsanjani's recognition of the need for modest political reforms should not be seen as a fundamental departure from Khomeini's legacy. The Islamic Republic remained a deeply repressive state that established clear boundaries of permissible political behavior. Factionalism and elections should not be confused with genuine pluralism. All of the major participants on the national scene retained their loyalty to theocratic rule and the imam's basic ideological convictions. For those intellectuals who dared to challenge the foundations of the state, journalists who probed its corrupt practices, ethnic minorities who sought a degree of cultural autonomy, and dissident clerics who called for the return of religion to the mosque, the Islamic Republic remained an intolerant government. The fact that the judiciary was arbitrarily employed against critics and elections were too often manipulated meant that rule of law and institutional accountability were missing from the system.

As part of his vision, Rafsanjani also toyed with the relaxation of cultural and social restrictions. The imposition of Islamic strictures on a youthful population was causing its own backlash and further alienating the young from the regime. Again Rafsanjani was shrewd enough to comprehend the need for tolerance: "Through suppression, pressure, and threat we can only partially preserve the façade of our society."[9] These aspects of the government's policies would be spearheaded by the president's brother, Muhammad Hashemi Rafsanjani, who headed the broadcasting services, and the minister of culture, Muhammad Khatami. Hashemi reintroduced Western programming and dismissed the conservatives' concerns as a sign of retrogression. Khatami, who had long perceived the need for greater artistic and literary diversity, was even more enterprising. The minister of culture claimed that "freedom of thought and respect for intellectual honor are among the prime goals of the revolution."[10] Under Khatami's auspices, the number of journals and newspapers went from 102 in 1988 to 370 in 1992.[11] However, once his liberal functionaries became controversial, President Rafsanjani was quick to abandon them.

The focus on economic reconstruction mandated a foreign policy of moderation.[12] While Khomeini had routinely rejected the prevailing international system, Rafsanjani acknowledged both its importance and interdependence. "If people believe we can live behind a closed door, they are mistaken. While we must be reasonably independent, we are in need of friends and allies around the world," declared the new president.[13] Hasan Ruhani, a leading parliamentarian and a close ally of Rafsanjani, similarly claimed, "The extraordinary events that have taken place in the world recently, as well as events that have taken place within our country, are persuading us to reexamine once more our position in the world."[14] The imam had scant interest in economic affairs and perceived that, for the sake of revolutionary empowerment, the nation had to suffer material shortages. Given the poor state of the economy, Rafsanjani and his allies could not remain indifferent to global opinion. The need to generate foreign investments and import much-needed technologies would lead the state to temper its revolutionary fervor.

The United States played a large role in Iran's geopolitical imagination, as Tehran found it difficult to conceive a coherent policy toward its most enduring foe. At the outset, the purpose of Rafsanjani's diplomacy was not so much to reconcile with the United States but to resist its pressures and attempts to isolate Iran. By cultivating ties with the European bloc, the new Russian Federation, and the Persian Gulf emirates, Iran tried to obstruct America's attempts to marginalize its influence. To be sure, Rafsanjani would at times entertain the possibility of reconsidering ties with the United States, but, given the opposition of both the conservative and the radical factions, he inevitably limited his horizons and tempered his ambitions.

As the Islamic Republic contemplated its future, a new supreme leader assumed center stage. In a hastily gathered conclave, the clerical oligarchs selected the former president as the theocracy's new standard-bearer. Khamenei was very much a compromise candidate whose selection reflected the contradictions of clerical rule. The initial choice for the august position of leader was Husayn Ali Muntaziri, who had become the heir apparent in 1985. Muntaziri had sufficient theological credentials and was a long-time adherent of the imam. However, in the late 1980s Muntaziri embarked on a more independent course, criticizing the regime's conduct and key policies. Despite his radical origins, he emerged as a detractor of economic mismanagement, the interference of the Revolutionary Guards in commercial activities, and the arbitrary execution of a large number of dissidents, who in many cases had already served stiff prison sentences. On the tenth anniversary of the revolution, Muntaziri disparaged the extravagant celebrations and instead called for an assessment of the regime's mistakes and misjudgments in the intervening decade.[15] Despite their close association, Khomeini recognized that his legacy would not be safe in the hands of the unruly Muntaziri and took the drastic step of dismissing his most intimate disciple.[16] With the removal of Muntaziri, the regime lost the one cleric who possessed adequate theological learning, as well as sufficient revolutionary credentials, to actually succeed the imam. Muntaziri's dismissal, however, hardly removed him from the national scene; instead, he gradually emerged as an advocate of democratic pluralism and foreign policy moderation.

In yet another compromise with political reality, Khomeini now had to oversee the revision of the constitution and the downgrading of its theological requirements for the position of supreme leader.[17] The existing esteemed clerics such as Ayatollah Muhammad Gulpayigani, Sayyid, Abu al Qasim Musavi Khu'i, and Shihab al-Din Mar'sashi Najafi simply could not be relied on since they all viewed Khomeini's concept of *vilayat-i faqih* (guardianship of the jurist) as an improper innovation. While the original constitution demanded that the leader be "recognized and accepted" by a majority of religious dignitaries, the new document emphasized "political and social" issues. Thus, revolutionary loyalty and political reliability were privileged over theological erudition. The regime had begun to separate Islamist ideology from Islamic political establishment and, in doing so, reducing religious requirements in order to sustain its ruling monopoly.

In light of the constitutional revisions, the Assembly of Experts focused on selecting a new leader. The regime loyalists finally rallied around Ali Khamenei, a midlevel cleric with an inconsequential record as president of the republic. A state born out of the musings of a grand ayatollah was entrusted to a mullah of minimal stature. In an ironic display, the guardians of the clerical state justified their decision by suggesting that service to an Islamic government counted as much as advancing religious learning. Ayatollah Ali Mashkini went so far as to claim that senior clerics were not suitable for the task of leadership, given their insufficient understanding of "political, social, and cultural issues facing Muslims."[18] In an even more bizarre display, the leaders of the state suddenly claimed that the imam had actually sanctioned the choice of Khamenei prior to his passing. Rafsanjani recalled that, in one of Khomeini's last meetings with the heads of the individual branches of government, he had pointedly dismissed any concerns regarding his succession. According to the ever-imaginative Rafsanjani, Khomeini pointed to Khamenei as his most suitable replacement. Equally implausible was the recollection of Abu al Qasim Khaz'ali, a member of the Guardian Council, who stated that, prior to his death, Khomeini repeatedly expressed his preference for Khamenei.[19]

Despite these professions of confidence in Khamenei and his spiritual stature, there was a concerted effort to enhance his standing by elevating him to the highest clerical rank of *marja' taqlid* (source of emulation). Muhammad Yazdi, head of the judiciary, and Ali Akbar Natiq-Nuri, speaker of the parliament, were among those who spearheaded the effort, stressing that Khamenei's position as head of state and the fact that Khomeini had designated him as the new leader should pave the way for his promotion. This was in direct contravention of Shiite norms, whereby the accumulated theological learning of a cleric would lead to his advancement through a subtle process of consensus among his peers. However, much as the Islamic Republic sought to impose discipline on the seminaries and ayatollahs outside the structure of the state, it could not compel them to accede to Khamenei's elevation. Sensing the reality, Khamenei himself pulled his name out of contention, claiming that the burdens of governing were too much to combine with the responsibilities of a *marja' taqlid*. However, the episode reveals the new supreme leader's overweening ambition and his determination to consolidate his power.[20]

As he assumed the mantle of leadership, Khamenei appeared at a disadvantage to the charismatic Rafsanjani. The new supreme leader did not possess the spiritual standing or political stature necessary to claim the initiative. However, Khamenei soon found himself allied with the republic's conservative faction. It is often suggested that, given his disdain for the radicals and the increasing competition for power with Rafsanjani, the new leader had no choice but to turn to the conservatives. All of this misses the point that, by temperament, Khamenei always perceived that the main mission of the Islamic Republic was to uphold its religious values and prevent popular pressures from altering the system. Thus, the union between Khamenei and the Right was not one of convenience but of ideological compatibility.[21]

The rise of Khamenei also coincided with the conservative forces' search for a new patron. As the Right looked at the national landscape, it grew concerned about Rafsanjani's penchant for pragmatism and the radical parliamentarians' populist tendencies. The Right may have agreed with Rafsanjani on the need to revitalize the economy, but it also called for a strict implementation of Islamic cultural standards and remained deeply suspicious of the West. For the conservatives who drew on the imam's authoritarian legacy, the most important task was to maintain the office of supreme leader and the prerogatives of the unelected branches of government. The clerical hard-liners emerged as the most vociferous defenders of absolute rule and displayed contempt for democratic practices. As Natiq-Nuri emphasized, "The main purpose of the regime is the implementation of the word of God."[22] Ayatollah Ibrahim Amin, another stalwart of the Right, similarly claimed that the "Leader's mandate is equal to that of the Prophet. Therefore, he is not responsible to the majority of the people, but only to God."[23] Given their philosophical outlook and ideological commitments, the conservatives preferred a ruling system in which despotism was masked by a veneer of participatory politics. While it is customary to suggest that Khamenei was dependent on the Right, it is also important to note their reliance on his office. Although they had cleverly ensconced themselves in powerful institutions such as the Guardian Council and the judiciary, they recognized that without Khamenei's support they could easily lose power.

The conservatives' foreign-policy orientation presented a complicated problem for Rafsanjani. On the one hand, they appreciated that, in the aftermath of the war and with the demands of the economy, a relaxation of tensions was necessary. However, the reactionary elements of the theocracy often looked at international relations through the prism of sustaining Iran's Islamic culture. As such, they would always be wary of normalizing relations with the West, which they believed could provoke a cultural onslaught. The dual themes of the "Great Satan and the "clash of civilizations" laced their pronouncements and defined their political identity. The United States remained a sinister source of cultural pollution whose influences and temptations had to be resisted. The fact that Iran's youth had long ceased paying attention to their ponderous theological tracts and demands for a puritanical social order was immaterial to a political class that perceived its legitimacy as deriving from God's will as opposed to popular approbation.

The anti-American pillar of the conservatives' ideology was only reinforced by Khamenei's ascension to the position of supreme leader. As president of the Islamic Republic during the war years, Khamenei had spent considerable time at the war front. Discarding his clerical garb for military khakis, Khamenei toured the battle scenes and saw firsthand the damage that the conflict had wrought on Iranian cities and villages. As with most members of the ruling elite, he came to blame the West for providing the chemical weapons and sophisticated arms to Iraq that had inflicted such damage on Iran. For Khamenei, the war's devastation was not an abstraction, and his eyewitness accounts came to shape his political outlook and condition his deep suspicion of the United States.

The post-Khomeini polity was nothing if not fractious, as a third faction, popularly known as the radicals, also emerged and pressed its own claims and ideological mandates. Unlike the other contending blocs, the radicals did not have a preeminent leader such as Rafsanjani or Khamenei, and they had sustained their influence largely because the imam appreciated their zeal and commitment. Moreover, the constitutional revisions had done away with the office of prime minster. The elimination of the post that the reliably leftist Mir Husayn Musavi had occupied deprived this faction of executive power. The radicals held many seats in the parliament but failed to appreciate the changing realities and believed instead that mere adherence to dogma and revolutionary ideals would resolve Iran's mounting problems. They saw any concession to pragmatism as abandoning Iran's revolutionary patrimony. Ali Akbar Muhtashami'pur, one of the leading radical deputies, now warned that the regime was not properly guarding the "honor and prestige of the Iranian system."[24]

In a perverse manner, the radicals even dismissed concentration on economic issues as a plot to dilute the revolution and normalize relations with the West. Muhtashami'pur stressed that the notion that the economy should be the foremost national concern was a pretext for abandoning the core of the revolution.[25] "If you set the economy as the principle and sacrifice everything to its altar, there would be nothing by which you could be powerful and free," he warned.[26] The radicals were quick to deride Rafsanjani's economic plans as "capitalist Islam" and insisted on a more dogmatic approach to state planning.[27] Indeed, given the passing of the imam and the end of the war, the task of sustaining revolutionary fires would be all the more challenging, thus necessitating a greater vigilance and determination on the part of the clerical regime.

To the extent that the radicals offered a solution to Iran's economic quandaries, it was the consolidation of the command economy. Advocating social justice as their overarching economic priority led them to call for wealth redistribution, an elaborate welfare system, and the nationalization of critical industries. Muhtashami'pur described the essential purpose of the state as "fighting inequality, poverty, class differences, and pursuing socio-economic justice."[28] A suspicion of private property and international lending organizations led them to propound the themes of self-sufficiency and sacrifice as a means of preserving Iran's independence. The nation had to be prepared to withstand economic deprivation, even falling living standards, in order to realize its divine mission of fortifying and exporting the theocratic order. The task of reconstruction and economic rehabilitation did not convince this faction to subordinate social justice to the imperatives of growth and efficiency.

The radicals' foreign-policy orientation emphasized anti-Americanism and the export of the revolution. Their postulations went beyond mere Islamist commitments and stressed the themes of anti-imperialism and Third World solidarity. To the radicals, Iran was not just an Islamist state but also a vanguard nation that could potentially lead the developing world's struggle against American hegemony. Unlike the conservatives, the radicals were not so much focused on America's seductive cultural influence but saw the United States as a rapacious imperial state. In their criticisms of the United States they ironically appropriated the slogans and themes that were popular in leftist circles in Latin America and Europe during the 1960s. A mixture of Islamist defiance and anti-imperialist zeal defined this faction's intense hostility to any efforts to forge new ties with the United States.

In one of the many paradoxes of the Islamic Republic, the radicals emerged as strong proponents of democratic pluralism. For them, the popular dimension of the republic was the most crucial source of legitimacy. Unlike other factions, the radicals were quick to stress that elections and plebiscites were the system's source of credibility and power.[29] A leading figure of the militant parliamentarians, Mahdi Karubi, noted that "without the vote of the people, the regime does not have legitimacy."[30] Given their base in the parliament, such comments may seem self-serving, but the movement's history reveals a sense of confidence that the citizens would embrace this vision should they be allowed to participate in the political process.

The radicals' most imaginative publication was the newspaper *Salam*, managed by Muhammad Musavi Khu'ini'ha, who had made his reputation as the spiritual leader of the students who had held the American diplomats hostage for 444 days. The anti-Americanism of *Salam* should not obscure its interest in social democracy. While the radicals advocated both antagonism toward the West and redistributive economic policies, they also emerged as vocal proponents of government accountability. The pages of *Salam* were filled with the most consistent and trenchant criticisms of the Rafsanjani tenure—its profligacy, corruption, and authoritarianism.

The fact that the newspaper was occasionally shuttered and its outspoken editor, Abbas Abdi, imprisoned demonstrates Rafsanjani's unwillingness to initiate political reforms that were a necessary complement to economic liberalization.

Given their populist tendencies, the radicals even challenged the prerogatives of the supreme leader and his absolutist pretensions. Although professing loyalty to the institution, they emphasized that it could not dominate all aspects of the social and political order. Muhammad Salamati, a radical parliamentarian, noted that "principally the faqhi is not supposed to think for everyone and present solutions for all issues."[31] In yet another rebuke to Khamenei, leftist deputy Husayn Hashimian stated that "Even the Prophet could not do much before the population at large gave him their mandate."[32] The radicals similarly attacked the Guardian Council as "rightist jurisprudence" and denounced its right to disqualify candidates for public office and negate parliamentary legislation.[33] A distinct limitation on the privileges of the nonelected institutions and empowerment of the citizenry were the hallmarks of this faction's political cosmology.

The intriguing aspect of the radicals was that they called for the export of the revolution, acclaimed the virtues of the command economy, and yet also embraced elections as the ultimate arbiter of politics. The popular Western notion that democrats are necessarily foreign-policy moderates and judicious economic planners is contradicted by the political demarcations of the Islamic Republic. Iran's radicals embraced social justice, defiance of the West, and democratic representation in equal parts. In essence, they managed to challenge both the pragmatists and the conservatives. The Islamic Republic was entering turbulent and uncharted waters as its institutions were pitted against each another. A populist parliament dominated by the radicals, a presidency led by Rafsanjani (an advocate of market economics), and a supreme leader who idealized a traditionalist Islamic society warily eyed one another. In the complex matrix of Iranian politics, the first faction that would lose power would be the hapless radicals.

The Theocracy Turns against Itself

Iran's politics would now be characterized by a series of shifting and tentative alliances, as every faction sought to monopolize political power. The arcane order that Khomeini had conceived, with its cantankerous politicians, differing ideological strands, and intrinsic competition between elected and appointed branches of government, could not function harmoniously in his absence. Khomeini had the power and the stature to mediate the disputes, punish and reward factions of his choosing, and prevent the system's instability from paralyzing the country. The imam's successors had neither the standing nor the desire to follow his lead.

Given the radicals' infringement on the prerogatives of both the new president and the supreme leader, Rafsanjani and Khamenei were quick to facilitate their marginalization. The 1992 parliamentary election was to be the occasion on which the radicals would be excised from the body politic. The election began with the reliably reactionary Guardian Council disqualifying a large number of radical deputies from running for office. Although this would be a routine practice of the council from this point on, the 1992 election was the first important occasion on which its supervisory powers were abused for political gain. The Rafsanjani-Khamenei alliance moved beyond electoral manipulation and used the mass media and the Friday prayer network to promote their message. The judiciary was similarly exploited for launching corruption investigations against prominent radicals such as Karubi and Muhtashami'pur. Despite the protestations of the disqualified candidates, Khamenei was quick to sanctify the council's verdict by stressing that people should vote for deputies who were inclined to cooperate with the executive branch. In an even more defiant rebuke, Khamenei disparaged the radicals as "those seditious people who have caused trouble for the government and told lies in their newspapers. People should not vote for their candidates."[34] Rafsanjani similarly chimed in: "I am convinced that our society in these elections will endorse our plan."[35] The contrived electoral process yielded the desired result—a conservative-dominated parliament. However, an ominous precedent had been established, as the institutions and practices of the Islamic Republic were manipulated for the purpose of marginalizing some of Khomeini's most dedicated followers.

Despite the machinations of the Guardian Council, the radicals' electoral misfortune had much to do with the unpopularity of their views. Their ideology was the product of the war and revolution. However, the death of the imam and the end of the war led the populace to look for stability and growth. The 1992 election debacle prove to be a watershed event, as many of the disqualified candidates retreated into private in order to reevaluate their dogma and identity. The radicals would remerge in the late 1990s as the reformers, having largely divested themselves of their reflexive anti-Americanism and statist economic perspective.

The 1992 parliamentary race also denoted the changing role of the supreme leader. Khamenei had been an active participant in the plot to oust a legitimate faction of the Islamic Republic. This stood in a stark contrast to Khomeini's behavior, as the imam had always sought to preserve a balance among his disciples and often protected a weak faction whose influence was threatened by its rivals. So long as a clerical cohort maintained its loyalty to the system and adhered to his basic ideological values, Khomeini would ensure that it had a role in the management of the state. As a politician who had ample confidence in his ability to move the masses, Khomeini felt no need to subvert his followers. Khamenei took a very different approach, as his desire to enhance his powers and advance the conservatives' cause mandated a tactical alliance with Rafsanjani to undermine the radicals, who were actively questioning the prerogatives of the unelected institutions. A combination of threats and opportunities was leading Khamenei to redefine the functions of his office. The need to disarm the democratic penchants of the populist politicians and the opportunity to ensure the ascendance of his reactionary allies meant that Khamenei was no longer a neutral arbiter in the Islamic Republic's debates. In due course, both Rafsanjani and the reformers would realize the difficulty of advancing their agenda in light of a supreme leader who was determined to ensure a conservative consolidation of power.[36]

The emasculation of the Left did not end the regime's internal conflicts. In fact, the remaining wings of the Islamic Republic increasingly assaulted each other. Rafsanjani perceived that, free from the obstructionism of the populist parliamentarians, he could move toward the implementation of his long-delayed reforms. This would entail borrowing from foreign lending organizations and accepting the restructuring mandates of the World Bank. The Islamic Republic would have to dispense with its rash initiatives and recognize that membership in the global economy required a more judicious foreign policy. The centrality of the economy was noted by Foreign Minister Ali Akbar Vilayati, who said, "Economic considerations overshadow political priorities."[37]

Rafsanjani's initiatives soon began to encroach on the conservatives' ideological imperatives and power base. Although both tendencies acknowledged the need to dismantle the command economy, which had come into existence during the war, they had different conceptions of what privatization meant. For Iran's reactionary ideologues, privatization implied a merchant class free of state intervention. The task of creating an industrial economy with a technocratic cadre was abhorrent to the conservative bloc. Given its paranoia about Western cultural influences, this group was averse to opening the system to foreign investments, much less implementing World Bank reforms. For this faction, the sanctity of private property implied empowering the bazaar and its opaque economic arrangements rather than creating a modern economy integrated into the global markets.

Beyond his economic measures, Rafsanjani faced an open rebellion when he attempted to loosen the suffocating cultural restrictions. Ayatollah Ahmad Jannati of the Guardian Council took the lead in admonishing the president and reminded him that the role of the state is to support "true Islamic culture by reinforcing [the] religious bedrock of the people and fighting all those who are anti-Islamic and Western-stricken."[38] The reactionary *Kayhan* newspaper summed up its own indictment of Rafsanjani: "Our criticism of the cultural policies of your government relate to the officials who neglected the destructive and degenerative trend that crept into the system after the war. It utilized the print media, art, and literature for a comprehensive assault against the integrity of the values derived from the revolution."[39] For the Right, the mission of the revolution remained rigorous enforcement of Islamic tenets. Despite Rafsanjani's professions, the moral police and law enforcement officials continued to harass and arrest those seeking a degree of personal and intellectual freedom. It seemed that, beyond the marginalization of the Left, the conservative and pragmatic factions shared limited interests.

Although initially hesitant, Khamenei had now emerged as the epicenter of the system and, in collaboration with the conservatives, did much to undermine Rafsanjani's presidency. The first salvo came in October 1992, when Khamenei pointedly deprecated the emphasis on reform over ideology. "The enemy is claiming that during the period of reconstruction, revolutionary spirit and morality must be set aside. Is this the meaning of reconstruction? It surely is not."[40] In his new role as protector of the revolution and its Islamic mores, Khamenei was fully endorsed by the conservative clerics. Natiq-Nuri stressed, "Liberalism is a real threat for the country and it must be eradicated. The building of a few roads and bridges and the completion of some development projects is not tantamount to upholding revolutionary values."[41] Khamenei had finally married his office to a powerful constituency, as the right wing stood with him against Rafsanjani and the remnants of the radical faction. By virtue of his institutional standing and a dedicated group of supporters, Khamenei managed to wrestle the national initiative away from the more popular Rafsanjani.

The conservatives' devotion to crafting a pristine Islamic society also distorted Rafsanjani's foreign policy. As we have seen, they had long identified the United States with domestic efforts to reform the Islamic Republic. Khamenei insisted that the United States was the "main propagator of corrupt, materialistic culture aimed at Iran."[42] To ensure Iran's Islamic identity, there had to be a stark commitment to battling America's influence. This meant opposition to the United States even in areas that could benefit Iran, such as economic relations. "Any rapprochement between America and Iran is out of question, and we will not permit American corporations to invest in Iran," announced the supreme leader.[43] Such perceptions would constitute an important obstacle to Rafsanjani's attempt to usher in a new international orientation.

In a pattern that would prove all too familiar, the conservatives employed their institutional power to thwart reform measures. The newly elected right-wing deputies now cynically embraced calls for social justice to obstruct economic practices that infringed on their privileges. Under the auspices of Khamenei, the president's pledged social liberalization policies were stifled, as Iran remained a country in the grip of onerous Islamic strictures. Iran was now paralyzed by the core contradictions between those professing ideology and the more moderate elements, which were pressing the cause of national interest.

In the end, the factionalism of the republic and the obstructionism of the conservatives ensured the failure of Rafsanjani's presidency. Despite some success in decreasing the state's role in the economy, the "era of reconstruction" did not lead to the much-promised liberalization. Spiraling inflation and unemployment rates eroded the standard of living of the average Iranian while a large number of college graduates could not find suitable employment. On the cultural front, Iran remained a repressive state struggling under the burden of religious impositions made all the more galling by the corruption of the clerical estate. Even in the international realm, the tentative openings would be hampered by frequent revolutionary spasms.[44]

However, despite Khamenei and the conservative bloc's absolutist pretensions, as well as their manipulation of the Islamic Republic's processes, Iran did not become a typical totalitarian state such as Saddam's Iraq. The constitutional structure that still invested some power in the elected bodies ensured that the Iranian people and their representatives would have a voice in the state's deliberations. Any faction could adjust its precepts and appeal to the masses for an opportunity to enter the presidency or parliament. The radicals proved the durability of the Islamic Republic's elite pluralism, as they would eventually transform themselves into reformers and return to power under the banner of the rule of law and freedom. Moreover, a faction that lost its standing could still maintain a degree of relevance by publishing newspapers and sustaining its party structure. As Khomeini had envisioned, for those who were part of the elite, the Islamic Republic was still a forgiving state. The conservatives may have had the preponderance of influence, but they never monopolized power and were never free from criticism and challenge.[45]

The New Look of the Islamic Republic

In the aftermath of Khomeini's passing, the Islamic Republic faced a real challenge about how to proceed. In Iran's moment of bewilderment, Rafsanjani initially captured the initiative by offering a different path and a new agenda. Despite the clerical oligarchs' occasional call for reform, it was Rafsanjani who propounded the notion that practical demands must transcend revolutionary mandates and that the formal state must supersede informal institutions. More important, he sensed that the legitimacy of the system had to be based on factors other than Islamist ideology and the ossified rhetoric of martyrdom. Rafsanjani did not so much transform the Iranian society as comprehend both how it had to change and how to accommodate that need. A nation ravaged by war, burdened by a decade of revolutionary turmoil, and witnessing a demographic explosion needed a leadership that acknowledged new realities and sought to address long pent-up demands. During the 1980s, the theocratic regime had stressed religious commitment over expertise, self-sufficiency over integration into the world economy, revolutionary defiance over realpolitik, and religious austerity over cultural emancipation. More than any other actor, Rafsanjani had the political acumen and intellectual suppleness to recognize that such policies were not feasible and that persisting in them could threaten the survival of the state.

Rafsanjani's experiment, however, reveals the system's limitations and its inability to balance the competing demands on it. He sought to construct a modern state while remaining loyal to the essential pillars of Khomeini's ideology. Such a balancing act may have been possible had the new president maintained a good relationship with the supreme leader. However, once Khamenei consolidated his power and developed ties with the conservative faction, he emerged as a serious obstacle to Rafsanjani's imaginative moves. As we have seen, Khamenei fundamentally altered the office of the supreme leader inasmuch as he was less interested in balancing factions then ensuring the conservatives' hegemony of power. As true heirs of the imam, the conservatives objected to attempts to diminish the regime's ideological determinations. The reactionary faction of the republic was committed to guarding the theocracy from excessive pragmatic intrusions.

Moreover, Khamenei's pattern of conduct further subverted Rafsanjani's presidency. Unlike his predecessor, Khamenei was far more interested in the details of the process. The imam paid scant attention to governance and saw his role instead as defining the overall direction of the state. Although Khomeini interfered at critical junctures to settle unresolved issues, he preferred to remain aloof from the day-to-day functions of the state. Khamenei, however, had spent his career not in the seminary but in the halls of government and was known as a master of bureaucratic intricacy. By nature, the new supreme leader would take a more active interest in the everyday tasks of the government, frequently interfere with the executive branch, and often usurp its prerogatives. As the ideological gap between Khamenei and Rafsanjani widened, their turf wars would further impede coherent planning.

To compound the difficulties, Rafsanjani's own personality did not contribute to the enactment of bold reforms. The president may have sensed the need for change, but, when confronted with resistance, he would often retreat and abandon his own declared principles. He articulated the imperative of development, yet proved reluctant to build an efficient state sector. He appreciated the necessity of political liberalization, yet his own authoritarian tendencies limited the scope of change. On his core objective of economic reconstruction, Rafsanjani's penchant for compromise and halfway measures ended up empowering the mercantile elite while drowning the country in foreign debt and massive corruption.

This retreat from pragmatism was evident in the realm of foreign affairs, as the conservatives' objections to the West as a source of cultural contamination pressed Rafsanjani toward self-defeating moves. Despite pressure from his economic advisers for a concerted opening to the West, Rafsanjani remained ambivalent, at times offering an olive branch, yet quickly retreating when faced with a domestic backlash. Terrorism would remain an instrument of policy, and the killing of dissidents abroad, as well as the providing of support for anti-Israeli forces, would go on as before. Iran would reach out to the Gulf states while being implicated in acts of violence against the incumbent regimes. In the end, their tentative and haphazard efforts would only generate more intrigue in the Arab world without diminishing the overall level of distrust.

The 1990s were a time of transition. The Islamic Republic was struggling to define its identity and its mission in the aftermath of its founder's demise and the end of the war with Iraq. As the regime's institutions and its factions sought to situate themselves in the altered political topography, tactical alliances would be forged and abandoned, and clerical politicians would shift allegiances and loyalties. However, Iran's transformations were taking place in the context of remarkable global changes confronting the Islamic Republic with demands that its fractured polity could not always meet.

6

Reconciliation Diplomacy and Its Limits

A S RAFSANJANI ASSUMED THE PRESIDENCY, HE SENSED THAT THE imperatives of economic reconstruction would have to guide his priorities abroad. Iran would have to be part of the global economy, mend fences with its neighbors, and come to terms with its erstwhile foes. Given the contentious nature of relations with the United States, he hoped that reconciliation with the European community and the Gulf states and the forging of constructive ties with Russia and China would be sufficient to meet Iran's requirements.

In his quest to reformulate Iran's international relations, Rafsanjani obtained tentative support from Khamenei and the conservative faction. The end of the cold war and the sudden empowerment of the United States meant that Iran had to approach Washington with caution. This sentiment was reinforced by the Gulf War and America's rapid eviction of Saddam from Kuwait. Given the global and regional realignments, Khamenei understood that counterbalancing the United States required good relations with Russia and China.

However, when it came to the European states and the emirates, Iran too often yielded to the temptations of militancy and terrorism. Moreover, ideological clashes with the Gulf rulers and persistent tensions with the Europeans complicated Iran's pragmatic trajectory. The Islamic Republic's hegemonic aspirations in the Persian Gulf and its continued questioning of the sheikdoms' legitimacy distorted attempts to reach out to the princely class. In the meantime, the clerical regime's penchant for terrorism made a sustained rapprochement with key European nations nearly impossible.

Despite his best efforts, Rafsanjani could not rescue Iran's policy toward these critical regions from its revolutionary traps. The imam's conservative disciples continued to embrace his animosities and looked with suspicion on attempts to adjust his legacy.

In the end, this proved a decade of restrained pragmatism, as Iran was neither a revolutionary state seeking to transform the region in its image nor just another member of the international community subtly advancing its practical interests. The Islamic Republic would pursue a bewildering range of policies that confounded both its critics and its allies.

Looking South: Iran and the Gulf States

The contradictory nature of Iran's foreign policy was most evident in the Persian Gulf. Given the centrality of the Gulf to Iran's economic vitality and practical security, Iran's new rulers understood the need for a different relationship with the sheikdoms. In an important departure from his predecessor, Rafsanjani acknowledged that Iran's own conduct was responsible for the emirates' unease about its aspirations. Even the Gulf states' subsidization of Iraq's war effort was blamed partly on Iran's ideological stridency. Rafsanjani stressed this point: "If we had demonstrated a little more tact, they would not have supported Iraq."[1] Deputy Foreign Minister Ali Muhammad Bihishti similarly conceded that it was time for Tehran to "turn [over] a new leaf."[2] To be sure, as a Persian, Shiite state, Iran would always be viewed with suspicion by the incumbent Sunni regimes. However, the revolutionary onslaught of the early years and the prolonged war with Iraq had created unprecedented tensions between Iran and its neighbors. The theocracy's isolation and its economic plight invited policies that were designed to reassure the Arab states of Iran's benign intentions.

The diplomatic necessity of reaching out to the Gulf states was reinforced by Iran's continued difficulties with Iraq.[3] The end of the war had hardly eliminated the challenge of Iraq, as the two parties could not come to terms on border demarcations, reparations, or even prisoner exchange. An economically hard-pressed theocracy had to be concerned with Saddam's rapid remilitarization program, which was widely believed to encompass nonconventional arms.[4] However, the reemergence of an aggressive Saddam also offered Iran a trump card, as the Iraqi strongman was proving to be a problem for the Gulf community. Baghdad's refusal to repay its loans and its territorial disputes with Kuwait exposed the latent fissures between the emirates and Iraq, which the war had largely concealed.

Iran's strategy for dealing with the Iraqi threat was described by Rafsanjani as "resistance in negotiations." Under the auspices of this policy, Tehran would continue its dialogue with Iraq while seeking to gain international and regional support for the full implementation of UN Security Council Resolution 598, which had formally ended the war. By improving ties with the sheikdoms, Iran hoped to turn the tables and actually isolate Iraq in its own Sunni-Arab environment.

In a flurry of activity, Iran's diplomats journeyed to the Persian Gulf capitals, where they called for the resumption of diplomatic and commercial ties and offered assurances of proper behavior. In a pointed acknowledgment of the prevailing order, Foreign Minister Vilayati stated that "Iran respects the independence of all and particularly its neighboring states and stresses détente and the pacific settlement of disputes."[5] As a gesture of its new attitude, Iran adjusted its propaganda campaigns and withdrew its provocative speedboat patrols, which often interfered with Gulf commerce. Tehran suddenly became a hub of activity with trade delegations, visiting dignitaries, and leading cultural figures attending various conferences and symposiums hosted by the Islamic Republic.

Iran's policy of moderation and pragmatism was designed not just to end its isolation but also to facilitate its great power pretensions. Tehran now shifted its focus away from the internal composition of the Gulf states and concentrated on influencing their international orientation. Deputy Foreign Minister Muhammad Javad Larijani emphasized this point: "Every country should be accepted as it is, as the status quo. We do not have to change any regime."[6] For Khomeini, the best means of ensuring the projection of Iranian power and the assertion of its revolutionary values was to overthrow the Gulf ruling class. The succeeding Islamic Republics would emulate Iran's theocratic model and accede to its regional leadership. Rafsanjani placed the emphasis on the international relations of the local states and perceived that a rapprochement might ease their concerns and lead them to accept Iran's primacy.

Along these lines, Iran began discussing a regional security arrangement whereby the stability of the Persian Gulf would be ensured by the indigenous actors as opposed to external powers. Instead of seeking to instigate Shiite uprisings and exhorting the masses to embrace Iran's revolutionary template, Tehran now called for greater economic and security cooperation. By implication this new policy accepted the legitimacy of the monarchical regimes and the sovereign privileges of the very states that the imam had long maligned. Tehran's insistence on a regional network was designed to facilitate the eviction of U.S. forces, thus ensuring its own preeminence. As we have seen, throughout the 1980s Khomeini's Gulf policy was driven by a mixture of Persian nationalism and Islamic militancy. Rafsanjani was much more motivated by the traditional Iranian ambition of dominating the Gulf than imposing an Islamist order on unwilling states.[7]

Beyond Iran's inherently contentious hegemonic claims, its assertion of power in the Persian Gulf continued to be obstructed by its complicated relationship with Saudi Arabia and the unresolved issue of the offshore islands. Iran's approach to Saudi Arabia reflected the revolutionary limits still imposed on Rafsanjani's pragmatic impulses. Most observers of Iran are quick to note its hostility toward the United States and Israel, but during the first decade of the revolution, it was the Saudi state that was the target of Tehran's most pernicious machinations. The fact that both countries predicated their legitimacy on the transnational mission of safeguarding Islam made them natural competitors. Throughout his life, Khomeini had castigated the Saudis as "palace dwellers" who masked their corruption through pious pretensions. For a vast array of the imam's disciples, the House of Saud, with its profligacy and Western indulgences, encapsulated all that was decadent in the princely order. The Iranian hard-liners persisted in condemning the Saudis as purveyors of "American Islam" and as ill suited for the exalted task of administering the holy sites.[8]

The Islamic Republic's ideological animosity was reinforced by the strategic tensions between the two states. Riyadh's ties to Washington and its purchase of sophisticated arms whose ostensible purpose was the deterrence of Iran greatly agitated the clerical regime. Such disagreements and concerns may have been better mediated within a rational diplomatic framework, but given the distrust between the two powers and the Saudis' perceptions of the unreliability of Iranian pragmatism, it was difficult to address mutual grievances constructively.

In a manner that the international community would find bewildering, Iran started speaking with multiple voices. While Rafsanjani and Vilayati pressed for better relations with the Saudi state, the hard-liners denounced such policy as betraying the essence of the revolution. The reactionary newspaper *Jumhuri-i Islami* took the lead and claimed that the "Saudi attitude toward the Islamic Republic during recent years, its attitude toward the Islamic Revolution, and its extensive support for the Iraqi Ba'athists during the bloody 1980–88 war cannot be forgotten."[9] The conservative daily *Risalat* similarly denounced any resumption of ties with Saudi Arabia as "surrender to the enemies of Islam."[10] In a gesture of accord with their conservative brethren, the radical parliamentarians also chimed in, and Speaker Mahdi Karubi stated that "Disputes between the Islamic Republic and Saudi Arabia are deep rooted and pertain to the fundamental quarrel between American-style Islam and the genuine Islam of the Prophet....There is no compromise in this dispute."[11] Khamenei finally ended the debate by castigating the Saudi rulers as "sinful idols of arrogance and colonialism."[12] Despite a tentative consensus across the political spectrum that Iran required a more nuanced policy in its immediate neighborhood, the theocracy could not emancipate itself from its burdensome ideological inheritance. The Islamic Republic failed to appreciate the difficulty of normalizing relations with the Gulf states while estranging the leading member of that community.

To further compound its problems, Iran continued to occupy the three small islands of Abu Musa and Greater and Lesser Tunb along the Strait of Hormuz, which had long been claimed by the United Arab Emirates (UAE).[13] Subsequent to Britain's departure from the Persian Gulf in 1971, the shah took over the islands, thereby beginning a dispute with the sheikdoms that persisted long after his departure from the scene. For the Gulf rulers, Iran's possession of the islands was an unacceptable indication of its imperial hubris. In a gesture of continuity with their monarchical predecessor, the clerical elite adhered to the shah's argument that the territories were an integral part of Iran. The unresolved nature of this dispute continued to hamper a more reasonable relationship between Iran and its immediate neighbors. Ironically, Rafsanjani's pragmatism was undermined by both the Islamic Republic's intense nationalism and its Islamist radicalism.

Over the years there would be repeated attempts to negotiate the status of the islands. Both bilateral and multilateral mechanisms would be employed only to fail. Iran never wavered from its contention that the islands were part of its territory, a claim denied by both the UAE and the Gulf Cooperation Council (GCC). At times tensions flared up on the islands, leading to military maneuvers and even the eviction of Arab residents. Ultimately, Tehran's failure to reach a suitable accord on a tangential issue such as its possession of three insignificant territories was seen by the Gulf Arabs as an indication that it was not serious about mending relations.

In the end, the altered Iranian position and its measured pragmatism were not sufficient to restore ties with the Gulf sheikdoms. After a decade of revolutionary militancy and mischief, Rafsanjani's more restrained approach was treated with caution. The skepticism deepened, as Khamenei and the clerical firebrands refused to temper their objections to the House of Saud. However, once more Saddam Husayn came to the rescue. On August 2, 1990, the impetuous Iraqi despot invaded Kuwait, hoping to utilize its oil wealth for the reconstruction of his devastated nation. Iraq's attack changed the political landscape of the Middle East by propelling the Arab princes toward a closer embrace of their Persian neighbor.

Iraq's invasion of Kuwait presented the theocratic regime with both opportunities and challenges. Saddam's foray offered Iran a chance to demonstrate its moderation, cooperate with the United Nations, and marginalize its historic foe. Yet Iraq's rash conduct also brought more than a half-million U.S. troops to Iran's periphery and renewed America's commitment to securing the Middle East's critical waterways. The latest crisis to grip the region thus proffered the Islamic Republic a series of balancing acts to contend with, as the theocratic regime had to reconcile its sense of Islamist solidarity with its strategic realism.[14]

To the surprise of many in the international community, Iran was among the first states to categorically condemn Iraq's invasion and demand its adherence to the UN resolution that called for its withdrawal. The Foreign Ministry stressed that Iran "considers Iraqi military action against Kuwait contrary to the stability and security in the sensitive Persian Gulf region and condemns it."[15] The Islamic Republic, which had spent many years denouncing the United Nations as an instrument of American imperialism, now upheld its mandate as a forceful expression of global consensus. In yet another ironic gesture, the clerical regime, which had plotted the overthrow of the Kuwaiti emirs, demanded the restoration of the Al-Sabah family as the sheikdom's legitimate rulers.

Along with embracing neutrality, Rafsanjani cleverly couched his arguments in Iran's own war with Iraq. The president noted that for eight years Iran had failed to convince the United Nations and the great powers of Saddam's nefarious ways. At a time when Iraq had undertaken another invasion and the international community had finally awoken to Saddam's true nature, Iran could not help but feel vindicated. In many ways, the war had validated Iran's claim that Iraq was the true source of instability and conflict in the Middle East.

Rafsanjani's pragmatic approach and Iran's neutrality during the war were not easy choices. Initially, debate within the clerical state pitted different factions against each other.[16] The radical politicians' behavior during the crisis was curious and irresponsible. On the one hand, they joined other groups in their condemnation of Saddam's aggression. However, in the radicals' cosmology, the American presence was a greater affront than Saddam's invasion. Given their paranoia and suspicions, they perceived that the war was a prelude to a larger U.S. strategy of militarily displacing ideologically unacceptable regimes. A number of radical politicians went even further and claimed that the imperative of resisting the United States necessitated forging an alliance with even the Iraqi regime. Ayatollah Sadiq Khalkhali, who had made a reputation as the hanging judge after sending many of the shah's officials to their death on trumped-up charges, once more stepped into the limelight and proclaimed: "We have always said death to America and death to Israel. Now we have to live up to these statements."[17] Ali Akbar Muhtashami'pur similarly echoed this view: "The Iranian nation has a religious duty to join the Jihad against the UN infidel forces, NATO forces and the Zionists."[18] The radicals' animosities toward the United States and the Arab ruling elite outweighed their disdain for Saddam's Ba'athist state.

Despite the radicals' protestation, Rafsanjani and Khamenei quickly settled the national course by pressing Saddam to relinquish his recent gain. At a time when Iran was seeking to attract investors and integrate into the global economy, the radicals' disastrous call for waging Jihad on Saddam's behalf was rejected by both the president and the supreme leader. Here we see the fluid nature of Iran's factions and personalities, as the conservatives and pragmatists, who were increasingly at odds, could still transcend their differences and defuse a domestic deadlock. Iran's unease about America's strategy and the arrival of a large contingent of U.S. troops in Saudi Arabia did not dramatically alter this calculus. Tehran's policy allowed it to project an image of responsibility by reinforcing its existing diplomatic overtures to the established authorities.

As the war clouds gathered over the Persian Gulf, the antagonists were rewarding Iran. Shortly after his invasion of Kuwait, Saddam capitulated to all of Iran's war aims. Baghdad now finally accepted Resolution 598, as well as the 1975 Algiers Accord, which offered Iran a favorable demarcation of the Shatt al-Arab waterway. The latter concession was particularly note-worthy: Saddam ostensibly went to war against Iran in part because of the inequities of the 1975 accord. The once-imperious Saddam was reduced to writing a plaintive appeal to Rafsanjani: "Oh President Ali Akbar Rafsanjani with our decision everything has become clearer and everything you wanted and on which you have been concentrating has been achieved."[19] In order to protect his eastern flank, Saddam had to agree to demands that he had often disparaged as an insult to Iraq's national dignity.

In a symbolically important move, UN Secretary General Javier Pérez de Cuéllar declared Iraq the aggressor for launching the Iran-Iraq war. The fulfillment of the long-standing Iranian demand potentially made Iraq responsible for reparations, which amounted to nearly $100 billion.[20] The war, which was proving a bonanza for Iran, yielded another gain when, in an act of folly, Saddam dispatched a number of his aircraft to Iran for safe-keeping. The Islamic Republic promptly expropriated the planes as payment on its larger reparations bill.

The benefits accruing to Iran were not coming just from Iraq and the UN, as some of its previous foes were also returning to the fold. With the exception of Saudi Arabia, Kuwait had long been one of Iran's staunchest critics and had done much to buttress Saddam's war effort. As we have seen, the clerical state had not helped its cause with its plotting of the assassination of Kuwaiti rulers. Tensions reached their peak during the reflagging crisis, when Tehran interfered with Kuwait's shipping activities. All of this seemingly changed, however, as the new Kuwaiti government in exile appreciated Iran's neutrality and its rebuff of Saddam's entreaties. Kuwaiti delegations now traveled to Tehran, promising better relations and apologizing for past misdeeds.[21] Although Iran's relations with its smaller Gulf neighbors would never be uncomplicated, the war did lower their inhibitions about dealing with the Islamic Republic.

In January 1991 sanctions were finally followed by an actual U.S. military intervention, which in turn led to a subtle change in Iran's studied policy of neutrality. The clerical regime allowed allied planes and ships to traverse its territory and pledged to rescue downed pilots. The exercise of U.S. power within the framework of the United Nations was not entirely unacceptable to Iran so long as there was a definite timeline to the departure of the American armies. It was hoped that, once the United States sufficiently degraded Iraq's military capabilities, it would quickly withdraw from the scene. However, as the war evolved, it presented Iran with some stark choices.

The initial dilemma confronting the Islamic Republic was the Shiite rebellion in southern Iraq. Having lost control over much of his territory, Saddam suddenly faced a Shiite revolt in key places such as Basra and Karbala. After a decade of calling and hoping for a Shiite upheaval, Iran seemed hesitant once the actual rebellion took place. Tehran refrained from large-scale military intervention and limited itself to modest logistical assistance. Although it seems that the Revolutionary Guards did enter Iraqi territory, their primary objective was the Mujahidin-i Khalq (MEK) installations and not the protection of their beleaguered coreligionists. Rafsanjani summed up Iran's position by claiming that the Iraqis "can do their own work."[22] The primacy of geopolitical calculations over Islamist designs was in full view, as Iran's policy was driven more by its fear of Iraq's disintegration than its hopes of Shiite empowerment.

In the country's first crisis since the passing of the imam, Rafsanjani demonstrated how Iran's priorities had altered. As tensions in the Persian Gulf intensified, Iran had behaved judiciously by placing national interests above revolutionary ideals. For his part, Khamenei sensed that the regional dangers necessitated accepting Rafsanjani's path and restraining the irresponsible elements within the clerical hierarchy. Although counterfactual history is always a precarious exercise, it is hard to envision the imam following a similar course. Khomeini's profound disdain for the United States and his well-honed animus toward the Gulf rulers may have motivated a less balanced policy. This is not to suggest that Iran would have been rash enough to enter the war on Saddam's behalf, but it might have been a less cooperative actor.

In the immediate aftermath of the war, the central focus of Iran's policy was its collective security proposal, which called for an alliance among the local regimes. The Islamic Republic perceived that its moderation and proper behavior had earned it the right to craft a new architecture for Gulf security. However, Tehran did not seek to be a mere participant. Instead, it demanded the exclusion of the United States and a new regional order that would encompass only the local actors. This was a convenient call for Iran, as the marginalization of a defeated Iraq had left the American presence as the last remaining barrier to its resurgence. However, while Iran was plotting its dominance over a prostrated Persian Gulf, the Arab countries and the United States were contemplating a very different future.

The March 1991 announcement of the Damascus Declaration and its "6+2 arrangement" disillusioned and infuriated Iran. The declaration called for an "Arab peace force" that comprised the GCC, as well as Egypt and Syria, to provide for the security of the Persian Gulf. This was to be an "example that would guarantee the effectiveness of the comprehensive Arab defense order."[23] Not only was Iran's neutrality during the war not acknowledged, but the Arab states also contemplated the creation of a regional defense network whose primary purpose was its containment. The fact that Syria was a participant in the arrangement caused momentary tensions in its alliance with Tehran, whose concerns were hardly assuaged by Hafiz al-Asad's pledge that the network was not aimed at Iran. As had often happened before, international developments had an impact on the theocratic regime's internal deliberations. Once Rafsanjani's pragmatism was seemingly discredited, the hard-liners felt free to criticize and undermine his approach. The voice of the conservatives, Jumhuri-i Islami, took the lead in castigating the Iranian officials who had invested in Arab and American goodwill.[24] In light of Iran's cooperative attitude during the war, a more inclusive system may have succeeded in tempering its militant tendencies. In the end, the Arab order was not to be, as rivalries among the Arab states and America's focus on the Israeli-Palestinian conflict proved to be the death knell of the nascent arrangement.

The demise of the Damascus Declaration did not pave the way for Iran's often-repeated calls for a regional security system. Saddam's continued presence and lingering concerns about Iran led the Gulf sheikdoms to cement bilateral defense ties with the United States. The agreements with Kuwait, Saudi Arabia, and Bahrain ensured that these countries' port facilities and installations would house U.S. forces and prepositioned equipment. The need to deter Iraq and contain Iran once more brought the United States and the emirates together. The evolving bilateral arrangements were more in line with the Gulf states' traditional international orientation, which had always relied on external powers to fend off the hegemonic aspirations of their more populous and powerful northern neighbors.

In the mid-1990s, Iran was still incapable of crafting a coherent Gulf policy. On the one hand, the theocratic regime remained devoted to its vision of a Persian Gulf that excluded foreign powers. Given the sheikdoms' numerous defense compacts with the United States and the active American role in the containment of Saddam, Iran's position seemed fanciful. Tehran's inability to implement its strategy let to a self-defeating, two-track policy that, while sustaining dialogue with the Gulf rulers, instigated terror attacks on their territory. As with many in the Middle East, Iran believed that the lesson of the 1983 Beirut bombing was that a spectacular act of terrorism could provoke America's withdrawal. Even if such a departure did not take place, it could increase the domestic price that the Gulf states paid for their intimate ties to Washington. Moreover, U.S. intelligence services have long attributed the 1996 bombing of the Khobar Towers in Saudi Arabia, which housed U.S. military personnel, to Iran.[25] Beyond strong circumstantial evidence, the incident certainly fits the pattern of Iranian behavior. However, as with previous acts of Iranian terror, the attacks not only failed to dislodge the U.S. presence but also further estranged the emirates. The stark contradiction of Iran's policy cannot be attributed to factionalism because it would be inconceivable for Rafsanjani not to have known about Iran's attacks on the United States.[26] It is here that Rafsanjani's unwillingness to impose discipline on the multilayered theocracy did much to undermine his own declared objective of normalizing ties with the Persian Gulf community.

In the end, during the Rafsanjani era, Iran made important gains and succeeded in reestablishing relations with key Gulf sheikdoms. However, the Islamic Republic's inability to devise a consistent policy of rapprochement and its insistence on America's withdrawal from a region that Washington had identified as vital to its national security prevented its integration into the new order. Had Iran transcended its ideological compunctions and acknowledged that the United States could play a constructive role in the Persian Gulf, it would have been a more important player in its immediate environment. Iran's resort to terrorism and its sporadic revolutionary denunciations of the princely class only honed the Gulf monarchies' suspicions. It would be Washington's task to maintain order in the Gulf, as the Arabs were more confident in U.S. power than Iranian ambitions. The Rafsanjani administration, which made the Persian Gulf the center piece of its foreign policy, ended its tenure still distrusted by the Gulf Arabs and largely isolated in its neighborhood.

Looking West: Iran and Europe

At the outset of the Rafsanjani administration there was an expectation that Iran's relations with the European states would improve. An Islamic Republic seeking to escape its isolation and a European Union in search of a more autonomous role in the post–cold war environment would put aside past grievances and cooperate on issues of common concern. However, the sporadic increases in trade and resumed diplomatic relations did not lead to the anticipated thaw. Once more, the burden of ideology, historical animosities, and the clerical regime's penchant for terrorism did much to undermine its attempt to normalize ties with the European states. The U.S.-Iranian confrontation too often hovered around Europe's policy, compelling it to choose between an indispensable ally and a problematic theocracy. Despite criticism in some American quarters of Europe's mercantile tendencies, whenever confronted with a choice between the United States and Iran, the Europeans opted for the Atlantic alliance.[27]

The best way to assess European-Iranian relations is to examine Tehran's approach to the three leading states: Britain, Germany, and France. These countries had the longest experience in the Middle East and constituted Iran's most important commercial partners. As the pivotal states of the continent, their priorities and concerns would have an inordinate influence on the overall direction of Europe's policy. To be sure, Iran would enjoy important ties with the Scandinavian countries, as well as Italy and Spain, but in the absence of a coherent policy toward the big three, Tehran could not fully come to terms with Europe.

By far the European country with the greatest impact on Iran's political imagination is Great Britain. For much of the twentieth century, Britain was the dominant Western power in Iran, exploiting its resources and manipulating its internal order. It was the British Empire that brought Reza Shah to power in 1921, thereby inaugurating the Pahlavi dynasty.[28] In 1941 Britain went a step further and—in conjunction with Russia— militarily occupied Iran and displaced the elder shah with his more compliant son. Although the U.S. government gets the lion's share of the blame for the 1953 coup, which deposed nationalist Prime Minister Muhammad Musaddiq, Britain is never far behind in Iran's demonology.[29] Even after Britain began its long decline in the postwar period, the ever-suspicious Iranians remained leery of its intentions. Sensing its sinister hands behind America's actions, Khomeini was swift in his denunciation of Britain as the "aged wolf of imperialism."[30] Given the mythology, history, and paranoia that conditioned Iran's image of the United Kingdom, it proved difficult for Whitehall to craft normal relations with the Islamic Republic.

Still, Britain never suffered a hostage crisis, and it maintained a diplomatic mission of some sort in Iran throughout the tumultuous revolutionary decade. At times, the two sides would expel each others diplomats, accuse their respective embassies of espionage, and mistreat each other's citizens. However, there was an incremental but steady improvement of relations. All of this came to a halt with the Rushdie affair. In order to galvanize the public behind the cause of the revolution, the imam issued a decree that was bound to isolate and ostracize his beleaguered nation.

Following the inauguration of the Islamic Republic, the expectation was that France would quickly emerge as Iran's most trusted European partner. Unlike Britain, France did not have a contentious history of intervention in Iran's internal affairs and had maintained correct and formal relations with successive Iranian governments. The fact that Khomeini had been provided a sanctuary in the Parisian suburb of Neauphle-le-Château further heightened the possibility of better ties. Upon his return to Tehran, the imam was quick to express his gratitude "to my French friends who gave me the opportunity to send my messages from Paris to Tehran."[31] For their part, the French intelligentsia seemed initially hopeful about a Third World revolution that denied despotism and had distinct anti-American overtones. The new rulers' clerical garb and religious idiom did not daunt a French intellectual class that pinned its hopes on a provisional government that had many French-educated leaders.[32]

All of this began to change, however, as the resurgence of religious fundamentalism and the vengeance of the mullahs disillusioned the French elite. France soon emerged as the principal home of Iranian dissidents, ranging from the fleeing monarchists to exiles of the Islamic Republic. The arrival of Bani-Sadr was followed by the establishment of MEK offices in Paris. Tehran's extradition requests were rejected by a state that had a humane tradition of caring for political refugees. Once the legal channels were rebuffed, the clerical regime opted for violence and plotted the assassination of numerous Iranian opposition figures who had fled its reign of terror. The high point of tensions came in 1986, when Paris was rocked by a series of explosions that it blamed on Iran. The key official behind these attacks was Iranian diplomat Valid Gorgi, whose expulsion triggered a diplomatic spat between the two states. Relations ruptured, and the Islamic Republic managed to estrange the one country that it initially hoped would act as a buffer against both American and British pressures.[33]

Beyond political disagreements, France's ties to Iraq emerged as yet another area of contention between the two states. Paris's relations with Baghdad had started in the 1960s, when the French republic began adopting a Middle East policy independent of both the United States and Britain. At a time when the conservative sheikdoms were under the influence of first the United Kingdom and later the United States, Iraq's radical regime offered France a way into the Persian Gulf. For its part, Baghdad welcomed such ties because it did not want an exclusive dependence on the Soviet Union and the Eastern bloc. François Mitterrand's socialist government agreed to major arms sales to Iraq, and the weaponry only grew in sophistication and quantity as the war progressed. Not surprisingly, the sales antagonized Iran, and Rafsanjani took the lead in denouncing them as "shameless acts by a socialist government which ignores human rights principles."[34]

As with the United States, Iran's violent interventions in Lebanon, a country with deep and historic ties to France, further aggravated relations between the two states. The infamous 1983 bombing of U.S. Marine barracks in Lebanon should not obscure the fact that Iranian terrorism also targeted French troops, killing fifty-eight military personnel that same year. France responded with its own retaliatory bombing of Bekka Valley, thereby bringing it into a confrontation with Iran's Revolutionary Guards. To be sure, the altercations did not lead to a prolonged severance of diplomatic and economic relations, but issues such as terrorism, human rights, and France's intimate ties to Saddam's regime did much to hinder normal relations.

Among the major European states, Germany managed to sustain a cordial relationship with Iran throughout the latter's revolutionary spasms.

Germany was not burdened by a torturous colonial history, and it did not have close ties to Iraq. Even more important, Bonn always took the position that dialogue and commerce were the best means of influencing the Islamic Republic and often demurred to America's insistence on sanctions and coercion. For its part, Tehran appreciated Germany's nuanced diplomacy and recognized the need to maintain stable ties with at least one important industrial power. The convergence of perspectives between the two states led to growing diplomatic and commercial exchanges, making Germany Iran's largest trading partner. All of this is not to suggest that Bonn took an uncritical view of Iran—despite Tehran's threats, Germany suspended nuclear cooperation with the clerical regime. In due course, escalating Iranian terrorism would compel even a tolerant Germany to reevaluate its policy and join the Western consensus against the Islamic Republic.

The European policy was never a purely bilateral affair, however. Broader regional issues and the U.S.-Iranian conflict had an impact on their approach. The first issue that thwarted a predictable reconciliation between Iran and the European community was the hostage crisis. The Europeans stood with their American ally in their condemnation of Iran's egregious and illegal conduct. Once the UN Security Council failed to impose sanctions due to the Soviet veto, many European countries voluntarily downgraded their economic relations with Iran. To be sure, the Europeans maintained their diplomatic representations, which actually played a useful role in mediating the crisis and providing a channel of communication between the United States and the revolutionary regime. Nonetheless, the hostage drama proved the difficulty of maintaining ties with an Iranian government at loggerheads with the United States. Once the Europeans had to make a choice, they opted for the American alliance as opposed to Iranian commerce.

On the heels of the hostage crisis came the war between Iran and Iraq, which once more presented the Europeans with uneasy choices. As with much of the international community, the European states chose to assist Iraq and perceived that the containment of Iran's revolutionary fervor required buttressing the unsavory Saddam. Given their historic ties, the French went furthest by providing Iraq with sophisticated aircraft and missile technology, which did much damage to Iran's oil installations. As permanent members of the UN Security Council, both Britain and France can be blamed for their lack of moral resolution, as Iraq's persistent use of chemical weapons went largely ignored by the United Nations. The "tanker war" of the late 1980s further entangled Europe in the U.S.-Iranian confrontation, as they joined the U.S. Navy in shielding Kuwaiti vessels from Iran's retribution. The close level of U.S.-European cooperation on all of these issues tended to obviate the possibility of a differentiated Western bloc that the Iranians could exploit.

Throughout the 1980s, there was a degree of unrealism in both Iran and Europe about the possibilities and potential of their relationship. The clerical regime falsely assumed that the lure of its trade could decouple the Western alliance and somehow divide the Europeans from the Americans. In the late cold-war era, the centrality of NATO to Europe's security concerns made such expectations seem fanciful. For their part, the European states similarly failed to note the impossibility of sustaining cordial ties with Tehran while providing arms to Iraq and siding with the United States in its many disputes with Iran. It was just such contradictions that did much to bedevil relations between the two parties.

Upon assuming power, Rafsanjani understood the need for improved relations with the European states.[35] The reconstruction program and its need for foreign technologies and investments, as well as the desire to escape its isolation, propelled Iran toward revisiting its outlook. Given the collapse of the Soviet bloc and the lack of a domestic consensus on an approach to the United States, the need for Europe became even more pressing. Once again, however, the evident logic of improved relations did not necessarily translate into the reality of better ties. The burden of Khomeini's ideological legacy and Iranian terrorism, which encompassed the targeted assassinations of dissidents abroad, did much to subvert Rafsanjani's pragmatic intentions. The Islamic Republic's paranoid style of politics meant that it always exaggerated threats to its security. It saw the killing of dissidents as a means of eliminating the opposition, as well as deterring internal plots. In the end, the Rafsanjani administration would end up in a place not that dissimilar from its predecessor, namely, with ruptured diplomatic ties and only a modest increase in trade.[36]

The European states initially embraced the new Iranian president and invested in his call for reconciliation with erstwhile foes. The European policy was soon labeled "critical dialogue," which suggested that, through diplomatic discussion and economic incentives, Iran could be persuaded to modify its behavior. The policy was not devoid of sanctions and pressure, as the Europeans periodically cut off official relations and reduced the level of trade. However, the sanctions were typically light, and the duration of severed relations often brief. Still, "critical dialogue" acknowledged that Iran was a multifactional polity with moderates and hard-liners battling each other for influence. From this perspective, a more judicious and inclusive approach was designed to empower the pragmatists and diminish the standing of the hard-liners. The European strategy would have its limits. In the end, it was difficult for either Britain or France to push Iran in the right direction with inducements while the United States not only remained on the sidelines but also actively undermined their stance by isolating the Islamic Republic.

The "critical dialogue" was not without its successes, as Iran soon began pressuring its Lebanese allies to release the remaining European hostages. It is important to recognize that the United States was not the only Western country that suffered at hands of Iran in Lebanon, as many French and German journalists and diplomats were also abducted, and European peacekeeping forces were often subject to Hezbollah's violence. Because he was instrumental in ending the hostage dilemma, Rafsanjani garnered a considerable degree of goodwill by facilitating the release of the captive Europeans.

Along this path, Rafsanjani also sought to tone down the Rushdie affair by differentiating between the religious validity of the fatwa and actual policy of the state. The Islamic Republic's evolving position was that a religious decree granted by an esteemed cleric could not be countermanded, but Iran had no intention of actually enforcing it. Foreign Minister Vilayati spelled out Tehran's position:

> We as a government are not going to send anybody to kill Salman Rushdie or to dispatch commandoes to kill somebody outside this country, whether this is Salman Rushdie or someone else. This is the official position of our government. But if you are asking about the fatwa, this is because we must divide the issues into two sections. First, the question of the fatwa; second, the position of the government.[37]

However tentative and ambiguous the renunciation of Khomeini's act may have been, it was initially acceptable to the European community. This tolerance soon subsided, however. Given Iran's multiplicity of voices and its continued attachment to terrorism, the Rushdie affair proved a more serious stumbling block for Rafsanjani. A thaw of sorts had taken place in Anglo-Iranian relations in 1992, and Foreign Secretary Douglas Hurd had even contemplated a visit to Tehran. But the emerging ties quickly refroze. Vilayati's statements were soon contradicted by many Iranian politicians, who insisted that the fatwa was irreversible. In the meantime, powerful religious foundations were still declaring their willingness to pay a bounty for Rushdie's head. These assertions were given more weight when Britain expelled a number of Iranian diplomats on the suspicion that they were actually plotting Rushdie's murder.[38] Whatever the validity of these charges may have been, Iran's inability to categorically distance itself from the imam's verdict obstructed its attempts to mend fences with London.

Nor did Iran see a significant improvement in its relations with France. Upon the inauguration of Rafsanjani as president, Paris had high hopes for resumed ties with Iran. The French were grateful for Iran's assistance in releasing their hostages in Lebanon and even reciprocated by imposing restrictions on the MEK's activities to the point of expelling some of its leadership.[39] Yet Iranian terrorism reared its head once more with the assassination of the shah's former prime minister, Shapur Bakhtiar, and other dissidents. As a consequence, relations were downgraded. Moreover, France, like many other European states, realized the difficulty of doing business in Iran given the country's increasing debt burden, the absence of the rule of law, and the lack of institutional transparency. Although trade between Iran and the European community increased during the initial phase of postwar reconstruction, it soon declined in response to Iran's mounting financial difficulties and its support for terrorism.

Perhaps no state was as patient and tolerant of Iranian malfeasance as Germany, whose approach to "critical dialogue" was focused less on criticism and more on dialogue. Even the 1992 assassination of Kurdish exiles in Berlin by Iranian agents did not lead to a reevaluation of relations. The German intelligence services actually used the occasion to open a discussion with their Iranian counterparts, particularly the notorious minister of intelligence, Ali Fallahian, who had been implicated in numerous internal and external killings. In 1993 Fallahian was invited to Bonn for a discussion on human rights and terrorism.[40] During his visit, the discussion also apparently addressed the fate of a German businessman held in Iran, Helmut Szimkus, and Ron Arad, an Israeli pilot shot down over Lebanon. However, far from focusing on human rights issues (in this case the plight of a German national and an Israeli aviator), Fallahian left Germany with computer technology that would improve the efficacy of Iran's intelligence system.[41]

The position of Helmut Kohl's government was assailed not just by the United States but also by German parliamentarians and the press, who claimed that Fallahian's visit contradicted the European Commission's own human rights declarations.[42] The respectful reception given to a terrorist mastermind did much to undermine the more valid assumptions of "critical dialogue," which acknowledged that simply isolating Iran was an ineffective means of altering its course of action. In the end, it would be the

German judiciary, with its dogged pursuit of Iranian terrorism, that would compel Bonn, and indeed other European states as well, to reconsider their approach and withdraw their envoys from Iran. As in the Persian Gulf, terrorism as an instrument of policy greatly undermined Iran's quest to reclaim its position as a legitimate member of the community of nations.

At the outset of the revolution, many political leaders in Iran anticipated a reasonable relationship with the European community. The Islamic Republic's slogan of "neither East nor West" implied not just antagonism toward the United States but also suspicion of the Soviets' intentions. The failure of Iran and Europe to establish normalized relations in the 1980s can be attributed to extraordinary events such as the hostage crisis, the war with Iraq, and Iran's revolutionary zeal. As the 1980s drew to a close, there was widespread hope that the rebirth of Iranian pragmatism and the European quest for a more independent post–cold war foreign policy would pave the way for resumed ties. Once more, however, Iran's self-defeating practices would obstruct the anticipated reconciliation. Tehran's wave of assassination of Iranian dissidents on European territory, the Rushdie affair, and its continued Islamist militancy prevented the emergence of relations that both parties seemingly desired. Iran's pragmatism proved tentative inasmuch as it was often subverted by internal machinations and the still powerful pull of ideology.

In the end, Iran's failure to move toward a different relationship with an accommodating Europe reflected the Islamic Republic's difficulty in balancing its competing mandates. The European states' modest diplomatic and economic offerings were ultimately insufficient to steer Iran away from its human rights abuses and terrorist attachments. The policy of "critical dialogue" may have succeeded in prolonging negotiations, but it did not solve the underlying quandaries facing the two parties. It is not that Iran did not realize its need for European trade and diplomatic engagement; nonetheless, that acknowledgment somehow failed to lead to an abandonment of its confrontational policies. President Rafsanjani, who shared many of the reactionary clerics' vindictive impulses, proved incapable of diverting Iran from its revolutionary excesses and living up to his pledge of pragmatically adjusting Iran's European policy.

Looking North: Iran and Russia

To the extent that Iran's foreign relations exhibited a degree of sustained realism, it forged ties with the Russian Federation. Given Russia's dire economic situation and Iran's need for arms, a lucrative commercial relationship evolved between the two states that soon involved the transfer of nuclear technology. As the price for this relationship, Iran refrained from pressing its Islamist message in the contested lands of central Asia and ignored Russia's suppression of Muslim rebels in Chechnya. A beleaguered Iranian state requiring arms and trade looked to an aggrieved former superpower seeking relevance and profits. The theocratic regime recognized that its national interests mandated stability on its northern frontier. This was a case in which Iran's factions came together and subordinated revolutionary values to more pragmatic considerations.

At the outset of the revolution, Iran's relations with the Soviet Union were cool and formal. The conflict between the United States and Iran did not pave the way for Soviet entry, as the prevailing slogan—"neither East nor West"—reflected Iran's continued ideological and practical disputes with the Soviet Union. The clerical regime viewed Soviet communism to be as hollow and inauthentic as other Western ideologies. The fact that Iran's youth had always been tempted by leftist tendencies made the Soviet state the object of particular distrust. The invasion of Afghanistan compounded these difficulties, as Iran not only condemned the attack but also provided assistance to the nascent Afghan resistance.[43]

Despite such ominous signs, the Soviet leadership initially hoped that the anti-imperialist character of the new revolution would somehow redound to its advantage. Like the United States, the Soviet policy toward the Middle East was conditioned by the cold-war rivalry. The Middle East's resources and waterways gave it geopolitical primacy in the superpowers' contest for global hegemony. Moscow's approach to Tehran reflected these concerns, as Iran's position along the Persian Gulf and its centrality to the international petroleum market made it a tantalizing prize in the superpowers' competition for influence. For the Soviet Union, which had long been on the margins of the region's politics, Iran's improbable revolution suddenly altered the balance of power by emboldening anti-American forces that loathed conservative monarchical states.

Beyond strategic calculations, the Soviet Union also had high ideological hopes for the unfolding Iranian revolution. As a state that took its Marxist cant seriously, the Soviets looked to Iran's revolution as a transition step to a socialist stage. Despite its religious character and prickly nationalism, Iran was seen as going through a predictable trajectory for a developing country and would soon dispense with its bourgeois impulses and embrace its true socialist calling. The presence of progressive forces in the revolutionary coalition, including the ardently pro-Soviet Tudah Party, led Moscow to believe that in due course things would go its way. Ironically, the Kremlin was hostile to the provisional government and much preferred the mullahs, who could be easily displaced. To say the least, this proved a short-sighted move.[44]

These tendencies led the Tudah to welcome the capture of the U.S. embassy by student militants. The hostage crisis would spark the collapse of the Bazargan government and provoke the severance of all ties between the United States and Iran. The secretary general of the Tudah Party, Nuraldin Kianuri, celebrated the capture of the diplomats: "As long as the hostages are in Iran, normalization of relations between the United States and Iran will not be possible."[45] In one of its typically flawed analyses, Tudah saw Iran's politics as a struggle between the provisional government and the revolutionary forces surrounding Khomeini. Free of the restraints of Bazargan and his cohort, the Islamist elements would yield to the vanguards of the working class and retreat to their seminaries. The imam would soon dash such hopes, however. He mercilessly persecuted the Tudah, thereby destroying a resilient Soviet proxy that had survived even the shah's secret police.

The Soviet Union's approach to the hostage crisis had to be more circumspect. Given Iran's transparently illegal conduct, Moscow had to walk a fine line between acknowledging the principles of diplomatic immunity and shielding Iran from international reprisal. The Soviet delegation at the UN accepted resolutions calling for the release of the diplomats without conceding to real punitive measures. *Pravda* subtly situated the hostage drama within the larger narrative of Iranian grievances: "The seizure of the American embassy is undoubtedly not in keeping with international conventions or respect for diplomatic privileges. This act, however, cannot be taken out of the overall conduct of American-Iranian relations."[46] Russia's behavior became even more problematic in the aftermath of its invasion of Afghanistan, as it sought to deflect attention from its own belligerence by portraying the United States as the aggressor in the Middle East.

The Soviet propitiation of the Islamic Republic endured the initial years of the Iran-Iraq war. Despite its long-standing ties to Iraq, Moscow greeted Saddam's invasion with alarm and adopted a neutralist posture. The fact was that, by 1980, Russia's relations with Iraq had somewhat cooled, as Saddam was threatening its Syrian client and forging a close relationship with the conservative Arab states. Moreover, Russia was concerned about the unpredictable consequences of the collapse of the theocratic regime. The Islamic Republic may not have been easy to deal with, but it was reliably anti-American. There was no assurance, however, that a successor government would sustain that level of hostility toward the United States. It is not that Leonid Brezhnev and the Politburo hoped for Iran's triumph, but a balance of power in the Persian Gulf better suited Russia's interests than the fall of either combatant.[47] Nonetheless, the Kremlin's latest overtures failed to mollify Iran, and Tehran remained opposed to Moscow's Afghan policy and continued to provide assistance to the rebels. The Soviet leadership was realizing the difficulty of forging relations with a radical regime in midst of a revolutionary whirlwind.

As with many facets of the Islamic Republic's international relationships, the year 1982 proved pivotal. Iran's decision to spurn various mediation efforts and invade Iraq provoked the Soviet Union and brought it out of its neutralist torpor. Just as Moscow feared the theocracy's collapse, it also did not want to see Saddam's leftist regime replaced by an Islamist one. The demise of the Ba'athist state might not only galvanize fundamentalist forces throughout the Islamic world, including central Asia, but also congeal the United States' military presence in the Persian Gulf. The smaller Arab emirates were bound to gravitate toward the American security umbrella to fend off Iran's moves. Thus, Moscow could potentially end up with both an intensified Islamist challenge as well as a reinforced U.S. presence on its southern periphery. The Soviet Union now began providing long-range missiles and other sophisticated armaments to Iraq, while its propaganda campaign criticized Iran's emerging religious dictatorship.[48]

Hardly cowed by the latest Russian moves, Tehran responded by increasing its aid to the Afghan resistance. Given its Islamist ideology, the clerical state could not remain indifferent to the Soviet invasion of a Muslim country, particularly at a time when Russia was providing significant military hardware to the secular Iraqi state, which had a checkered history of persecuting its own religious class. The tensions between the two powers paved the way for the clerical regime's effective destruction of the Tudah. Not only was Iran's oldest Communist party banned, but many of its leaders were also forced to make public recantations. The subsequent trials asserted that a sinister Soviet cabal had penetrated Iran's key institutions with the aim of overthrowing the regime.[49] In yet another swipe at the Soviet Union, Iran expelled a contingent of Russian diplomats for interfering in its domestic affairs and executed a number of the convicted Tudah leaders despite Moscow's appeals. *Pravda* noted Iran's open hostility: "As for the anti-Soviet campaign that has been launched in Tehran, it only darkens the relationship between our countries and people, harming above all the interest of Iran itself."[50]

Despite the growing discord, Tehran realized that its relationship with Moscow had to be more nuanced and calibrated. The Soviet power was too close and its trade too valuable, given Iran's estrangement from the West. Disagreements over Afghanistan and Iraq also had to be balanced with competing needs. In a sense, the Islamic Republic's policy toward the USSR was more measured then its stance toward the United States, which was always conditioned by ideological stridency and historical animosities. In its approach to the Soviet Union, Iran had to compartmentalize and agree to disagree. Thus, while Tehran continued to object to Soviet moves in Afghanistan, it curtailed neither diplomatic nor commercial relations with Moscow.

In the aftermath of the Iran-Iraq war and the Soviet Union's expressed commitment to leave Afghanistan, the relationship between the two powers underwent a noticeable thaw. The first indication of this was, oddly enough, the bizarre episode in which Khomeini took it upon himself to write a letter to Mikhail Gorbachev and call on the Soviet premier to reform his system according to the tenets of Islam.[51] In a surprise move, the Kremlin treated Khomeini's absurd missive with respect and dispatched Foreign Minister Eduard Shevardnadze to Tehran in the hope of improving relations.[52] Rafsanjani reciprocated in June 1989, when he visited Moscow and signed a $6 billion arms deal. In a gesture of magnanimity toward his Soviet hosts, Rafsanjani pledged to purge the slogan of "neither East nor West" from Iran's official lexicon. Two events—the death of Khomeini and the collapse of the Soviet Union—would prove turning points in Iran's relationship with its northern neighbor. The uneasy coexistence now led to strategic cooperation.

The rapid collapse of the Soviet Union confronted Russia with difficult exigencies and the task of defining its interests in an altered geopolitical landscape. Boris Yeltsin and the new governing elite sought to revive Russia's decrepit economy through close association with the United States and the European community. Beyond acute economic problems, Yeltsin also had to deal with the emergence of the newly independent states in central Asia and a series of ethnic convulsions and wars triggered by the breakup of the Soviet Union. All of this was taking place in the psychological background of a once-great power that was having to adjust to its shrinking frontiers and marginalized place in the international system. Initially, the Middle East and Iran were low priorities for the bewildered Kremlin, which was seeking improved ties with the United States.

By 1993, the pro-American tilt in Russia's foreign policy was being eclipsed by nationalism.[53] The recalcitrant states of the Middle East would be the obvious beneficiaries of such a reorientation since they provided Russia with both a strategic outpost and a market for its surplus defense products. However, Moscow's policies could never be categorical. Russia had to remain cognizant of American sensibilities and its place in a global economy dominated by the United States.

For its part, the Islamic Republic was also adjusting to the post–cold war realignments. Like many Third World countries struggling for autonomy within the international order, the collapse of the Soviet Union initially proved disturbing to Tehran. The cold war competition had regulated U.S. power and imposed some restraints on Washington's ambitions. In the absence of the Soviet constraint, the United States would be free to project its power and pressure unruly states such as Iran. The fact that the demise of the Soviet state coincided with a massive deployment of U.S. forces to the Persian Gulf and an expressed American commitment to contain "outlaw" regimes alarmed the clerical elite.

As Russia became more assertive and Iran more concerned, the ties between the two states began to strengthen. The Islamic Republic eased Russia's fears by pledging that the arrangements between the two states would be predicated on strategic considerations largely devoid of the ideological conflicts that plagued U.S.-Iranian relations. At a time when Washington was busy contemplating the expansion of NATO and imposing ever more stringent sanctions on Iran, both sides were concerned about the unencumbered exercise of American power.

It is important to grasp the extent to which the clerical state was prepared to cast aside past grievances in order to cement its relationship with the Yeltsin administration. As with the European states, Russia had provided missiles and aircraft to Iraq, which were used to target Iranian cities and civilians. However, the collapse of the Soviet Union and the rise of the Russian Federation were somehow greeted by Iran as a new beginning. In a fortuitous twist of history, the demise of the Soviet state coincided with the rise of a practical leadership in Tehran willing to take advantage of opportunities that the dogmatic Khomeini might have missed. The fact that the Islamic Republic could not transcend its antagonism of the United States made pragmatism toward Russia even more compelling. Vilayati conceded that relations between the two powers had "never been this good in the past five hundred years."[54] Even Khamenei and the conservatives understood that Iran's need for trade and diplomatic assistance made the preservation of the Russian card a strategic necessity.

The first substantial manifestation of the renewed rapprochement between the two states was Russia's agreement to provide Iran a light-water nuclear reactor over America's objections.[55] The plant was initially contracted by Germany, which refused to complete the project once the Islamist revolutionaries assumed power. However, Russia saw the billion-dollar deal as a windfall for an atomic industry in dire need of funds. The sale of nuclear installations was also an indication that a resurgent Russia would be less concerned with America's qualms.[56] Having gained its footing, the Yeltsin government seemed determined to find occasions for expressing its autonomy from Washington. Moreover, unlike the United States, Russia did not view Iran as a rash, unpredictable militant state but as one that was cooperating in the stabilization of its "near abroad." Its more charitable assessment of Iran's intentions, its ample commercial incentives, and its desire to defy the United States brought Moscow ever closer to Tehran.

On the surface, the independence of central Asia, with its historic cultural and commercial ties to Iran, should have whetted the Islamic Republic's appetite for expansion. After all, as a vanguard Islamist state, Iran had long arrogated to itself the obligation of spearheading the cause of fundamentalism. However, Rafsanjani was determined not to complicate relations with his newfound Russian ally and thus guided Iran's policy toward the promotion of stability as opposed to the export of the revolution. Given Iran's estrangement from the West and its need for Russian arms and commerce, Tehran had to be cautious. The clerical regime's embrace of stability was not just a gesture of deference toward Russia but also a recognition that its practical concerns could best be ameliorated through a more tempered approach.[57]

In an unusually judicious assessment, Iran understood the limited appeal of its governing template to the newly independent central Asian region. The Islamist awakening that may have tempted Iran never materialized, as after decades of Communist rule, the central Asian masses desired economic rejuvenation rather than assertion of their religious identity. Given its geographic location and its proximity to the Persian Gulf, Iran focused on offering itself as a bridge between these states and the global markets. It invested heavily in its infrastructure, seeking road and railway connections to the republics. As Rafsanjani noted, "For links between north and south, the east and west, these countries and Europe, everything should cross Iran—oil, gas, pipelines, railways, communication routes and international airports."[58] Numerous trade and economic agreements were signed with these states, particularly Turkmenistan and Kazakhstan. While the United States, Turkey, and Pakistan were eager to enter central Asia, Iran realized the benefits of cooperating with Russia and de-emphasized ideology.[59]

Far from instigating fundamentalist uprisings, Iran even sought to mediate conflicts between various Islamist movements and the new governments. Tehran developed good relations with Christian Armenia and sought to settle its dispute over Nagorno-Karabakh with Muslim Azerbaijan. In a similar vein, Iran constructively addressed the civil war in Tajikistan between the Islamist opposition and the Russian-backed government. The Islamic Republic realized that its influence in central Asia, the viability of its economic prospects in the region, and its ties to Russia mandated advancing stability along its northern frontier.

The extent of Iranian pragmatism became further evident during the Chechnyan conflict. As Russian soldiers massacred Muslim rebels and viciously assaulted the civilian population, Iran remained largely silent. On occasion, Tehran would complain and call on various multilateral organizations to address the humanitarian consequences of the war. Unlike its approach toward Hezbollah and the Palestinian militants, Iran did not embrace the cause of Chechnya and did not offer military assistance to the insurgency. Nonetheless, the clerical state's reticence did not stem entirely from its fear of antagonizing Russia but also from its own concern for the cause of territorial integrity. As a multiethnic country, Iran has always been alarmed about the impact of separatist movements on its national cohesion. A combination of respect for Moscow and qualms about its internal order led Iran to look the other way as Russia annihilated the Chechnyan opposition.[60]

After years of conflict with the Soviet Union, the emerging rapprochement with the Russian Federation was an important triumph for Rafsanjani's pragmatism. The factors that brought the two powers together were unique and had much to do with the changing international balance of power. Both parties were disturbed by the post–cold war unipolar system and America's unchallenged preeminence.[61] Although Russia and Iran faced different predicaments, the former seems to have opted for a balance between its ties with the West and its continuing interests in the Middle East. For its part, Iran comprehended that one way of fending off American pressures was to cultivate a close economic and security partnership with Russia. In an even more surprising move, the two powers cooperated in central Asia. The conservative and pragmatic factions of Iran's leadership managed to place stability over revolutionary mandates and refrained from exploiting tensions and difficulties among the newly independent republics in the north. Thus, in the handling of its relations with Russia, Iran managed to embrace the type of realism that was absent from its dealings with Western Europe and the Persian Gulf sheikdoms. Recognizing its need for Russian trade and diplomatic support and recognizing that inflaming fundamentalist fires in central Asia could only provoke instability on its frontiers, Iran opted for caution. And it was this caution that Moscow amply rewarded.

Looking East: Iran and China

On the surface, the Islamic Republic of Iran had much in common with the People's Republic of China. Two ancient nations with long-standing grievances against the West had managed to achieve their independence through revolutionary upheaval. The historic commonalities, however, were diminished by a more recent memory, namely Beijing's close ties to the shah. It was not lost on Iran's revolutionaries that, in the latter stage of their struggle, Chinese leader Hua Guofeng had arrived in Tehran as a gesture of solidarity with the beleaguered monarch. The ever-suspicious Khomeini did not exclude China from his expansive indictment: "Our youth must know that China and Russia, like the U.S. and Britain, feed on the blood of our people."[62] However, Iran's enmity proved short lived, as a combination of strategic necessity and shared historical narrative soon brought the two countries together.[63]

Despite Beijing's close association with the shah, many within the clerical estate had long admired China. From the outset, Islamist leaders such as Rafsanjani were attracted to the Middle Kingdom and its triumphant journey from servitude to autonomy. China was one of the few states in the developing world that had experienced a genuine revolutionary transformation, one that had upended its political and economic foundations. Moreover, China had managed to advance and prosper in defiance of both superpowers, which at various times colluded to arrest its surge of influence. Iran's elite was often fascinated by the so-called China model, whereby an autocratic state managed to create economic prosperity. Whether seen as a defiant state challenging Western hegemony or a nonrepresentative polity that had deciphered the secrets of economic growth, China had a special place in the clerics' political imagination.

Iran's self-perception has always been peculiar. A combination of righteousness and victimization constitutes a core part of Iranians' national identity, and they are acutely sensitive to perceived slights. Iran is a proud and ancient civilization that demands acknowledgment of its historical grandeur in even the most routine of diplomatic exchanges. Treated like a pariah state and regularly denounced by the United States as an outlaw nation, the Islamic Republic craved respect but felt that its dignity was constantly under assault. The one state that best understood Iran's dilemma and effectively exploited it to its advantage was China, which enjoyed more diplomatic success with Iran than any other nation. The themes of anti-imperialism, Third World solidarity, and respect for Persian accomplishments laced Beijing's public pronouncements. Among China's first acts after the revolution was a private apology for Hua Guofeng's ill-timed visit and pledges of equality as the basis of renewed relations.[64] The rhetoric of common struggle and shared historical experience cut through the clerical elite's suspicions and paved the way for cooperative ties. At a time when Iran was subject to harsh and unyielding censure from the West, it appreciated China's deferential treatment and gradually excluded Beijing from its "neither East nor West" framework.

The theocratic regime's revised attitude toward China was not exclusively the product of its public relations campaign but also an appreciation of its strategic importance. In view of the fact that Iran stood isolated from both the United States and the Soviet Union, it required a reliable diplomatic and economic partner. A country in the midst of revolutionary chaos and at odds with much of the international community could not afford to alienate the last remaining significant power. Although this might have been pragmatism born out of compulsion, Beijing did ease Iran's reorientation through its blandishments and commerce.

As with the Soviet Union, the hostage crisis put China in a delicate and difficult position. Beijing had to craft a balance between the two antagonists, prodding Iran toward accepting the principles of diplomatic protection while acknowledging its grievances against the United States. The Chinese Foreign Ministry's statement reflected these tensions: "We always hold that the internal affairs of each country should be managed by its own people and there should be no interference in [the] internal affairs of all countries. But at the same time we hold that the principles guiding international relations and the accepted diplomatic immunities should be universally respected."[65] As such, China abstained from many critical UN votes, which displeased both Iran—which hoped for its veto—and the United States, which wanted a unanimous condemnation of Tehran's act.

Iran's dealings with most states have a clear breaking point, a distinct demarcation that ushers in a new era. The Iran-Iraq war was one such occasion, and the Islamic Republic became more isolated and its enmities grew deeper. Despite ritualistic calls by many foreign embassies for the conflict to end, China genuinely desired a quick termination of a war that was imperiling its strategic and financial position. As part of its economic modernization plan, China had begun important trade negotiations with the Sunni Arab bloc, which was siding with Saddam Husayn. These emerging commercial ties precluded an open-ended alliance with Iran. Yet Beijing also feared that an isolated Iran would turn to the Soviet Union and further enhance the power of its archrival. Once more, Beijing opted for neutrality, accepting certain UN mandates while selling arms to both belligerents. Given that Iraq already had access to the Gulf states' considerable financial reserves and Western arms, Iran stood to benefit from China's practice of neutrality.

As the war progressed and international embargoes were imposed on Iran, China became the Islamic Republic's main source of arms.[66] Through barter arrangements that involved the exchange of oil for weapons, Iran obtained much-needed aircraft, missiles, and tanks. For the sake of appearances, North Korea would at times be used as the conduit, but the deals were between Beijing and Tehran. It is estimated that, by the mid-1980s, Iran was securing 70 percent of its arms from China and North Korea.[67] During the latter stages of the conflict, China even provided Iran with Silkworm missiles, which greatly disrupted the Gulf shipping. The arms sales were designed not just to secure profits but also to cement a relationship that was valuable to both sides.

Although the war served to disrupt Iran's relations with both the European states and the Soviet Union, it actually led to a dramatic enhancement of its ties with China. Vilayati captured the mood in Tehran: "It is rare to find two neighboring countries with a history of a thousand years that have no record of dispute or contradiction."[68] It is a tribute to China's diplomatic acumen and its ability to placate Iranian nationalism that, unlike other powers, it never paid a price for providing weapons to Iraq.

Far from being infuriated by China's diplomacy, Iran was pressing for a broad anti-imperialist front against the United States that would feature the Islamic Republic and China as the leaders. During his 1985 visit to China, Rafsanjani emphasized this theme by calling for "solidarity among Third World and oppressed nations against both superpowers."[69] In a more specific claim, Rafsanjani asked his host to join Iran "to remove the cancerous tumor of imperialism in our region."[70] Although the visit garnered Iran additional contracts and pledges of arms sales, the anticipated alliance against the superpowers never materialized.

In the end, China's competing mandates meant that it had to observe certain limits in its dealings with Iran. Deng Xiaoping's policy adjustments ranked the task of economic revitalization as the most important priority. Mao's struggles in the Third World and his radical shibboleths had to be left behind as Beijing focused on an economic policy that required Western technologies and investments. China would have to balance its relations with Tehran and Washington and on occasion rebuff Iran's more radical initiatives. A more tempered Islamic Republic that did not relish challenging international conventions and antagonizing the United States was in China's best interest.

The ascendance of Rafsanjani and his pragmatic allies usually signaled a departure from previous Iranian policies and a mending of relations with erstwhile enemies. This was not entirely the case in Sino-Iranian relations, however, as Rafsanjani's tenure continued the existing pattern of cooperation. Upon concluding the war, Rafsanjani had already paid tribute to Beijing: "China had been cooperative with Iran during the war and the resulting hardships."[71] Once more, economic and strategic factors coincided to buttress the existing consensus for improved ties. The monumental task of reconstruction at a time when Iran continued to face sanctions from the Western countries made Chinese investments even more valuable. Moreover, as we have seen, the clerical leadership was always intrigued by the "China model" of rapid economic growth spearheaded by an autocratic regime. As Mahdi Karubi, speaker of the parliament, conceded, "In the process of implementing postwar reconstruction, Iran hopes to borrow from China's experience."[72] The economic motivations were reinforced by both China's and Iran's concerns regarding the assertiveness of American power in the post–cold war environment. Both states were very anxious about the emerging unipolar international system and the prospect of unrivalled American primacy. To be sure, the typical tension between a confrontational Iran and a China that required American trade persisted, yet both nations still appreciated the importance of cooperation in the shadow of the menacing U.S. hegemony.

Beyond commercial dealings, an expansive military and nuclear trade evolved between the two countries during the 1990s. As a state seeking to develop and modernize its armed forces, Iran turned to a willing China and signed a large number of contracts. Iran often paid for the weapons through shipments of oil, as an industrializing China was growing ever more dependent on Middle Eastern energy supplies. Even more ominous were agreements on transferring nuclear technology and China's pledge of constructing several atomic reactors in Iran. The nuclear issue would be the subject of much contention in Sino-American relations and compel Beijing to retreat from some of its promises to Iran. The nuclear agreements and their subsequent cancellations demonstrated the difficulties of dealing with both Washington and Tehran and of China's unwillingness to antagonize the United States for the sake of Iran's approbation.

During the initial two decades of the revolution, Iran's relations with China flourished more than those of any other country partly because they were uncomplicated by issues of terrorism and human rights. Far from seeing China's sizeable Muslim population as a constituency to mobilize, Iran largely ignored their plight. The various episodes of Chinese Muslim unrest in the 1980s were studiously ignored by an Islamic Republic that still required China's assistance to prosecute its war with Iraq. During his 1989 visit to Beijing, Khamenei even made the remarkable claim that "the Muslims of China are satisfied with the policies of the Chinese government with regard to Muslims and the freedom of faith."[73] Given the fact that no political party or religious minority had freedom of action in China, such spurious assertions by a cleric were obviously designed to placate Beijing. Once more, Iran suppressed its Islamist instincts because of the stakes involved in Sino-Iranian relations.

Nor did human rights constitute an obstacle in dealings between the two states. Indeed, the issue of human rights abuse actually brought the two powers together, as they both regarded condemnations of their abysmal records by the United States as a crass Western conspiracy to undermine their respective regimes. The Islamic Republic was vociferous in its support of China and its massacre of protesting students at Tiananmen Square. For its part, China found little objectionable in Iran's rigged elections or in its persecution of dissidents and intellectuals. Unlike China, the Western countries could never remain indifferent to Iran's human rights violations.

During Rafsanjani's tenure, Iran failed to sustain favorable ties with either the European states or the Persian Gulf community. Both the Europeans and the Gulf states Arabs desired a better relationship with Iran and were prepared to accommodate the Islamic Republic's legitimate concerns after the tumultuous Khomeini decade. However, the regime's ideological compulsions often surfaced and then hampered Rafsanjani's more tempered approach. Terrorism, the assassination of dissidents, hegemonic aspirations, and periodic challenges to the legitimacy of the princely class obstructed attempts at reconciliation with such pivotal actors. All of this is not to suggest that the Islamic Republic's international orientation did not undergo important changes. Khamenei and Rafsanjani managed to come together in making sure that Iran behaved responsibly during the Gulf War. However, given the tentative nature of its moderation and its sporadic lapses into radicalism, Iran did not obtain the confidence and trust of either the European leaders or the Arab monarchs.

Unlike its approach to Europe and the Persian Gulf, Iran's policy toward Russia and China was marked by a greater degree of pragmatism and moderation. As Iran became estranged from the West, it proved more judicious and realistic in its dealings with Moscow and Beijing. An internal consensus across the political spectrum ensured a consistent Iranian approach toward these states. Iran's bickering clerics recognized that their need for technology and financial credits meant that they could not alienate the emerging industrial giant of the East or the new Russian Federation. The fact that all three powers were concerned about the evolving nature of the post–cold war international order and the prospects of a menacing American hegemony provided them with further incentive for cooperation. Tehran recognized that the price it had to pay for this relationship was to arrest its ideological proclivities.

Iran's international orientation had evolved considerably beyond the rigid, revolutionary parameters of the 1980s. Pragmatism and careful calibration of national interests became important variables in Iran's foreign policy considerations. The conservatives were not immune to such impulses, and Khamenei in fact collaborated with Rafsanjani in improving Iran's ties with its eastern neighbors. However, ideology was not completely eclipsed by pragmatic calculations. For many within the theocratic state, Iran's charge remained the redemption of Khomeini's Islamist mission. In terms of its approach to Western Europe and the Persian Gulf region, Iran could not divest itself from its radical heritage. In the Rafsanjani era, Iran remained the most peculiar of states—a country that was simultaneously capable of both revolutionary agitation and pragmatic adjustment. Put simply, Iran was a nation in the midst of a prolonged and unresolved identityc risis.

7

The Satans

DURING THE SECOND DECADE OF THE REVOLUTION, THE UNITED States remained a looming presence for Iran, and its policies were debated in the parliament, presidential office, universities, and the streets. On the surface, policymakers in both Tehran and Washington seemed to recognize that the prevailing acrimony was not serving their mutual interests. Rafsanjani was not beyond reevaluating U.S.-Iran relations and exploring the possibility of some type of accommodation. However, ideological pressures and disagreements on regional developments prevented the emergence of a more rational relationship between the two states. At times, the door would be cautiously opened, and the politicians from both countries would gingerly peek inside, only to retreat for fear of a domestic backlash.

Whatever pragmatic impulses Iran may have displayed toward the United States, its approach to Israel remained mired in ideological stridency and the competition for power in the post–cold war Middle East. The decade of the 1990s was a watershed era in the region. On the one hand, the incumbent Arab regimes began to shed the mantle of intransigence and genuinely contemplated a peace compact with Israel. On the other hand, the decade also witnessed the rise of Islamist movements determined to inflict violence on both Israel and its Arab interlocutors. Both Tehran and Jerusalem sensed ample opportunities in the new Middle East: Israel sought a diplomatic settlement with its neighbors while Iran seemed determined to empower the Islamist militants.

Iran's policy would move beyond the rigid revolutionary parameters of Khomeini's tenure. A new pragmatic faction led by Rafsanjani understood that the radical spasms of the previous decade had too often undermined Iran's national interests. However, this tendency had to coexist with the imam's dedicated disciples, who continued to occupy important seats of power. The pitfalls of ideology and strategic antagonisms caused Tehran and Washington to line up on opposite sides of the region's conflicts. Indeed, the 1990s witnessed some of the most acute confrontations between the United States, Israel, and Iran.

The Debate

As the Islamic Republic considered its approach to the United States, its internal debate quickly transcended geopolitics and took place in a distinctly cultural terrain. For many hard-liners within the clerical estate, the challenge of the United States was not limited to a strategic rivalry but also involved an assault on Iran's national identity. The notion of Western imperialism seeking to superimpose its mores on Iran is nothing new: Throughout the twentieth century leftist and secular writers bemoaned America's encroachment. Yet the postrevolutionary elite on a quest to revive traditional customs and religious values was particularly sensitive to America's cultural temptations. While previous intruders and invaders of Iran had sought wealth and power, the American challenge was at once more perplexing and more pernicious. For Iran's hard-liners, the United States remained the "Great Satan" and "the global arrogance," whose influences had to be resisted.

No one more clearly embodied these sentiments than Ali Khamenei. For the supreme leader, the United States was always devious and arrogant, and its policies were mere cover designed to advance its nefarious purposes. To preserve the integrity and authenticity of Iran's Islamic path, one had to resist America's blandishments and forego the rewards that resumed relations might offer. Khamenei made his suspicions clear: "America appears with a deceitful smile but has a dagger behind its back and is ready to plunder. That is its true nature."[1] In the end, Khamenei perceived that Iran "has nothing to talk to them about and no need for them."[2]

Iran's ruling mullahs have an impressive propensity to document their thoughts in a variety of speeches, articles, and published texts. As clerics who underwent extensive scholastic training to achieve their status, they have a professorial reverence for the written word and spend an inordinate amount of time publishing their memoirs and opinions while still in office. In 1996 the supreme leader demonstrated that penchant when he published an important book, *Farhang va tahajum-i farhangi,* which was largely devoted to dissecting America's cultural attacks on Iran. Khamenei betrayed his thesis early: "We have to believe that we are subject to the cultural assault of our enemies."[3] Iran's Islamic revolution constituted the Muslim world's most momentous defiance of the West. For this reason Iran was subjected to America's pressures and censure. For Khamenei, it was not Iran's behavior but its uncompromising embrace of an Islamist ideology that had provoked Washington's animus. Given its vanguard role, the Islamic Republic had to persist with its struggle against America's machinations, however long and costly that struggle might be.

The hard-liners were particularly worried about the impact of renewed ties on Iran's vulnerable youth. They equated the young Iranians' fascination with America's cultural products with yet another U.S. plot to colonize Iran intellectually. The speaker of the parliament, Ali Akbar Natiq-Nuri, captured this sentiment by differentiating between the United States and previous empires, stressing that, while in the past, armies and armadas were the preferred imperial tools, today "they dominate by attacking thoughts and ideologies and promote their culture of corruption and decadence."[4] The Islamic Republic tirelessly launched unsuccessful campaigns against satellites and communication networks. Such devices, according to the head of the Guardian Council, Ahmad Jannati, were like "poison poured in the mouth of people."[5] Although Iran might benefit from an economic relationship with the United States, it was feared that America's presence would have a debilitating impact on the revolutionary commitment of the younger generation, which was already moving away from the imam's ideals.

Given their suspicions of the United States and fears of a cultural onslaught, for the hard-liners, opposition to the United States was not just a calculated foreign policy move but also a means of preserving the revolution. The United States was seen as a formidable threat not only because of its armed forces and its regional ambitions but also because of the lure of its ideals and seductive culture. America was the one nation with the capacity to subvert Iran's character and turn the masses against the republic. As we have seen, secular intellectuals had long complained about the process of Westernization, but the reactionary mullahs, unsure of the Islamist loyalty of their subjects, found the concept of the West at once more frightening and more ominous. Any engagement that brought the menace of America closer to the land of Islam was a danger that had to be avoided.

The hard-liners' incendiary rhetoric, however, conceals the emergence of pragmatic elements that sought to balance the theocracy's ideological claims with its practical imperatives. Rafsanjani and his allies sensed a possibility for a more compartmentalized relationship with the United States, whereby Iran would resist America's cultural influences yet resume cooperative commercial dealings. Rafsanjani may have been the leader of this cohort, but he was by no means its only representative. Technocrats in the ministries, university professors, and liberal clerics realized that the altered international landscape necessitated setting aside self-defeating animosities. Given the needs of the reconstruction program and Washington's commitment to defend the Persian Gulf in light of Saddam's aggression, they saw a more reasonable relationship as a national necessity. The pragmatic forces displayed far more confidence in the resilience of Iran's indigenous culture and believed that the Iranian people were quite capable of maintaining their identity and dealing with foreigners at the same time.

As the executive in charge of the country's economy, Rafsanjani challenged the conservatives' core conviction that Iran's independence was contingent on its self-sufficiency and even isolation. "There is so much machinery in the country that depends on foreigners to a large degree. There are so many projects which cannot be completed with the country's own resources," declared Rafsanjani.[6] These views naturally called for a different relationship with the United States, whose approbation was necessary for Iran's integration into the global economy.

Once more, though, Rafsanjani did not display the courage of his convictions and failed to directly confront his conservative detractors. Given Iran's contested political terrain and the provocative nature of improving relations with the "Great Satan," Rafsanjani too often insisted that the United States must take the first step and demonstrate its goodwill before Tehran could reciprocate. Such expressions of respect implied tangible concessions, such as releasing Iran's assets, which had been frozen at the time of the hostage crisis, and relaxing the increasingly burdensome sanctions imposed by the Reagan administration. Once granted such dispensations, Rafsanjani felt he could press the conservatives toward a modification of their views. Indeed, this would remain a perennial Iranian argument, namely, that any improvement of relations must begin with measurable American compromises. For both Democratic and Republican administrations such demands would prove untenable.

Rafsanjani's pragmatism was further debilitated by the limits of his imagination. Despite his professions of moderation, Rafsanjani wholeheartedly shared the conservatives' disdain for Israel. As we have seen, in the 1980s he went so far as to publish a book that stressed the inauthentic nature of Israel and the spurious reasons marshaled to justify its establishment.[7] To be sure, Khamenei ordinarily opted for a more inflammatory approach, frequently calling for the eradication of Israel and contesting the narrative of the Holocaust.[8] Ultimately, however, there was rarely much difference between the president and the supreme leader. Both opposed diplomatic efforts to resolve the Arab-Israeli dispute. Iran would pay a price for its animosity in terms of sanctions and the opprobrium of being designated a terrorist sponsor. However, in the end, the regime seemed to calculate that the benefits it derived from its posture outweighed the penalties.

The remarkable aspect of the theocracy's approach to the Jewish state was its constancy. Indeed, the tone and tenor of the debate remained largely unchanged from what they had been in the 1980s. Far from distancing themselves from Khomeini's malicious legacy, the clerical rulers proudly guarded their patrimony. The Islamic Republic even claimed that Israel was a greater threat to the cohesion of the Islamic world than the United States. The mullahs' antagonism toward Israel did not stem from any specific policy disagreements but from its mere existence. As a prominent conservative paper noted, the United States some day may "cease to be a major enemy, but as long as the Zionist regime exists in any part of Palestine, the struggle will continue."[9] Such rhetoric was not designed to placate a particular constituency or garner the acclaim of Arab street but reflected the deep-seated ideological objections that the clerical community has long harbored.[10]

At this point the U.S. policy also suffered from its own conceptual failures. Haunted by the Iran-Contra affair, successive administrations rarely opted for a creative approach. The fact that Iran was not the main concern of the United States lessened the need for an inventive policy. Iraq and the Arab-Israeli peace process would consume much of America's effort and leave little time for the prickly theocracy. Although at various junctures, policymakers were intrigued by the changing nature of the Islamic Republic, in the end, untangling the Iranian puzzle proved too cumbersome. After tentative approaches, the United States inevitably settled on a policy of containment, however flawed and ineffective that policy may have been.

As Tehran contemplated its approach to Washington, it did so with a divided house. A powerful segment of the clerical leadership simply refused to consider an alternative relationship with the "Great Satan." Struggling to define a coherent policy, the Rafsanjani administration ended up embracing the notion that the only way to break the internal stalemate was for the United States to take the first step. Of course, Rafsanjani would at times move beyond such rigid parameters, only to be rebuffed by clerical backlash and American indifference. In the meantime, Iran maintained its unbending opposition to Israel and continued to denounce the Jewish state in an incendiary manner. Such rhetoric could have been cast aside had it not been complemented by Iran's support for a variety of militant and terrorist organizations plotting against Israel. The Islamic Republic seldom appreciated the contradiction inherent in calling for better ties with the United States and undermining the security of one of America's most important allies.

The Bush Administration and the Limits of Realism

George H. W. Bush assumed the presidency at a time of momentous changes around the world. The end of the cold war, the collapse of the Soviet Union, and the resounding victory over Saddam made a new Iran policy a low priority. Seldom has an administration been more judicious in managing an entire range of foreign policy challenges, as the once-discredited president is now widely acclaimed for his deft handing of a multiplicity of crises. The task of reconfiguring European security and devising a new Middle East order made the Islamic Republic a second-tier issue. Still, Iran could not be ignored or wished away.

The Bush administration's practical realism augured a potentially different relationship with Iran. In his inaugural address, Bush promised Tehran that "goodwill begets goodwill," a clear signal that proper behavior might entail a revised U.S. policy. However, in the end, the contentious issues that had historically divided the two countries would bedevil the initial pragmatism evident in both capitals. A fairly predictable cycle was one more at hand—at the beginning of nearly every administration there is hope for a less hostile relationship with Iran. Soon stubborn realities, domestic politics, and the usual misunderstandings intrude, leading to charges and countercharges of who was responsible for squandering the lost opportunity.

Given the absence of links between the two states, Iran began to convey its messages to Washington in a more indirect manner. In 1990, in an explosive article in the newspaper *Ittila'at*, Vice President Ata'Allah Muhajirani called for the resumption of interactions with the United States: "If we do not give priority to the interests of the state and the revolution, we will end up losing an opportunity for our revolution, our state, and our people."[11] In essence, Muhajirani claimed that, given the power of the United States and its dominance over global affairs, a posture of defiance ill served Iran's national objectives. In a clever move, Muhajirani cast his arguments in religious terms and emphasized that the Prophet of Islam often negotiated with the enemies of God. A policy of considered dialogue could potentially lead to the release of Iran's frozen assets and even pave the way for greater integration into the world economy. The vice president stressed that the revolution did not intend Iran's complete isolation, particularly at a time of economic interdependence and rapid communications. Given Muhajirani's official position and close ties to Rafsanjani, it appeared that his article was meant to test the waters in both Tehran and Washington.

The heretical notion that Iran might require better relations with the United States unleashed the full force of clerical denunciation. *Kayhan*, the mouthpiece of the hard-liners, castigated Muhajirani for suggesting that the United States was the key to "solving all our problems."[12] The radical parliamentarian Ali Akbar Muhtashami'pur, in a typically strident gesture, noted that compromise with the United States would threaten Iran's "identity, revolutionary prestige, and image."[13] The limited overture by Muhajirani had provoked a conservative rebuke with a concerted media campaign that depicted such views as the sinister designs of hidden hands. Despite these reactions, Rafsanjani pressed ahead, and ironically Lebanon became the arena of possible cooperation between the two nations.

In the late 1980s Lebanon was undergoing its own transformations, as the region finally paid closer attention to a civil war that had been raging for nearly fifteen years. In October 1989, under Saudi mediation, the Taif Accord offered a power-sharing arrangement to Lebanon's confessional communities. Although Iran and Hezbollah initially denounced the agreement, they both eventually conceded to its logic. More temperate figures such as Muhammad Husayn Fadlallah stressed the impracticality of Islamic rule in a religiously diverse Lebanese society. An exhausted population was ready for peace, and Hezbollah's relevance was contingent on its acceptance of the new realities. Hezbollah's participation in the 1992 elections constituted its belated willingness to advance its objectives within the prevailing system.[14] An Iran preoccupied with its own concerns was also reconsidering its priorities and began pressing for stability as opposed to continued sectarian confrontation. Hezbollah's decision to take part in the elections was partly facilitated by Khamenei, who gave his blessing to those calling for engagement in the political process rather than its outright rejection.[15]

In a direct signal to the United States, Rafsanjani took the lead: "I wish to say—I address the White House—that Lebanon has a solution; the freedom of the hostages is solvable."[16] In the aftermath of the Iran-Contra affair, Washington was not eager for secret meetings and quiet bargains and instead relied on the United Nation's emissary, Giandomenico Picco, to serve as a mediator. The pace of the release of the American hostages proved painfully slow, as Rafsanjani found it difficult to establish a consensus either in Tehran or Beirut.[17] The final hostage was not released until 1991, thereby provoking the Bush administration's complaints about the lack of Iranian goodwill. An exasperated Bush betrayed his frustrations by noting that the United States and Iran were "no closer at this moment" to a different relationship.[18] In the delicate diplomacy of putting together the necessary factions in Iran and Lebanon, Rafsanjani could placate neither the United States' legitimate concerns for a quick release of its citizens nor his clerical detractors, who pointed to America's failure to acknowledge his efforts.[19] In the end, a variety of intervening events would overshadow Iran's cooperation in Lebanon and lead to renewed confrontation.

As we have seen, the Gulf War provided opportunities for both parties to assume a different posture and establish better relations. Iran had hoped that its neutralism and its practical assistance to the allied war effort would bring about some type of American reciprocity. However, the strategic differences between the two states remained largely unmediated by the conflict. The Islamic Republic was not willing to forfeit the waterways to American predominance and continued to press for the eviction of all foreign forces. Khamenei insisted that the "region's security is the business of regional nations."[20] This was not just an innovation of the Islamic Republic, as successive generations of Persian monarchs had asserted the same hegemonic claim. Such gestures were completely unacceptable to the American architects of a "new world order," who perceived that the stability of the international system and the resolution of its many conflicts was the responsibility of the remaining superpower. In its triumphant mood, Washington was hardly willing to yield the security of the Persian Gulf to an antagonistic Iran.

Indeed, after its successful defeat of Saddam's armies, the United States began moving its foreign policy in a direction that was bound to disappoint Iran. Beyond the ill-fated Damascus Declaration, the Bush administration embarked on a massive militarization of the region not just through its own deployments but also through vast arms sales to the Gulf emirates. Since a coherent Gulf security architecture eluded the United States, the Bush team settled for bilateral arrangements with the sheikdoms, complemented by nearly $23 billion in weapons sales by 1991. Both Washington and Tehran failed to adjust their ambitions in a manner that would not only improve their relations but also establish a durable foundation for the long-term stability of the Persian Gulf. The tensions between the two states soon moved beyond the Gulf waters, as they embarked on very different policies in the wider Middle East.

The early 1990s were a heady time for the Bush administration. It had easily evicted Saddam from Kuwait and redeemed the most fundamental tenet of international law: state sovereignty. After the war, Washington sought to craft a regional consensus behind an Arab-Israeli settlement. A new Middle East would be born, one that focused its energies and resources on economic development and political modernization. The time for resolving the four-decade conflict, which had provoked so many senseless wars, was finally at hand.

The Madrid International Conference, which convened in October 1991, was the capstone of American diplomacy.[21] The conclave featured not just Israel and its Arab neighbors but also the European community and the still extant Soviet Union. The meeting was to establish a framework for resolving the Arab-Israeli dispute, as well as a mechanism for dealing with issues such as economic growth, arms control, and environmental concerns. But as American diplomats gathered to contemplate the future, the old Middle East lurked in the background, holding fast to its animosities and antagonisms.

The United States was not the only power that sensed new opportunities in the region. As the mullahs gazed across the Arab world, they saw an entire range of Islamist parties challenging the decrepit Arab ruling class and seeking to reclaim the Middle East for the path of God. Islamism as a political force appeared in the ascendant with the Islamic Salvation Front in Algeria, al-Gama'a al-Islamiyya in Egypt, and Hezbollah in Lebanon all contending for power. The complexion of political opposition appeared to be changing, with Islamic fundamentalist groups displacing Arab nationalist parties. For a clerical regime at odds with both the United States and the Arab states, the new fundamentalist surge was a unique chance to assert its influence and demonstrate its appeal. Iran offered material assistance to Islamist opposition forces in places as varied as the Persian Gulf and North Africa.[22]

In defiance of Washington, Iran organized a counterconference to Madrid that featured all of the leading rejectionist states and radical Islamic organizations. In addition to the usual denunciations of the United States and Israel, the clerical rulers focused their ire on the incumbent Arab regimes. Rafsanjani led the charge: "The weak and miserable Arab governments have agreed to negotiations with Israel, thinking their problems are finished. These signatures haven't the least value."[23] Khamenei followed suit by claiming that the Arab leaders' participation would cause them to be "hated by their nations."[24] The problem was that the more Iran allied itself with Islamist movements and plotted against the peace process, the more difficult it became for any American administration to develop confidence in its pledges of moderation.

Consistent with its recent history, Iran soon expressed its hostility through terrorist attacks. On March 17, 1992, a bomb destroyed the Israeli embassy in Buenos Aires, killing twenty-nine people. Two years later Argentina became the scene of another Hezbollah attack as a bomb devastated a Jewish center and killed eighty-six civilians. Hezbollah would not be Iran's only instrument of terror, as the Islamic Republic established close ties with Hamas and the Palestinian Islamic Jihad. It must be stressed that these groups had their own motivations for striking Israel and were not pliable agents of the mullahs. A shared determination to obstruct the peace process brought Iran and the militant Islamists together, for they all perceived that Israel's integration into the region would work against their interests. Iran and the Islamist groups established mutually reinforcing relationships, as the terrorist organizations were provided with Iranian logistical support while Tehran could strike at Israel indirectly—and thus with a degree of impunity.[25]

Israel was not the only target of Iranian-sponsored terrorism. Tehran now emerged as a benefactor of Islamist parties struggling against Arab monarchies and dictatorships. Hezbollah unquestionably remained the principal jewel in Iran's crown, but the theocracy was hardly parsimonious in establishing ties with fundamentalist forces seeking to supplant the prevailing secular order. Along with Sudan and Syria, Iran managed to sustain the fires of Islamic militancy that were raging throughout the Middle East.

In the end, despite initial anticipations, the theocratic state and the Bush administration failed to usher in a new relationship. Washington's hope for improved ties with Tehran soon disappeared, as its post–Gulf War preoccupations with restructuring the Middle East brought it into direct confrontation with Iran. The U.S. policy was not without its failures of imagination, however. A more inclusive approach to security in the Persian Gulf might have enticed the clerics toward further cooperation. The reality remains that Iran was not rewarded for its constructive behavior during the Gulf War or its assistance in the release of the American hostages in Lebanon. Once the resolution of the Arab-Israeli dispute became America's foremost regional priority, an antagonistic approach toward Iran was nearly inevitable.

For its part, Tehran perceived an entire range of U.S. policies as deliberately designed to limit its influence and contain its power. From Iran's perspective, the strategic gains that resulted from Saddam's defeat in the Gulf War would quickly evaporate if a new Middle East came into existence. Excluded from America's Gulf security discussions and squeezed by a peace process that was bound to isolate it, Iran fought back by cultivating ties with rejectionist forces that were similarly at odds with America's mandates. Despite his belief that Iran could benefit from better ties with the United States, Rafsanjani shared the conservatives' animus toward the peace process. And once Washington identified the clerical regime as the main obstacle to the execution of its strategy, conflict was bound to displace diplomacy.

The Clinton Administration and the Politics of Peacemaking

The first post–cold war election in the United States witnessed a repudiation of the Bush presidency and its emphasis on international relations. An economically hard-pressed population hoping for a peace dividend turned to Governor Bill Clinton and his pledge to refocus national energies on domestic concerns. The challenges and quandaries of the Middle East would now belong to a Democratic administration that would soon develop its own expansive vision for the region.

Having soured on George Bush, Rafsanjani once more hoped for a different policy from the United States. In its typical manner, the Islamic Republic began sending subtle signs through press commentary. The *Tehran Times,* a newspaper with close ties to the Foreign Ministry, editorialized that "any sign of goodwill will be responded [to] by goodwill on the Iranian side."[26] Rafsanjani soon moved beyond press feelers and openly declared that improved relations "would not be in contradiction with Iran's objectives."[27]

It is hard to see how much authority or leeway Rafsanjani actually had since his position was soon assailed by the conservatives. The *Kayhan* thundered against naïve leaders who believed that Iran's problems would be solved only if the country reestablished relations with America.[28] Yet another conservative stalwart, the *Risalat,* went so far as to stress that Iran's integration into the global economy was bound to undermine its quest for self-reliance.[29] Instead of directly confronting the hard-liners, Rafsanjani hoped that Washington would somehow rescue him from his dilemma. The president seemingly felt that, armed with a dramatic gesture of reconciliation from the United States, he could deflect domestic criticisms and press ahead. Alas, such gestures of unilateral concessions to the Islamic Republic were not about to come from the Clinton White House.

The new American administration assumed power with its own criticisms of its predecessor's policies. Freed from the task of containing the Soviet Union, the United States no longer needed to make tawdry bargains with unsavory states. The focus of U.S. policy was democratic enlargement and the establishment of ties with like-minded states. Regimes that were outside the democratic community of nations were to be ostracized, contained, and isolated. These "outlaw states" with their despotic internal arrangements and revisionist foreign policies did not adhere to the norms that America sought to uphold.[30] The Islamic Republic found itself in a difficult position confronting an administration focused on individual rights, democratic representation, and moderate international affairs.

The personalities and policies of the Clinton administration portended further difficulties for Iran. The new secretary of state, Warren Christopher, came into office with his own long and thorny legacy with the mullahs. As the lead U.S. negotiator during the hostage crisis, Christopher had developed well-honed animosities toward Iran. Among his first acts was to condemn the clerical regime: "Wherever you look, you find the evil hand of Iran in this region."[31] Buttressed by a team of colleagues that included many staunch advocates of democracy, the secretary of state's antagonism militated against reaching out to Tehran.

The two states' differing regional priorities further reinforced the trend toward confrontation. The Clinton team came into office sensing a unique opportunity to resolve the conflict between Israel and its neighbors. The process that was launched in Madrid and complemented by secret Oslo negotiations between Israelis and Palestinians finally placed the elusive breakthrough within sight. In many respects, Iran policy was a function of the broader context of Arab-Israeli relations, and the barometer that measured Iranian moderation was its approach to the peace process. Christopher made his antagonisms clear: "The enemies of peace are determined to kill this historic chance for reconciliation. As we promote peace, we must also deal with the enemies of peace."[32] Moreover, the Clinton administration was wary of the experience of its two Republican predecessors, in which sporadic negotiations with Iran had failed to solve the fundamental problems between the two nations. It was time to invest in diplomatic efforts to achieve a workable peace instead of aspiring to the chimera of reconciliation with a deeply problematic theocracy.

The eventual U.S. policy became known as "dual containment," the notion that the United States would no longer lean toward either Iran or Iraq in sustaining a balance of power in the Persian Gulf. As Martin Indyk, a senior White House official, explained:

> We do not accept the argument that we should continue the old balance of power game, building up one to balance the other. We reject that approach not only because its bankruptcy was demonstrated in Iraq's invasion of Kuwait. We reject it because of clear-headed assessment of the antagonism that both regimes harbor towards the United States and its allies in the region. And we reject it because we don't need to rely on one to balance the other.[33]

Given America's unrivaled power and the unsavory nature of both Saddam's Iraq and theocratic Iran, Washington wanted to shape the essential parameters of Gulf politics while simultaneously isolating its regional competitors. With regard to Iran, "dual containment" would translate into economic warfare, as the United States would not only curtail its own trade with Iran but also pressure its allies to limit their commerce.

"Dual containment" was a peculiar departure from traditional U.S. policy, which at least acknowledged that Iran and Iraq were significant regional states whose influence had to be shaped by an active U.S. policy.[34] Since the departure of the British forces from the Persian Gulf, the United States had hoped that Iran and Iraq would balance out and contain each other. In the 1970s, it was the shah who took the lead in preserving the security of the Gulf by checking the ambitions of the Ba'athist state. In the 1980s, the United States and much of the international community buttressed Saddam's war machine in order to negate the revolutionary ambition of the radical theocracy. "Dual containment" discarded that admittedly problematic task of relying on one objectionable state to counterbalance another. Instead, Washington now embraced the presumption that it could preserve stability in the Persian Gulf largely by itself. This entailed not just a substantial U.S. troop presence but also a massive infusion of arms into the region. The problem was that America's allies had a limited appetite for confronting Iran. In a further blow to regional stability, America's intrusive establishment in states such as Saudi Arabia stimulated militant Islamist forces aggrieved at an alien presence in proximity to Islam's holiest shrines.

The discord between the United States and Iran was nowhere more evident than in the issue of the Israeli-Palestinian peace process. Oslo hit Tehran like a thunderbolt. Iran's inflammatory attacks became even sharper

as Arafat's "treachery" was condemned from pulpits and podiums throughout the Islamic Republic. Khamenei castigated Arafat as "that puny ill-
reputed blackguard," whose crime was greater than Anwar Sadat's acceptance of the Camp David Accords. According to Iran's supreme leader,
Sadat had at the very least betrayed the Arab cause for the sake of territory,
whereas Arafat had obtained only a series of promises that would never be
implemented.[35] In the meantime, 270 Iranian parliamentary deputies
signed a letter that emphasized their continued commitment to the "annihilation of Israel from the world map."[36] Iran did not curb its incendiary
rhetoric, however, and in fact became the patron of the radical Islamic
forces struggling against a Middle East that was seeking to come to terms
with its past.

The tragic history of the region repeated itself once more. Given the
asymmetry of power between Israel and its opponents, spectacular suicide
bombings designed to shock the Israeli public and galvanize the Palestinian
population became the preferred tactic. Under the auspices of Hezbollah,
Hamas and the Palestinian Islamic Jihad conducted attacks that the clerical
rulers in Tehran often applauded.[37] Iran would never claim actual responsibility for these gruesome acts of terror, but it also made no secret of its
approval. Foreign Minister Ali Akbar Vilayati plainly stated that "Iran is the
main supporter of Hamas and Hezbollah and their struggle against
Israel."[38]

It is important to comprehend that Iran's objective in assisting the
rejectionist forces was not merely the creation of mayhem in Israel but also
the intimidation of Arab rulers. As Islamist groups emerged defiant and
triumphant, they captured the public's imagination across the Middle East.
In turn, Arab governments hesitated to move forward. The typically timid
Arab regimes were already concerned about their constituents' inflamed
opposition to the Oslo Accords. The terrorists' popularity caused these
states to recoil from giving Israelis and Palestinians the support they needed
as they embarked on the precarious exercise of peacemaking. Iran and its
allies thus created a situation in which Arab leaders became passive observers rather than responsible stakeholders in one of the most important
turning points in the region's recent history.

Despite decades of inflammatory denunciations of the Jewish state by
the Iranian clerical class, the year 1996 witnessed a particularly callous act.
Iran, which had seldom displayed good public relations acumen, chose to
celebrate the assassination of Prime Minister Yitzhak Rabin. *Jumhuri-i
Islami* exclaimed that everyone throughout the world was "rejoicing
over the slaying of this bloodthirsty Zionist."[39] Natiq-Nuri blamed the

assassination on Israel itself: "Zionists should have known when they open the door to terrorism that they themselves would be victims of the plots they hatched for others.[40] The assassination of Rabin was followed a few months later by a devastating series of bombs in Tel Aviv and Jerusalem that killed fifty-nine civilians. The Israeli politicians, led by the new prime minister, Shimon Peres, blamed Iran for Hamas's violent outburst. Although operational linkages are difficult to substantiate, given Iran's routine resort to terrorism and its close ties with Palestinian militants, the charge of its complicity gained widespread acceptance. The campaign of terrorism finally unhinged the power of the Labor Party, as the conservative skeptics of the peace process, led by Benjamin Netanyahu, assumed leadership in Israel. Not for the first time in the history of the Middle East would violence derail the promise of peace.

At a time when the United States and Iran were at loggerheads, an expanding level of trade had gradually evolved between the two nations.[41] Through various subsidiaries, U.S. firms continued to export to Iran while America emerged as one of the largest purchasers of Iranian oil. Given the intensifying tensions between the two states and pressures developing within Congress, the Clinton administration was bound to consider a more strenuous sanctions policy. To avert such a possibility, Iran sought to offer a tantalizing billion-dollar oil exploration deal to the American firm Conoco. As with the Iran-Contra affair, many have interpreted this offer as an attempt by Iran to pursue a more pragmatic policy toward the United States.[42] Certainly, for Rafsanjani and his allies the deal had the advantage of potentially easing tensions with the Clinton White House, which was growing impatient with Iran's machinations. However, a more compelling motivation seems to have been an attempt by Iran to sustain its lucrative commercial relations with U.S. subsidiaries without necessarily adjusting its objectionable policies.

The Conoco offer reflected the limits of Rafsanjani's authority and imagination. The deal was a crass means of influencing an administration mainly concerned with Iran's support for terrorism and its opposition to important U.S. objectives. This is not to suggest that Rafsanjani was insincere about his desire to reach out to the United States, as he plaintively confessed that "We invited an American firm and entered a deal for a billion dollars. This was a message to the United States that was not properly understood."[43] However, no commercial incentive could have assuaged a Washington establishment that was attributing its peace process frustrations to Iranian intrigue. The proper path for placating the United States would have been for Iran to abandon its opposition to Israel and the

diplomatic efforts to resolve the conflict between Jerusalem and its neighbors. However, given Rafsanjani's own attachment to these policies, all he
was prepared to do was offer an oil deal.

The response of the Clinton administration was to cease all trade with
Iran. Assistant Secretary for Near Eastern Affairs Robert Pelletreau defended
the imposition of the sanctions by claiming that this was the best means of
making Iran pay "for flouting the norms of law-abiding nations."[44] This
theme was echoed by Undersecretary for Political Affairs Peter Tarnoff,
who similarly stressed that these prohibitions were designed "to counter
Iran's rogue activities."[45] Iran's policy toward the United States was caught
in a set of contradictory pressures that ensured its failure. On the one hand,
Iran's reactionaries, who had ample institutional power at their disposal,
continued to persist with their anti-American crusades. Rafsanjani seemed
disinclined to challenge policies that did so much to antagonize the United
States. In a corresponding gesture, the U.S. position steadily hardened, further undermining calls from clerical pragmatists for the relaxation of
tensions.

This economic pressure on Iran took an extraterritorial dimension in
August 1996, when the president signed into law the Iran-Libya Sanctions
Act (ILSA), which sought to punish international firms that invested more
than $20 million in Iran's energy sector. It is important to note that many
of these initiatives were coming out of the Republican-controlled Congress,
including an absurd measure by Speaker Newt Gingrich to allocate $18
million for the overthrow of the Islamic Republic.[46] Nonetheless, ILSA did
give the president the option of a waiver that he could employ if he deemed
it in the nation's interest. The Iran-Libya Sanctions Act, which called on the
United States to penalize European and Japanese firms, caused a predictable uproar among the allies. The call for secondary sanctions violated
America's own often-declared commitment to free trade, complicated its
dealings with its important partners, and had virtually no impact on the
volume of Iran's commerce. ILSA would never be invoked by successive
administrations even as they acquiesced to its periodic renewal. The legislation may have reflected Congress's frustrations and hostilities toward
Iran, but it was ultimately too provocative and divisive to serve as a viable
tool of American diplomacy.

The nadir of relations between the two states came with the terrorist
attack on the Khobar Towers, which housed American servicemen in Saudi
Arabia. As the previous chapter explains, strong circumstantial evidence
tied Iran to the bombing, which was carried out by its Saudi surrogates.

The resort to terrorism not only further estranged Iran from the United States but also strained its relations with the Gulf monarchies. For a country seeking to escape its isolation, the Khobar Towers bombing was a dramatic step back.

By the end of Rafsanjani's tenure, it was difficult to make the case that his diplomacy toward the United States was either judicious or imaginative. Certainly the pragmatic president continued to hold out hope for a different relationship with the United States. Iran's proper behavior during the Gulf War, its assistance in the release of the American hostages held in Lebanon, and its press feelers to the newly inaugurated Bush and Clinton administrations were neither modest nor useless gestures. However, Iran also pressed for the eviction of U.S. forces from the Persian Gulf area and used terrorism against the United States and its Israeli and Arab allies. Rafsanjani cannot escape blame, as he readily joined the conservatives in the execution of many of these policies. Too often Rafsanjani's conciliatory moves were negated by his own conduct.

In retrospect, Iran could not fully transcend the legacy of its founder and the revolution's innate antagonism to the "Great Satan." Rafsanjani believed that he could break that pattern of hostility if Washington would offer him a meaningful package of economic incentives. Armed with these concessions, perhaps he could have arrested Iran's descent toward radicalism. In the opaque backroom politics of the Islamic Republic, the president believed that he might have been able to persuade the supreme leader that a constructive relationship with the United States could do much to enhance Iran's national interests. In this sense, Rafsanjani may have underestimated Khamenei's and the hard-liners' attachment to anti-Americanism as an enduring pillar of the revolution. At any rate, such unilateral and preemptive gestures were not forthcoming from Washington.

Although there is much in Iran's approach that can be criticized, it is still difficult to make a good case for America's coercive containment doctrine. Ultimately, U.S. sanctions and military deployments on Iran's periphery failed to compel the theocracy to adjust its policies. The Bush and Clinton administrations perceived in the post–cold war environment an opportunity to realign the politics of the Middle East. Although such grand transformations are often attributed to George W. Bush, his predecessors sensed that, with the end of the cold war and the Oslo process, they could unlock the doors to a new Middle East. Such an altered region would focus its energies on issues of economic interdependence and political renewal as opposed to its ancient feuds and conflicts. There was little room in this reconceptualized Middle East for recalcitrant regimes such as the Islamic Republic. Despite occasional flirtations with engagement, Iran was seldom offered a path toward rehabilitation, as its influence was seen as too unsavory and its government too reactionary for redemption. The American animus, Rafsanjani's reticence, and the hard-liners' antagonism made a pragmatic approach unworkable. Rafsanjani should be credited with seeing how Iran's animosity toward the United States was subverting its national interests, but in the end, he proved a feeble agent of reform.

PART III

The Age of Reform

8

The Odyssey of the Reform Movement

T HE ISLAMIC REPUBLIC IS OFTEN DEPICTED AS A TYPICAL authoritarian regime with a rigid political order and a militant foreign policy. A state ruled by reactionary clerics who had scant respect for either the people's aspirations or global public opinion was destined to remain in the clutches of clerical despotism. Yet Iran gave birth to one of the most intellectually vibrant democratic movements in the contemporary Middle East. A land of perennial surprises would defy the cynicism of its detractors, as Iran would be the only place in the region where elections did not follow a preordained script. For a moment in time, Muhammad Khatami and the reformers appeared on the verge of establishing a novel form of government—an Islamic democracy.

In the realm of foreign affairs, Khatami's presidency illustrates the uneasy interplay of revolutionary values and pragmatic considerations that was conditioning Iran's international orientation. Khamenei and the ideologues acknowledged that Iran's core national interests required a different approach to the Arab world and Europe. It would have been difficult for Khatami to implement his détente policies without Khamenei's consent. Yet the hard-liners' ideological compulsions would manifest themselves clearly on the issue of the United States. For the conservatives, who perennially anguished about America's cultural temptations and its sinister strategic designs, the prospect of a more normal relationship with the "Great Satan" was still beyond the pale. Iran would persist with its bewildering mixture of pragmatism and ideological stridency and thereby cause many to doubt its expressions of reform.

From the perspective of nearly a decade later, it is easy to foresee the ultimate failure of the reform movement. The strength and determination of the clerical hard-liners to sustain their anachronistic definitions of proper rule were perhaps underestimated. However, it would be too harsh to suggest that Khatami's tenure was without its successes. A more nuanced judgment would have to concede an imperfect record, one that triumphed more abroad than it did at home.

The Genesis of the Reform Movement

By the mid-1990s, as the Rafsanjani presidency was hobbling to its inglorious end, Iran was undergoing subtle changes. While the ruling elite were preoccupied with their petty rivalries and foreign policy misadventures, the nation's social landscape was experiencing a pronounced transformation. An impressive array of the regime's own loyalists, who had found themselves marginalized by the defenders of the orthodoxy, were relinquishing their revolutionary inheritance. Radical parliamentarians who had been excised from power put their time in exile to good use, as they abandoned their statist economic preferences and tempered their anti-Americanism. Veteran politicians such as Sa'id Hajjariyan and Abdullah Nuri began to consider an Islamic Republic that was responsive to its constituents' demands. The activists' cause was empowered by the emergence of dissident clerics such as Mohsen Kadivar, pioneering investigative journalists such as Akbar Ganji, and courageous academics such as Hashem Aqajari. The universities were finally awakening from their torpor, and students' organizations and women's groups began taking their place at the forefront of the coalition for change. The rise of the reform movement was an acknowledgement that the Islamic Republic's rigidity had alienated a large segment of the public. The ruling elites' continued insistence on ossified rhetoric in the midst of a changing Iran would only endanger the revolution.[1]

To the extent that the reform movement had an intellectual forerunner, it was the famed thinker Abdul Karim Soroush, who had become one of Khomeini's disciples in the 1960s, while he was still in high school. In the aftermath of the revolution he proved a zealous partisan by purging the universities' personnel and curriculum on behalf of the imam's cultural revolution. In the battle to reclaim academia from leftist influences, Soroush engaged in heated polemical debates with Marxist and secular scholars. He even wrote a number of books and articles that defended the government and castigated Marxism as a "satanic ideology."[2] In due time, his commitment to the cause of Islamic tyranny waned, and he found himself at odds with the theocracy he had once acclaimed.

By the early 1990s, Soroush was advocating his notion of a religious democratic government, whereby faith and freedom would not only coexist but also complement one another. In Soroush's conceptualization of Islam, the essence of the sacred texts would remain constant while their interpretations would vary with the demands of the time. For Soroush, a "social understanding of religion is combined with rationality for people's satisfaction."[3] The Prophet's emphasis on consultation and consensus within the community of believers was seen as justifying modern ideas such as pluralism and diversity of opinion. Islam would be the pathway to the construction of a religious polity that was still based on a popular mandate. In essence, Soroush argued that there was nothing divine about the clerical monopoly of power.

Beyond his many lectures and published books, Soroush further influenced the debate in the monthly magazine *Kiyan*. A periodical inspired by Soroush, *Kiyan* became a forum for dissecting the official reading of Islam and subjecting it to critical inquiry. The prerogatives of the supreme leader and the centrality of elected institutions were among the many topics mooted in the pages of *Kiyan*. A new set of writers, committed revolutionaries revolting against the stale Islam of the ruling clergy, captured a growing audience. Suddenly names such as Hamid Reza Jalayi'pur and Masha Allah Shams-al Va'izin became popular folk heroes on college campuses and among a youth looking for a new direction.

The voices of reform were not limited to the universities and intellectual circles. In fact, many clerics outside the corridors of power made their own contributions to the cause of pluralism. The most authoritative challenge to the Islamic Republic came from Ayatollah Muntaziri.[4] The aging cleric, ousted from power and harassed by the hard-liners, became a thundering advocate for democratic rule. A radical figure in the 1980s and one of the architects of Iran's constitutional order, Muntaziri had mellowed with age and seemingly understood the dangers of unaccountable rule. Once ensconced in his secluded exile, Muntaziri turned on Khamenei with a vengeance, questioning his meager theological credentials and his suitability for such a high office. In 1999 he published a short book, *Hukumat-i Mardumi va Qanun-i Asasi*, which not only refuted the supreme leader's absolutist pretensions but also questioned the Guardian Council's right to reject candidates for public office and parliamentary legislation. Muntaziri still believed in the institution of supreme leader but now stressed that its powers had to be circumscribed by popular will. Given the dissent of one of the elders of the revolution, suddenly heretical notions such as term limits and even making the position of supreme leader an elective one were openly discussed.

It would be Muntaziri's prized student, Mohsen Kadivar, who further pressed the boundaries and challenged the foundation of theocratic rule. In a seminal study, he contested the very notion of *vilayat-i faqih*. "It is neither required by religion nor dictated by denomination; that is, it is not part of imami jurisprudence," concluded Kadivar.[5] Khomeini's ideas, which had always contradicted normative Shiite traditions, were now contested by an enterprising young cleric. By carefully examining the canons, Kadivar exposed the flimsy theological foundation of the imam's ideas. For Muntaziri's disciple, a proper government was based on popular consent. He emphasized that "If a government is not accepted by the people, even if its laws are in congruence with Sharia it lacks legitimacy."[6] Provocatively, Kadivar placed the collective will above religious decree as the basis of authentic rule. This stood in stark contrast to the reactionary mullahs, who professed that the Islamic Republic required neither popular approbation nor democracy to ensure its credibility.

In essence, the reform movement sought to redefine the structure of the Islamic Republic and reconceptualize the relationship between the public and the state, as well as religion and democracy. Islam, with its inclusive values, was to sanction popular participation in the political process. The reformers emphasized the republican pillar of the state and insisted that the legitimacy of the system had to be predicated on elections. This was not just a rejection of the clerical hegemony of power but also a repudiation of Khomeini's legacy. To protect themselves from retribution, the reformers constantly cited Khomeini and his words to authenticate their standing. However, at its core, a movement that emphasized the need for the public's consent, respect for global opinion, and the relaxation of cultural restrictions was a denial of the imam's politics of intolerance. In this sense, the conservatives were right to be dubious about the reformers' professed loyalty to Khomeini's vision.

The presidential election of 1997 would constitute the reformers' public debut. As their standard-bearer they chose Hujjat al-Islam Sayyid Muhammad Khatami, a former minister of culture who was dismissed due to pressure from the conservatives. Khatami was initially derided by the Right as a mere spokesman for a narrow circle of out-of-touch intellectuals. However, on closer look he appeared a more formidable candidate. His time at the Hamburg Islamic Institute, a decade as minister of culture, and his leadership of the National Library of Iran had led him to reach out to secular thinkers and verse himself in Western philosophical traditions. Unlike his many counterparts, Khatami was neither corrupt nor a participant in the shadowy violent wing of the Islamic Republic. His approach to Islam was to emphasize its tolerant side, as he often stressed that religion should not be interpreted to justify dictatorship in the guise of a divine mandate.[7] Khatami had a unique appeal. His intellectual curiosity, inclusive personality, and incorruptible nature made him an ideal person to craft a national coalition. In due time, though, the qualities of moderation and temperance, which made him such an appealing candidate, would work against him in office, as he would yield too easily to the hard-liners.

As the election approached, the reformers found they had advantages that might not have been initially evident. A coherent intellectual argument and ideological solidarity had brought together the differing strands of the movement. In their quest for power, the reformers were assisted by Rafsanjani and his pragmatic allies. Although the relationship between the reformers and the incumbent president would eventually fray, at this stage Rafsanjani's help provided them with an indispensable network of financial and political support. Having been frustrated and undermined by the reactionary forces at every turn, Rafsanjani was in no mood to concede to their latest power grab.

For their part, the conservatives settled on the speaker of the parliament, Ali Akbar Natiq-Nuri, as their candidate. Freely indulging in the Right's dogmatic rhetoric, Natiq-Nuri stressed the themes of cultural offensive and Western attacks on Iranian identity. In contrast to Khatami, Natiq-Nuri blamed the West for "spreading corruption and obscenity, propagating debauchery and homosexuality."[8] Demonstrating how profoundly out of touch he was, the speaker claimed that national progress should not be measured by financial gain but by spiritual attainment. For a populace experiencing economic distress, this message proved remarkably insensitive, particularly coming from a politician known for his corruption.

In their arrogance, the conservatives quickly sought to deflate the public's exuberance for the election by essentially suggesting that the leadership had already made the choice. Khamenei signaled his preference: "In selecting the next president, the ulema are the trusted and acceptable references for the people."[9] Given that the Friday prayer leaders and the official pulpits of the Islamic Republic were busy acclaiming the virtues of Natiq-Nuri, Khamenei's choice was all too evident. To further clarify the issue, the conservative oligarch Ayatollah Muhammad Reza Mahdavi-Kani said, "We guess that the esteemed Leader favors Natiq-Nuri."[10] Khamenei's long-term devotion to the cause of the conservative consolidation of power left no doubt that he would prefer a reliable hard-liner to succeed the problematic Rafsanjani.

By contrast, Khatami was running an exhilarating campaign that was promising a new dawn. Khatami subtly alluded to the supreme leader's powers and criticized those "who think that they hold a monopoly on the correct reading of the *vilayat-i faqih*."[11] The campaign's primary slogan was the rule of law and the primacy of the constitution as the foundation of the state. In a clever appeal to the youth, Khatami eschewed the conservatives' paternalism and condescension and insisted that, "rather than estranging them, we must involve the young in the policies and economic affairs of the country."[12]

While Khatami was cautious in his rhetoric and circumspect in his claims, many other reformers were much bolder in their denunciation of the prevailing order. Ganji openly stressed that "We think the election of the Leader with term limits does not conflict with Islamic divine law."[13] Hasan Yusufi Ishkavari, a prominent liberal cleric, similarly pointed out, "What was promised was that the clergy would be involved in their own business and at most would have a supervisory role."[14] The varying sentiments within the reform movement would do much to bedevil Khatami's tenure in office.

Although the campaign evolved largely around domestic issues, Khatami did not entirely neglect foreign policy. The reformist candidate called for Iran's reintegration into the community of nations and its reconciliation with its estranged neighbors. Along this path, he explicitly rejected the conservatives' isolationist position on international relations. "We may be able to close the door to a certain extent, and in some areas. But given the way the world is progressing, tomorrow it would be impossible to close the doors," claimed Khatami.[15] For the hard-liners, relations with the West were always seen as a conspiracy, a ploy to undermine the pillars of the Islamic regime. As an intellectual at ease with Western ideas and as a politician who placed the nation's interests above ideological imperatives, Khatami called for breaking down the walls of mistrust and transforming Iran into just another nation.

Within the circumscribed context of the Islamic Republic, the two candidates presented a real choice. Natiq-Nuri epitomized the complacent conservative establishment, which was pledging the same rhetoric of resistance. The economic anxieties and political aspirations of average Iranians found no room in the speaker's discourse. Khatami, on the other hand, was seen as a symbol of hope, a humble cleric attuned to the concerns of the masses. He promised a brighter future of rejuvenation at home and moderation abroad. The choice for the public proved surprisingly easy. In a stunning upset, Khatami captured 69 percent of the votes and carried nearly every city, locality, and district in the country.

The 1997 presidential election was remarkable for a number of reasons. This was the first time in the history of the Islamic Republic that the people's demands had countermanded the ruling oligarchs' preferences. The clerical elite, which had embraced Natiq-Nuri, had to accept the repudiation of their candidate at the ballot box. Moreover, the election demonstrated how the electorate had changed, as increased literacy, urbanization, and women's participation in the workforce had created a more informed and involved citizenry. The American politicians who routinely condemn Iran's elections as contrived and without consequence would be wise to temper their rhetoric with a more informed view of history.

Khatami's election also stands as a landmark in modern Middle Eastern history. The region is not without its routine electoral cycle, as presidents and parliaments are elected at normal intervals, usually with 95 percent of the votes. For a region cluttered with monarchical autocracies and presidential dictatorships, the notion that the public could deny power to the establishment's choice must have seemed strange.

The challenge for the empowered reform movement was to move from contemplation of change to the implementation of its ideals. The reformers' hope quickly faded into trepidation, as the aggrieved conservatives still maintained ample institutional power. Nonetheless, in their moment of triumph, the reformers might have overestimated the likelihood of a successful conservative backlash. Suffering an unmistakable public rebuke, the humiliated reform faction seemed disoriented and unsure about how to proceed. A window had opened slightly, and if the reform movement was to succeed, it had to transcend its inhibitions and pry the window further ajar.

Failure at Home

As a cautious politician who tended to accommodate his rivals, Khatami utilized a strategy that one could describe as "pressure from below, negotiations from the top." This was an incremental approach that sought to reclaim the elected institutions while continuously expanding civil society and media outlets to sustain popular mobilization. In the meantime, the conservative oligarchs were treated carefully and assured that the purpose of the reforms was not to undermine the republic but merely to liberalize the tenets of Islamist rule.

At the outset, Khatami seemed ready to press ahead and remove the many obstacles in his way. His overwhelming national mandate seemed to have energized him. "I am determined to fulfill my promises and I believe that the atmosphere is conducive and will improve day by day."[16] The first challenge the new president faced was to persuade the skeptical and conservative parliament to confirm his cabinet. Two appointments particularly enraged the Right—Ata' Allah Muhajirani as minister of culture and Abdullah Nuri as minister of interior. As Rafsanjani's vice president, Muhajirani had infuriated the hard-liners by suggesting that the time had come for the resumption of relations with the United States. Muhajirani was also committed to a relaxation of the censorship laws, which governed not just the newspapers but also theater arts, books, and other cultural expressions. For his part, Nuri's progressive views and intimate knowledge of the security apparatus made him a vexing problem for the clerical reactionaries. However, the parliament confirmed the entire list of Khatami's appointments, as the conservatives were still too unsure about how to grapple with the reform phenomenon. Such deference would not be offered for long.

The conservative critics of the reform movement have ordinarily been seen as a band of reactionary clerics fending off liberalism in order to protect their political power. It is important to note that many conservatives see themselves as defending principles just as noble and lofty as those professed by the reformers. They viewed their totalitarian conception of Islam as benefiting the believers. The hard-liners were offering the populace their own national compact, one that exchanged freedom for salvation. The achievement of a pristine religious order meant that the masses had to trust the clerical elders and blindly follow their commands. Comfortable with their self-professed verities and at ease with their authoritarian political structure, they would employ all means to achieve their desired ends.

As the conservatives regained their composure, they began to recognize that the reform movement was not just an organizational challenge but also an intellectual dilemma. A coterie of conservative mullahs now emerged to refute the reformist version of a tolerant Islam and offered their own justifications for clerical despotism. Khamenei set the stage: "The enemies of Islam are seeking to separate religion from politics. Using seductive Western concepts such as [a] pluralistic competitive system and bogus democracy, the Westerners are trying to present a utopian picture of Western societies and portray them as the only salvation for our Islamic society."[17] Typically, archconservative Ayatollah Muhammad Taqi Misbah-Yazdi went further: "We must shut the mouths of those who call for a new reading of Islam."[18] By depicting the reformers as agents of the West, the conservatives were hardly subtle. In their view, having failed to overthrow the Islamic Republic by Iraq's invasion and economic sanctions, Washington had finally found internal accomplices willing to discharge its plot under the guise of democratic reforms.

Despite decades of advocating elections and plebiscites, suddenly the hard-liners viewed such measures with suspicion. Not unlike Khomeini, they saw elections as acceptable only if they validated their own decisions and preferences. If democracy implied a form of government that would infringe on their rights and privileges, then it had to be resisted. Ayatollah Abbas Va'iz Tabasi, the powerful custodian of the Imam Reza Shrine, stressed, "Islam does not accept a democratic government and does not accept majority rule."[19] Misbah-Yazdi was more categorical in his claim that the office of the supreme leader was "the continuation of divine rule. Opposing it would be equal to apostasy and negation of Islam."[20]

By 1998, the contours of the cynical conservative stratagem of subverting the reform movement were becoming apparent. Through the institutions they dominated and the terror networks they controlled, the conservatives sought to undermine the newly installed reformist government.[21] The parliament would impeach key ministers, and the judiciary would imprison prominent reformers and close down newspapers on flimsy charges, while vigilante groups and security forces would be unleashed to harass student gatherings and assassinate prominent intellectuals. The purpose of this strategy was not just to intimidate the reformers but also to disillusion the public and provoke its political passivity.

The first officials targeted by the conservatives' acts of retribution were Tehran's enterprising mayor, Ghulam Husayn Karbaschi, and the minister of interior, Abdullah Nuri. Karbaschi had not only transformed Tehran into a more cosmopolitan city but had also mobilized its resources behind Khatami's presidential bid. As head of the Ministry of Interior, Nuri had been busy purging the conservative holdovers and getting his organization ready for the unbiased administration of the elections. The conservative deputies in the Majlis now accused both men of abuse of power. Given that Karbaschi was outside its jurisdiction, however, the parliament quickly voted for articles of impeachment against Nuri.

Shortly after the parliament's improper act, the judiciary stepped in with its contrived charges, convicted both men, and sentenced them to

considerable jail sentences. Iran's judiciary would now emerge as the linch-
pin of the right-wing plot against the reformers. The judiciary was no ordinary body of learned jurists interpreting the law impartially. By the
mid-1990s, the head of the judiciary, Ayatollah Muhammad Yazdi, had
begun recruiting former Ministry of Intelligence interrogators into judicial
service.[22] Suddenly the regime's brutal enforcers and intelligence operatives began masquerading as judges, sentencing journalists, activists, and
clerical dissidents to prison.

The impeachment and imprisonment of Karbaschi and Nuri did much
to condition the future of the reform movement. Khatami's failure to protect his able lieutenants only emboldened the conservatives toward further
implementation of their strategy. The ease with which the conservatives
dispensed with two pillars of the reformist government proved that, by
exploiting key state agencies, they could silence important voices with
impunity. Had the reactionaries been rebuffed at this early stage, their
nefarious plan might have been aborted. However, the more Khatami vac-
illated, the more obvious became the divisions within the reform movement. While the president moved ahead cautiously, his younger followers
were demanding more forceful action. In due course, a growing and
unbridgeable gap evolved between Khatami and his coalition partners.

Through similar extralegal methods, the conservatives sought to regu-
late the public debate. The press had emerged as the reform movement's
most effective means of mobilizing mass opinion. Under the auspices of
Muhajirani's Ministry of Culture, Iranian media experienced one of its
most dynamic periods. A remarkable range of newspapers and magazines
began debating issues ranging from women's rights to theological reform.[23]
The numbers were indeed impressive: In 1998 Iran saw 880 new publications with an estimated readership of 12 million.[24] Given its vibrancy, the
press became the conservatives' next target. Once more, the right-wing
assault on the media went through the judiciary. Soon the most popular
and accessible newspapers were closed down on the vague charge of damaging the national interest.

The conservatives' early successes indicate the reformers' conceptual
failures and their excessive reliance on the media to shape public attitudes.
The reform movement's organizational engine should have been the political parties because such associations give expression to popular sentiments
and allow a group to develop a national network. The reformers' preoccupation with civil society and newspapers caused them to avoid the more
tedious and important task of building a resilient grassroots infrastructure.
No less a figure than Hajjariyan, the organizational genius behind Khatami's

election, recognized this reality and urged the new president to behave as a leader and set up a viable party.[25] Khatami's typical response to such demands was to claim that "Unfortunately, it is not up to the government to establish parties; the people must do that themselves."[26] Although this is technically accurate, the masses still looked to the reformers, who were at the helm of power, for guidance and direction. Once the conservative backlash came, the absence of an effective national mechanism capable of galvanizing the population did much damage to the cause of democracy.

The right-wing attack on the reformers was not limited to manipulating judicial procedures, as terror and targeted assassinations were also part of their arsenal. After all, the Islamic Republic was a government ordained by God, and thus its preservation required vigilance and violence. Khamenei openly justified terrorism: "Is violence bad or good? It is neither bad or good. Legal violence is good. It is necessary."[27] The head of the Revolutionary Guards, Yahya Rahim Safavi, was even more explicit: "We must behead some, cut off the tongues of others. Our language is the language of the sword and the seekers of martyrdom."[28]

Such assertions can hardly be dismissed as idle threats, as the hardliners had developed an impressive coercive capability both within and beyond the state. Among the vigilante groups at their disposal was the notorious Ansar-i Hezbollah, which was largely composed of returning war veterans repulsed by the increasingly materialistic and irreligious direction of Iranian society. Moreover, the reactionary seminaries in Qum could always be counted on to provide the necessary religious sanction for the killings, while powerful foundations furnished the required funding. The terror of the Right was a coordinated affair, and all of these groups had links with state organizations such as the Ministry of Intelligence and the Revolutionary Guards.

In November 1998 Iran was shocked by the news of the brutal murder of nationalist politician Daryush Furuhar and his wife at their home. This was followed by the equally grotesque killings of intellectuals Majid Sharif and Muhammad Ja'far Puyandah. Initially, the conservatives brazenly implicated the reformers in the murders. Iran's state television network, which was controlled by the archconservative Ali Larijani, even broadcast a program called "The Light," which made the scurrilous charge of reformers' involvement.[29] In the conservative circles, rumors surfaced that perhaps the liberal Minister of Interior, Nuri, might have had a hand in the killings. Given the reform government's commitment to the rule of law and institutional accountability, an investigation was mandatory. In due time, the committee that looked into the serial murders revealed that the

Ministry of Intelligence was responsible. Although this was an unprecedented acknowledgement by the government, soon the hard-liners imposed limits on the investigation that transformed it into another national farce.

The attempt to quash the examination was led by Khamenei himself, who insisted that only the so-called rogue elements within the Ministry of Intelligence were responsible for the killings. The supreme leader stressed his confidence in the system's probity: "Based on my twenty-years of experience in serving the state and government, I cannot believe that there is a decision-maker in the state who could be responsible for the murders."[30] What Khamenei did not reveal was that it would be impossible for the killing of such prominent politicians and intellectuals to have taken place without his consent.[31]

The reformist government must bear its own measure of blame for the essential coverup of the killings. The intrepid investigative journalist Akbar Ganji has revealed that Khamenei agreed to an investigation only after obtaining Khatami's assurance that it would not implicate any official beyond Deputy Minister of Intelligence Sa'id Imami.[32] Imami appears to have been chosen as the fall guy, and his timely suicide in prison (from drinking hair tonic) precluded his implicating more senior officials. It appears that as a price for his acquiescence, Khatami obtained the dismissal of Minister of Intelligence Qurban'Ali Durri Najafabadi and replaced him with the reliably reformist Ali Yunasi. Even this proved a short-term remedy as many of the bad elements of the intelligence community were simply relocated to the Revolutionary Guards. Ganji's account was unintentionally corroborated when the investigating committee incredulously arrived at the conclusion that the killings were carried out by a few unsavory actors without the knowledge of the security services' leaders. An episode that has usually been presented as a reformist breakthrough in upholding new standards of governance, in retrospect, appears a perversion of justice. The fact that Khatami conceded to the sham verdict did much to evaporate the moral stature of the reformist government.

The most determined blow against the reform movement, however, came in July 1999, with the violent suppression of the student demonstrations. The act that sparked the protest was the banning of the newspaper *Salam*, which enjoyed a wide readership among the student population. The initial protest at the University of Tehran soon turned into six days of rioting that encompassed nearly every city in the country. The student demonstrators were joined by many other elements, including the labor unions, thereby producing the largest protest marches since the 1979 revolution. The students' slogans reflected the scope of their frustrations, as they chanted "Death to despotism" and "Freedom of thought, always, always." This protest by the children of the revolution reflected the way in which the initial promise of creating an accountable and democratic religious government had been squandered by a theocratic autocracy. The riots fully crystallized the fissures within the reform movement by pitting establishment figures calling for patience against student agitators demanding immediate change.

After some initial equivocation that concerned his right-wing supporters, Khamenei recovered his resolve and quickly denounced the demonstrations as a foreign plot to overthrow the Islamic Republic. This was clear permission for the violent suppression of the student protesters. An even starker warning came from the commanders of the Revolutionary Guards, who collectively warned Khatami that "our patience has run out, we cannot tolerate the situation any longer."[33] The state prevailed, and the students, who were demanding political rights and economic justice, were brutally put down. The July 1999 riots transformed both the reform and conservative movements in important and irrevocable ways.

Khatami's tentative and ambiguous response to the students' pleas disillusioned his youthful supporters, who had always been wary of his excessive caution. The president faced a choice: He could either defend the regime and its excesses or stand with the students in their demand for fundamental change. Despite his deeply held democratic convictions, Khatami proved too much a man of the system. His penchant for order overwhelmed his desire for change. Confronted by students chanting "Khatami, where are you?" he merely urged them to be tolerant and return to their campuses. Although the reformers would go on to contest elections and push for more progressive legislation, in retrospect, the once-exhilarating movement died that terrible summer.

The student demonstrations also had an impact on the conservatives' calculations, as they now saw the reformers as a real threat to the regime's survival. Natiq-Nuri recalls Khamenei's strong endorsement in the midst of the crisis when he declared that "the faith of Gorbachev and the Soviet Union, God forbid, can befall us."[34] For the already alarmed reactionaries, the student marches proved that the reform movement might just succeed in overthrowing the Islamic Republic. Not only did the student protests need to be firmly suppressed, but the entire institutional power of the state also had to be dedicated to the cause of emasculating and subverting the Khatami government. The essential strategy of negating the reform movement through manipulation and terror did not change; on the contrary, it was pursued with even greater vigor.

Khatami's claim that the theocracy could liberalize itself if only the reformers controlled the remaining elected branches of government was offered yet another opportunity. The parliamentary election of 2000 was seen as critical because it would not only validate popular sentiment but also wrest away an important and historic institution from the conservatives. Despite the typical electoral irregularities and the Guardian Council's arbitrary vetting of the candidates, the reformers triumphed at the ballot box. However, by this time, the hard-liners had a well-honed strategy of containment that cynically employed the Guardian Council to veto parliamentary measures while Khamenei intervened on occasion to prevent bills from even being considered. Given the hard-liners' determination to deny the citizens' aspirations, it is hard to see how continued legislative activity or lofty speeches could have advanced reform.[35]

The conservative strategy could not have succeeded without Rafsanjani's complicity. The gap between a movement seeking transparency and accountability and a politician devoted to self-aggrandizement and self-enrichment could not have been greater. There was no room in the reformist universe for Rafsanjani's corruption and ties to terrorism. The former president's humiliation at the ballot box when he failed to gain a seat in the parliament (much less its speakership) further propelled him toward the reactionary elements. In the complicated organizational web of the Islamic Republic, disagreements between the legislative branch and the Guardian Council would be dispatched to Rafsanjani's Expediency Council for resolution. As a sheaf of rejected bills made their way to Rafsanjani's office, he cooperated with the conservatives in ensuring their burial. It is hard to see what Rafsanjani gained from his part in suffocating the reform enterprise, as Khamenei and the hard-liners would never concede to his return to the helm of power.

The symbolic end of the reform movement came in March 2000 with the attempted assassination of Hajjariyan. Although the brilliant strategist somehow survived the point-blank shots, his impaired state essentially removed him from the national scene. As usual, the assailant was given a superficial sentence, and no further inquiry was made concerning the true source of the plot. It is undeniable that right-wing vigilante groups were involved with the backing of the clerical hard-liners. Hajjariyan had long been the embodiment of the reform effort, and his physical condition was a telling metaphor of the status of democratic empowerment in Iran.

The student riots and the attempt on Hajjariyan's life seem to have further weakened Khatami's resolution. The idealistic yet tentative president finally understood how difficult it would be to liberalize the regime and appeared to recoil from that task. He rebuked the hard-liners and cautioned his supporters but generally seemed unable to either lead or rule. In 2001, after much public soul searching, Khatami ran for another presidential term and managed to win. However, by this time it was a hollow victory. The issue at hand was not whether he would run but whether he had a realistic strategy for overcoming the obstructionism of a confident right wing. Khatami would press for constitutional amendments that limited the Guardian Council's oversight powers, only to be rebuffed. The parliament would pass bills, only to have them vetoed. In the meantime, the closure of newspapers and the arrest of dissident politicians continued apace.

Nearly a decade after the demise of one of the most intellectually scintillating democracy movements in the history of the Middle East, it is important to contemplate how it failed to achieve its objectives. To begin with, Khatami was a flawed leader who was unsuccessful in capitalizing on his fleeting moment. Because the initially shell-shocked conservatives were bound to recover, Khatami had at most a year to enact his agenda. It is here that his insistence on gradualism proved self-defeating, as the reformist momentum could not be sustained in the long run. What did it mean to stress the rule of law in a state where judicial proceedings were often shams? How could an expanded civil society and newspapers triumph over reactionaries willing to shed blood? How could elections and the passing of legislation change a system whose unelected branches were devoted to negating the collective will? To succeed, Khatami had to quickly transform himself from a popular politician into a protest leader who challenged the institutional power of the clerical hard-liners with the street power of the masses. And this he simply could not do.

Beyond Khatami's irresolution, the reformers' quest to authenticate their claims by continually invoking Khomeini's words and legacy only trapped them in the framework and language of the regime. By insisting that change could come through only the processes and deliberations of the Islamic Republic, they accredited the government's arbitrariness. Ultimately, the conservatives were seen as the imam's more plausible heirs, and their abuse of power was seemingly sanctioned by the reformers' assertion that the state was the only legitimate authority. The reformers could never make the transition from a loyal opposition to a movement seeking genuine change. Once it became apparent that the president and the parliament could not deliver on their pledged liberalization, to a large segment of the public the notion of patient participation in politics lost its meaning.

The other glaring shortcoming of the reform movement was its lack of focus on the economy. To be sure, Khatami and his ministers made the cogent case that rule of law had to precede viable economic reforms. Still, the inordinate number of intellectual debates regarding the parameters of civil society baffled the average citizens, who had hoped that the reformers' ascendance would somehow alleviate their economic distress. The fact that any structural economic changes would challenge the financial power of the conservatives, as well as of Rafsanjani and his allies, made the government even more hesitant. The reformers' failure to connect with both the labor force and the hard-pressed middle class further limited their national reach.

In the end, yet another actor must also assume responsibility for ensuring the failure of the reform movement—Ayatollah Khomeini. A silent and pervasive source of stagnation was the legacy of the imam whose speeches the reformers so often cited. Khomeini had succeeded in creating a governing order that could not adapt to the expectations of its citizenry. As the imam had intended, the unelected branches of the government placed restraints on the democratic sentiments he so ardently despised. The Islamic Republic survived the reformist challenge and remained true to Khomeini's vision of a religious autocracy.

The reformers' challenges abroad were no less daunting than their domestic project. Two decades of rhetorical excess and revolutionary militancy had created an image of a rogue state with no respect for international norms. By 1997 Iran was at odds with its neighbors, locked in a perennial conflict with the United States and estranged from Europe. By demonstrating respect for global opinion and altering critical policies, the reformers hoped to alter Iran's tarnished image. This would involve not just a change of rhetoric but also a fundamental transformation of policies. It would be beyond Iran's borders that Khatami would find his greatest and most durable successes.

Success Abroad

Although Khatami's tenure in office is routinely decried as a failure, in the realm of foreign relations his achievements were nothing less than momentous. In contrast to his domestic agenda, during his first two years in office he moved boldly and energetically to alter Iran's international orientation. During Khatami's tenure Iran, which had essentially been a pariah state noted for its sponsorship of terrorism, became a country whose leader was welcomed throughout the world.

For Khatami and the reform movement the concept of democratic accountability at home was married to a responsible foreign policy. A regime beholden to popular approbation would also be respectful of international norms. Khatami stressed that "our civil society neither seeks to dominate others nor does it submit to domination. It recognizes the right of all nations to self-determination and access to the necessary means for honorable living."[36] Gone were the days when terrorism and violence were the principal currencies of Iranian policies. As Khatami noted, "Foreign policy does not mean guns and rifles but utilizing all means to convince others."[37] The essence of this vision was its implicit acknowledgment that Iran's isolation stemmed partly from its own conduct. It was Iran's penchant for terrorism and subversion and its irresponsible statements that had placed it outside the community of nations.

Khatami showcased his new international policies in Tehran during the annual meeting of the 1997 Organization of the Islamic Conference. The clerical reformer quickly rejected the idea that Islamic civilization was sealed off from the outside world and could recapture its glory by looking to its past. Khatami insisted that preserving "our common Islamic homeland does not mean being reactionary, negating scientific achievement, and isolating ourselves from the contemporary world."[38] The Iranian president championed a dialogue of civilizations in which all sides were mutually respectful and learned from each other's traditions in a spirit of genuine inquiry. This was in stark contrast to Harvard professor Samuel Huntington's then popular clash-of-civilizations thesis, which simplistically asserted that, in the post-Communist era, global conflicts would proceed along civilizational fault lines. In an ironic twist, bombastic claims of civilizations clashing were now emanating from prestigious American universities instead of Tehran's presidential podium.

Khatami quickly changed the prevailing Iranian discourse on the West. As we have seen, for the hard-liners the West was an agent of cultural imperialism, whose intent was the subversion of Islamic rule. The West was sinister, decadent, cruel, and exploitive. While acknowledging the West's preeminence, Khatami stressed its beneficial facets. Science, literature, and a form of government that balanced faith and reason were all byproducts of a Western civilization that Iran could learn from. In an era of rapid communications and global economy, an exchange of ideas was both inevitable and constructive. The new president stressed that "We must try and establish a dialogue.... This is the way we can bring about coexistence without enmity."[39] Such temperate and sophisticated calls for civilizational harmony had almost never been voiced by a leading official of the Islamic Republic.

In contrast to their domestic disagreements, in the realm of international affairs, Khamenei offered Khatami a degree of support. Khatami's foreign policy agenda was indeed expansive, as he sought to reconcile with Saudi Arabia, normalize relations with the European community, and reach out to the United States. The supreme leader was apparently supportive of the first two objectives yet remained highly skeptical of any diplomatic overture to the United States. Khamenei understood that Iran's national interests required a different relationship with its neighbors, as well as its European trading partners. He would prove unhelpful on the issue of the United States, but at least in the initial stages of Khatami's presidency he was willing to allow him a degree of leeway.

The new era of reconciliation began in the Persian Gulf. The *Tehran Times* captured this sentiment by noting that Iran's policy was predicated on "détente, mutual respect and dialogue."[40] Defense Minister Ali Shamkhani similarly claimed that "all our brothers in the region should know that Iranian forces will never be used against them."[41] The issue that had always obstructed a rapprochement with the Gulf states was Iran's tense relations with Saudi Arabia. In the end, Rafsanjani never abandoned violence as a means of registering Iran's opposition to a variety of Saudi policies. But Khatami recognized that normalization of ties with the emirates could not come about without a better relationship with Saudi Arabia, and this entailed abandoning terrorism and subversion as tools of statecraft.

In a series of meetings and conclaves, Iranian officials assured their Saudi counterparts that Tehran had no intention of subsidizing Islamist opposition movements active in their country or aggravating relations between the kingdom and its sizeable Shiite minority. Another issue that divided Tehran from Riyadh was the theocratic regime's call for the expulsion of all U.S. forces from the Persian Gulf region. In the past, the Saudi refusal to accede to Iran's demands had triggered terrorism. Khatami now subtly suggested that Iran was prepared to coexist with the Saudi position and that disagreements on the presence of U.S. forces would not trigger a violent reaction. Iran seemingly believed that, through a "good neighbor" policy, the local states might in time accept its claim that the best means of securing the Gulf was through an indigenous alliance network. Khatami dispensed with harsh rhetoric and unyielding demands and stressed that "cultivating confidence is the first and most appropriate strategic approach to ensuring regional security by regional powers themselves."[42] In essence, Iran was willing to live in a Persian Gulf whose balance of power would be determined by the United States for at least the immediate future.

It is important to note that the ensuing normalization of relations would not have taken place without the rise of Prince Abdullah in Saudi Arabia. A nationalist leader skeptical of the United States and eager to initiate his own domestic reforms, Abdullah sensed in the ascendance of Khatami a unique opportunity to improve relations between the two states. At a time when the peace process seemed to have stalled and America's containment of Iraq through military reprisals and economic sanctions was becoming unpopular in the Arab world, Abdullah needed to ease tensions with his northern neighbor.[43]

In 1999 Khatami became the first sitting Iranian president to visit Riyadh. Upon arriving on Saudi soil, Khatami stated that his trip was designed to "get closer to a more sensitive and more fruitful understanding in the region."[44] The visit soon bore fruit, as a number of economic, cultural, and diplomatic agreements were signed. The collapse of the oil market in the late 1990s put inordinate pressure on both countries' economies because it came at a time when they particularly needed to create jobs for their youthful constituents. At OPEC, the collaboration between the two states did much to stabilize the petroleum market. Moreover, they both took the unprecedented measure of establishing a mechanism for dealing with internal security issues such as drug trafficking and money laundering. This began a dialogue between the two nations' intelligence organizations that opened the lines of communications on matters such as domestic unrest and terrorism. The fact remains that such cooperative measures could not have been fostered so long as Iran was ruled by unreliable mullahs dedicated to undermining the princely class throughout the Persian Gulf region. The rise of Khatami offered the House of Saud sufficient confidence to proceed with negotiations and agreements that benefited both parties.

Khatami's path of détente found a similarly receptive audience in Europe. During the latter stages of Rafsanjani's presidency, EU-Iranian relations had reached their nadir. Terrorism and continuing disagreements over the Rushdie fatwa had dramatically strained this link. At the time of Khatami's inauguration, the European envoys had been withdrawn, and trade between the two parties had dramatically lessened. Khatami and his new foreign policy team would have to tackle these thorny issues and offer concessions to the Europeans comparable to those given to the Saudis. Khamenei was quick to offer his support. Differentiating between Europe and the United States, he claimed that "We do not look at all countries in the same light; we respect the countries that have healthy relations with us."[45] The endorsement of the supreme leader was critical for the president, who was touching on sensitive issues bound to antagonize key conservative oligarchs.

The election of Khatami and the hopes of domestic liberalization had already made Europe a more receptive audience to Iran's entreaties. As a gesture of reconciliation, Khatami ended the long-standing practice of assassinating Iranian dissidents in Europe. Although it is customary to label Iran as one of the most active sponsors of terrorism, Khatami succeeded in shutting down an important aspect of Tehran's portfolio of violence. For a president with tentative control over the security services, this was no small achievement.

It was also during Khatami's presidency that the issue of the fatwa against Rushdie was finally settled. Foreign Minister Kharrazi declared conclusively that "The government of the Islamic Republic of Iran has no intention, nor is it going to take any action whatsoever to threaten the life of the author of the *Satanic Verses* or anybody associated with his work, nor will it assist or encourage anybody to do so."[46] After decades of living underground, the beleaguered author was finally allowed to pursue a more normal life and resume his literary pursuits.

In response to Iran's moves, the European policy evolved from "critical dialogue" to "constructive engagement." The new policy brought about a lifting of the prohibition on ministerial meetings and the full resumption of commercial relations. In July 1998 Italian prime minister Romano Prodi became the first European official to travel to Iran since the imposition of the diplomatic embargo on such high-level visits. Khatami would eventually embark on his own European tour that would take him to Italy, France, and the Vatican. Not long into his tenure, Khatami had managed to achieve two out of his three diplomatic objectives. The United States, however, would prove his most vexing challenge.

In his approach to America, Khatami moved gingerly and carefully. Conscious of the conservatives' deep-seated reservations, Khatami seemingly embraced the Rafsanjani formula, namely that the United States would have to first offer substantial concessions as a gesture of its seriousness and goodwill. The Khatami strategy envisioned a gradual exchange of scholars, activists, and athletes that would ease mutual suspicions. Such exchanges in conjunction with U.S. economic concessions would hopefully provide him with sufficient leverage to influence the conservatives at home, particularly the incredulous supreme leader. After all, Khamenei had acquiesced to a series of compromises that made a rapprochement with both Europeans and Saudis possible. In this sense, Khatami underestimated the extent of the hard-liners' opposition to any thaw in U.S.-Iranian relations.

Moreover, the notion that the Clinton administration would offer unilateral inducements in the hope of Iranian moderation at some distant future date was fanciful. Washington may have been willing to pursue a policy of give-and-take, but that was the limit of America's forbearance.

In January 1998, in his boldest overture to the United States, Khatami agreed to be interviewed by CNN. With the passage of time, the remarkable nature of that memorable interview and Khatami's willingness to defy the Islamic Republic's red lines and sacred symbols have become only more obvious. Khatami expressed regret for the hostage crisis, denounced terrorism in all its forms, and communicated a willingness to establish a commonality between Iran's theocratic regime and an American republic founded by the Puritans. Khatami was the first Iranian leader to acknowledge America's sensitivities and interests. "No one ever had the intention of insulting the American nation, and we even consider the American government a legitimate and lawful representative of its people," declared the Iranian president.[47] For the American public, whose country was routinely denounced as the "Great Satan" and whose leadership was caricatured as tools of capitalists and Zionists, Khatami's statements must have seemed revolutionary. More than any other Iranian official, Khatami recognized that, given the legacy of mistrust between the two countries, the best means of forging new ties was to transform the United States from an enemy into a rival.

Although much of the CNN interview focused on internal politics and relations with the United States, the issue of Israel resurfaced. Much has been said about Khatami's crass denunciations of Israel as a racist and terrorist state and his claim that the peace process was bound to fail. However, in the same interview, Khatami declared that "We do not intend to impose our views on others or stand in their way."[48] For the first time, Iran seemed to be adjusting its dogmatic stance and accepting the realities of the region and the pragmatism of the local actors.

Khatami's comments on Israel were neither improvised nor haphazard. Rather, they stemmed from a larger debate that the reformers were injecting into Iran's body politic. The clerical state's calls for the eradication of Israel and its periodic conferences pledging to reclaim Jerusalem through a holy war seemed at odds with the sentiments of the Middle East in the late 1990s. The critical question was, who was the legitimate representative of the Palestinian people? Was it Hamas, as the hard-liners insisted, or the Palestinian Authority, as the reformers maintained? The reformers were pressing the state to recognize that Iran's stance was popular only with radical Islamists, rejectionists, and terrorists. In his inaugural address, Khatami unveiled his position and stressed that Iran was prepared to advance an agreement that was predicated on UN resolutions.[49] Given the fact that those resolutions had conceded a two-state solution, Iran's reformist leader subtly stipulated the authority of the land-for-peace formula. It was during Khatami's tenure that the Islamic Republic finally agreed that it would respect a peace compact acceptable to the Palestinians. To be sure, the critics could scoff at this concession and insist that such rhetorical alterations did not eliminate Iran's support for Hezbollah or Hamas, yet this was still an important breakthrough for a country known for its unrelenting hostility toward the Jewish state.

Khatami's CNN interview was followed by some modest yet important gestures of moderation. The Iranian navy ceased its many provocations and acted with respect toward the patrolling U.S. vessels. Iran also shut down Iraqi oil-smuggling activities that had long been carried on in its ports and facilities. In a series of messages, unofficial Iranian emissaries with close ties to the government journeyed to Washington and met with American functionaries to reinforce the substance of Khatami's interview. The message was the same each time: Khatami was engaged in a difficult internal struggle, and a more accommodating American attitude could expedite the process of reform. However, in this respect the beleaguered president would not receive much assistance from influential corners in either Washington or Tehran.

The issue of improving ties with the United States would pit the theocracy's factions and ideologies against one another. The idea of dialogue with the American people may have been grudgingly accepted by the conservatives, but the notion of official relations with Washington was still beyond the pale. Since one of their principal ideological pillars was antagonism toward the United States, Khatami would confront a solid wall of conservative opposition.

The hard-liners' reaction to Khatami's interview was swift, categorical, and uncompromising. Khamenei led the charge by claiming that the United States was seeking to "bring about instability and insecurity to the nation."[50] Vilayati, now serving as Khamenei's foreign policy advisor, insisted that "No intelligent person can accept negotiating with the United States."[51] In the meantime, *Kayhan* focused more closely on Khatami's interview: "It's a shame that instead of expressing regret, the president did not try to convey the grievances of the Iranian nation to the American people."[52] It is important to note that the conservatives did not always contest the notion that Iran could benefit from a more tempered approach to the United States. Nonetheless, they continuously warned that better ties with the "Great

Satan" would somehow expose their pristine republic to the suffocating cultural contamination of the United States. Not unlike his predecessor, Khatami hoped to break the internal stalemate and soften Khamenei's stance by gaining substantial concessions from the unlikeliest of sources—the United States itself.

The rise of Khatami and the reform movement caught a skeptical Washington establishment mired in the lessons of the Iran-Contra affair flat footed. The United States' "dual-containment" policy remained largely unaltered, as the administration wanted to see more palpable changes in areas such as terrorism and the peace process before embarking on a fundamental revision of its policy. Nearly six months after Khatami's interview, President Clinton made his first important foray into the Iran debate: "We believe that Iran is changing in a positive way, and we would like to support that."[53] This statement was followed by Secretary of State Madeleine Albright's call for Iran to join the United States in devising a "roadmap to normalized relations."[54] Still, the administration, which was concerned about Khatami's ability to effect real change in Iran, often invoked the catchphrase "good deeds, not good words." Khatami had hoped for measurable concessions from the United States to disarm his domestic critics, while the Clinton team hoped for important adjustments from Iran before embracing Khatami.[55]

Two years after Khatami's CNN interview, Albright responded with one of the most thoughtful and impressive speeches given by a U.S. official on the subject of Iran. In an important gesture of contrition, Albright apologized for America's role in the coup against Musaddiq in 1953. The secretary acknowledged that the "coup was clearly a setback for Iran's political development."[56] In another magnanimous gesture, Albright similarly expressed regret for America's assistance to Iraq during its war with Iran. The secretary then moved beyond lofty words and lifted the sanctions on Iran's carpets, pistachios, and caviar, all of which were among Iran's most lucrative exports.

Khamenei's response to Albright's gesture was insensitive and incendiary. The supreme leader betrayed his suspicion when he even denounced America's contrition "as just another ploy laying the ground for their sinister plots."[57] In an address to a large gathering of the faithful, Khamenei declared that "They admit that they supported and backed the dictatorial, oppressive, corrupt and subservient rule of the shah for 25 years. And they are now saying that they supported Saddam Husayn in his war against Iran. What do you think the Iranian nation, faced with this situation and these admissions, feels?"[58] It is at times suggested that a specific line in Albright's speech—"Despite the trend toward democracy, control over the military, judiciary, courts, and police remains in the unelected hands"—caused the conservative backlash. However, it was not so much the content of the speech but its timing that undermined its impact. As we have seen, the hard-liners had always been leery of resumed relations with the United States. The pragmatism that Khamenei and his allies displayed toward Europe was to obviate dealing with America. Moreover, in the aftermath of the student riots of 1999, Khatami simply did not have the authority or the resolution to wage an internal turf war against the hard-liners on the provocative issue of normalizing ties with the United States. Had the speech been given two years earlier, when Khatami was at the zenith of his power, he might have been able to press the theocracy toward a revision of its policies. As things stood, in spring of 2000, Albright's speech fell on deaf ears.

As he approached the end of his tenure, Khatami crafted a "letter for tomorrow," which sought to sum up the predicament of his presidency for posterity. He placed the tribulations of his reform movement within the larger context of Iranian history, with its tendency toward authoritarian-ism and its preference for "violence over logic." Even at this stage, Khatami continued to push his template of gradualism, with its emphasis on "mod-eration, flexibility and rationality."[59] In the end, he perceived himself as beset by "myopic opponents" and "impatient friends." Khatami was a decent, modest man who was genuinely liberal, but he had the misfortune of trying to tame reactionary forces that had no compunction about main-taining their political hegemony in the face of popular resistance.

However, Khatami's evaluation of his presidency was not entirely fair to his record of achievement. The reformist leader accomplished more in the international realm than any of his predecessors. By the time he left office, Iran had normalized relations with its Arab neighbors, as well as the European community. In terms of his approach to the United States, Khatami's policy of incremental change and confidence-building measures did not result in a political accommodation. It was difficult for Khatami to dismantle the wall of mistrust while the conservatives were busy fortifying it. To be sure, the United States' response to the important changes unfolding in Iran had all of the hallmarks of bureaucratic inertia and intellectual complacency. As so often in the past, Washington and Tehran once more failed to transcend their animosities and suspicions and forge a new rela-tionship. Ironically, it would be the most spectacular terrorist attack in U.S. history that offered the two parties another chance to revisit their relationship.

9

September 11 and the Politics of Fear, Hope, and Necessity

THE TERRORIST ATTACK ON THE AMERICAN HOMELAND ON September 11, 2001, was a defining moment in recent U.S. history. For decades, successive administrations had relied on unrepresentative regional governments to provide stability. The United States had exempted itself from paying too close attention to the Arab order with its decaying institutions, religious extremism, and a political culture that often condoned violence against the "infidels." George W. Bush, who had hoped his presidency would focus on domestic problems and great power rivalries, now had to confront a Middle East with all of its pathologies and resentments.

As Washington settled down to deal with the quandaries of the region, it would question traditional foreign policy doctrines and instruments. The notion of containment and diplomacy would be displaced by preemption and coerced democratization. The best means of dealing with the long-term challenges of a deeply dysfunctional region would be through a transformation of its political order rather than the forging of new compacts with despotic rulers. However, reality often upended ideological certainties. In order to prosecute its wars against the Taliban and Saddam Husayn, the administration was compelled to deal with autocratic regimes that it disdained.

On the surface, there was no better candidate for regime change than the Islamic Republic of Iran. It had a long-standing enmity toward the United States, ties to terrorism, and a penchant for weapons of mass destruction. However, the administration's approach was a contradictory mixture of denouncing the clerical state and contemplating its ouster while also engaging it in order to achieve its war aims against Iran's more problematic neighbors. No administration has had a harsher rhetoric and yet more extensive diplomatic discussions with Iran than the Bush team. It would be America's need of Iran that would condition its approach, and when that need evaporated, Washington's policy would become one of more sustained opposition.

For their part, the clerical leaders realized that a certain threshold had been crossed and that their relationship with a range of terrorist organizations and their secret nuclear program would now be seen in a different light. Paradoxically, Khatami and the reformers came to see 9/11 as a unique opportunity to mend fences with the United States. Even more intriguing was the conservatives' recognition that they would have to dispense with their cherished taboo of not having official talks with Washington in light of the exigencies of the times. There was an element of fear in the conservatives' calculations inasmuch as they were concerned about how the Islamic Republic would fare in the age of global war against terrorism. Moreover, the hard-liners saw nothing particularly wrong with cooperating with an America that seemed determined to vanquish their historic nemeses. Once the United States became engulfed in its Iraq misfortunes, the conservatives' anxieties quickly faded, and their traditional hostilities resurfaced.

The period of 2001 to 2003 stands as one of the most pivotal phases in U.S.-Iranian relations. A combination of fear, hope, and necessity would drive the two antagonists into an uneasy and tentative relationship that was bound to be shattered in the midst of recrimination and mutual accusations of bad faith.

9/11

As the news broadcast across the world displayed the grisly images of the collapsing Twin Towers in New York and the Pentagon's burning façade, the Iranian public's reaction was both extraordinary and instinctive. Khatami was one of the first leaders to offer his condolences, and he took to the airways and expressed his "deep sympathy to the American nation, particularly those who have suffered from the attacks."[1] In the meantime, the streets of Tehran were filled with spontaneous demonstrations and candlelight vigils in which Iranians conveyed grief and solidarity with the American public. The Iranian people have always harbored pro-American sentiments, but the outpourings in Tehran seemed to have caught both the regime and its critics off guard. On the day of America's trauma, a distant nation seemed to have felt a genuine bond of kinship with the latest victims of senseless terror.[2]

Such generosity of spirit, however, was rarely evident among the conservative forces. Khamenei maintained his silence and did not credit the statements of his own president. The right-wing papers such as *Kayhan* and *Jumhuri-i Islami* were filled with conspiracy tales about how secret cabals in the White House had engineered the attacks in order to justify America's interventions in the Middle East. The pulpits of the Islamic Republic were similarly manned by reactionary clerics such as Ayatollah Jannati and Ayatollah Mashkini, who casually dismissed the notion that the United States was a victim of terrorism. Indeed, it would be a staple of right-wing discourse that the tragedies of 9/11 were a deliberate plot to alter the region's political landscape for the sake of America's aggrandizement.

Nonetheless, for the reformist government, 9/11 was neither a conspiracy nor a threat but an opportunity to revisit ties with the United States. As we have seen, upon assuming the office of president, Khatami had established three foreign policy objectives: normalization of relations with Saudi Arabia, reconciliation with the European community, and a meaningful overture to the United States. After the failure of the Clinton initiative and the conservative backlash, the reformers perceived that a new relationship with the United States was beyond their reach. In the aftermath of 9/11, such detachment from America was seen as impossible. The United States was coming to the Middle East with a massive troop presence and grand designs. As Foreign Minister Kharrazi conceded, "The presence of America affects the whole region and we cannot remain indifferent."[3] For Khatami, this was a second chance to reach out to the new U.S. administration and prove that Iran could be a reliable partner.

The fortuitous aspect of all of these assumptions was that America's first target of retribution was the state of Afghanistan, which was anathema also to Iran. Afghanistan had always been the place where U.S. and Iranian interests roughly coincided. Throughout the 1980s, both parties opposed the Soviet occupation and did much to aid the Islamic resistance. The departure of Soviet forces may have provoked America's retreat, but Iran had no choice but to be interested in the chaos next door. The flow of drugs and refugees meant that Iran could not remain passive and had to directly protect its concerns. The 1990s saw a competition for power between Iran and a Pakistani state that had come to see Afghanistan as a necessary bridge to the markets and resources of newly independent central Asia. It was Pakistan and its intelligence services that would greatly facilitate the ascendance of the Taliban. If the reactionary Islamist group could provide a degree of stability, then that was fine with Islamabad. The fact that the Taliban imposed a medieval version of Islam on that hapless nation and offered sanctuary to Osama bin Laden and al-Qaeda was acceptable to a cynical Pakistani leadership. For Iran, the rise of the chauvinistic Sunni militants was an unmitigated disaster. The Taliban's persecution of the Shiites and its murder of ten Iranian diplomats in the summer of 1998 nearly caused a war between the two states. Iran would actively aid the Northern Alliance, the coalition of militias and politicians that continued to oppose the Taliban. Those links and associations would prove invaluable as the United States suddenly became preoccupied with a nation it had spent decades trying to ignore.

Khatami was quick to realize the advantages of cooperating with the United States, particularly given the intersecting objectives of the two countries. As a religious intellectual who saw Islam and democracy as compatible, Khatami found the Taliban a particular affront to his sensibilities. "Islam and Quran must not be used as instruments for propagating violence, terror and destruction," declared the Iranian president.[4] However, beyond his condemnation of the Taliban's perversion of religion to justify its draconian rule, Khatami understood that the demise of the radical Sunni group would not only enhance Iran's security but also provide an avenue for reconciliation with the United States. Khatami openly acknowledged this perception: "Afghanistan provides the two countries a perfect opportunity for improving their relations."[5]

In a momentous decision, Khamenei agreed to cooperate with the United States as it prepared to invade Afghanistan. It is difficult to believe that Khamenei, with his well-honed enmity toward the United States, saw the events the same way that Khatami did. Nonetheless, as the guardian of Iran's national interests, Khamenei appreciated the acute danger confronting his country. He may well have looked at diplomacy at this stage as a means of deflecting America's anger and forestalling whatever designs it may have had on his homeland. The atmosphere of fear in Tehran was palpable, as the White House was eerily looking at the recalcitrant states of the Middle East as potential targets of its vengeance. Moreover, so long as the Bush administration's ire was focused on the detested Taliban, the hard-liners had no compunction about cooperating with the "Great Satan." Despite the Islamic Republic's ritualistic objections to a Western attack on a Muslim country, Tehran was ready to assist the United States' war effort in Afghanistan. For different sets of reasons, Khatami and Khamenei had come together in their determination to aid America's first campaign in its unfolding war against terrorism. It would now be up to Washington to take advantage of the opportunities that the theocracy suddenly proffered.

Pax Americana

It is sometimes easy to forget that prior to the 9/11 attacks, the Bush administration was seen as following the realist paradigm that had largely governed U.S. foreign policy in the postwar years.[6] The preoccupation with a rising China, management of the Atlantic alliance, opening up Latin America, and further pursuit of a missile defense system were the foremost priorities of the new administration. Given that a central lesson of the Clinton tenure was that time and energy spent on the region's intractable conflicts would seldom be rewarded, the Middle East was not regarded as a pressing issue. Certainly there were hawkish voices within the corridors of power agitating for a more aggressive approach to Iraq, but initially the principal voice of the administration's policy was the cautious Secretary of State, Colin Powell. There was much confidence in foreign capitals that, despite his lack of experience, Bush was in the able hands of a superb team.

The 9/11 tragedies had a profound impact on the administration's international orientation.[7] In a stark departure from the realist tradition, the character of the regime was seen as the most important determinant of its actual conduct. Thus, authoritarian governments would necessarily be prone to acquire and use weapons of mass destruction, sponsor terrorism, and create conditions that yielded radicals and extremists. Condoleezza Rice, the national security advisor, captured this sentiment best:

> Our experience of this new world leads us to conclude that the fundamental character of regimes matters more today than the international distribution of power.…The goal of statecraft is to help create a world of democratic, well-governed states that can meet the needs of their citizens and conduct themselves responsibly in the international system.[8]

Bush was even more dramatic: "We understand that history has called us into action, and we are not going to miss that opportunity to make the world more peaceful and more free."[9] Stability could not rest on the shoulders of despotic regimes. Instead, the only way to create a peaceful order was to help give birth to like-minded democratic governments. The administration suddenly arrogated to itself the presumption that the United

States was uniquely suited to transform the political culture of a complicated region that it poorly understood.[10]

On September 20, 2002, the White House went so far as to articulate its vision with the publication of a new national security strategy document.[11] It said that the most urgent threat facing the United States would be the "crossroads of radicalization and ideology." To combat tyrannical regimes about to acquire weapons of mass destruction, America would exercise the "right of self-defense by acting preemptively."[12] Traditional tools of statecraft such as deterrence and containment were dismissed as relics of a distant and discredited past. Regime change was the proper avenue for disarmament and the most suitable manner of preventing the proliferation of dangerous technologies. The old balance of power had to be discarded in favor of one that sought a balance that supported "human freedom."[13] A safe world was one that was molded in America's image.[14]

Bush's missionary impulses were buttressed by the ascendance of a neoconservative cohort ensconced in key positions of power.[15] From their perches in the vice president's office, the Defense Department, and the National Security Council, the neoconservatives suddenly found a receptive audience in a beleaguered president searching for answers to thorny problems. Deputy Secretary of Defense Paul Wolfowitz, Undersecretary of Defense Douglas Feith, and senior White House official Elliott Abrams invoked democratic ideals to justify a muscular foreign policy. This was consistent with the history of the neoconservative movement, which first burst onto the foreign policy scene by opposing the Nixon administration's détente with the Soviet Union. In their traditional guise of resisting non-democratic governments, they stressed that the 9/11 attacks proved that the false stability of the Middle East only masked a deeply disturbed political order. The best means of achieving true stability was not by dealing with decrepit incumbent regimes but by supplanting them with democratic polities. Although Iraq would become their central focus, they were also critical of America's allies, such as Saudi Arabia and Egypt.

The neoconservatives' postulations were given a veneer of intellectual credibility when prominent academics such as Bernard Lewis validated their misperceptions. The renowned scholar of the Middle East confidently declared that an invasion of Iraq would lead the Iranians to besiege the United States with calls of "come this way."[16] Lewis proved that he was better at chronicling the past than predicting the future. In reams of opinion pieces in the *Wall Street Journal*, television appearances, and public lectures, he continued making prognostications that ill served his academic pedigree and stature.

In the end, the administration's absolutist pretensions were somewhat undermined by its own internal divisions and the impracticalities of its vision.[17] The State Department, with its traditional penchant for diplomacy, was in favor of improving relations with Iran and continuing to work with America's allies in the Middle East, however problematic they might be. Moreover, as the administration focused on displacing the Taliban and later Saddam's government, it required assistance from nondemocratic states such as Saudi Arabia, Pakistan, and Kuwait. The notion that the United States could transform the region's deep-seated political culture was too impractical to serve as a viable policy guide.

Despite its black-and-white rhetoric, the administration settled on a discursive approach that often contradicted itself. The United States would not abandon its ambition to democratize the Middle East but would pursue it in an ineffective manner. On the one hand, many within the administration made the remarkable claim that somehow an invasion of Iraq would provoke a larger wave of democratization throughout the region. In the meantime, when it came to America's allies, Washington opted for a gradual democracy-promotion policy that did not differ much from its predecessors. America's efforts would focus on assisting with election commissions and voter registration programs, as well as supporting civic awareness. The anemic Arab civil society was the subject of particular fascination, as the lure of the community of nongovernmental organizations (NGOs) proved difficult to resist. To its credit, the administration did stress the need for economic reform but then recommended a set of entirely unproductive measures such as the Microfinance Consultative Group. Quite naturally, women's rights campaigns, a literacy corps, and legislative exchanges further complemented Bush's lackluster efforts. The region's reigning autocrats quickly realized that they had little to fear from the United States expressed commitment to liberalize their societies.

On the issue of Iran, the administration would follow the same pattern of contradictory policies. On the one hand, the notion of regime change gained widespread currency within the neoconservative circles in the bureaucracy and the broader Washington community. The pages of neoconservative publications such as *The Weekly Standard* and *Commentary* were filled with stories about an Iranian public eager to revolt if only given a positive indication by the United States. The complexity of Iran's internal struggle was largely ignored, and the reform movement was dismissed as another ruse to dilute the confused and gullible Westerners. The possibility of engagement and the negotiation of restraints on Iran's behavior were seen as the naïve proposals of pusillanimous apologists. The president seemed receptive to such messages, as he was genuinely affronted by the clerical autocracy, its abuse of its citizens at home, and its terrorism abroad.[18]

However, such concerns did not lead to a complete abandonment of dialogue and diplomacy. As the administration planned its military attacks on Afghanistan and later Iraq, it seemed open to negotiations with the very same Islamic Republic it had so often denigrated. Bush's approach toward Iran was molded by a combination of ideology and opportunism. When it suited the United States, the administration would negotiate with Iran. And when the need for Iranian assistance diminished, Washington would return to its themes of regime change and freedom. Although this posture did not lead to a normalization of ties, it did lead to tactical cooperation.

Iran and America's Wars

The first test of the relationship between the United States and Iran came in October 2001, when after weeks of futile (and indeed senseless) negotiations, the Bush administration decided to intervene militarily in Afghanistan. The objective of Operation Enduring Freedom was not just to apprehend Osama bin Laden and dismantle the al-Qaeda infrastructure but also to depose the Taliban. The Islamic Republic quickly made known its readiness to assist the U.S. operation. Foreign Minister Kharrazi openly declared that "We have some common points with the U.S. over Afghanistan."[19] The reality remains that America's quick overthrow of the Taliban and the rapid success of its invasion were partly facilitated by Iran's cooperation. Iran allowed the use of its airspace and agreed to rescue downed U.S. pilots. Tehran also made available its port facilities, which were important for the delivery of humanitarian assistance to the impoverished and displaced Afghan people. Even more important were Iran's connections to the Northern Alliance and its appeals to them to join forces with the arriving U.S. troops. At this juncture, the United States even saw the Revolutionary Guard's Quds Brigade—which the Americans would later characterize as a terrorist organization—as a helpful auxiliary force.

Iran's assistance did not end with the prosecution of the war, as Tehran emerged as a helpful actor in the reconstitution of Afghanistan. At December 2001 Bonn Conference, Iranian officials were instrumental in getting the long-time leader of the Northern Alliance, Burhanuddin Rabbani, to relinquish his claims to power in favor of the U.S.-supported Hamid Karzai. Kharrazi disappointed many of Iran's allies by insisting, "Our objective is to help with formation of a broad-based government which we believe could help lead to the return of peace and stability in Afghanistan."[20] A month later at the Tokyo Conference, Iran once more stepped forward and pledged $530 million for reconstruction of war-torn Afghanistan. As the interests of the United States and Iran coincided, they proved easy collaborators with ample intermingling among their representatives. The administration that had pledged moral clarity in its foreign relations had no inhibitions about dealing with a theocracy that actively suppressed its citizens and supported Hezbollah and other terrorist groups. The need to stabilize Afghanistan overwhelmed the Bush administration's ethical concerns.

Iran's helpful behavior can be dismissed as the natural reaction of a state seeking to protect its own concerns. After all, Iran had poor relations with the Taliban, and the demise of a hostile Sunni force would do much to relieve the pressure on its vulnerable eastern frontier. The Karzai government was not only open to better relations with Tehran but was also sensitive to its preferences and claims. Moreover, the removal of the Taliban further marginalized Pakistan's influence and paved the way for the projection of Iranian power. The Islamic Republic now flooded Afghanistan with its traders, missionaries, and intelligence operatives. Although such self-serving calculations may have motivated Khamenei and the conservatives, the reformers genuinely saw Afghanistan as a bridge to a better relationship with the United States.

On January 3, 2002, the cooperative relations between the two states came to a momentary halt with the Israeli capture of Karine A, a ship full of Iranian arms seemingly bound for the Palestinian Authority. This event has raised many questions that have yet to be conclusively resolved. Were the Iranian arms actually intended for Hezbollah, and did they have to be sent by an unusual sea route because Syria had begun restricting its air space? Another explanation that has gained some plausibility is that the arms were dispatched by hard-line elements without Khatami's consent or even foreknowledge. There is some tentative evidence to support this claim. At that time, Iran's reformist deputy, Davud Sulaymani, complained on the floor of the parliament about "illegal power centers providing excuses for external attacks."[21] The parliament even threatened investigations, only to be rebuffed by Khamenei. Khatami's own spokesman, Abdullah Ramazanzadah, talked of "minority groups that interfere in foreign policy."[22] In the absence of official documentary evidence, it is impossible to chart with any confidence the deliberations within the Islamist state on such a sensitive issue. However, at a time when the regime was denying its involvement in the affair, for such important officials to not just implicate the state but also imply that specific elements unduly jeopardized Iran's national interests suggests that the Khatami government may not have known that these activities were taking place.

The question then becomes, why did the hard-line elements try to disrupt the nascent ties between the United States and Iran? It is too simplistic to suggest that they were trying to scuttle the cooperative relations between the two nations, as those activities received Khamenei's approbation. An alternative suggestion is that Iranian officials perceived that they could easily compartmentalize their relations with the United States and support terrorist activities on one front while actively dealing with Washington on issues of common concern. The Islamic Republic, which had never been able to divest itself from the Israeli-Palestinian conflict, may have hoped that its constructive posture on Afghanistan would modulate America's response. If so, this proved a grave miscalculation. The Bush administration, which was already prone to consider Iran a rogue actor bent on undermining regional order through subversion, now had further evidence to that effect.

In his January 2002 State of the Union address, President Bush made one of the most contentious speeches of his tenure.[23] Facing a gallery of lawmakers, the president castigated Iran as a member of an "axis of evil," along with North Korea and Iraq. Bush rebuked Iran as a "major sponsor of terrorism" and condemned its unelected leaders for oppressing the citizenry. In an even more direct threat, he stressed that, in the post-9/11 environment, the United States "would not permit the world's most dangerous regimes to threaten us with the world's most dangerous weapons." Although in retrospect, the speech seems to have been designed to prepare the American public for the administration's decision to invade Iraq, the inclusion of Iran also reflected Washington's concern about its latest transgression.[24] A recalcitrant theocracy that sustained its ties to terrorist organizations and seemed determined to develop weapons of mass destruction could not but feel threatened by Bush's denunciation.

To reinforce the president's message, administration officials began their own criticisms of Iran and even dismissed its more cooperative attitude since 9/11. National Security Advisor Rice claimed that Iran's penchant for terrorism "belies any good intention it displayed in the days after the world's worst terrorist attack in history."[25] Vice President Dick Cheney similarly condemned "Iran's apparent commitment to destroy the Israeli-Palestinian peace process and unstinting efforts to develop weapons of mass destruction."[26] The notion that the United States should aid the reformers and somehow buttress the moderate Khatami government was pointedly dismissed by the senior White House official Zalmay Khalilzad.

"Our policy is not about Khatami or Khamenei, reform or hard-line; it is about supporting those who want freedom, human rights, democracy, and economic and educational opportunity for themselves and their fellow countrymen and women."[27] Iran's complex internal political order and the struggles between reformers and hard-liners became a caricature, as simplistic assertions about promoting freedom and changing the regime replaced thoughtful assessment.

Iran's response to the "axis of evil" speech was predictably incendiary and uncompromising. Khamenei condemned Bush as "thirsty for blood" and claimed that "the Islamic Republic of Iran is proud to be the target of the rage and hatred of the world's greatest Satan."[28] Khatami, who traditionally eschewed harsh rhetoric, confined himself to rejecting Bush's speech as "bellicose, insulting, and anti-Iranian."[29] The reformist faction of the parliament also chimed in: "The position taken by the U.S. president under the obvious influence of the Zionist regime is a threat to world peace and security."[30] For a U.S. administration that made outreach to the Iranian people one of its principal objectives, the speech was counterproductive. The Iranians may not have been pleased by the nature of their government, but, as a deeply nationalistic population, they did not appreciate an impudent American politician disparaging their nation and equating it with the hermitic state of North Korea and the genocidal Saddam Husayn.

The curious aspect of the "axis of evil" speech, however, was that it did not actually end the ongoing dialogue between the two states. At times, the president's address has been elevated to a watershed moment in U.S.-Iranian history. The actual course of events belies such a dramatic conclusion, however. The looming war in Iraq caused both sides to transcend their animosities and reconsider diplomacy as the best path forward.

It is here that the Bush administration's opportunism is in full view, as it had no qualms about engaging a state that it had just condemned as a member of an "axis of evil." Despite its concerns about Iran's mischievous interventions in the Israeli-Palestinian peace process and its nuclear ambitions, the United States recognized the need for Tehran's cooperation as it focused on displacing Saddam's regime. In one of the ironies of U.S.-Iran relations, Zalmay Khalilzad, who had dismissed the prospects of reform in Iran and blatantly called for a change of regime as the best means of dealing with the theocracy, led the negotiations on behalf of the United States. In this sense, Iran benefited from the administration's obsession with Saddam and its determination to invade Iraq at all cost.

Iran's own calculations featured the same combination of fear and hope that had propelled it toward negotiations in the first place. Even though many reformers were genuinely offended by Bush's address, they did not give up the wish of rekindling a better relationship with the United States. To be sure, there was less confidence in Washington, as the reformers began to sense that America's antagonism would be difficult to moderate. Still, they wanted to leave the door open to the possibility of enhanced relations. Mohsen Mirdamadi, head of the parliament's foreign affairs committee, confessed, "We should use opportunities to pursue a policy of détente. Naturally, when pursuing a policy of détente we could present and continue with our independent policy and maintain our international status."[31] Given the fact that reconciliation with the United States had been an important pillar of reformist international policy, they were unwilling to relinquish it even in the face of America's belligerence.

Fear rather than hope seems to have motivated the conservatives. The hard-liners' defiant posture concealed their concern that they might yet emerge as a target of America's retribution. In a rare public expression of anxiety, Khamenei declared that the "axis of evil" speech "could put Iran in the firing line of a U.S. war on terror."[32] Rafsanjani, who had fully ensconced himself in the right-wing camp, similarly stressed, "It is true that one has the impression that Bush has a sparrow's brain in a dinosaur's head. That is why we must be vigilant about the accusations of this supercilious man."[33] Ali Shamkhani, minister of defense, followed suit, stating, "General preparedness must be raised, everyone must sense that they are in danger."[34] As the United States stalked the Middle East looking for militants to tame, it behooved the theocracy to act with caution. Moreover, so long as the United States seemed determined to dislodge another one of Iran's historical foes, the clerical rulers saw little reason not to be responsive.

As the Bush administration launched its second invasion of a Middle Eastern country in less than three years, Iran was circumspect and helpful. Once more, Tehran pledged to assist downed pilots and offer humanitarian assistance. Iran similarly pressed its Shiite allies to cooperate with the American invaders. Since the first Gulf War, when the elder Bush simply stood by as the Shiites were massacred by Saddam's war machine, suspicion had characterized their attitude toward the United States. The clerical regime's intimate relations with the leading Shiite parties such as the Supreme Iraqi Islamic Council and the Da'wa Party proved beneficial to Washington. In the end, the war would have a dramatic impact on Iran.

The speed of the U.S. attack and its quick dispatch of Saddam's vaunted forces shocked the Islamic Republic. Iran had fought Iraq for eight years without securing even a modest change of the boundaries. A senior Iranian official confessed that "The fact that Saddam was toppled in just twenty-one days is something that should concern all countries in this region."[35] Many officials within the theocratic state were convinced that Iran was next. Mohsen Reza'i, former head of the Revolutionary Guards, expressed this concern: "Any action in Iraq is a prelude to one against Iran."[36] Reformist journalist Hamid Reza Jalayi'pur also noticed the clerical elite's disquiet: "I think the sounds of the cruise missiles in Iraq were heard in Iran very well."[37]

By the spring of 2003, the Islamic Republic seemed ready to extend its cooperation with the United States. The Iranians hoped that, as in Afghanistan, the task of stabilizing Iraq would draw Washington back to Tehran. Khatami declared to his cabinet that "talking with the U.S. is in the interest of Iran."[38] Rafsanjani echoed these sentiments: "In the past we missed certain opportunities or took late or wrong measures or even did not take action. Our ideology is flexible."[39] This is not to suggest that Iran was prepared to abandoned all of its prohibitions and openly acquiesce to America's demands as Muammar Qaddafi did in Libya. Even when greatly distressed, Khamenei maintained his red lines and stressed that "Some peoples' words and thoughts have become all about negotiations with the U.S. They say hold talks so that the U.S. does not threaten, obstruct, or exert pressure. No! Negotiations would not solve any problems."[40] Nonetheless, there seems to have been an intense internal debate within the theocracy about how to approach the United States at the zenith of its power. Although the hard-liners maintained their skepticism, they were prepared for continued talks as a means of deflecting America's regime-change designs.

In May 2003 an event shrouded in considerable controversy took place. A reported Iranian proposal offering broad-based agreement on all issues of concern was faxed to the U.S. State Department. According to some accounts, Iran was prepared to abandon its support of Hamas and the Palestine Islamic Jihad, pressure these groups to come to terms with Israel, agree to the disarmament of Hezbollah, and fully cooperate with international authorities in ensuring that its nuclear program was for peaceful purposes.[41] The proposal became commonly known as the "grand bargain," where an intractable theocracy essentially sued for peace.

There is ample reason to doubt the authority of this proposal, particularly given the fact that it involved a well-meaning but overtly ambitious Swiss ambassador in Tehran and a series of dubious Iranian characters such as the unreliable envoy to France, Sadiq Kharrazi. Given the lack of documentary evidence, one cannot determine the credibility of the document or whether it was approved by Khamenei. A circumstantial case, however, can be made that during the spring of 2003, Iran was trying to probe America's intentions and was open to a diplomatic outreach. Nonetheless, as we have seen, Khamenei and the hard-liners were still against the normalization of relations with the United States and opposed concessions to it. The notion that the theocratic regime was prepared to abandon its cherished Hezbollah disciple or relinquish its long-standing opposition to Israel seems doubtful. To avert a possible U.S. attack, Iran was probably trying to engage in protracted negotiations. Still, whatever the credibility of the offer, the Bush administration's decision not to consider the document was a lapse of judgment born out of arrogance and ideological excess. The failure to follow through was a gross case of diplomatic malpractice.

In the spring of 2003, Washington was transforming itself into an imperial capital mired in the hubris of "shock and awe." During the period between the collapse of Saddam's regime and the rise of the Sunni insurgency, American officials were confidently proclaiming their ability to transform the Middle East, rout out evil, and install democratic polities throughout the region. This was not an age for diplomatic compacts with unsavory states or strategic hesitation. The United States had finally found the key to a stable Middle East, namely, coercive democratization. The fall of Saddam's statue in central Baghdad reminded the reigning despots that their time had ran out. Prior to the invasions of Afghanistan and Iraq, the administration had perceived that it needed Iran's cooperation, but there was no longer any such compulsion. Iran's diplomatic overtures were met with silence, if not outright antagonism.

The event that finally led to the termination of U.S.-Iranian dialogue was predictably terrorism. For some time, the United States had been complaining that Iran had not been sufficiently vigilant in apprehending al-Qaeda personnel traversing its territory. All of this came to a head on May 12, 2003, when three explosions took place near Western housing complexes in Riyadh and killed seven Americans. Through its intercepts, U.S. intelligence revealed that al-Qaeda personnel, particularly the high-ranking Saif al-Adel, had masterminded the attacks from their sanctuaries in Iran. The immediate impact of the assault was the termination of discussions between Washington and Tehran.[42]

The bombings, however, raised troubling questions regarding the nature and direction of Iran's foreign policy. Given the deep-seated enmity between a Shiite theocracy and a radical Sunni terrorist organization, how does one account for such an operational association? Moreover, given the fact that the most prized diplomatic accomplishment of the Khatami government was the normalization of relations with Saudi Arabia, why would Iran be complicit in attacks in Riyadh? As with most aspects of Iranian terrorism, this episode is veiled in its own share of mystery, making all explanations necessarily tentative. The fact that al-Qaeda personnel were located in eastern Iran, where government control is at best lax, may suggest that whatever sanctuary they enjoyed was without authorization. An alternative assessment would be that a degree of operational ties existed between the Iranian intelligence apparatus and elements of al-Qaeda, given their shared animosity toward the American enterprise unfolding in the Middle East. In the past, Iranian intelligence and the Revolutionary Guards have taken initiatives that contradicted the official policy of the Khatami government. Perhaps certain elements within the regime saw a benefit in holding high-value al-Qaeda targets as bargaining chips and potential leverage in any discussions with the United States. Whatever their motivations, the May bombings in Saudi Arabia ended the Bush administration's flirtation with the Islamic Republic. However, even if the attacks had not taken place, it is doubtful that the faltering cooperation between the two states would have persisted. By May 2003 Washington believed that it did not need Iran to execute its regional strategy.

While America's motivation for dealing with Iran evaporated in the spring of 2003, the theocratic hard-liners' desire to accommodate the United States vanished soon thereafter. As the United States became mired in the Iraqi quagmire of its own making, the conservatives' fears and anxieties about its intentions disappeared. Suddenly the United States no longer looked like a menacing giant capable of overthrowing regimes with quick, decisive military strikes. As the Sunni insurgency drained the mishandled American occupation, the clerical hard-liners regained their confidence. The only faction that continued to be interested in a normalization of relations with the United States was the reformers. However, by 2004, a series of devastating elections had led to their gradual displacement by a younger cadre of militant reactionaries even more contemptuous of the United States than their conservative elders.

Despite the fact that the period 2001–2003 has been the subject of considerable controversy, it appears that influential corners in both Tehran and Washington were not ready for a fundamental transformation of the relationship between the two nations. Fear, opportunism, and sporadically overlapping common interests may have led the two sides toward tactical dealings, but such transactions were ultimately insufficient to induce either the clerical hard-liners or the Bush administration to transcend their animosities. The only actors in this melodrama who behaved with courage and a genuine desire for peace were President Khatami and the reformers, who suddenly found themselves beset by another challenge from the right.

PART IV

Hegemony at Last?

10

The Rise of the New Right

THE 1990S ARE OFTEN SEEN AS A DECADE OF ECONOMIC RECON-
struction and political reform. Intellectuals, businessmen, and technocrats dominated the public sphere in Iran as the country seemed to be
distancing itself from its revolutionary heritage. The clerical reformers
were seeking to reconcile democracy and religion, while the younger generation was moving away from a political culture that celebrated martyrdom and spiritual devotion. However, beneath the surface of innovation
and reform there evolved a war generation—pious young men who had
served on the front lines of the Iran-Iraq conflict. This cohort of austere
veterans maintained its revolutionary zeal and commitment to Khomeini's
original mission. From this segment of society emerged some of Iran's
more important future leaders: Mahmoud Ahmadinejad, Sa'id Jalili, and
Mujtaba Samarah Hashemi.

As the reform movement swept Iranian politics, the younger conservatives were hardly inactive. Given the generous benefits that the state provided for them, many of the returning veterans entered universities and
earned advanced degrees. They soon set up newspapers, organized their
own associations, and developed links with militant clerics and security
services who shared their disdain for materialism and talk of freedom,
which was enchanting the population. These were the years of academic
preoccupation, intense organization, and development of a vision for the
future of Iran.

The young reactionaries defined their ideology by calling for a return
to the "roots of the revolution." The New Right would often romanticize

the 1980s as a pristine decade of ideological solidarity and national cohesion. Its adherents saw it as an era when the entire nation was united behind the cause of the Islamic Republic and was determined to assert its independence in the face of Western hostility and Saddam's aggression. Khomeini and his disciples were dedicated public servants free of corruption and crass competition for power, traits that would characterize their successors. Self-reliance and self-sufficiency were the cherished values of a nation that sought to mold a new Middle East. As with all idealized recollections, the conservative view of the 1980s has a limited connection to reality. For most of the Iranians, the first decade of the revolution was a time of economic privation, encroaching autocracy, and an endless war that nearly destroyed the country.[1]

Beyond its piety and calls for reclaiming the revolution, the emerging conservative movement was not without an argument. As we have seen, the hard-liners had traditionally disparaged democracy as an alien import unsuited for an Islamic society. The antidemocratic message was now propagated under the banner of development. The focus of the Right was on creating a strong state that concentrated on economic efficiency and an equitable distribution of wealth. The inadequacies and inefficiencies of the reformist government were attributed to its political experimentations and its neglect of the everyday needs of the population. The conservative faction now self-consciously labeled itself the I'tilaf-i Abadgaran-i Iran-i Islami (Alliance of the Developers of Islamic Iran) and pledged a new order of prosperity and equality. The function of the government was not to cultivate a balance between reason and religion but to provide social services and ensure the society's economic viability. A vision of practical authoritarianism began contesting the reform movement's call for pluralism and the rule of law. Although the conservative ascendance would have much to do with its cynical manipulation of institutions under its command, popular frustrations with the reformers should not be discounted. The mood of the country seemed to be shifting from political reform to economic development.

Although the conservatives' primary focus was on internal affairs, they did not neglect foreign relations. The international orientation of this group was shaped by the devastating Iran-Iraq war. In the veterans' self-serving narrative, Iran's failure to overthrow Saddam had more to do with superpower intervention and less with their poor planning and lack of resources. The Western states and the United Nations, which failed to register even a perfunctory protest against Iraq's massive use of chemical weapons, were to be treated with suspicion and hostility. The notion of struggle and sacrifice were to displace civilizational dialogue and détente. As with Khomeini, a central tenet of the younger conservatives' foreign-policy perspective was that Iran's revolution was a remarkable historical achievement that the United States could neither accept nor accommodate. The Western powers would always conspire against an Islamic state that they could not control. The only means by which Iran could secure its independence and achieve its national objectives was through confronta-tion. The viability of the Islamic Republic could not be negotiated with the West; it had to be claimed through steadfastness and defiance.

In an even more ominous development, the young reactionaries brought a new style of politics to Iran. Given their background in the mili-tary and security services, they transferred a war mentality to domestic debates. During the war they had waged a jihad to protect and preserve the revolution. The postwar struggle against the forces of liberalization was just as critical. Once more, nefarious enemies were plotting against the revolution and seeking to erode its foundations through secularism and material greed. This was to be a jihad against the "internal enemies" of dis-sent and reform, which were the new subversive tools of counterrevolu-tionary activism.

In the turbulent politics of the Islamic Republic, violence and terror were not uncommon means of political control. However, even in the con-text of Iran's bloody politics, the new breed of conservatives had a particu-lar attachment to terrorism. Violence was not only a permissible but also a mandatory response against those seeking to undermine God's republic. As Ansar-i Hezbollah warned, "This will be the decade of settling scores with the seditionists by the friends of the revolution. And in this stage, the hands of the Hezbollah in repelling this sedition will not be tied."[2] Yet another leading conservative newspaper reinforced this message: "If imple-menting Islamic objectives would not be possible except by violent means, then that becomes necessary."[3]

In an attempt to signify their independence, the callow reactionaries rejected both Rafsanjani's and Khatami's tenures as sixteen years of devia-tion from the true revolutionary path. Rafsanjani's focus on economic reconstruction through integration in the world economy was dismissed as cultivating dependence on the West. Moreover, as devout religious lay-men, they were offended by his corruption and ostentatious lifestyle. Too often Rafsanjani reminded them of the shah, a dishonest and complacent politician who had surrounded himself with sycophantic aides who outdid each other in praising him. Khatami's tenure was seen as even more dan-gerous, as there was a real fear that the reform movement would convulse the state and precipitate its downfall. In essence, both the pragmatists and the reformers were blamed for the population's lack of fidelity to the imam's message. Rafsanjani's corruption and Khatami's treasonous message had diverted the youth from the task of revolutionary activism.

While the younger conservatives seemed antiestablishment, their cause was embraced by important members of the old guard. Prominent hard-liners such as the head of the Guardian Council, Ahmad Jannai, and the former minister of intelligence, Muhammad Muhammadi Ray'shahri, were among the elders of the revolution who saw much merit in the younger cadre. Despite extensive support within the clerical estate, it would be the archconservative Ayatollah Muhammad Taqi Misbah-Yazdi who would emerge as the mentor to the rising stars of the New Right. These informal relationships were buttressed by the Haqqani theological school, which did its part in training younger clerics who would ensconce themselves in the judiciary and the coercive apparatus of the state.

A long-time disciple of Khomeini, Misbah-Yazdi had taken his place within the ranks of the politicized clergy shortly after the revolution.[4] As the director of the Imam Khomeini Educational and Research Institute and a member of the Assembly of Experts, he has played an important role in the state's deliberations. Misbah-Yazdi had been an champion of totalitarian Islam for many years and seldom shied away from advocating violence against those calling for more tolerant view of religion. "The Prophets of God did not believe in pluralism. They believed that only one idea was right," stressed the dogmatic cleric.[5] He had renounced Khatami "as a betrayer of the Islamic Revolution" and was himself accused of sanctioning the series of killings in the late 1990s.[6] One of the peculiarities of the Islamic Republic is the orderly nature of its violence, as even the right-wing vigilante groups looked to their spiritual guides for affirmation of their conduct. Given Misbah-Yazdi's open advocacy of retribution against the reformers, he was always suspected of granting the necessary religious justifications for murdering dissidents. Misbah-Yazdi's complicity is further evidenced by the fact that he routinely condemned those killed by the militant groups as enemies of Islam and thus worthy of assassination.

If Misbah-Yazdi was the spiritual guide to many younger reactionaries, the Haqqani School was their intellectual home.[7] The school's founding predated the revolution, coming into existence in 1964 with the intended purpose of battling leftist ideologies popular among the youth. In the mid-1990s, however, the school came fully into its own when the head of the judiciary, Ayatollah Muhammad Yazdi, recruited many of its graduates into the bureaucracy, particularly the Special Court of Clergy, the Islamic

Propagation Center, and the various branches of the intelligence community. The graduates of this institution would be responsible for the press closures, the prosecution of progressive clerics, and the commission of violence against the reformers. During Ahmadinejad's presidential tenure, two of its most notorious alumni, Ghulam Husayn Muhsinii'j'i and Mustafa Pur Muhammadi, would respectively serve as ministers of Intelligence and Interior.

By far the most important institution to serve as the foundation of the conservative resurgence was the Revolutionary Guards. The Islamic Republic's own "Praetorian Guard" had fully come into its own, with vast commercial holdings and an expanded reach into the economy. Many of the guardsmen were assuming civilian roles and eyeing public office as a reward for their military service. Iran's elections would now feature the presence of former military officers whose ideological commitments and ability to deliver patronage made them an attractive choice for many voters. With their institutional connections and simple message of stability and prosperity, they would prove a formidable force in national affairs.

The New Right could not have reached the heights of power without the indispensable support of Ali Khamenei. The supreme leader not only appreciated their zeal but also shared many of their concerns. Moreover, as we have seen, the popular notion of Khamenei as a balancer of factions is belied by the historical record. Since his ascension to the post of supreme leader, Khamenei has relentlessly pursued the twin objectives of consolidating his power and ensuring the political hegemony of the conservative movement. In his younger disciples he found a cadre that revered his office and was ready to submit to his demands. While members of the old guard, such as Rafsanjani and Khatami, constantly challenged his verdicts and even questioned his authority, the younger conservatives were prepared to accept his command without question. A new political tendency now arrived on the scene, composed of the supreme leader's office, a group of ultraconservative clerics, and a dogmatic generation of war veterans. Those present at the creation of the revolution were being increasingly marginalized, as the Islamic Republic was undergoing its own subtle succession.

The Means of Ascent

By the early years of the twenty-first century, a shift was occurring in Iran's politics that reflected the conservatives' success in fending off the reform movement. A combination of the public's disenchantment with the political process and clever populism underpinned the conservatives' electoral surge. The systematic negation of parliamentary legislation and the obstruction of Khatami's initiatives by the unelected agencies of the state had already disillusioned those who looked to politics as a means of realizing their democratic aspirations. The middle class and the student movement were growing indifferent to national affairs and beginning to turn inward. As such, the electorate was shrinking and becoming limited to those who saw government as an institution that would mitigate economic adversity. The locus of elected politics was moving to the lower class, provincial towns, and those susceptible to the message of development. This is not to suggest a simplistic demarcation with the rich and the young suddenly abandoning the public sphere to the urban poor and the rural dwellers. However, there was a noticeable movement away from the type of electorate that had ensured Khatami's victories to a smaller one that was more attuned to populist rhetoric.

The first test of the conservative strategy came in the local council elections of February 2003. Unlike the parliamentary and presidential races, the Guardian Council does not vet the candidates for the municipal elections, thus making them the most unregulated contests in Iran. Approximately 200,000 candidates competed for 180,000 seats nationally.[8] The conservative program focused on reforming the economy while also touching on issues of social propriety and Islamic cultural mores. The reformers largely stuck to their theme of continuing the existing process of political liberalization through gradual pressuring of the system. In a stunning turnaround, the conservatives managed to recapture nearly all of the seats they had lost in 1999. The composition of the voters was also changing, as the middle and upper classes in large urban areas largely stayed away from the ballot box. This was an election that was dominated by the provincial towns and the poor, who looked to politicians to deliver financial relief. Although the overall national turnout was 48.87 percent, in the key city of Tehran it hovered around 24 percent.[9] This pattern occurred throughout the country. The overall national participation was respectable, but it was the result of a high turnout in remote areas.

The Islamic Republic had reached an impasse. The electoral process was no longer providing a viable path for liberalization of the theocracy. Given the hard-liners' emasculation of the presidency and the reduction of the parliament to a mere debating society, elected institutions could not effectively discharge their mandate. As Amir Muhibbian, the influential editor of the conservative daily *Risalat,* noted, "Iran's reformers are like poker players whose bluff has been called. The game is over."[10] In confirmation of Muhibbian's prognosis, 153 reformist parliamentarians acknowledged in an open letter that "The majority of Iranians are waiting for reforms but have reached the conclusion that their votes are meaningless."[11] Still, many within the reform camp soothed themselves by believing that the council results were an anomaly and that the public would come out and support their cause during the more consequential legislative races.

The conservatives' quest for power went into overdrive on the eve of the parliamentary election of 2004. Khamenei set the stage for a more agreeable parliament: "There is no knot that cannot be united and every conflict has a solution."[12] Ayatollah Ali Mashkini, head of the Assembly of Experts, was more explicit in his denunciation of the reformers for not taking "steps to eradicate unemployment, the sickness of the economy, high prices and the young people's propensity toward immorality."[13] The conservative campaign once more emphasized the themes of economic rejuvenation and faith-based communitarian virtues. Gulam Ali Haddad Adil, the future speaker of the parliament, emphasized this theme: "We believe that economic growth should be accompanied by social justice. We have certain criticisms about abnormalities in society; therefore, we would try to expand Islamic values, ethics, and spirituality in the country."[14] There was even talk of Iran's becoming an "Islamic Japan."

However, despite the strength of their coalition and the resonance of their message, the conservatives were leaving nothing to chance. In a brazen act of electoral manipulation, the Guardian Council disqualified twenty-five hundred reformist candidates, including eighty incumbents, from running for office. In an absurd claim, the Guardian Council decreed that the eighty sitting members of the parliament were actually religiously unqualified to hold their position. The reformers retaliated by staging a sit-in at the Majlis and denouncing the "parliamentary coup." Such appeals not only failed to impress the ruling authorities but also were largely greeted with popular apathy. A disqualified reformist parliamentarian, Muhammad Sadiq Javardi Hisar, acknowledged this reality: "The sit-in came far too late, and the reformers have not raised effective short-term demands among the people."[15] After making a number of speeches, Khatami failed to support the disqualified legislators, one of whom was his own brother, Deputy Speaker of the Parliament Muhammad Reza Khatami. Once Khatami was seen on the television casting his ballot in the transparently rigged elections, his once-powerful claim on the imagination of Iran's youth and the modern middle class largely evaporated.

In the end, the second most important elected institution in Iran fell to the conservatives. The reform movement now stood largely repudiated because it had failed to provide either political freedom or material gain for its constituents. Despite their overreach, the conservatives ran a more effective campaign by concentrating on people's economic distress and ending the gridlock. The tensions, conflicts, and bottlenecks of the previous seven years had convinced many that perhaps conservative control could lead to an expeditious resolution of the deep-seated and persistent economic problems. The Iranian electorate, which had already shrunk as a result of middle-class indifference, seemed to have become more practical and less concerned about the lofty promises of civil society and civilizational dialogue. Like the radical parliamentarians of the early 1990s, the reformers were beset by the conservatives' cynicism, as well as their lack of understanding of the public's mood.

Iran's Improbable President

Iran's presidential election of 2005 began with more than 1,014 aspirants registering as potential candidates. The Guardian Council eventually narrowed that list to a mere eight politicians. This radical reduction can be misleading. The final slate of candidates in fact reflected the broad range of ideologies present within the confines of the Islamic Republic. Iran's religious polity can never be mistaken for a democratic government, but average citizens were offered an array of choices as they contemplated their next president.

As the campaign began, initially all eyes were fixed on Iran's most durable politician, Hashemi Rafsanjani, who after months of speculation had finally thrown his hat into the ring. Rafsanjani presented himself as the savior of Iran at the moment of its economic distress and international isolation. The reform movement was represented by the former minister of education, Mustafa Mu'in, who ran a courageous campaign by pledging to reinvigorate civil society. In the center of the national spectrum was the former speaker of the parliament, Mahdi Karubi, who had gone through his own share of reinventions during his twenty-year career. Among the conservatives, much of the focus was on the flamboyant Revolutionary Guardsman and former head of the national police, Muhammad Qalibaf. Many of his youthful supporters, who were enthralled by his modern campaign, seemed to have forgotten his role in suppressing the 1999 student demonstrations and the charges of corruption that swirled around him. The candidate who was largely ignored was the archconservative mayor of Tehran, Mahmoud Ahmadinejad. The dismissal of his candidacy was not without justification, as he made no impression on public opinion polls and ran a lackluster campaign that eschewed even talk of political reform.

Mahmoud Ahmadinejad was an unusual politician. A forty-nine-year-old engineer, he had joined the Revolutionary Guards in 1986 and served largely in the northern frontier of Kurdistan.[16] Subsequent to the war, he had held a number of posts, including the governorship of Ardebil. In 2003 he was appointed mayor of Tehran by the conservative local council. Although a relatively obscure national figure, he belonged to the new generation of hard-liners, who were gradually assuming the reins of power. He was closely associated with Misbah-Yazdi and seemed to enjoy the support of the Basij forces and the urban poor. As one of the austere veterans of the war who had grown concerned about society's lack of religious devotion, he viewed public office as a means of revitalizing the imam's original mission. Throughout his career he proved a stern advocate of reactionary Islam and often stressed the importance of revolutionary values as guiding principles of national affairs.

Ahmadinejad's tenure as mayor presaged some of his moves as president. He deliberately avoided concerted economic planning and relied instead on rash populist measures such as handing out loans to his low-income constituents. While his predecessor focused on building recreational facilities and public parks, he concentrated on refurbishing mosques and religious centers. Ahmadinejad was meticulous in taking care of his supporters, as most of the city contracts were awarded to members of the Revolutionary Guards and the Basij. As a gesture of solidarity with and remembrance of his fellow veterans, he even sought to bury the remains of war dead throughout Tehran's parks and universities.[17] However, the idea of turning the nation's capital into a giant cemetery appalled most of its citizens and compelled the mayor to back down. Nonetheless, the remains of some of the war martyrs were eventually buried in seventy-two locations throughout Tehran. Even more dramatic was his use of city coffers to subsidize his fellow conservatives' political activities. Although Ahmadinejad and his allies criticized their competitors' corruption, the misuse of public funds for political purposes constitutes its own form of malfeasance. Whatever disdain the upper-class residents of Tehran may have had for their uncouth mayor, the urban poor, various members of the Revolutionary Guards, and the fiery clerics greatly admired him.

The other aspect of Ahmadinejad's rhetoric that would perplex much of the international community was his obsession with the Hidden Imam. According to Shiite canons, the final imam disappeared in the year 874, and his return will spell the end of time. Ahmadinejad was not alone in believing this, as a mixture of theology and folklore has long conditioned public piety in Iran. During the 1990s, a revivalist movement of sorts was sweeping certain sectors of society, particularly the poor, whose difficult economic situation propelled them toward a more intense embrace of religion. For decades, a steady stream of pilgrims had journeyed to Jamkaran, a site south of Tehran where the Hidden Imam is supposed to reappear. The traditional clergy were contemptuous of this unorthodox gesture and condemned it as mere superstition. Not so Ahmadinejad, who became an ardent proponent of Jamkaran and even built a rail link that connected Tehran to the shrine. Beyond a demonstration of his religiosity, this was also smart politics. Many lower- and working-class residents of Tehran believed in the redemptive powers of Jamkaran and thanked the new mayor for providing them a convenient means of reaching their spiritual destination.

Ahmadinejad's prominence on the world stage today belies the fact that, when he embarked on his presidential run, he was a lonely figure. Although he had a modest following among the younger militants, the larger conservative establishment, manned by the old guard, was dismissive of his quest. Given the number of conservatives running for the presidency, it was feared that they might split the vote and thereby facilitate a reformist victory. Thus, a coordinating council was formed and led by former speaker of the parliament Ali Akbar Natiq-Nuri to choose a single nominee. Not only was Ahmadinejad not that candidate, but he also came under much pressure to terminate his quixotic campaign. Mustafa Chamran, a member of Tehran's city council and a close ally of Ahmadinejad, confessed, "There is widespread pressure on Ahmadinejad to withdraw. Everyone wants him to leave the race, but he himself is not prepared to go."[18] In the end, no right-wing newspaper or association backed Ahmadinejad during the first round of the elections. Registering in the low digits in all of the opinion polls and limiting his campaign to calls for respecting war martyrs, the young, stubborn mayor was expected to gradually disappear from the scene.

Iran's ninth presidential election would be one of the most unusual in the country's history.[19] Not only was this the first election to go into a second round of voting, but many of the politicians running for the office also misjudged the mood of their constituents. On the eve of the elections, the reformers were peculiarly confident about retaining the office of president.[20] Reflecting how out of touch they had become, they once more focused on the theme of liberalizing the theocracy from within the system. After eight years in power, they were unable to demonstrate any tangible improvements in the lives of the less privileged segments of society. In addition, their reformist slogans failed to motivate the middle class, the intelligentsia, and the student and women's movements, which were the backbone of their previous triumphs. Mu'in certainly went further than Khatami in indicting the regime's repressive tendencies and openly denouncing the reactionary forces that had greatly thwarted the reform agenda. However, the prevailing stalemate had convinced many Iranians that it was time for a practical agenda as opposed to another unfeasible crusade. Deprived of a successful record and a convincing argument, Mu'in proved vulnerable to the conservatives' charges that he did not care about the poor and the working class. His fifth-place showing would further damage the reform movement's prospects as a significant force in the country.

Rafsanjani's core argument was that as a long-term practitioner of politics he was the only person capable of resolving Iran's manifold problems. Since leaving the presidency in 1997, Rafsanjani had been a restless figure, trying to find ways to reclaim an office of significance. As we have seen, his attempt to regain the speakership of the parliament in 2000 proved disastrous. Still, Iran's most wily politician somehow convinced himself that 2005 was his time. He widely intimated that, given his status and stature, he could effectively challenge the increasingly unaccountable Khamenei. In many ways, this was a competition not so much between Rafsanjani and other candidates but between the former president and the supreme leader. The once-intimate allies had gradually turned against each other, as Khamenei's quest for self-aggrandizement militated against the reemergence of Rafsanjani. It was no secret that Khamenei disapproved of Rafsanjani's candidacy and had sought to discourage his rival from running. Once Rafsanjani disregarded that advice and openly proclaimed that he would restore the powers of the presidency and, in essence, marginalize the supreme leader, the die was cast. Khamenei was not about to concede the presidency to a figure who pledged to confront him.

On the surface it was easy to dismiss the candidacy of Mahdi Karubi, a perennial fixture on the national scene. Karubi began his career as a radical politician devoted to exporting the revolution and constructing a command economy. By 2005, he had been transformed into a pragmatic reformer who was a frequent and daring critic of both Khamenei and the Guardian Council's abuse of power. Among Iran's politicians, he possessed an independent streak and a willingness to defy the established authorities. Despite the pervasive caricaturing of his campaign, the former speaker seemed to have sparked a real connection with the masses. More than any of his counterparts, he would prove a victim of electoral corruption that too often plagued the politics of the Islamic Republic. Indeed, in the absence of voting fraud, it is entirely possible that Karubi would have become Iran's president.

To the extent that the 2005 election had a conservative frontrunner, it was Qalibaf. The former Revolutionary Guard commander was rumored to be Khamenei's choice and a favorite of many hard-liners. However, Qalibaf soon ran a campaign that forfeited all of his advantages. In order to make himself attractive to the younger generation, he discarded his military fatigues for fashionable Western sunglasses and white suits. In yet another miscalculation, he went so far as to claim that he would emulate Reza Shah, the autocratic, modernizing father of the deposed monarch.[21] To be sure, the elder Pahlavi, with his strong-man reputation, was enjoying a revival among an Iranian population with a traditional penchant for dictatorial saviors. The problem for Qalibaf was that Khamenei and his devoted disciples neither shared the Pahlavi nostalgia nor appreciate Qalibaf's turning away from Islamism in favor of monarchical themes. Khamenei may have calculated that his hegemonic grip on power would not be secure in hands of a politician prone to advance his personal cause by sacrificing revolutionary values. Hovering over all of this were credible charges of corruption, as other Revolutionary Guard commanders implicated Qalibaf in unsavory business practices. As the guardian of the state, Khamenei understood that the legitimacy of the religious government was being threatened by charges of financial corruption and elite thievery.

The election results stunned both the nation and the international community. Although Rafsanjani managed to come out on top with 21.5 percent of the votes, the little-known mayor of Tehran came in second with 19.5 percent of the electorate. Since no candidate had captured the necessary 50 percent threshold, a runoff between the top two vote getters was required. There was an immediate disagreement between the reformist Ministry of Interior and the Guardian Council regarding the propriety of the vote. Although the Ministry of Interior is statutorily responsible for certifying the election results, the Guardian Council once more stepped beyond its boundaries and approved the outcome.

All of the leading candidates, particularly Karubi, who had come in third, complained about corruption in the process and vote rigging. In the backroom politics of the Islamic Republic, it is difficult to discern with complete accuracy the actual course of events. However, it appears that at the last minute Khamenei transferred his support from Qalibaf to Ahmadinejad. It was at that time that the entire institutional arm of the state was mobilized on behalf of Ahmadinejad, with the Revolutionary

Guard and Basij commanders ordering their foot soldiers to vote for the mayor. Muhammad Baqir Zulqadr, deputy commander of the Revolutionary Guards, confirmed these rumors: "Fundamentalist forces, thank God, won the election thanks to the smart and multi-front plan and through the massive participation of the Basij."[22] Such massive participation was seemingly buttressed by vote fraud and ballot stuffing. Despite his anticorruption concerns, the supreme leader was apparently willing to countenance certain irregularities for the sake of political expediency.

During the runoff campaign, the two remaining contenders for the presidency could not have run more different campaigns. Rafsanjani did not even deign to leave Tehran and limited himself to giving interviews largely to Western reporters about how he was uniquely qualified to save Iran from all of its troubles.[23] Rafsanjani's campaign not only displayed his arrogance but also demonstrated how the elders of the revolution had grown complacent. Under the banner of resisting fascist encroachment, many reformers and centrist politicians gravitated toward Rafsanjani. However, their political endorsements failed to impress the average citizen, who recalled Rafsanjani's tenure as a time of economic inefficiency and mismanagement.

In contrast to his jaded campaign during the first round, Ahmadinejad seemed to have found a message and a vision during the runoff period. The mayor of Tehran presented himself as a humble servant of the public whose principal aim was to "put Iran's petroleum income on people's table." He traveled to faraway towns that seldom saw a presidential candidate and spoke of relieving their financial burdens. Iran needed "an Islamic economy, one based on justice, whose aim is human progress," declared Ahmadinejad. Given his sense of religiosity, he seemed genuinely affronted by the state's corruption and denounced those who used their government service to "line their pockets." In a clever move, Ahmadinejad highlighted his modest home and the fact that he had driven the same car for twenty years and packed his own lunch every day. In a country where high office was seen as prelude to self-enrichment, he stood as a modest man devoted to the nation. For the forgotten rural voter in a distant province or the hard-pressed urban resident struggling with everyday needs, both the messenger and his message were appealing.[24]

On June 24, 2005, Ahmadinejad scored a landslide victory, capturing 64 percent of the votes to Rafsanjani's 36 percent. Although the turnout was not as large as in previous elections, it was still a respectable 60 percent. Rafsanjani and his allies were quick to charge voting irregularities. Although the conservatives had no compunction about rigging votes, Ahmadinejad's victory could not be attributed to fraud. A largely exhausted population unimpressed with Rafsanjani's reincarnation and disillusioned with the reform movement was willing to concede the state to the conservatives.[25] In his acceptance speech, Ahmadinejad declared that "Today is the beginning of a new era."[26] No one at that time realized just how turbulent that new era would be.

The ascendance of Ahmadinejad to the office of president represented a transformation of Iranian politics away from the struggle between reform and reaction to one in which the conservatives dominated the entire government. The Islamic Republic would not be entirely free of internal discord, however, as the competition for power pitted various strands of the New Right against each other. However, all of these actors were devoted to the revolution and revered the office of the supreme leader. For Khamenei, Ahmadinejad's election was a triumph of the strategy that he had launched a decade earlier. Khamenei was finally heading a regime whose politicians yielded to his judgments without undue protest, shared his dogmatic values, and viewed him as the arbiter of all of their debates. The elders of the revolution (such as Rafsanjani) would remain on the national stage, but theirs was a passing age, as Iran had entered a new epoch.

The trajectory of Iran's politics also confounded the West's anticipation of a forward historical progression. At the outset of the reform era, it was widely assumed that Iran was abandoning its revolutionary past and moving inexorably toward a pluralistic future. Even the setbacks and tribulations of the reform movement were dismissed as momentary hiccups on a longer journey whose conclusion was certain. After all, despite sporadic reactionary backlashes, previous revolutions had come to dispense with their radical heritage. Such presumptions overlooked not only the degree of the conservatives' determination to retain power but also their sincere belief that they were serving God's will. Under Khamenei's auspices, the hard-liners crafted a well-delineated strategy of gradually yet relentlessly reclaiming all of the relevant state institutions. For the first time since the inception of the Islamic Republic, a single faction had managed to marginalize all of its competitors.

As the newly revamped Islamic Republic contemplated its international relations, the usual interplay of ideology and pragmatism continued to spark its share of disputes. However, factionalism became less of a relevant factor in the regime's deliberations. The reformers and pragmatists would complain about the direction of the state and petition the supreme leader to limited effect. Although a certain degree of disagreement is intertwined in the Islamic Republic's political fabric, the cast of national-security decision makers now dramatically narrowed. It is too simplistic to suggest that Iran had reached the age of consensus, but the domestic transformations were bound to have an important impact on its approach to the world.

11

The Ahmadinejad Era

THE RISE OF THE NEW RIGHT PORTENDED IMPORTANT CHANGES in Iran's foreign policy. A mixture of Islamist ideology and ultranationalism would condition the new rulers' perspective. As with all of their predecessors, the conservatives believed that Iran had a right to emerge as the preeminent power of the region. Such nationalistic claims, however, were complemented by an Islamist outlook that closely identified with Palestinian and Arab opposition forces struggling against both the United States and Israel. Still, Iran did not return to the frenzied early days of the revolution, as even the New Right recognized that a less belligerent approach was the best means of ensuring Iran's ascendance in the Middle East. Unlike in the 1980s, the Islamic Republic refrained from denouncing either the Persian Gulf monarchies or the Egyptian and Jordanian regimes as illegitimate and—worse—plotting their overthrow. In keeping with the traditional practice of power politics, Iran was more concerned about these states' external orientation than their internal composition.

Nor has the New Right embarked on a path of exporting its revolution to the fertile grounds of Iraq. The opposition of the senior Iraqi clerics and Shiite politicians has convinced Iranian officialdom that its policy next door should be guided by practical concerns rather than grand ideological postulations. As such, Tehran's promotion of its Shiite allies is intended to prevent the rise of a state dominated by a Sunni elite, whose pan-Arab aspirations have led to tense relations, even war, with Iran. Tehran has no illusion that Iraqi Shiites are willing to subordinate their communal interests to Iran's national ambitions but hopes that a Shiite-dominated government will provide it with a sympathetic and accommodating neighbor.

The debates that are gripping Iran today focus on how the regime can consolidate its sphere of influence and best exploit its status as an emerging hegemon. Can Iranian predominance surge forward in coexistence with or defiance of the United States? As is customary with the Islamic Republic, even the New Right is divided in assessing its newfound fortunes.

New Tendencies within the New Right

As the conservatives assumed political power, their previous cohesion began to erode. Once confronted with the task of governance, this faction learned that some of its latent disagreements were beginning to undermine its unity of purpose. While campaigning against the reformist government, it was easy for the hard-liners to denigrate all aspects of their rule, but now that they were in command of the state, they had to wrestle with issues ranging from the nuclear portfolio to the charting of Iran's course in the turbulent Middle East. For the sake of simplicity, we can divide the New Right along militant and realist lines. For the militants, ideological impera-tives remained the primary focus of their policy, while the realists appreci-ated the need to modify their rhetoric and even objectives along more pragmatic lines. In the actual practice of foreign policy, the differences between these two groups prove limited.

On one side of the spectrum stood the militants, led by Ahmadinejad. Drawing strength from the Revolutionary Guards, particularly its intelli-gence apparatus, the Basij paramilitary force, and various clerical hard-liners, this group has been busily consolidating its authority over key components of the bureaucracy. For the militants, their most formative experience was Iran's prolonged war with Iraq. A pronounced suspicion of the United States and the international community, which had tolerated Saddam's war crimes, characterizes the perspective of those who fought on the front lines. Given their Islamist commitments and ardent sense of nationalism, they believe the Islamic Republic has a right and indeed an obligation to emerge as the leading power of the Middle East.

A central tenet of the militants' perspective is that enemies are always lurking about and plotting to subvert the theocratic state. Civilizational dialogue and integration into the global community have limited value for those who stress that only through a dogmatic stance can Iran claim its rightful place in the international order. "Confrontational diplomacy" was to be the new norm, as Iran had to be vigilant in the defense of its prerogatives. From militancy on the nuclear issue to asserting regional influence, this faction would be less prone to compromise than any of its predecessors.

The rise of Ahmadinejad and his allies injected a new, strident voice into Iran's foreign-policy deliberations. However, the obsessive international focus on the charismatic president runs the risk of disregarding or underestimating other political forces within Iran. In fact, the new generation of conservatives also features important actors pressing for a more tempered approach toward international politics. Ironically, evidence suggests that this tendency has also been shaped by the seminal experience of the Iran-Iraq war. In the aftermath of the war, many officials within the intelligence and security services, as well as combatants from the Revolutionary Guards, began contemplating their nation's future path. Among the leading members of this group are the mayor of Tehran, Muhammad Qalibaf; the speaker of the parliament, Ali Larijani; and the former minister of defense, Ali Shamkhani. Their writings and speeches reflect the conclusion that the end of the cold war and Iran's unique geographic location positioned it naturally as the preeminent state of the region. However, for too long the ideological edges of the regime and its unnecessarily hostile approach to the West have thwarted those ambitions. They argue that the only way for the Islamic Republic to reach its desired status is to behave in a reasonable manner while increasing its power. Such an Iran would have to impose some limits on the expressions of its influence, accede to certain global norms, and be prepared to negotiate mutually acceptable compacts with its adversaries.

In the broader story of the conservative ascendancy, the most underreported issue is this bifurcation among the second generation of rightwingers. In fact, many members of the more cautious realist group have moved into positions of influence within the Islamic Republic's key institutions, including the parliament and the military. Given the realists' role in such organizations and their links with traditional clerical networks, they are in position to press their claims and assert their influence.

It is important to stress that, despite their differences on economic affairs, the conservatives largely agree on core security issues. Given the displacement of Iran's historic enemies in Afghanistan and Iraq, as well as the decline of America's influence, they all sense that it is a propitious time for the Islamic Republic to claim the mantle of regional leadership. Iran has finally been offered a rare historical opportunity to emerge as the predominate power in the Persian Gulf region and as a pivotal state in the Middle East. This sentiment has best been captured by an influential editorial in the conservative daily *Kayhan:*

> A new Middle East is being formed in which America's old opponents have become powerful and popular and one by one they are pulling in countries that do not go along with America. The expansion of Iran's spiritual power in the Middle East has confronted America's historical interests in the region with unprecedented danger.[1]

As we have seen, the young reactionaries are hardly the first rulers of Iran to aspire to regional hegemony. What is new is that the New Right is now convinced that the goal of regional predominance, which eluded its predecessors, is within its grasp. Whether they are correct in their assessment of America's power or the willingness of incumbent Arab regimes to accommodate their aspirations is less relevant. The salient point is that such perceptions condition their approach to international affairs.

In its path of self-aggrandizement, Iran has to be prepared to pay a price. Ayatollah Jannati, the head of the Guardian Council, has stressed this point: "We have to have perseverance. We will tolerate sanctions and enmities and continue in our Islamic stance."[2] While serving as the deputy secretary of the Supreme National Security Council, Ali Husayn-Tash similarly noted, "A nation that does not engage in risks and difficult challenges, and a nation that does not stand up for itself, can never be a proud nation."[3] In essence, the New Right has redefined Iran's national interests by privileging strategic gain over economic growth. Western politicians, who insist that financial penalties will somehow distract the theocracy from its planned course, do not fully appreciate the hard-liners' mindset.

A key disagreement within the New Right centers on the necessity of relations with the United States. For Ahmadinejad and his allies, America is both a source of cultural contamination of the sacred Islamic lands and a rapacious capitalist power exploiting indigenous resources. As such, Iran's ambitions can never be reconciled with U.S. interests. Coexistence with the "Great Satan" is viewed as tantamount to an appeasement of evil. Ahmadinejad has plainly declared that "Our nation is on the path of progress, and on this path has no significant need for the United States."[4] Not since Khomeini has there been an Iranian faction so fundamentally averse to dialogue and compromise with the United States.

In contrast to Ahmadinejad and the firebrands, the more restrained hawks claim that Iran's predominance cannot be truly ensured without a more rational relationship with the United States. In a revealing address, Larijani stated, "We may be sure that the Americans are our enemy. Working with enemies is part of the world of politics. I believe that a strategy of curbing and reducing disruptions and normalizing relations is itself beneficial."[5] Although the U.S. presence in the Middle East is bound to diminish, for this faction, America's power can still present a barrier to Tehran's resurgence. A less contentious relationship with the United States may ease America's distrust and pave the way for the projection of Iran's influence.

Hovering over this debate remains Ali Khamenei. As a stern ideologue with his own considerable suspicions of the United States, Khamenei finds Ahmadinejad's fiery denunciations of the West and his assertive Islamism appealing. The supreme leader certainly shares the militants' opposition to any relations with the United States. "Having ties with the U.S. does not decrease the danger which that country poses to Iran. Therefore, restarting relations with that country is not to the benefit of Iran no matter what some talkative people say."[6] As we have seen, Khamenei anguishes over America's seductive cultural influences and how closer relations between the two nations can subvert the theocratic rule.

Nonetheless, as a long-term survivor of the Islamic Republic's treacherous politics, Khamenei comprehends that excessive zeal and unnecessary provocations could entangle Iran in difficulties that may be hard to manage. Khamenei is not just the guardian of the regime's ideology but also a head of state responsible for protecting its national interests. In that capacity, he has sporadically been receptive to the realists' arguments and has accepted the principle of negotiations with the United States over Iraq and the nuclear issue. To be sure, the leader has been at pains to draw distinctions between tactical talks on a limited set of issues and the full-scale normalization of relations. Still, Khamenei cannot always tolerate Ahmadinejad's fanaticism and at times has to rein in his adventurous disciple.

Today the landscape of the Middle East is rapidly changing. America's declining fortunes in Iraq and Afghanistan, Hezbollah's victory over Israel in the summer of 2006, and the rise of Hamas as an elected party have presented Iran with opportunities to project its influence. In the meantime, the apparent success of Ahmadinejad's nuclear diplomacy has seemingly validated his claim that, should Iran remain steadfast, the Western powers will grudgingly accept its new status. As the supreme leader watches over the state, he must balance competing and at times conflicting interests.

The best manner of assessing Iran's foreign policy during the turbulent Ahmadinejad tenure is to focus on three issues that have dominated Tehran's foreign-policy priorities: the nuclear challenge, civil strife in post-war Iraq, and the Arab-Israeli conflict. By examining these topics one can get a better sense of the interplay of Islamist ideology and nationalistic mandates, which is conditioning Iran's international orientation.

Nuclear Politics

Iran's nuclear ambitions did not commence with the onset of the Islamic revolution. It was in fact the shah who first launched the country's efforts to build the bomb. The remarkable aspect of the nuclear program is not just its continuity but also the fact that the same set of assumptions that guided the shah has motivated his clerical successors. A combination of deterrence and a desire to project power in the Middle East have conditioned Iran's nuclear aspirations under two very different regimes.[7]

One of the seminal dates in Iran's nuclear history is 1972, the year the shah declared that Iran would build a nuclear apparatus designed to generate twenty-three thousand megawatts of power.[8] Two years later the country established the Atomic Energy Organization of Iran and committed itself to constructing approximately forty reactors. In addition to the United States, Iran obtained assistance from West Germany, France, and South Africa. The Iranian nuclear program encompassed technologies critical for the construction of nuclear weapons, namely, an indigenous uranium-enrichment and reprocessing network.

From the beginning there were suspicions that the shah desired not just an alternative source of energy but nuclear arms as well. Given his declared objective to become the regional hegemon, a nuclear capability was central to his national-security perspective. Asadollah Alam, the shah's minister of court and one of his closest confidants, stated in his posthumously published diary that "HIM [His Imperial Majesty] has a great vision for the future of this country, which, though he denies it, probably includes the manufacturing of a nuclear deterrent."[9] In the aftermath of the revolution, the shah's former foreign minister, Ardashir Zahidi, confessed the following:

> The Iranian strategy at that time was aimed at creating what is known as surge capacity, that is to say to have the know-how, the infrastructure, and the personnel needed to develop a nuclear

military capacity within a short-time without actually doing so. But the assumption within the policymaking elite was that Iran should be in a position to develop and test a nuclear device within 18 months.[10]

Akbar I'timad, the head of Iran's nuclear program during the monarchy, has similarly recalled, "I always suspected that part of shah's plan was to build bombs."[11] The Washington establishment, which was nurturing the shah's desire to act as the policeman of the Persian Gulf, not only looked the other way but also actively assisted his pursuit of such weaponary.

Paradoxically, the revolution, with its tumult and disorder, initially derailed the nuclear program. The cultural revolution launched by the Islamic Republic closed the universities and impeded all aspects of Iran's scientific research. However, beyond the chaos of the early revolutionary days, it appears that Khomeini was skeptical about the program and viewed it as another ploy for making Iran dependent on the West. Sharing the imam's disapproval, Prime Minister Bazargan curtailed the construction of the Bushehr plant. Given Iran's financial difficulties, Bazargan was hardly inclined to devote precious resources to a program whose utility he doubted. The Atomic Energy Organization may not have been shuttered, but its activities were drastically curtailed.

Two officials emerged at this time as benefactors of the nuclear industry, Speaker of the Parliament Rafsanjani and Prime Minister Mir Husayn Musavi. Subsequent to the collapse of the provisional government, these two functionaries became even more relevant and pressed for the resumption of Iran's nuclear activities. Reza Amrullah, the former head of the Atomic Energy Organization, recalled, "During the first days of the revolution, it was Hashemi Rafsanjani and Mir Husayn Musavi who stood with the program."[12] The exigencies of the war demonstrated to these politicians the value of the "strategic weapon." Given their control over the important levers of power and their proximity to Khomeini, they managed to sustain the nuclear program. During the 1980s Iran could hardly boast of having an impressive nuclear network, but the fact that its program was not completely shut down had much to do with the efforts of the speaker and the prime minister.

Subsequent to Musavi's departure from government in 1989, Rafsanjani remained the politician most interested in the nuclear industry. However, despite Rafsanjani's long-term investment in the atomic project, Iran's program did not make impressive gains during his tenure. Iran was still recovering from the devastation of the war and had a difficult time reconstituting its scientific establishment, particularly in the sensitive area of nuclear research. Tehran in fact attempted to build up its infrastructure, but its efforts were often plagued by corruption, inefficiency, and misman-agement. Moreover, pressures exerted by the United States were effective in denying Iran a reliable international partner. For example, U.S. diplomacy was instrumental in dissuading the European states and even China from cooperating with Iran. It was not until 1996 that Iran managed to secure Russian assistance for the reconstruction of the Bushehr plant. Even more ominously, Iran appeared to have commenced a relationship with the A. Q. Khan network and acquired important technologies and designs.[13] Still, a combination of U.S. vigilance and Iranian incompetence retarded Rafsan-jani's nuclear aspirations.

Throughout the 1990s, Iran's nuclear progress reflected a degree of complacency. Although Western foreign ministries would routinely express their concerns about Tehran's proliferation tendencies, there was misplaced confidence that international efforts had managed to derail Iran's nuclear trajectory. The Iranian threat that garnered the most attention was its pen-chant for terrorism and its efforts to destabilize the Middle East. All of this changed, however, with a series of devastating revelations in August 2002.

The first shock came when an opposition group announced that Iran had constructed an elaborate enrichment facility in Natanz, approximately two hundred miles south of Tehran. The complex task of enriching ura-nium was thought to be beyond Iran's technological capability. At Natanz, Iran had already installed 160 centrifuges with a commitment to eventually operate more than fifty thousand such machines. In addition, Iran was active in developing its plutonium capabilities. The heavy water facility at Isfahan and the nearly completed plant in Arak demonstrated a diversified path to nuclear empowerment. The scope of the program showed that Iran was moving along the path of self-sufficiency and was increasingly relying on its own technologies and scientists for completion of the program.[14]

The nuclear industry that Rafsanjani revived was obviously enhanced by his reformist successors. Indeed, the indications are that the reformers were far more efficient and capable in this realm than the Rafsanjani administration. The question then becomes, why did these two very differ-ent governments come to attach so much value to the nuclear program? Why did Iran invest so much money and undertake so many risks to develop its nuclear capacity? What sort of threats and opportunities actu-ated Iran's nuclear ambitions?

It is impossible to understand Iran's nuclear calculations without con-sidering its war with Iraq. That conflict shaped the Islamic Republic's defense doctrine and molded its values and outlook. The security of Iran would be contingent on its own efforts, as legal compacts and international conventions were unlikely to provide it with any protection. The fact that Saddam had used chemical weapons against Iran with impunity demonstrated that the Western powers' hostility toward the clerical regime would always overcome their moral compunctions. Moreover, as we have seen, the chemical agents proved successful in turning the tide of battle and ultimately forcing Iran to acquiesce to an armistice. The fact that Iran had insufficient retaliatory power and could not protect its citizens from unconventional attacks was critical to its decision to end the war.

Iran's experience during the war validated the strategic importance of nuclear capability. As chapter 4 explains, in the concluding stages of the conflict, the commander of the Revolutionary Guards insisted that a successful prosecution of the war required atomic weapons. Rafsanjani was even blunter:

> With regard to chemical, bacteriological, and radiological weapons it was made very clear during the war that these weapons are very decisive. It was also made clear that the moral teachings of the world are not very effective when war reaches a serious state and the world does not respect its own resolutions and closes its eyes to the violations and all the aggressions which are committed in the battlefield. We should fully equip ourselves both in the offensive and defensive use of chemical, bacteriological and radiological weapons.[15]

Ata' Allah Muhajirani, who served as Rafsanjani's vice president and would go on to become Khatami's progressive minister of culture, similarly noted, "Muslims must cooperate to produce an atomic bomb regardless of U.N. efforts to prevent proliferation."[16] For many key officials of the theocratic state, the best means of preserving the regime's security and Iran's territorial integrity was through possession of the bomb.

If the war looms large in Iran's nuclear designs, its unpredictable neighborhood seems to be less of a factor. It is hard to see how atomic weapons can prevent instability in central Asia or Afghanistan from sweeping into Iran. Nor has Israel's nuclear arsenal proven a sufficient threat to Iran to account for its ambitions. To be sure, Iran and Israel have had tense relations since the inception of the Islamic Republic, but both sides have been careful to subsume their conflict within well-delineated parameters and have assiduously avoided a direct military confrontation. Iran has chosen to register its opposition to Israel by supporting terrorist organizations and

Palestinian rejectionist forces. A careful examination of the clerical leaders' rhetoric on the nuclear issue reveals that the need to deter Israel is seldom mentioned. To the extent that Israel features into Iran's nuclear discourse, it is to point to the international community's hypocrisy: While critical of Iran's program, it has remained largely silent about Israel's growing armory. Terrorism and proxy war have been Iran's preferred method of dealing with its Israeli nemeses. All of this may change should Israel engage in precipitous action and attack Iran's nuclear installations. Such a move might finally succeed in elevating the Iranian-Israeli confrontation beyond its current status and transforming Israel into a type of enemy whose deterrence mandates a nuclear shield.

Nor does Pakistan's nuclear inventory constitute a leading motivation for Iran's program. During the 1990s Iranian-Pakistani competition over influence in Afghanistan led to tensions between the two states. Iran does indeed anguish over the possibility of a radical Sunni regime coming to power in Karachi and assuming control of the nuclear arsenal. Nonetheless, given that Pakistan has not been a significant power in Iran's immediate neighborhood, it is at best a secondary concern for Tehran.

In the aftermath of 9/11, Iran's nuclear appetite should have diminished, as the changing Middle East seemingly offered it an unprecedented degree of security. The need to deter Iraq and offset its designs no longer worried the theocratic state. Indeed, the Shiite-dominated government in Baghdad looked forward to establishing constructive relations with its Iranian neighbor. Although the Taliban presented a lesser danger than Saddam, it was a thorny problem that required periodic military deployments and even skirmishes in the border areas. The removal of the Taliban and its replacement with yet another friendly regime further eased Iran's dilemmas. Certainly Israel and Pakistan sustained their nuclear programs, but they were not the primary threats that conditioned Iran's nonconventional aspirations. The one adversary, however, that appeared even more menacing was the United States.

For decades, U.S.-Iranian relations had been mired in a pattern of confrontation and animosity. The two powers even clashed militarily during the Iran-Iraq war. The end of that conflict hardly diminished their mutual hostilities, as Iranian terrorism and America's sanctions policy continued to fuel their antagonism. However, during the Bush presidency this conflict was ratcheted up to a new level. The speed with which the United States overthrew Saddam made a pronounced impression on the clerical elite. America had not just arrived in Iran's back yard but had come with ambitions to displace despotic regimes who pursued weapons of mass destruction and had ties with terrorist organizations. Given the asymmetry in the conventional balance of power, the United States could not be deterred by Iran's armed forces or even the threat of retaliation with chemical weapons. After all, the Bush administration was hardly dissuaded from invading Iraq when it perceived that Saddam possessed chemical munitions. More so than any other factor, the need to negate the American challenge immeasurably enhanced the case for an Iranian bomb.

It was Khatami's misfortune that the nuclear crisis erupted during his presidency. For the reformers, the nuclear program was seen in the context of Iran's overall international relations and thus had to be balanced with other concerns. Given their desire to integrate into the global order, the reformers took the threat of UN censure seriously. Hasan Ruhani, secretary to the Supreme National Security Council, acknowledged that "Being a revolutionary state does not mean that we discard everything and put ourselves on a road of confrontation with the West."[17] The reformist government may have hoped to maintain both its nuclear program and its commercial relations, but, once threatened with sanctions, it quickly came to terms with the international community. In 2003 negotiations with the European states of Britain, France, and Germany (EU3), Tehran agreed to suspend its program and adhere to the additional protocol of the Nuclear Nonproliferation Treaty (NPT), which promised a more stringent inspection regime.[18]

Khatami's suspension of the program was not a cynical ploy designed to avert American retribution. This was a genuine attempt to determine what Iran could gain in terms of security assurances and economic concessions for its voluntary act of suspension. Although Iran insisted that it would never relinquish its right to enrich uranium, it was open to a prolonged freeze for the right price. The reformers, who privileged cooperative relations with the West over nuclear empowerment, were willing to concede to the demands of the great powers.

The possibility of an Iran-EU3 agreement establishing the basis for a durable accord was undermined by a combination of American hostility and conservative ascendance. From 2003 to 2005 the Bush administration limited itself to denigrating the talks and pressuring the Europeans to be more aggressive. In the meantime, the 2004 elections produced an Iranian parliament that routinely denounced the reformers as naïve accomplices of cynical Europeans. The domestic political landscape, as well as the regional situation, were changing in a manner that buttressed the hard-liners' dogmatic position. The Europeans' inability to offer a meaningful package of incentives, America's declining fortunes in Iraq, and the rise of the New

Right militated against a compromise solution. The European and Iranian negotiators were hopelessly attempting to craft a deal that was somehow acceptable to both American and Iranian hawks. All of this was bound to change as Iran elected a new president.

Even before his assumption of power, Ahmadinejad had made clear his contempt for Khatami's patient strategy. The presidential candidate derided Iran's negotiating team: "Those who are handling the talks are terrified and before they even sit down to talks they retreat 500 kilometers."[19] The hardliners continually denounced the reformers as capitulating to Western imperialism and relinquishing Iran's legitimate rights. The advocates of "confrontational diplomacy" insisted that Iran could gain more by being aggressive.

Given its determination to eclipse America's power, the New Right seems to consider the acquisition of nuclear-weapons capability an important objective. Ayatollah Misbah-Yazdi has declared this task a "great divine test," while the mouthpiece of the extreme Right, *Kayhan*, has openly called for acquiring "knowledge and ability to make nuclear weapons that are necessary in preparation for the next phase in future battlefield [*sic*]."[20] Larijani has similarly stipulated that "If Iran becomes atomic Iran, no longer will anyone dare to challenge it because they would have to pay a too high of a price."[21] While the Rafsanjani and Khatami administrations looked at nuclear weapons as tools of deterrence, for the conservatives they are a critical means of solidifying Iran's preeminence in the region. As such, the current leaders of the Islamic Republic have no intention of bartering the program away for commercial contracts or security guarantees, which they openly scoff at. A hegemonic Iran requires a robust and extensive nuclear infrastructure.

The one issue that provokes a slight but perceptible disagreement within the New Right is the necessity of negotiations. The militants dismiss diplomacy and suggest that Washington is not interested in proliferation but is merely exploiting the nuclear issue to multilateralize its coercive policy. Given the United States' immutable hostility toward Iran, any concession on the nuclear program would only lead to further impositions. Ahmadinejad has stressed, "If this issue is resolved they will bring up human rights. If human rights is resolved, they will bring up animal rights."[22] Thus, the militants dismiss negotiations and call for Iran to press ahead with its activities irrespective of international concerns and sensitivities.

The realists agree that the enhancement of Iran's influence necessitates a weapons capability. However, as Iran plots its nuclear strategy, they recognize the importance of offering confidence-building measures to a skeptical international community. All of this is not to suggest that Iran is inclined to suspend the program or to relinquish its critical components, but they are more open to dialogue. Moreover, the realists stress that a reasonable Iran can potentially gain the support of the European states, China, and Russia, thus isolating the United States and undermining its sanctions policy.

The ultimate arbiter of Iranian politics and the person responsible for setting the national course remains Khamenei. Thus far, Khamenei has crafted a strategy that has combined elements from both sides' perspectives. On the one hand, he has been effusive in his praise for Ahmadinejad's defiance on the nuclear issue. "Among the significant characteristics of the ninth government is its justice-seeking and its campaign against global hegemony which are among the mottos of the revolutionary government," he has insisted.[23] Khamenei has also echoed Ahmadinejad's claims that any "setback will encourage the enemy to become more assertive."[24] A supreme leader who survived the internal challenge of the reform movement and the external threat of American intervention seems at ease with Ahmadinejad's nuclear advocacy.

Nonetheless, Khamenei cannot always afford Ahmadinejad's bellicosity and has been receptive to the arguments of his more judicious disciples. He has accepted the realists' advice on diplomacy and has maintained Iran's basic commitment to the Nuclear Nonproliferation Treaty. Under the auspices of the supreme leader, Iran has negotiated a work plan with the International Atomic Energy Agency (IAEA) designed to shed more light on its current and past nuclear activities. And Iran's officials have continued to meet with Javier Solana in his capacity as representative of the Security Council and Germany. Such compromises are anathema, however, to the militants, who view all diplomatic initiatives as an encroachment of Iran's sovereign prerogatives.

The maturing of the nuclear program has generated patriotic fervor, and the regime has certainly done its share to promote the importance of the atomic industry as a pathway to scientific achievement and national greatness. From issuing commemorative stamps to celebrating the enrichment of miniscule quantities of uranium, the clerical regime believes that a national commitment to the cause of nuclear self-sufficiency can once more revive its political fortunes. As a conservative newspaper has conceded, "Atomic energy has become the glue that has reinforced the solidarity of the nation."[25] The problem with this approach is that, once such a nationalistic narrative is created, it will be difficult for the government to offer any concessions without provoking a popular backlash. After years of proclaiming that this is the most important issue confronting Iran since the nationalization of the oil industry in 1951, the government will find that meekly suspending the program will challenge the legitimacy of the state. The Islamic Republic's deliberate strategy of marrying Iran's national identity to the cause of nuclear aggrandizement makes the task of diplomacy even more daunting.

The pattern of Iranian procurement suggests that this is not a crash program but one of sustained progress. Given the flexible confines of the NPT and its stipulation that member states have a right to develop an entire spectrum of capabilities for civilian use, Iran can advance its program while adhering to the treaty. At some point, Tehran will have to choose between continuing its civilian pursuits and crossing the weapons threshold. In the next several years, the thorny issue of Iran's proliferation will likely preoccupy the United States and its allies. The diplomatic challenge is to craft an accord that satisfies Iran's nationalistic desire for a domestic enrichment apparatus while granting the international community sufficient confidence that those capabilities will not be misused for military purposes. Barring such an imaginative solution, Iran's nuclear imbroglio could easily provoke an altercation that would destabilize the Middle East for years to come.

Iraq: Revolution or Stability?

Unlike with the nuclear issue, there has been a widespread consensus across Iran's political spectrum on how to handle Iraq. The policies of both the reformist government and its hawkish successors were more pragmatic than ideological. Given that Iraq's complex sectarian makeup militates against theocratic rule, Iran has recoiled from exporting its revolution next door. Despite routine accusations by the United States, Iran is interested in defusing the existing civil war and sustaining Iraq as a unitary state. Moreover, Tehran comprehends that the best means of realizing its objectives in Iraq is not through violence but the democratic process, which is bound to strengthen the Shiite community. A functioning and legitimate Iraqi state would be equipped to neutralize the insurgency, sap Ba'athists of their remaining power, and incorporate moderate Sunnis into an inclusive governing order.

During its seven-decade monopoly of power, the Sunni minority dismissed and relegated the Shiites to the margins of the society. The Ba'athist regime went on to extract a cruel revenge for any signs of Shiite political agitation and demands for representation commensurate with its demographic power. The esteemed men of religion would be persecuted, the Shiites' southern habitat would be subjected to a manmade ecological disaster, and the ancient shrine cities reduced to squalor. The Ba'athist malevolence was nowhere more evident than in its treatment of the Shiite uprising of 1991, when at the behest of the first Bush administration, the Shiites rose up to reclaim their society. The Ba'athists' retaliation was brutal: Summary executions, the razing of cities, and massive deportations became the order of the day.[26]

The fortunes of history rarely change with the rapidity that confronted the Sunni minority in 2003. The U.S. invasion, accompanied by expectations of "democratic transformation," irrevocably altered Iraq's political landscape. The Shiites, confident of their numerical majority, viewed the democratic process with optimism and proved patient with the vicissitudes of the postwar order. The remarkable aspect of Iraq was the way in which the Shiite clerical estate managed to preserve its essential infrastructure of influence. Despite the Ba'athist onslaught, the ayatollahs' quietism allowed them to maintain their seminaries and mosques. At a time when all organized political activity was viciously suppressed, the clerical class would assume prominence. Ironically, Iraqi society had undergone decades of forced secularization, but the Shiite political parties that now emerged would be led by either clerics or men of religious devotion. The United States had to adjust and deal with religiously oriented parties that did not always share its views.

As with most political movements, the Shiite bloc was beset with its own tensions and disagreements. For the senior clergy, led by Ayatollah Ali Sistani, the tradition of quietism and guidance prevailed over direct engagement in public affairs.[27] In his role as guardian of the Shiites' interests, Sistani pressed for elections and plebiscites as the best means of consolidating political gains. The message of the patient and gradual acquisition of power in cooperation with the occupying U.S. forces was acceptable to the returning exiles such as the venerable Da'wa Party and the Supreme Iraqi Islamic Council. Nonetheless, the forbearance of the elders would be contested by the firebrand cleric Muqtada al-Sadr, who compensated for his lack of theological erudition with the street power of radical politics.[28] Sadr's blend of Shiism and nationalism, his willingness to confront the United States, and his calls for an Islamic state brought him popular acclaim, particularly among the poor and disaffected.

The Shiite enterprise of consolidating power through elections was pressured by a Sunni rebellion. The Sunnis' response to the new order was hardly passive acquiescence. Accustomed to the privileges of power, they spawned a radical insurgency that was at times linked to al-Qaeda. The bombing of markets and mosques, assassinations, and abductions taxed Shiite patience and eventually triggered a counterreaction that led to a sectarian civil war. Anger, suspicion, and prejudice divided neighborhoods and cities along a confessional line that is proving difficult to bridge.[29]

Beneath the reality of carnage, violence, and civil war, Iraq remains the only Arab state that is gradually undergoing a transfer of power from the Sunni minority to a Shiite-dominated state. Although the Middle East has a reputation for political volatility, the incumbent regimes have easily deflected challenges to their rule. Regardless, Iraq is experiencing an unprecedented transformation. Its political culture has completely changed through a combination of occupation, violence, and pluralism. And it is this process that has confronted Iran with both historical opportunities and important challenges.

As the Islamic Republic contemplates its policy in Iraq, it has to contend with a number of difficult positions. Tehran's overarching objective is to prevent Iraq from once more emerging as an ideological and strategic threat. Thus, it is critical for the theocratic regime to ensure the Shiites' political primacy. However, Iran must also guard against any spillover from a civil war that is threatening Iraq's territorial cohesion. Dismemberment of Iraq into three fledging states at odds with each other would present Iran with more instability in its immediate neighborhood. In the meantime, Iran desires a withdrawal of American forces, as its hegemonic aspirations can never be ensured so long as a sizeable contingent of U.S. troops remains in the area. To pursue its competing goals, Iran has embraced a contradictory policy of pushing for elections and accommodating responsible Sunni elements while at the same time subsidizing Shiite militias who are bent on violence and disorder.[30]

Since the demise of Saddam, the region's Sunni princes and presidents have anguished over the rise of a "Shiite crescent" and how a mini-Islamic Republic is being created at least in the southern portion of Iraq.[31] However, this is a mischaracterization of an Iranian policy that is seldom motivated by the export of the revolution. The leaders of the theocratic state grasp the fact that Iraqis are not about to subordinate their national cause to Iran's mandates. Muhammad Jaffari, deputy of the Supreme National Security Council, noted this reality: "After the fall of Saddam, the Iraqi clerical leaders entered politics. However, as preferred by Ayatollah Sistani, they opted to guide, not lead. In Iran, the Imam chose to lead the revolution."[32] In 2003, Foreign Minister Kamal Kharrazi similarly stressed, "No Iranian official has suggested the formation of an Iranian-style government in

Iraq."[33] As such, Iran's promotion of its Shiite allies is designed not to impose its template on an unwilling Iraqi nation but to ensure that its government features actors prone to engage with Iran.

To a great extent, Iran's policy today is driven by its own prolonged war with Saddam's Iraq. Iran is a country that lives its history. The war is far from a faded memory—it is debated in lecture halls, street gatherings, and scholarly conferences. After more than two decades of reflection, a relative consensus has finally emerged within Iran's body politic that suggests that the cause of Iraq's persistent aggression was the Sunni domination of its politics. The minority Sunni population sought to justify its monopoly of power by embracing a radical pan-Arabist foreign policy that called for Iraq to lead the Middle East. Thus, the Sunnis were ruling Iraq not for crass parochial purposes but for the larger cause of Arab solidarity. Such a posture inevitably led to conflicts between Iraq and its neighbors. One of the primary victims of the Sunni misadventures was the Islamic Republic. However, Iraq is a land of sectarian divisions and contrasting identities. The Shiites and Kurds also possess a foreign-policy orientation, but it is one that calls for a better relationship with Iraq's non-Arab neighbors. An Iraq that no longer serves as an instrument of Sunni aggrandizement can be counted on to behave with moderation and judiciousness.

The differing perceptions held by Iraq's Sunnis and Shiites are nowhere more evident than in their assessment of the Iran-Iraq war. For the Sunnis, this was a struggle between Arabs and Persians designed to check Iran's regional ambitions. It was an occasion where Iraq's defiance redeemed the Middle East for the Sunni world. For the Shiites, Iran is not a menacing Persian hegemon but a coreligionist that has often stood with them. Despite the fact that the Shiite conscripts manned the front lines of the war, a very different historical perception pervades the Shiite community. In the Shiite narrative, both Iran's and Iraq's Shiites were Saddam's victims and suffered at his hands. The Shiite populace would vote for exiles who spent decades in Iran without concern for their loyalties, whereas the Sunnis would often castigate those very same politicians as traitors. The Shiite leaders would apologize for the war, whereas many Sunnis considered it the high point of their national achievement. The sectarian divide has even managed to infiltrate the historical memory.

Contrary to Washington's claims, the clerical state has always seen its fortunes as best served by elections and plebiscites. In a strange twist of fate, Iranian hard-liners, who have done much to subvert pluralism at home, have emerged as proponents of liberal rule in Iraq. Ayatollah Jannati, who in his capacity as head of the Guardian Council has done immense damage to the cause of democratic change in Iran, confessed, "Iraq is undergoing a promising election stage. The election results are very good so far."[34] Beyond strengthening the more congenial Shiites, a democratic Iraq will likely be a federal state devolving much of its power to the provinces. In such a governing structure, Iraq is unlikely to have a robust, centralized state seeking supremacy in the Persian Gulf. It would be much easier for Iran to exert influence over a divided and weak Iraq with many contending actors than a strong, cohesive regime.

Given Iran's interest in the stability of Iraq, the question remains, why is Tehran providing sophisticated munitions to recalcitrant Shiite militias? Iran's model of operation in Iraq is drawn from its experiences in Lebanon in the early 1980s. At that time, Iran amalgamated a variety of Shiite parties into the lethal but popular Hezbollah. Since the removal of Saddam, Iran has similarly been busy strengthening the Shiite forces by subsidizing their political activities and arming their militias. Iran hopes that the Shiites will continue to exploit their demographic advantage to solidify their gains. But should the political process fail, they must be sufficiently armed to win the civil war. The purpose of Iran's military dispatches is not necessarily to provoke a confrontation with the United States but to maintain the viability of the Shiite forces. The problem is that, once such arms cross the border, it is hard for Iran to maintain operational control over them, and it is entirely possible that some of them have been used against U.S. personnel.

Iran's interest in stability is reinforced by its belief that a period of calm may ease America's path out of Iraq. Even Ahmadinejad has stipulated that "the more this government [Iraq] is successful in establishing security, the weaker the foreigners' reasons will be to continue their occupation of Iraq."[35] Iran's ambassador to Iran, Hasan Kazimi Qumi, has also stressed, "In an insecure Iraq, the occupying military forces have a pretext to extend their presence. Therefore, it is logical for Iran to seek security in Iraq."[36] An Iraqi regime that can claim a degree of coherence can finally provide Washington with the necessary justification.

To the extent that Iran has a cure for Iraq's ills, it is regional mediation that both Iran and Saudi Arabia lead. Iran as the leading Shiite power and Saudi Arabia as the foremost Sunni state would come together to press their respective allies toward a new national compact featuring a loose federal arrangement that would encompass the moderate Sunnis, along with the Shiite and Kurdish parties. As Ahmadinejad declared, "We are prepared with the help of our regional friends and neighbors such as Saudi Arabia and others to fill the vacuum in the interest of the region."[37] Along this path, Iran has dispatched a number of emissaries to Riyadh to enlist Saudi and Gulf Cooperation Council (GCC) support. Once the Gulf sheikdoms transcend their suspicions of the Persians and the Shiites, the region can move collectively toward a measured solution to Iraq's tribulations.

Such subtle mediation is hardly in evidence today, as the United States is increasingly claiming that its problems in Iraq stem from Iranian malfeasance. In the midst of the recriminations and accusations, the United States fails to understand that in the end a more constructive dialogue with Iran may yet achieve its goal of restoring stability to Iraq. One high-ranking foreign ministry official, Abbas Araqchi, has pointedly offered a different direction to the United States: "It is useless to accuse Iran of supporting foreign fighters or sending arms. Why should we do that? We have the same interests in Iraq."[38] A diplomatic framework has yet to be established to realize these shared objectives. A more proper strategy would not deny that Iran should have influence in Iraq but seek ways to harmonize U.S.-Iranian policies. Both parties have interests in sustaining the territorial integrity of Iraq, empowering the democratic process, and tempering the civil strife. Once Washington stops dedicating itself to expunging Iran's presence in Iraq, it can begin the process of effective coordination. It is incongruous to suggest that the United States has sufficient interests in Iraq to the point of mandating its invasion and occupation, whereas the country next door should have no role in its neighbors' affairs.

Ahmadinejad vs. Israel

As we have seen, since the inception of the Islamic Republic, strategic considerations and ideological values have coincided to produce an enduring enmity toward Israel. During Ahmadinejad's tenure, the theocracy's hostility toward the Jewish state became even more alarming, as he not only pledged the destruction of Israel but also denied the historical reality of the Holocaust. Iran's defiant posture was reinforced by Hamas's election and Hezbollah's triumph over the much-vaunted Israeli armor. In a region accustomed to defeat and despair, the two Islamist parties were widely acclaimed for their virtue and valor. In such a milieu, Tehran saw little reason to abandon its unyielding opposition to Jerusalem. Despite occasional grumblings about Ahmadinejad's rhetorical excesses, the conservatives largely stood by their president as he offended world opinion with his inflammatory rhetoric.

In one of its rites of passage, the Islamic Republic holds an annual conference that brings together reactionaries and radicals from across the Middle East to denounce Israel. The international press, as well as the

Iranian public, usually dismisses such conclaves as yet another expression of the theocracy's peculiarity. It was at one such gathering, titled "The World without Zionism," that Ahmadinejad uttered his infamous call for the eradication of Israel. Unlike previous Iranian politicians—most of whom routinely engage in such crass displays—Ahmadinejad did not go unnoticed by the outside world.[39] As his words captured headlines throughout Western capitals, an undaunted Ahmadinejad pronounced the Holocaust a "myth." For a politician determined to revitalize Khomeini's mission, denying Israel's legitimacy and casting doubt on the well-documented sufferings of the Jewish people was unexceptional.

In his subsequent musings on this subject, Ahmadinejad has suggested the relocation of Israel to Europe. On his first trip abroad, Ahmadinejad embarrassed his nation, as well as his Saudi hosts, by declaring:

> Some European countries insist on saying that Hitler killed millions of innocent Jews in furnaces, and they insist on it to the extent that if anyone proves something contrary to that they condemn that person and throw him in jail. Although we don't accept this claim, if we suppose it is true, our question for Europeans is: Is the killing of innocent Jews by Hitler the reason for their support to the occupiers of Jerusalem? If the Europeans are honest, they should give some of their provinces in Europe—like Germany, Austria, or other countries—to the Zionists and the Zionists can establish their state in Europe.[40]

The Iranian president even turned himself into a free-speech advocate and defended the rights of the Holocaust deniers to publish their distortions. To demonstrate his point, he organized a conference to examine the Holocaust, which featured a disreputable gallery of neo-Nazis, anti-Semites, and just plain racists. It was an ill-suited and unfortunate occasion for a country with a rich civilization and a history of tolerance toward the Jews.

The tragedy of Ahmadinejad's rhetoric is that he was expressing sentiments that have been emanating from the pulpits and platforms of Iran for three decades. The calls for the destruction of Israel and the provision of platforms for Holocaust deniers are ordinary aspects of political life in the Islamic Republic. The Iranian officialdom seemed genuinely shocked by the international outcry, as this was the first time that it had been held accountable for its odious claims. There would be some backtracking and attempts to explain away the discourse, but, given that such statements were an important dimension of Khomeini's legacy, it would prove difficult for Tehran to extract itself from its latest predicament.

Despite international condemnations, Khamenei supported his president, and there were no signs of divergence between the two leaders. The supreme leader's own denunciations of Israel certainly made him receptive to Ahmadinejad's arguments. Moreover, Khamenei has indulged in his own share of Holocaust speculations. "From a psychological standpoint, the Israelis are engaged in very important activities. All politicians, all reporters, all intellectuals, all officials, all experts of the West should bow their heads to commemorate the gas chambers. That is, they should all endorse a tale the authenticity of which is not clear and regard themselves as indebted because of that story," declared the leader.[41] Although Khamenei may appear more circumspect than his bombastic president, it is obvious that the clerical oligarchs found little that was objectionable in Ahmadinejad's historical rendition.

As Iran's governing elite rallied behind Ahmadinejad, the reformist faction once more distinguished itself by its vociferous condemnations of his claims. Khatami rebuked his successor: "We should speak out even if a single Jew is killed. Don't forget that one of the crimes of Hitler, Nazism, and German National Socialism was the massacre of innocent people, among them many Jews."[42] Sa'id Hajjariyan, a key reformist figure, noted the damage that Ahmadinejad had caused: "In the eyes of the world, Iran is an unpredictable country with bizarre and undiplomatic comments."[43] The nature of the reformers' response once more demonstrates that the United States made a grave error in not seriously engaging Tehran during their time in office. The Khatami government, which had subtly acknowledged the reality of a two-state solution and was open to a new relationship with the United States, stands in stark contrast to the Ahmadinejad regime.

The question remains, why did Ahmadinejad choose to indulge in such strident rhetoric at a time when Iran was already in conflict with the international community over its nuclear violations? To be sure, Iran's nuclear diplomacy was greatly complicated by its president's pledge to annihilate a member of the United Nations. However, it would be too facile to suggest that Iran was developing its nuclear arsenal to preemptively obliterate Israel. The laws of deterrence still hold, and the theocracy comprehends that such a move would ensure its own demise. Iran's rulers should not be caricatured as messianic politicians seeking to implement obscure scriptural dictates for ushering in the end of the world through conflict and disorder. As with most leaders, they are interested in staying in power and will recoil from conduct that jeopardizes their domain.

The attacks on Israel can best be understood in the context of the Islamic Republic's ideology, as well as its attempt to reach out to the masses in the Middle East. Ahmadinejad and the Iranian clerical elite genuinely believe in Khomeini's dictum—that Israel is an artificial construct imposed on Islam's realm by the forces of imperialism. However, they also employ such rhetoric as a means of appealing to public opinion in an inflamed region. The carnage in Iraq, the failure to make even the slightest progress toward a Palestinian-Israeli compromise, and the Arab rulers' inability to stand up to Washington have generated a popular clamor for a leader willing to defy the United States and Israel. As a cagey politician, Ahmadinejad recognizes that his callous denunciations of Israel and his contemptible denials of the Holocaust actually enhance his popularity in a region relying on conspiracies to explain its predicament. Through his use of Islamic discourse and his appeals to local grievances, Ahmadinejad has managed to leapfrog the sectarian divide and allow a Shiite, Persian country to capture the imagination of the Sunni Arabs. As such, his unrelenting religious exhortations are designed not to prepare a path for the return of the Hidden Imam but to advance the cause of Iranian influence.

The year 2006 would emerge as one of the more critical years in the Middle East, as events in Palestine and Lebanon measurably strengthened Iran's anti-Israeli resolve. In a free and fair election, the radical Islamist party, Hamas, with its historical links to Iran, managed to defeat the ossified and corrupt Palestinian Authority.[44] As the United States struggled to recover from the latest mishap of its ill-conceived democracy-promotion agenda, Iran was quick to embrace its triumphant ally. As *Jumhuri-yi Islami* noted, "To help the position of Abu Mazen [Muhammad Abbas, president of the Palestinian Authority] means confronting the Hamas government that has been established with the majority of the votes of the Palestinian nation. It means supporting the government of Salam Fayyad, who is supported by the Zionist regime that has no legitimacy."[45] Suddenly there were two Palestinian governments, with Iran standing by the one with a reputation for probity and efficiency. Tehran's embrace of Hamas became even closer when the radical group survived Israel's attack three years later.

In the summer of 2006, the sporadically volatile Israeli-Lebanese border became the scene of yet another Middle Eastern tragedy.[46] On July 12, Hezbollah guerrillas attacked an Israeli patrol, killed three soldiers, and captured two more. In a subsequent skirmish, three more Israeli troops were killed. Hezbollah seemingly anticipated a limited Israeli strike and then negotiations over an exchange of prisoners. Instead, what took place was a full-fledged war that lasted thirty-four days and destroyed much of the recently rebuilt Lebanon. Throughout the conflict, Hezbollah managed to sustain its rocket attacks, which terrorized much of northern Israel.

In the end, the Shiite guerrillas succeeded against Israel's formidable military far better than Arab armies had during four previous Arab-Israeli wars. Hezbollah's miscalculation became the basis of its regional acclaim, thereby benefiting not just its own reputation but also the stature of its Iranian patron.

The regional reaction to the war crystallized the fissures in the Middle East. At the initial stages of the conflict, the leading Arab capitals, particularly Cairo and Riyadh, were eerily silent. Uneasy about the rising Shiite power, the Sunni regimes hoped that Israel would be able to strike a blow against at least one Shiite force. Iran stood with its protégé and decried all efforts to marginalize and destroy Hezbollah. As the war proceeded and Hezbollah survived the onslaught, the Arab rulers lost their street.

Suddenly protest marches and the seething anger of the Arab population compelled the reigning governments to retreat and call for a ceasefire. Mustafa Chamran, one of Ahmadinejad's close allies, best captured the position of the Arab states: "Some Muslim countries with the aim of destroying Hezbollah and upending Shiite enclaves supported Israel. But once Hezbollah won, they quickly changed their policies and supported it."[47] An Iran that had always seen both strategic and ideological value in supporting Hezbollah would now embrace its disciple even more warmly.

The recent events led to a perceptible shift in Iran's policy toward the Arab-Israeli peace process. During Khatami's tenure, Iran had decided that it would concede to a peace treaty that was acceptable to the Palestinians. Beginning a concerted assault on that stance, the conservative forces insisted that Iran would oppose an accord even if it proved acceptable to the Palestinian leadership. Ahmadinejad articulated this point: "Anybody who takes a step toward Israel will burn in the fire of the Islamic nation's fury."[48] Ayatollah Muhammad Reza Mahdavi-Kani, one of the elders of the revolution who still commanded respect among the new guard, similarly stated, "A peace agreement that calls for recognition of Israel is not acceptable."[49] To the extent that Iran has a solution to the conflict, it is a referendum that features all Palestinians, including those of the Diaspora. Given the numerical realities, this was a means of ensuring Israel's demise through a plebiscite.

Ultimately, whether Iran will sustain its opposition to a peace treaty that proves acceptable to the Palestinians and the leading Arab states remains an untested proposition. Given the breakdown of diplomatic efforts, there is no viable process or agreement for Iran to oppose or obstruct. Would Iran grudgingly acquiesce to a compact or continue a lonely struggle against a regional consensus for peace? During the reformist era, this was an easy question to answer. Today, one must be cautious about claiming that Tehran would not uphold the mantle of the opposition irrespective of the cost.

The New Right has managed to achieve a degree of consensus on key international issues that eluded its predecessors. Under the auspices of the supreme leader, his more obedient, youthful disciples have come to an agreement on the need for nuclear self-sufficiency and regional aggrandizement that necessitates a commanding presence in Iraq. However, it is great power pretensions more than ideology that define the New Right's ambitions. This is not to suggest, however, that Islamism no longer drives the policies of Iran's rulers. As we have seen, on the issue of Israel, a strident ideological voice has entered the debate and reversed the moderation of the reformist government. However, Iran's inflammatory denunciations (even of Israel) can be partly attributed to its attempt to mobilize the region behind its leadership. A defiant Iran flanked by Hezbollah and Hamas is standing firm against Zionist encroachment and has captured the imagination of the Arab masses.

The one issue that presents a source of division for the New Right is its approach to the United States. The more pragmatic elements may be prone to a diplomatic settlement that remains unacceptable to the more hardline faction. The core question that divides the younger conservatives is whether Iranian preeminence can best be achieved through a more tempered relationship with the United States or open confrontation with the "Great Satan." A more calibrated U.S. policy could potentially expose the divisions within the ruling conservative elite and strengthen the more realist elements.

The Iranian approach to the world was conditioned by tensions between pragmatism and revolutionary values during the tenures of Rafsanjani and Khatami. However, it underwent a marked change during the reign of the New Right. A "war generation," with its imperial ambitions and austere Islamism, has come to power and is redefining the parameters of Iran's international relations and pressing its newfound advantages to their limits. Iran is well along the path of achieving a nuclear-weapons capability while emerging as the pivotal state of the Middle East. One can argue that Khamenei's gamble of investing so much authority in his younger disciples has thus far paid handsome dividends.

Conclusion

THE ISLAMIC REPUBLIC OF IRAN HAS ENTERED THE TWENTY-first century in an enviable position. During its first three decades in power, the theocratic regime has survived a brutal war, domestic unrest, and American hostility. By choice and chance, Iran has now emerged as a leading power of the Middle East, whereby its preferences and predilections have to be taken into consideration as the region contemplates its future. As the clerical leaders gaze across the region, they see a crestfallen American imperium eager to extract itself from Mesopotamia, an Iraq preoccupied with its simmering sectarian conflicts, and a Gulf princely class eager to accommodate their power. The challenge of Iran has never been greater, and the ability of the United States to manage the surging power of the Islamist state will go a long way toward stabilizing the Middle East.

Despite occasional calls for regime change and fanciful hopes that somehow it can provoke another revolution, the basic U.S. policy toward Iran remains one of containment. In a return to its glorious past, successive administrations have taken a page from the United States' early cold-war struggle with the Soviet Union, when the Western powers successfully frustrated Moscow's expansionist designs. By directly projecting its own power and conceiving a broad-based Arab alliance, the United States aims to check and if possible to reduce Iran's influence. The only intriguing aspect of this strategy is that its persistent failure has yet to disabuse the Washington establishment of its utility.

To begin with, this paradigm is predicated on the fallacy that Iran can be compared to the Soviet Union and that the cold-war model is applicable to the Middle East. While during the early stages of the anti-Communist struggle, the United States and its European allies shared the same assumptions and agreed on the same tactics, no such consensus exists in the Middle East. The Arab regimes may decry Iran's ambitions, but they are loath to participate in the type of aggressive containment strategy that could unduly antagonize the Islamic Republic. Even in the Persian Gulf, with its proximity to Iran, there is no uniform anti-Iranian agreement. Unlike Saudi Arabia, Kuwait, and Bahrain, the states of Qatar and the United Arab Emirates do not have a Shiite minority problem and enjoy extensive economic relations with Iran. Far from seeking a confrontational policy toward Tehran, these states fear that escalating tensions between the United States and Iran threaten to reverse the normalized relations they have enjoyed with the clerical regime since the mid-1990s. Even the perennially suspicious House of Saud has settled on a policy of integrating Iran into the existing Gulf framework instead of isolating and ostracizing it. Moreover, U.S. allies will assess their capabilities and vulnerabilities, shape alliances, and pursue their interests, all the while understanding that they are susceptible to an Iranian influence predicated on religious and economic ties. A containment strategy build on porous Arab solidarity is bound to fail.

Moreover, in practical terms it is hard to see how a viable containment structure can be conceived. For close to half a century the Arab world saw Iraq's military as its bulwark in the Persian Gulf. The United States dismantled that military in 2003. With no other armed forces in the Gulf able to contain Iran, the United States will have to shoulder that responsibility—by maintaining large numbers of troops in the region indefinitely. Given the visceral anti-American sentiments pervading the Gulf today, other than Kuwait, it is hard to see how any of these states can countenance a return of substantial U.S. forces in their territory. In any realistic conception of its containment strategy, the United States will be relying on weaker regional actors to contain the rising one—the largest country in the Persian Gulf region in terms of size and population, not to mention the most socially and culturally dynamic one. Large-scale arms sales to the Gulf states will not change that reality.

For U.S. policymakers, who rely so much on their reading of history to substantiate their policies, their grasp of recent Middle Eastern history is curiously lacking. The last time the United States rallied the Arab world to contain Iran (in the 1980s), Americans ended up creating a political culture that facilitated the rise of Sunni militancy. It was this milieu that produced the Taliban and al-Qaeda. The results may again be similar this time around. Containment will mobilize Sunni extremism as the ideological barrier to Shiite Iran. This was the consequence of Saudi Arabia's rivalry with Iran in South Asia in the 1980s, as well as the reason radical Salafis quickly mobilized to contain Hezbollah's soaring popularity in the summer of 2006. Whereas during the cold war, confronting communism meant promoting capitalism and democracy, in the Middle East version, it will mean promoting Sunni extremism. It is here that Washington's containment strategy comes into full confrontation with its goal of defeating radical Islam.

The realities of the Middle East are bound to defeat Washington's cold-war fantasies. That is not to say that Iran does not pose serious challenges to U.S. or Arab interests. However, the vision of a grand U.S.-Arab alliance to contain Iran is not achievable, will not work, and may make things worse by sinking Iraq, Afghanistan, and Lebanon into greater chaos, inflaming Islamic radicalism, and further committing the United States to a long and costly presence in the Middle East. In considering its policy, the United States requires a more imaginative leap forward.

The Middle East is a region continuously divided against itself. In the 1960s, radical Arab regimes contested the legitimacy and power of traditional monarchical states. In the 1970s, Islamic fundamentalists rejected the prevailing secular order and waged war against the incumbent Arab regimes. In the 1980s, much of the Arab world supported the genocidal Saddam Husayn as he sought to displace Iran's theocracy. And now, the Middle East is once more fracturing, this time along sectarian and confessional lines, with the Sunni states clamoring to redress Shiite ascendance. The tragedy of the U.S. policy is that, in the name of preserving the balance of power, it has taken sides in the region's conflicts, thus exacerbating tensions and further widening existing cleavages. Outside the Arab-Israeli dispute, the United States has shown limited interest in mediating conflicts and bringing antagonists together. It sided with the conservative monarchies against Arab socialist republics, acquiesced to the secular states' brutal suppression of fundamentalist opposition, supported both Saudi power and the Iraqi war machine in order to temper Ayatollah Khomeini's Islamist radicalism, and is now being tempted by an alignment with the Sunni states against the so-called Shiite crescent. Along every step of the way, as America has become mired in the region's rivalries, it has seen its goal of stability slipping ever further away.

Instead of focusing on reviving a shattered balance of power, the United States would be wise to aim for regional integration and the fostering of a framework where all of the powers see it in their own interest to preserve the status quo. Washington is correct in sensing that a truculent Iran poses serious challenges to America's concerns, but the evolving strategy of containing Iran through antagonistic alliances and military deployment is simply not tenable. Iran is an opportunistic state seeking to assert predominance in its immediate neighborhood. The task at hand is to conceive a situation whereby Iran wants to be contained—in other words, sees benefit in limiting its ambitions and abiding by the prevailing norms. Dialogue, compromise, and commerce, as difficult as they may be, are a means of providing Tehran with a set of incentives to adhere to international norms and commit to regional stability. America's acknowledgement that Iran will have influence in Iraq can finally induce the two states to cooperate in realizing their many intersecting objectives in that hapless nation. Both Washington and Tehran want to preserve the territorial integrity of Iraq and prevent its civil war from engulfing the Middle East. Resumed diplomatic and economic engagement between the two states and collaboration on Iraq may presage an arrangement for restraining Iran's nuclear program within the limits of its Nuclear Nonproliferation Treaty obligations. Then the United States may finally get to the point where Iran sees some benefit in reining in its regional ambitions.

An engagement strategy with Tehran need not come at the expense of America's relationships with Iran's Arab neighbors. Instead of militarizing the Persian Gulf and shoring up shaky alliances on Iran's periphery, Washington can move toward a new regional security system that features all of the local actors. Such a framework can involve a treaty that pledges the inviolability of the borders, arms-control pacts that proscribe certain categories of weapons, a common market with free-trade zones, and a mechanism for adjudicating disputes. For the Gulf states, such an order would have the advantage of bringing the Shiite-dominated states of Iran and Iraq into a constructive partnership, thus diminishing the sectarian conflict, whose perpetuation threatens regional cohesion. For Iran, the new order offers it an opportunity to legitimize its power and achieve its objectives through cooperation rather than confrontation. And for an Iraqi regime that is often belittled and ostracized by its Sunni neighbors, such an arrangement could help dissipate the canard that it is a mere subsidiary of Iran. Indeed, such a concerted diplomatic strategy would afford the leading states of Saudi Arabia and Iran a means of transcending their zero-sum competition in Iraq and press their allies toward a new national compact that, although dominated by the majority Shiite populace, would still recognize the interests of the Sunni and Kurdish minorities. This would be far more preferable than engaging in a proxy war, which could easily get out of hand.

None of this can come about without active American participation and encouragement. The Gulf states will require the reassurance of a U.S. role if they are going to entrust their defense needs to a new regional order. For an Islamic Republic whose chief contender for preeminence remains the United States, membership in such a framework has no value unless it enjoys Washington's approbation. In a curious manner, a new situation can be created in the Persian Gulf, whereby all of the relevant states are not just cooperating with one another but also sensing the need for a continued U.S. presence. In this context, the United States is not seeking to enforce a balance of power but upholding a regional arrangement that has the essential consent of all of the relevant regimes. An American presence by invitation is more easily emplaced than one that is predicated on fear, anxiety, and coercion.

Today the center of gravity in the Middle East has shifted from the Arab east to the Persian Gulf. It is not the Israeli-Palestinian conflict that will decide the future of the Middle East but the failed and failing states of Iraq and Afghanistan, where Iranian power and influence have ample room to expand. These conflicts will determine the nature of Middle East politics and the role that Iran will play in it—whether it will support or undermine its stability. The Palestinian issue is important for Israel's security, stability in the Levant, and America's image and prestige. Nonetheless, the main power brokers and the salient issues that will shape this region are all in the Gulf. It is more likely that peace in the Persian Gulf will bring peace to the Levant than the other way around.

Engaging Iran and regulating its rising power within an inclusive regional-security architecture and institutions will present the best way of addressing the concerns of America's Arab allies, stabilizing Iraq, and even giving a new direction to negotiations over Iran's nuclear program. A regional-integration strategy that all of the relevant actors are invested in is more sustainable, and its maintenance will tax U.S. resources the least. Ultimately, security for Arabs and Israelis will be more achievable if Iran is part of the region and is vested in its stability rather than excluded from it.

Afterword

MORE THAN THIRTY YEARS AFTER AYATOLLAH RUHOLLAH Khomeini came to power—and two decades after his passing—the Islamic Republic of Iran remains an outlier in international affairs. Unlike other non-Western, revolutionary regimes that, over time, eschewed a rigidly ideological approach to foreign policy and accepted the fundamental legitimacy of the international system, Iran's leaders today remain largely committed to upholding Khomeini's worldview. The resilience of Iran's Islamist ideology as guide for successive generations of policymakers is striking. One cannot argue that the present-day foreign policy of China is being structured according to Mao Zedong's Thought, nor is Ho Chi Minh the guiding light behind Vietnam's efforts to integrate into a larger Asian community of nations. Iran's leadership, however, continues to implement policies derived, in part, from Khomeini's ideological vision—even when such policies are detrimental to other stated national interests of the country, such as enhancing economic development and cementing Iran's rise as a regional power.

This continues to puzzle Western observers—why Iran has not yet become a postrevolutionary country. What makes this case more peculiar is that by the late 1990s, Iran did appear to be following in the footsteps of states like China and Vietnam, at least in terms of its foreign policy. Yet this evolution was deliberately halted and to some extent reversed after the election of Mahmoud Ahmadinejad to the presidency in 2005. Paradoxically, it has been a younger generation of Iranian leaders who have rejected the more pragmatic, nonrevolutionary approach of some of their elders in favor of reclaiming the legacy of Khomeini.

The success of Khomeini's vision stems partly from its malleability. Revolutionary states often find it difficult to maintain any semblance of fidelity to ideology as pragmatic concerns take increasingly center stage in foreign policy. Over time, ideological pronouncements ossify into straightjackets that constrain policy flexibility. This was the phenomenon well known to Soviet diplomats, who found it increasingly necessary to engage in intellectual gymnastics and selective, out-of-context quotations taken from writing of Vladimir Lenin to justify policies such as détente with the United States and peaceful coexistence with capitalist states. Yet, because adherence to the ideology legitimated the Soviet political system, the regime was loath to break completely with the Marxist tenets.

Khomeini might reasonably be described as a fanatic, but he was willing to inoculate his version of Islamism with a sufficient degree of pragmatism to allow flexibility in policymaking without having to jettison the ideology altogether. For instance, Khomeini acknowledged that Iran's interests required pursuit of economic and political ties with a variety of non-Muslim states—among them China, Cuba, Japan, and Korea. As the Iran-Iraq war dragged on, Khomeini also reconceptualized the role of the Islamic state, to not simply being the guardians of past Islamic traditions, but also capable of issuing new rulings that could contradict previous stances or existing traditions. In order to preserve the interests of the state, Khomeini had to terminate his Islamist quest to displace Saddam with a more acceptable ruler. The Imam's preferences were always tilted toward his transnational mission of Islamic redemption, and he did seem indifferent to the calamitous consequences of his policies. Nonetheless, the imperatives of ruling did lead Khomeini to inject a measure of pragmatism in Iran's governing fabric.

The onerous and complicated legacy of Khomeini, however, would often frustrate his more enterprising disciples. The Imam bequeathed to his successors a state that quickly lapsed into paralyzing factionalism. As such, Iran could never chart a cohesive, predictable foreign policy. The Islamic Republic would witness momentous realignments in the international order. From the marginalization of Iraq to the collapse of the Soviet Union, Iran confronted challenges that it could not easily manage given its domestic squabbles. A state that was capable of both pragmatism and revolutionary radicalism did not always prove a reliable interlocutor. As soon as hints of moderation became obvious, another arm of the state would engage in activity that undermined the promise of a new opening. Such contradictory impulses were particularly evident in the case of Iran's relations with the European community and Saudi Arabia. The need to have better relations with these important states may have been obvious to some within the theocratic establishment, but the cyclical nature of Iran's foreign policy often impeded normalized ties.

When Rafsanjani assumed the office of the presidency in 1989, he concluded that the imperatives of economic reconstruction would have to guide his foreign policy priorities abroad. Iran would have to be part of the global economy, mend fences with its neighbors, and come to terms with its foes. This, of course, was the starting point by which postrevolutionary leaders in China and Vietnam had also begun the process of de-ideologizing foreign policy. Rafsanjani did not see himself as breaking with the Imam's injunctions. He supported Khomeini's overall goal of independence from the global system, and was uneasy about approaching the "Great Satan." However, for the conservative faction of the republic, led by Khamenei, such pragmatic modifications at times went too far. As we have seen, under the banner of national interests, the conservatives tentatively supported some of Rafsanjani's moves. Iran did behave judiciously as America dislodged Saddam from Kuwait, and the hardliners were amenable to forging economic relations with the European states. The conservatives, however, did not allow for such national interest calculations to circumscribe their ideological proclivities. Iran continued to sponsor terrorism, remained committed to the export of its revolution, and seemed indifferent to the sensitivities of its major trading partners. The clash of ideals and interests that Khomeini often held in check ultimately bedeviled his disciples.

For their part, Khatami and the reformers similarly viewed themselves as upholding the Islamic Republic's pledge of being responsive to the political aspirations of its constituents. The expansion of civil society groups, critical media, and political parties was seen as buttressing the pluralistic aspect of Iran's constitution. Khatami's pursuit of a moderate foreign policy stemmed from his belief that democratic accountability at home mandated easing tensions abroad. Iran could not have undertaken a democratic enterprise with all its difficulties and dislocations while subject to international pressures, threats, and sanctions. A certain international environment had to be created in order to enable important domestic changes. In this respect, Khatami went far in pressing the reluctant conservatives to sanction his attempts to come to terms with the European community and Saudi Arabia. He changed Iran's discourse on America and even Israel. By being respectful of America's historical achievements and conceding to a peace compact that would be acceptable to the Palestinians, Khatami tackled long-held positions of the Islamic Republic. It was ultimately the fear that the reform movement would provoke a "Gorbachev phenomenon" and gradually engulf the state that led Khamenei and his allies to utilize terror and judicial manipulations to subvert a peaceful movement for change.

The election of 2005 may have eased the problems of factionalism, as Khamenei's disciples were in control of all the relevant organs of the state. However, a government more attuned to ideological inclinations and at ease with its suspicions of the West could not untangle Iran's foreign policy dilemmas. Ahmadinejad's odious rhetoric and relentless pursuit of a nuclear program in the face of international censure caused Iran's growing isolation. For a while, Iran's malfeasances were mitigated by the Bush administration, whose unilateralism and seeming disdain for the opinion of even its closest allies caused many to blame Washington for the U.S.-Iranian impasse. The more the Bush administration resisted dialogue and diplomacy, the less the Islamic Republic was blamed for its defiance. All this would change as two events in 2009 would face the conservative oligarchs with their most momentous quandaries.

In January 2009, Barack Obama became the President of the United States with the pledge of engaging Iran, directly and without preconditions. After decades of insisting on respectful treatment, the Islamic Republic suddenly confronted an American politician who called for a "new beginning." "We know that you are a great civilization, and your accomplishments have earned the respect of the United States and the world," declared Obama's New Year's message to Iran.[1] For the clerical oligarchs who relied on American animosity and inflamed rhetoric to affirm their revolutionary identity, such statements were indeed unsettling. Engagement became an even greater challenge to Iran than United States' hostility and plots. The Islamic Republic would send confusing signals, but in the end, Khamenei and his cohort seemed incapable of overseeing a transformation of U.S.-Iranian relations. Pragmatism had its limits, and dealing with the "Great Satan" and dispensing with the anti-Americanism as the core element of the Islamic Republic's values proved too much for the heirs of Khomeini.

On June 12, 2009, the Islamic Republic changed forever. A placid election featuring an array of lackluster candidates suddenly turned into an intense contest for political power. For decades, the Supreme Leader Ali Khamenei had gradually consolidated his authority by vesting control of all governing institutions to pliable young reactionaries.

Suddenly, the elders of the revolution, led by the former Prime Minister Mir Hussein Musavi, threatened to disrupt this delicate plan. Musavi campaigned on good governance and restoring Iran's place in the international community. A pointedly uncharismatic candidate who had been out of the limelight for decades suddenly captured the popular imagination. The crestfallen reformers, burdened businessmen, young idealists, women seeking equality, and even revolutionaries tired of Ahmadinejad's bombast and incompetence rallied around an improbable politician.

In an ominous break with tradition, moments after the polls closed, Iran's official organs began declaring Ahmadinejad the victor by an impressive 2:1 ratio. In a coordinated campaign, the hardliners' media outlets quickly followed suit with Keyhan and other reactionary newspapers celebrating the incumbent's landslide. The morning after the election, Khamenei hailed the vote as "divine assessment" and warned the opposition of "provocative behavior."[2] The regime must have perceived that through warnings and display of power it could overcome the crisis of a transparently contrived election. Not for the first time, the guardians of the revolution miscalculated.

The ensuing street protests led to the birth of the Green Movement. As with the reformers, the Green Movement would be a coalition of disenchanted clerics, disgruntled elders of the revolution, restive youth, disenfranchised women, and impoverished elements of the middle class. The regime would manage to regain the control of the street through brute violence against its own citizens, show trials where regime loyalists would confess to fantastic crimes, and continued repression. For its part, the Green Movement lacked a coherent ideology, modes of organization, and even identifiable leaders, as Musavi seemed more of a spectator than a leader. However, the essential link between state and society was broken during the June riots. The Islamic Republic was never a typical totalitarian state as its democratic procedures and elected institutions provided the public with a means of expressing their preferences. The fact remains that the republican pillar of the regime provided it with a veneer of legitimacy. And it was that legitimacy along with the republican dimension of the regime that evaporated.

Iran today is entering a period of prolonged transition. For now, the Islamic Republic will endure, as many illegitimate autocracies in the Middle East continue to linger. The mixture of strident nationalism, Islamism, and pragmatism that guided its foreign policy for the past three decades will remain intact. Given the alienation of the population and the fragmentation of the elite, however, the regime will not be able to manage a succession crisis. For all his faults, Khamenei is the glue that keeps the Islamic Republic together. Unlike 1989, should Khamenei pass from the scene, the system is too divided and lacks a sufficient social base to easily choose another successor. In the process of consolidating the power of the conservatives and safeguarding his preeminence, Khamenei may have ironically ensured that his republic will not survive him.

Notes

INTRODUCTION

1. Islamic Republic News Agency (IRNA) (June 1, 2008).

CHAPTER 1

1. Baqer Moin, *Khomeini: Life of the Ayatollah* (New York: St. Martin's, 1999), 199–223; Daniel Brumberg, *Reinventing Khomeini: The Struggle for Reform in Iran* (Chicago: University of Chicago Press, 2001), 98–120; Hamid Dabashi, *Theology of Discontent: The Ideological Foundation of the Islamic Revolution in Iran* (New York: New York University Press, 1993), 409–485; and *Iran: A People Interrupted* (New York: New Press, 2007), 180–190.

2. For Imam's important work see Ruhollah Khomeini, *Hukumat-i Islami* (Tehran, 1980); Hamid Algar, trans., *Islam and Revolution: Writings and Declarations of Imam Khomeini* (Berkeley: Mizan, 1981); *Kashf-i Asrar* (Tehran, 1944); *Nashq-i Ruhaniyyat dar Islam* (Qum, Iran, 1962).

3. Evrand Abrahamian, *Khomeinism* (Berkeley: University of California Press, 1993), 13–39.

4. Shahrough Akhavi, *Religion and Politics in Contemporary Iran: Clergy-state Relations in the Pahlavi Period* (Albany: State University of New York Press, 1980) 23–60; Hamid Algar, "Religious Forces in Eighteenth- and Nineteenth-century Iran," in *Cambridge History of Iran*, ed. Peter Avery, Gavin Hambly, and Charles Melville, vol. 7, *From Nadir Shah to the Islamic Republic* (New York: Cambridge University Press, 1991), 705–732.

5. Venessa Martin, "Khumaini, Knowledge, and the Political Process," *Muslim World* (January 1997): 1–16; Alexander Knysh, "Irfan Revisited: Khomeini and the Legacy of Islamic Mystical Philosophy," *Middle East Journal* (Fall 1992): 631–653; Hamid Algar, "Religious Forces in Twentieth-century Iran," in *Cambridge History of Iran*, ed. Peter Avery, Gavin

Hambly, and Charles Melville, vol. 7, *From Nadir Shah to the Islamic Republic*, 750–752 (New York: Cambridge University Press, 1991).

6. For an important assessment of Murtaza Mutahhari's views see Hamid Dabashi, *Theology of Discontent: The Ideological Foundation of the Islamic Revolution in Iran* (New York: New York University Press), 147–216; Ali Husayn Muntaziri, *Khatirati-i Ayatollah Husayn Ali Muntaziri: Bih inzimam-i kulliyah-i payvast ha* (Los Angeles, 2001).

7. A. Davani, *Ayatollah Burujirdi* (Tehran, 1993); M. T. Falsafi, *Khatirat va mubarizat-i Hujjat al-Islam Falsafi* (Tehran, 1997), 99–120; M. Rezavi, *Hashimi va Inqilab* (Tehran, 1997), 94–100; Venessa Martin, *Creating an Islamic State: Khomeini and the Making of a New Iran* (London: Tauris, 2000), 48–69; Farhang Rajaee, *Islamism and Modernism: The Changing Discourse in Iran* (Austin: University of Texas, 2007), 68–74.

8. Ruhollah Khomeini, *Kashf al-Asrar* (Tehran, 1942), 32.

9. Rajaee, *Islamism and Modernism*, 66.

10. Algar, "Religious Forces in Twentieth-century Iran," 743–750.

11. Moin, *Khomeini*, 66.

12. For the 1964 crisis see Ervand Abrahamian, *Iran Between Two Revolutions* (Princeton, N.J.: Princeton University Press, 1982), 473–495; Hamid Algar, "Imam Khomeini, 1902–1962," in *Islam, Politics, and Social Movements*, ed. Edmund Burk and Ira Lapidus, 263–288 (Berkeley: University of California Press, 1988); also Hamid Algar, "The Oppositional Role of the Ulama in Twentieth-century Iran," in *Scholars, Saints, and Suffis: Muslim Institutions in the Middle East since 1500*, ed. Nikkie Keddie, 231–255 (Berkeley: University of California Press, 1972); Ihsan Tabari, "The Role of Clergy in Modern Iranian Politics," in *Religion and Politics in Iran: Shiism from Quietism to Revolution*, ed. Nikkie Keddie, 47–72 (New Haven, Conn.: Yale University Press, 1983).

13. Shaul Bakhash, *The Reign of the Ayatollahs: Iran and the Islamic Revolution* (New York: Basic Books, 1984), 34.

14. Fahmi Huwaydi, *Iran Min al-Dakhil* (Cairo: Al-Ahram Center, 1988), 113.

15. Ali Shari'ati, *Islamshinasi* (Collected Works, nos. 16–18) (Tehran, 1981); also *Jahat-giri-i tabaqati-i Islam* (Tehran, 1980); *Khvudsazi-i inqilabi* (Tehran, 1977). For important works on Shari'ati see Ali Rahnema, *An Islamic Utopian: A Political Biography of Ali Shariati* (London: Tauris, 1998); Hamid Dabashi, "Ali Shariati's Islam: Revolutionary Uses of Faith in Post-traditional Society," *Islamic Quarterly* 28(4) (1983); Mansoor Moaddel, *Class, Politics, and Ideology in the Iranian Revolution* (New York: Columbia University Press, 1993), 130–154; Brad Hanson, "The Westoxication of Iran: Depictions and Reactions of Behrangi, Al-E Ahmad, and Shariati," *International Journal of Middle Eastern Studies* (February 1983).

16. Jalal Al-e Ahmad, *Gharbzadegi* (Lexington, Ky.: Mazda, 1982); Mehrzad Boroujerdi, *Iranian Intellectuals and the West: The Tormented Triumph of Nativism* (Syracuse, N.Y.: Syracuse University Press, 1996), 52–65; Ali Mirsepassi, *Intellectual Discourse and the Politics of Modernization* (New York: Cambridge University Press, 2000), 96–127; Sepehr Zabih, *The Left in Contemporary Iran* (London: Croom Helm, 1986), 113–157; Afsaneh Najmabqdi, "Iran's Turn to Islam: From Modernism to a Moral Order," *Middle East Journal* (Spring 1987): 202–217; Maziar Behrooz, *Rebels with a Cause* (London: Tauris, 1999), 3–47; Ervand Abrahamian, *Radical Islam: The Iranian Mojahedin* (New Haven, Conn.: Yale University

Press, 1989), 81–105; Farzin Vahdat, "Post-revolutionary Discourses of Muhammad Mojtahed Shehbestari and Mohsen Kadivar: Reconciling the Terms of Mediated Subjectivity," parts I and II, *Critique: Critical Middle Eastern Studies* (Spring/Fall 2000); Arshin Abid-Moghaddam, *Iran in World Politics: The Quest for the Islamic Republic* (New York: Columbia University Press, 2008), 44–54.

17. Michael Fischer, *Iran: From Religious Dispute to Revolution* (Cambridge, Mass.: Harvard University Press, 1980), 61–104; Said Arjomand, "Shiite Islam and the Revolution in Iran," *Government and Opposition* (Summer 1981); also, "The Ulama's Traditional Opposition to Parliamentarianism, 1907–1909," *Middle Eastern Studies* (April 1981); Hamid Dabashi, "The End of Islamic Ideology," *Social Research* (Summer 2000).

18. R. Hrair Dekmeijian, *Islam in Revolution* (Syracuse, N.Y.: Syracuse University Press, 1985), 131–135.

19. Khomeini, *Hukumat-i Islami.*

20. Roy Mottahedeh, *The Mantle of the Prophet: Religion and Politics in Iran* (New York: Simon and Schuster, 1985); Shahrough Akhavi, *Religion and Politics in Contemporary Iran: Clergy-state Relations in Pahlavi Era* (Albany: State University of New York Press, 1980), 91–117; Hamid Dabashi, "Shiite Islam: The Theology of Discontent," *Contemporary Sociology* (March 1986): 178–181; David Menshari, "Shiite Leadership in the Shadow of Conflicting Ideologies," *Iranian Studies* (1980): 119–145; James Bill, "Power and Religion in Contemporary Iran," *Middle East Journal* (Winter 1982).

21. Marvin Zonis and Daniel Brumberg, "Shi'ism as Interpreted by Khomeini: An Ideology of Revolutionary Violence," in *Shi'ism, Resistance, and Revolution,* ed. Martin Kramer, 47–66 (Boulder, Colo.: Westview, 1987); Hossein Seifzadeh, "Ayatollah Khomeini's Concept of Rightful Government: The Velayat-e Faqih," in *Islam, Muslims, and the Modern State,* ed. Hussein Mutalib and Taj ul-Islam Hashmi (London: Macmillan, 1998); Said Amir Arjomand, "Ideological Revolution in Shi'ism," in *Authority and Political Culture in Shiism,* ed. Said Amir Arjomand (Albany: State University of New York, 1988), 178–210.

22. H. E. Chehabi, "Religion and Politics in Iran: How Theocratic Is the Islamic Republic?" *Daedalus* (Summer 1991): 72–74.

23. For an important study on Khomeini's theological ideas see Abdulaziz Sachedina, *The Just Ruler (al-sultan al-'adil) in Shi'ite Islam: The Comprehensive Authority of the Jurist in Imamite Jurisprudence* (New York: Oxford University Press), 119–232.

24. Hamid Algar, "Ayatollah Khomeini: The Years of Struggle and Exile, 1962–1978," June 3, 2007 (www.Baztab.com).

25. Quoted in Nikki R. Keddie and R. I. Cole, eds., *Shi'ism and Social Protest* (New Haven, Conn.: Yale University Press, 1986), 8.

26. Ruhollah Khomeini, *Siyasat-i Khariji va ravabit-i bayn al-milal az didgah-i Imam Khomeini* (Tehran, 1987), 44.

27. Maridi Nahas, "State-system and Revolutionary Challenge: Nasser, Khomeini, and the Middle East," *International Journal of Middle Eastern Studies* (November 1985): 507–527.

28. Ruhollah Khomeini, *Sahifah-i nur: majmu'ah-i rahnumudha-yi Imam Khomeini* (Tehran, 1982), vol. 1, 19.

29. *New York Times* (June 4, 1989).

30. For important studies on the Mossadeq period see Mark J. Gasiorowski and Malcolm Byrne, eds., *Mohammad Mossadeq and the 1953 Coup in Iran* (Syracuse, N.Y.: Syracuse University Press, 2004); Homa Katouzian, *Musaddiq and the Struggle for Power in Iran* (London: Tauris, 1990); Stephen Kinzer, *All the Shah's Men: An American Coup and the Roots of Middle East Terror* (Hoboken, N.J.: John Wiley and Sons, 2003).

31. Khomeini, *Sahifah-yi Nur* (Tehran: Islamic Republic's Documentation Center, 1982), vol. 1, 139.

32. Ibid., 136.

33. Nikki R. Keddie, *An Islamic Response to Imperialism: Political and Religious Writings of Sayyid Jamal ad-Din al-Afghani* (Berkeley: University of California Press, 1983); Emmanuel Sivan, *Radical Islam: Medieval Theology and Modern Politics* (New Haven, Conn.: Yale University Press, 1985), 50–83; Johannes Jansen, *The Dual Nature of Islamic Fundamentalism* (Ithaca, N.Y.: Cornell University Press, 1997), 26–49.

34. Richard P. Mitchell, *The Society of the Muslim Brothers* (London: Oxford University Press, 1969), 160–272.

35. Algar, trans., *Islam and Revolution,* 35.

36. Adeed Dawisha, *Arab Nationalism in the Twentieth Century: From Triumph to Despair* (Princeton, N.J.: Princeton University Press, 2003), 252–315; Mansoor Moaddel, *Islamic Modernism, Nationalism, and Fundamentalism: Episode and Discourse* (Chicago: University of Chicago Press, 2005), 195–320.

37. Among the most important studies on Iran's revolution are Charles Kurzman, *The Unthinkable Revolution in Iran* (Cambridge, Mass.: Harvard University Press, 2004); Marvin Zonis, *Majestic Failure: The Fall of the Shah* (Chicago: University of Chicago Press, 1991); and Nikki R. Keddie, *The Roots of Revolution: An Interpretive History of Modern Iran* (New Haven, Conn.: Yale University Press, 1981), 142–183.

38. Abrahamian, *Radical Islam,* 186–224.

39. Seyed Mohammad Ali Taghavi, "Fedaeeyan-i Islam: The Prototype of Islamic Hardliners in Iran," *Middle Eastern Studies* (January 2004): 151–165.

40. James Bill, "Power and Religion in Revolutionary Iran," *Middle East Journal* (Winter 1982): 22–47; Farideh Farhi, "Ideology and Revolution in Iran," *Journal of Developing Societies* 6 (January/February 1990): 98–112; Ahmad Ashraf, "Bazaar and Mosque in Iran's Revolution," MERIP Reports 113, *Iran since the Revolution* (March/April 1983): 16–18; Robert Dix, "The Varieties of Revolution," *Comparative Politics* (April 1983): 281–294.

41. Haggy Ram, "Crushing the Opposition: Adversaries of the Islamic Republic," *Middle East Journal* (Summer 1992): 426–439; Gregory Rose, "The Post-revolutionary Purge of Iran's Armed Forces: A Revisionist Assessment," *Iranian Studies* (Spring/Summer 1984): 153–194; Richard Cottam, "Inside Revolutionary Iran," *Middle East Journal* (Spring 1989): 168–185.

42. Mehdi Bazargan, *Shoray-e enqelab va dowlat-e movaqat* (Tehran, 1982), 27.

43. Shaul Bakhash, *Reign of the Ayatollahs,* 55.

44. Riza Hassan, "Iran's Islamic Revolutionaries before and after the Revolution," *Third World Quarterly* (July 1984): 675–686; Eric Rouleau, "Khomeini's Iran," *Foreign Affairs* (Fall 1980): 6–12.

45. *New York Times* (Oct. 21, 1979).

46. Eliz Sanasarian, "Ayatollah Khomeini and the Institutionalization of Charismatic Rule in Iran, 1979–1989," *Journal of Developing Studies* (1995): 189–194.

47. Behzad Yaghmaian, *Social Change in Iran: An Eyewitness Account of Dissent, Defiance, and New Movements for Rights* (Albany: State University of New York, 2002), 208–210.

48. A. William Samii, "Iran's Guardian Council as an Obstacle to Democracy," *Middle East Journal* (Autumn 2001): 644–646.

49. Said Amir Arjomand, "The State and Khomeini's Islamic Order," *Iranian Studies* 13 (1980): 155.

50. Fred Halliday, "The Iranian Revolution and Great Power Politics: Components of the First Decade," in *Neither East nor West: Iran, the Soviet Union, and the United States,* ed. Nikki R. Keddie and Mark Gasiorowski, 250–256 (New Haven, Conn.: Yale University Press, 1990).

51. R. K. Ramazani, "Khumayni's Islam in Iran's Foreign Policy," in *Islam in Foreign Policy,* ed. Adeed Dawisha, 9–32 (New York: Cambridge University Press, 1983); Nikki R. Keddie, "Iranian Imbroglios: Who's Irrational?" *World Policy Journal* (Winter 1987–1988): 29–54.

52. *Kayhan* (Mar. 21, 1980).

53. Miron Rezun, "The Pariah Syndrome: The Complexity of the Iranian Predicament," in *Iran at the Crossroads* (Boulder, Colo.: Westview, 1990), 76.

54. *Jomhuri-ye Islami* (Oct. 21, 1980).

55. Husayn Ali Muntaziri, *Khatirat-i Ayatollah Husayn Ali Muntaziri* (Tehran, 2001), 244.

56. Farhad Kazemi and Jo-Anne Hart, "The Shi'i Praxis: Domestic Politics and Foreign Policy in Iran," in *The Iranian Revolution and the Muslim World,* ed. David Menashri, 58–63 (Boulder, Colo.: Westview, 1990).

57. Suzanne Maloney, "Politics, Patronage, and Social Justice: Parastatal Foundations and Post-revolutionary Iran," PhD diss., Fletcher School of Law and Diplomacy, Tufts University, 2000.

58. For the relationship between revolutions and external conflicts see Stephen Walt, "Revolution and War," *World Politics* (April 1992): 321–368; Theda Skocpol, "Special Revolutions and Mass Military Mobilization," *World Politics* (January 1988): 147–168.

59. Asghar Schirazi, *The Constitution of Iran: Politics and the State in the Islamic Republic,* trans. John O'Kane, 8–161 (London: Tauris, 1997); Ali Ghessari and Vali Nasr, *Democracy in Iran: History and the Quest for Liberty* (New York: Oxford University Press, 2006), 77–98.

60. Ervand Abrahamian, *A History of Modern Iran* (New York: Cambridge University Press, 2008), 165.

61. Shireen Hunter, "Iran and the Spread of Revolutionary Islam," *Third World Quarterly* (April 1988): 736.

62. Hamid Algar, trans., *Constitution of the Islamic Republic of Iran* (Berkeley: Mizan, 1980), 19.

63. *New York Times* (Nov. 21, 1980); "An Interview with Muhammad Musavi-Khu'iniha," www.emrouz.com, Oct. 31, 2005.

64. Khatarat-e Ayatollah Mahdavi Kani (Tehran: Markaze-Esnad Enqelab-e Islami, 2007), 283–284.

65. Ibid., 282.

66. Hashemi Rafsanjani, *Khutbaha-ye Jum'eh* (Tehran: 1982), 167.

67. Said Amir Arjomand, *The Turban for the Crown: The Islamic Revolution in Iran* (New York: Oxford University Press, 1988), 146.

68. Shahrough Akhavi, "The Ideology and Praxis of Shi'ism in the Iranian Revolution," *Comparative Study of Society and History* (January 1983): 216–217.

69. *Kayhan* (Oct. 23, 1979).

70. Mohsen Milani, "The Transformation of the Velayat-e Faqih Institution: From Khomeini to Khamenei," *Muslim World* (October 1992): 178.

71. Ibid.

72. Ali Akbar Natiq-Nuri, *Khaterat,* vol. 2 (Tehran, 2005), 52.

73. Kasra Naji, *Ahmadinejad: The Secret History of Iran's Radical Leader* (London: Tauris, 2008), 27.

74. Maziar Behrooz, "Factionalism in Iran under Khomeini," *Middle Eastern Studies* (October 1991): 597–614; Shahrough Akhavi, "Elite Factionalism in the Islamic Republic," *Middle East Journal* (Spring 1987): 181–201.

75. Muhammad Reyshari, *Khaterat: Tasis vezaret-e Etelaat,* vol. 3 (Tehran, 2006), 84.

76. Ibid.

77. H. E. Chehabi, "The Political Regime of the Islamic Republic of Iran in Comparative Prospective," *Government and Opposition* (Winter 2001): 48–70.

CHAPTER 2

1. Homa Katouzian, "Problems of Political Development in Iran: Democracy, Dictatorship, or Arbitrary Government?" *British Journal of Middle Eastern Studies* (1995): 12–19.

2. Mohsen Milani, *The Making of Iran's Islamic Revolution: From Monarchy to Islamic Republic* (Boulder, Colo.: Westview, 1988), 172–173.

3. For a documentary record of Bihishti's meeting with U.S. officials, see http://www.tabnak.ir, Apr. 23, 2008.

4. James Bill, *The Eagle and the Lion: The Tragedy of American-Iranian Relations* (New Haven, Conn.: Yale University Press, 1988), 283–284.

5. Sadiq Khalkhali, *Az ayyam-i talabagi i ta dawran-i hakim-i shar'-i dadgahha-yi Inqilab-i Islami/nivishtah-i Sadiq Khalkhali* (Tehran, 2001), 314–352.

6. Husayn Ali Muntaziri, *Khatirat-i Ayatollah Husayn Ali Muntaziri: Bih inzimam-i kulliyah-i payvast ha* (Los Angeles, 2001), 218.

7. Zbigniew Brzezinski, *Power and Principle: Memoirs of a National Security Advisor, 1977–1981* (New York: Farrar, Straus, Giroux, 1985), 475–476.

8. Kenneth Pollack, *The Persian Puzzle: The Conflict between Iran and America* (New York: Random House, 2004), 154.

9. Hashemi Rafsanjani, *Engelab va Pirouzi* (Tehran, 2004), 370.

10. Babak Ganji, *The Politics of Confrontation: The Foreign Policy of the USA and Revolutionary Iran* (London: Tauris, 2006), 133.

11. Massoumeh Ebtekar, *Takeover in Tehran: The Inside Story of the 1979 U.S. Embassy Capture* (Vancouver: Talonbooks, 2001), 50.

12. Muhammad Reza Mahdavi-Kani, *Khatirat-i Ayatollah Mahdavi-Khani* (Tehran, 2007), 219.

13. Iransamanehm, Nov. 5, 2007, http://www.asrrian.com.

14. Ali Akbar Hashemi Rafsanjani, *Inqilab va piruzi: karnamah va khatirat-i sallah-yi 1357 va 1358* (Tehran, 1983), 373.

15. Hamid Ansari, *Muhajir-i qabilah-i Imam: nigahi bih zindaginamah-i yadgar-i Imam Hazrat Hujjat al-Islam va al-Muslimin Hajj Sayyid Ahmad Khomeini* (Tehran, 1996), 154–155.

16. Yahya Rahim Safavi, *Az janub-i Lubnan ta janub-i Iran: Khatirat-i sadar sar lashkar duktur Sayyid Yahya Rahim Safavi* (Tehran, 2006), 134.

17. For new studies on the hostage crisis see Mark Bowden, *Guests of the Ayatollah: The First Battle in America's War with Militant Islam* (New York: Atlantic Monthly Press, 2006); David Harris, *The Crisis: The President, the Prophet, and the Shah—1979 and the Coming of Militant Islam* (Boston: Little, Brown, 2004); David Farber, *Taken Hostage: The Iran Hostage Crisis and America's First Encounter with Radical Islam* (Princeton, N.J.: Princeton University Press, 2005).

18. Warren Christopher, ed., *American Hostages in Iran: The Conduct of a Crisis* (New Haven, Conn.: Yale University Press, 1985), 72–144; Jimmy Carter, *Keeping the Faith: Memoirs of a President* (Fayetteville: University of Arkansas Press, 1995), 462–490; Barry Rubin, *Paved with Good Intentions: The American Experience and Iran* (New York: Oxford University Press, 1981), 311–313.

19. *Kayhan* (Nov. 8, 1980).

20. Rafsanjani, *Inqilab va piruzi*, 373.

21. Dilip Hiro, *Iran under the Ayatollahs* (London: Routledge and Kegan Paul, 1985), 139.

22. Said Amir Arjomand, *The Turban for the Crown: The Islamic Revolution in Iran* (New York: Oxford University Press, 1988), 130.

23. *Ettela'at* (Apr. 8, 1980).

24. Paul Ryan, *The Iranian Rescue Mission: Why It Failed* (Annapolis: Naval Institute Press, 1985); Pollack, *Persian Puzzle*, 167–170; Zbigniew Brzezinski, "The Failed Mission: The Inside Account of the Attempt to Free the Hostages in Iran," *New York Times Magazine* (Apr. 18, 1982); also Brzezinski, *Power and Principle*, 487–500; Rubin, *Paved with Good Intentions*, 301–304.

25. Faber, *Taken Hostage*, 62.

26. Shaul Bakhash, *The Reign of the Ayatollahs: Iran and the Islamic Revolution* (New York: Basic Books, 1990), 149.

27. Http://www.farsnews.com (July 3, 2007).

28. *Kayhan* (Apr. 3, 1985).

29. Trita Parsi, *Treacherous Alliance: The Secret Dealings of Israel, Iran, and the United States* (New Haven, Conn.: Yale University Press, 2007), 110–125.

30. Samuel Segev, *The Iranian Triangle: The Untold Story of Israel's Role in the Iran-Contra Affair* (New York: Free Press, 1988); Trita Parsi, "Israeli-Iranian Relations Assessed: Strategic Competition from the Power Cycle Perspective," *Iranian Studies* (June 2005): 247–269.

31. James Bill, "U.S. Overture toward Iran, 1986–1986: An Analysis," and Eric Hooglund, "The Policy of the Reagan Administration toward Iran," in *Neither East nor West: Iran, the Soviet Union, and the United States,* ed. Nikki R. Keddie and Mark Gasiorowski (New Haven, Conn.: Yale University Press, 1990): 180–200.

32. Robin Wright, *In the Name of God: The Khomeini Decade* (New York: Simon and Schuster, 1989), 132.

33. For various perspectives see Robert McFarlane, with Zofia Smardz, *Special Trust* (New York: Cadell and Davies, 1994); George Schultz, *Turmoil and Triumph: My Years as Secretary of State* (New York: Maxwell Macmillan International, 1993); Robert Gates, *From the Shadows: The Ultimate Insider's Story of Five Presidents and How They Won the Cold War* (New York: Simon and Schuster, 1996); Peter Kornbluh and Malcolm Byrne, *The Iran-Contra Scandal: The Declassified History* (New York: New Press, 1993); U.S. Congress, House of Representatives Select Committee to Investigate Covert Arms Transactions with Iran and Senate Select Committee on Secret Military Assistance to Iran and Nicaraguan Opposition, *Report of the Congressional Views* (Washington, D.C., 1987).

34. John Tower, Edmund Muskie, and Brent Scowcroft, *The Tower Commission Report* (New York: Times Books, 1987), 27.

35. Bob Woodward, *Veil: The Secret Wars of the CIA, 1981–1987* (New York: Simon and Schuster, 1987), 433.

36. Pollack, *Persian Puzzle,* 231.

37. Peter Kornbluh, "The Iran-Contra Scandal: A Postmortem," *World Policy Journal* (Summer 1987); Cheryl A. Rubenberg, "U.S. Policy toward Nicaragua and Iran and the Iran-Contra Affair: Reflections on the Continuity of American Foreign Policy," *Third World Quarterly* (October 1988): 1467–1504.

38. U.S. Congress, House of Representatives and Senate Select Committee to Investigate Covert Arms Transactions with Iran, *Report of the Congressional Committee Investigating the Iran-Contra Affair* (Washington, D.C., 1987), 280.

39. *Kayhan* (Nov. 14, 1986).

40. Ibid. (Nov. 13, 1986).

41. Ibid. (Nov. 4, 1986).

42. Baqer Moin, *Khomeini: Life of an Ayatollah* (New York: Tauris, 1999), 264–265.

43. R. K. Ramazani, "Iran and the United States: 'Islamic Realism'?" in *The Middle East from the Iran-Contra Affair to the Intifada,* ed. Robert O. Freedman, 169 (Syracuse, N.Y.: Syracuse University Press, 1991).

44. *Kayhan* (Nov. 26, 1986).

45. Ibid. (Nov. 28, 1986).

46. Ali Ansari, *Confronting Iran: The Failure of American Foreign Policy and the Next Great Crisis in the Middle East* (New York: Basic Books, 2006), 112–115; Wright, *In the Name of God,* 190–192.

47. Quoted in Wright, *In the Name of God,* 187.

48. Gary Sick, "Slouching toward Settlement: The Internationalization of the Iran-Iraq War, 1987–1988," 219–246, in Keddie and Gasiorowski, eds., *Neither East nor West.*

49. Ervand Abrahamian, *Tortured Confessions: Prisons and Public Recantations in Modern Iran* (Berkeley: University of California Press, 1999), 124–129; Amnesty International, *Iran, Violations of Human Rights* (London: Amnesty Press, 1991), 12.

50. Miron Rezun, "The Internal Struggle, the Rushdie Affair, and the Prospects for the Future," in *Iran at the Crossroads: Global Relations in a Turbulent Decade,* ed. Miron Rezon (Boulder, Colo.: Westview, 1990), 207.

51. *Newsweek* (Mar. 6, 1989).

52. Ibid.

53. *Kayhan* (Nov. 11, 1989).

54. Shahram Chubin and Charles Tripp, *Iran and Iraq at War* (Boulder, Colo.: Westview, 1991), 131.

CHAPTER 3

1. *Asnad-i inqilab-i Islami* (Tehran, 1995), 166–212.

2. A representative sample of Khomeini's views on Israel and Jews can be found in *Filastin va Sahunism* (Tehran, 1984); *Azadi-yi Aqaliyat-ha Mahzabi* (Tehran, 1984–1985); *Filastin az didgah-i Imam Khomeini* (Tehran, 1997), 13.

3. *The Imam versus Zionism* (Tehran: Ministry of Guidance, 1984), 21.

4. Ibid., 25.

5. Behrouz Souresrafil, *Khomeini and Israel* (London: Researchers, 1988), 24.

6. Shaul Bakhash, "Iran's Relations with Israel, Syria, and Lebanon," in *Iran at the Crossroads: Global Relations in a Turbulent Decade,* ed. Miron Rezun, 118–120 (Boulder, Colo.: Westview, 1990).

7. Ruhollah Khomeini, *Hukumat-e Islami* (Tehran, 1980), 7.

8. Ibid., 121.

9. *Kayhan* (Feb. 11, 1979).

10. Ibid. (June 23, 1982).

11. Ali Akbar Hashemi Rafsanjani, *Isra'il va Quds-i Aziz* (Qum, 1984), 45.

12. Ali Akbar Vilayiti, *Iran va mas'alah-i Filastin: Bar asas-i asnad-i Vizarat-i Umar-i Kharijah* (Tehran, 1997), 13.

13. David Menashri, *Post-revolutionary Politics in Iran: Religion, Society, and Power* (London: Cass, 2001), 267.

14. *Sharq* (Aug. 2, 2007).

15. *Washington Post* (Feb. 19, 1979).

16. *Kayhan* (Feb. 18, 1979).

17. Ibid. (Feb. 19, 1979).

18. Nader Entessar, "Israel and Iran's National Security," *Journal of South Asian and Middle Eastern Studies* (Summer 2004): 5–6.

19. *Kayhan* (Nov. 23, 1980).

20. Ibid. (June 20, 1983).

21. Http://www.tabank.com (Aug. 13, 2008).

22. Sohrab Sobhani, *The Pragmatic Entente: Israeli-Iranian Relations, 1948–1980* (New York: Praeger, 1989), 148.

23. Trita Parsi, *Treacherous Alliance: The Secret Dealings of Israel, Iran, and the United States* (New Haven, Conn.: Yale University Press, 2007), 106.

24. Souresrafil, *Khomeini and Israel*, 72.

25. Sobhani, *Pragmatic Entente*, 149.

26. *International Herald Tribune* (May 29, 1982).

27. Ari Bar-Menashe, *Profits of War: Inside the Secret U.S.-Israeli Arms Network* (New York: Sheridan Square, 1992), 201.

28. Itamar Robinovich, *The War for Lebanon, 1970–1985* (Ithaca, N.Y.: Cornell University Press, 1985), 120–135.

29. Shimon Shapira, "The Origins of Hizballah," *Jerusalem Quarterly* (Spring 1988): 115–130; Martin Kramer, "The Moral Logic of Hizballah," in *Origins of Terrorism: Psychologies, Ideologies, Theories, States of Mind*, ed. Walter Reich (New York: Cambridge University Press, 1990), 131–160; Martin Kramer, "Hizbullah: The Calculus of Jihad," in *Fundamentalism and the State: Remaking Polities, Economies, and Militance*, ed. Martin Marty and R. Scott Appleby (Chicago: University of Chicago Press, 1996); Meir Hatina, *Islam and Salvation in Palestine* (Tel Aviv: Moshe Dayan Center for Middle Eastern and African Studies, 2001), 107–117; Daniel Byman, *Deadly Connections: States that Sponsor Terrorism* (New York: Cambridge University Press, 2005), 79–117; R. K. Ramazani, *Revolutionary Iran: Challenge and Response in the Middle East* (Baltimore: Johns Hopkins University Press, 1986), 175–194.

30. Selim Nasr, "Roots of the Shi'i Movement," MERIP Reports (June 1985), 10–16; Augustus Richard Norton, "The Origins and Resurgence of Amal," and Joseph Olmert, "The Shi'is and the Lebanese State," in *Shiism, Resistance, and Revolution*, ed. Martin Kramer (Boulder, Colo.: Westview, 1987).

31. Fouad Ajami, *The Vanished Imam: Musa Sadr and the Shia of Lebanon* (Ithaca, N.Y.: Cornell University Press, 1992); Yitzak Nakash, *Reaching for Power: The Shi'a in the Modern World* (Princeton, N.J.: Princeton University Press, 2006), 113–128; Yann Richard, *Shi'ite Islam: Polity, Ideology, and Creed* (Cambridge, Mass.: Blackwell, 1995), 121–139.

32. For the most incisive account of Iran's historic involvement in Lebanon see H. E. Chehabi, *Distant Relations: Iran and Lebanon in the Last 500 Years* (London: Tauris, 2006), particularly 201–231; Mahmud Faksh, "The Shi'a Community of Lebanon: A New Assertive Political Force," *Journal of South Asian and Middle Eastern Studies* (Spring 1991): 33–56.

33. Ali Akbar Muhtashami'pur, *Khatirati-i siyasi*, vol. 2 (Tehran, 2000), 79–120; Mustafa Chamran, *Lubnan: Guzidah'i az majmu'ah-i sukhanrani'ha va-dast nivishtah-ha-yi sadar-i pur-iftikhar-i Islam Shahid Duktur Mustafa Chamran dar barah-i Lubnan* (Tehran, 1985).

34. *Kayhan* (June 2, 1982).

35. Ibid. (June 1, 1982).

36. *Washington Post* (June 9, 1989).

37. Abbas William Samii, "A Stable Structure on Shifting Sands: Assessing the Hizbullah-Iran-Syria Relationship," *Middle East Journal* (Winter 2008): 35.

38. Ibid.

39. Judith Harik, "Hizballah's Public and Social Services and Iran," in Chehabi, *Distant Relations,* 259–289; Haleh Vaziri, "Iran's Involvement in Lebanon: Polarization and Radicalization of Militant Islamic Movements," *Journal of South Asian and Middle Eastern Studies* (Winter 1992).

40. Asad Abukhalil, "Syria and the Shiites: Al-Asad's Policy in Lebanon," *Third World Quarterly* (April 1990); Augustus Richard Norton, *Amal and the Shi'a: Struggle for the Soul of Lebanon* (Austin: University of Texas Press, 1987), 41–55.

41. Augustus Richard Norton, *Hezbollah: A Short History* (Princeton, N.J.: Princeton University Press, 2007), 36.

42. Marius Deeb, "Shia Movements in Lebanon: Their Formation, Ideology, Social Basis, and Links with Iran and Syria," *Third World Quarterly* (April 1988): 683–698; As'ad Abukhalil, "Ideology and Practice of Hizballah in Lebanon: Islamization of Leninist Organizational Principles," *Middle Eastern Studies* (July 1991): 390–403.

43. Norton, *Hezbollah,* 38.

44. Ibid., 30.

45. Ramazani, *Revolutionary Iran,* 185.

46. Ibid., 190.

47. *Middle East Insight* (June 1987): 5–17.

48. Anoushiravan Ehteshami and Raymond Hinnebusch, *Syria and Iran: Middle Powers in a Penetrated Regional System* (London: Routledge, 1997), 57–116; Hussein Agha and Ahmad Khalidi, *Syria and Iran: Rivalry and Cooperation* (London: Printer, 1995), 1–9.

49. Shireen Hunter, "Iran and Syria: From Hostility to Limited Alliance," in *Iran and the Arab World,* ed. Hooshang Amirahmadi and Nader Entessar, 208–210 (New York: St. Martin's, 1993); Ehteshami and Hinnebusch, *Syria and Iran,* 27–57, 87–116.

50. Ehteshami and Hinnebusch, *Syria and Iran,* 97.

51. Agha and Khalidi, *Syria and Iran,* 10–14; Elie Chalala, "Syria's Support of Iran in the Gulf War: The Role of Structural Change and the Emergence of a Relatively Strong State," *Journal of Arab Affairs* (October 1988).

52. *Ettela'at* (Sept. 27, 1990).

53. Joseph Olmert, "Iranian-Syrian Relations: Between Islam and Realpolitik," in *The Iranian Revolution and the Muslim World,* ed. David Menashri, 177 (Boulder, Colo.: Westview, 1990).

54. Hashemi Rafsanjani, *Karnamah va khatirat-i 1361: Pas az buhran* (Tehran, 2001), 159.

55. Christin Marschall, "Syria-Iran: A Strategic Alliance, 1979–1991," *Orient* (March 1992): 438–441; Robin Wright, *In the Name of God: The Khomeini Decade* (New York: Simon and Schuster, 1989), 108–130.

56. Fadia Nasrallah, "Factors behind the Amal-Hezbollah War," *Middle East International* (March 1990); Olmert, "Shi'is and the Lebanese State."

CHAPTER 4

1. Ali Husayn Muntaziri, *Matn-i Kamil-i khatirati-i Ayatollah Husayn Ali Muntaziri: bih hamrah-i pay vast'ha* (Spånga, Sweden, 2001), 244.

2. Amazia Baram, "The Impact of Khomeini's Revolution on the Radical Shi'i Movement of Iraq," in *The Iranian Revolution and the Muslim World,* ed. David Menashri, 142 (Boulder, Colo.: Westview, 1990).

3. F. Gregory Gause III, "Iraq's Decisions to Go to War, 1980 and 1990," *Middle East Journal* (Winter 2002): 65.

4. Shahram Chubin and Charles Tripp, *Iran and Iraq at War* (Boulder, Colo.: Westview, 1988), 53–68; Gause, "Iraq's Decisions to Go to War," 63–69; Eric Davis, *Memories of State: Politics, History, and Collective Identity in Modern Iraq* (Berkeley: University of California Press, 2005).

5. Efraim Karsh, "Geopolitical Determinism: The Origins of the Iran-Iraq War," *Middle East Journal* (Spring 1990): 265–267; Mohssen Massarrat, "The Ideological Context of the Iran-Iraq War: Pan-Islamism versus Pan-Arabism," in *Iran and the Arab World,* ed. Hoochang Amirahmadi and Nader Entessar (New York: St. Martin's, 1993), 28–41.

6. For important accounts of Saddam see Marion Farouk-Sluglett and Peter Sluglett, *Iraq since 1958: From Revolution to Dictatorship* (London: Tauris, 1990), 255–269; Phebe Marr, *The Modern History of Iraq* (Boulder, Colo.: Westview, 1985); Charles Tripp, *A History of Iraq* (New York: Cambridge University Press, 2000), 193–275; Kannan Makiya, *Republic of Fear: The Politics of Modern Iraq* (Berkeley: University of California Press, 1989).

7. Marr, *Modern History of Iraq,* 67.

8. Ibid.

9. Majid Khadduri, *The Gulf War: The Origins and Implications of the Iran-Iraq Conflict* (New York: Oxford University Press, 1988), 80–81.

10. R. K. Ramazani, *Revolutionary Iran: Challenge and Response in the Middle East* (Baltimore: Johns Hopkins University Press, 1986), 61.

11. Ralph King, *The United Nations and the Iran-Iraq War* (New York: Ford Foundation, 1987), 15–17.

12. Chubin and Tripp, *Iran and Iraq at War,* 38.

13. Islamic Republic News Agency (IRNA) (Oct. 20, 1980).

14. *Jumhuri-i Islami* (Nov. 25, 1981).

15. Saskia Gieling, *Religion and War in Revolutionary Iran* (London: Tauris, 1999), 149.

16. *Jumhuri-i Islami* (Sept. 30, 1980).

17. *Ittila'at* (Sept. 27, 1980).

18. Sayyad Ali Shirazi, *Khatirat-i salha-yi nabard: Khatirat-i shahid' Ali Sayyad Shirazi/ intikhab va sadah-nivisi-i Mohsen Mumini* (Tehran, 2009), 209.

19. *Le Monde* (Jan. 1, 1981).

20. *Kayhan* (Jan. 7, 1985).

21. James Bill, "Morale and Technology: The Power of Iran in the Persian Gulf War," and Hamid Algar, "The Problem of Retaliation in Modern Warfare from the Perspective of Fiqh," in *The Iran-Iraq War: The Politics of Aggression,* ed. Farhang Rajaee (Gainesville:

University of Florida Press, 1993); Claudia Wright, "Religion and Strategy in the Iran-Iraq War," *Third World Quarterly* (October 1985): 839–852.

22. Khadduri, *Gulf War*, 95.

23. John Parott, "The Response of Saudi Arabia to the Iran-Iraq War," *Journal of South Asian and Middle Eastern Studies* (Winter 1986); James Bill, "The Arab World and the Challenge of Iran," *Journal of Arab Affairs* (October 1982); Itamar Rabinovich, "The Impact on the Arab World," and Barry Rubin, "The Gulf States and the Iran-Iraq War," both in *The Iran-Iraq War: Impact and Implications,* ed. Efraim Karsh (New York: St. Martin's, 1989); Saideh Lotfian, "Taking Sides: Regional Powers and War," in *Iranian Perspectives on the Iran-Iraq War,* ed. Farhang Rajaee (Gainesville: University of Florida Press, 1997).

24. The principal propagator of this view was Ahmad Khomeini, who years after the war suggested that his father was prepared to end the conflict in 1982.

25. Http://www.aftabnews.ir/ (July 7, 2008).

26. Hashemi Rafsanjani, *Karnamah va khatirat-i 1361: Pas az buhran* (Tehran, 2001), 43, 75.

27. *Kayhan* (June 12, 1982).

28. Ali Khamenei, *Dar maktab-i jum'ah: Majmu'ah-i khutbah'ha namaz-i jum'ah-i Tehran,* vol. 2 (Tehran, 1982), 333.

29. *Ittila'at* (Sept. 31, 1981).

30. Shirazi, *Khatirat-i sallah-yi nabard,* 318.

31. *Kayhan* (June 12, 1982).

32. Ibid. (June 4, 1981).

33. Ibid. (June 26, 1981).

34. *I'timad* (Oct. 18, 2006).

35. Rafsanjani, *Karnamah va khatirat-i 1361,* 234.

36. Http://www.tabank.ir (Sept. 15, 2008).

37. *Kayhan* (June 23, 1982).

38. Ruhollah Khomeini, *Dar justuju-yi rah az kalam-i Imam: Daftar 2, jang va jihad* (Tehran, 1984), 142.

39. Chubin and Tripp, *Iran and Iraq at War,* 164.

40. IRNA (Aug. 22, 1986).

41. Hashemi Rafsanjani, *Dar maktab-i jum'ah: majmu'ah-i khuabah 'ha-yi namaz-i jum'ah-i Tehran,* vol. 2 (Tehran, 1982), 333; *Markaz-i Madarik-i Farhang-i Inqibal-i Islami* (Tehran, 1987), 80.

42. *Kayhan* (Apr. 2, 1985).

43. Chubin and Tripp, *Iran and Iraq at War,* 173.

44. R. K. Ramazani, "The Iran-Iraq War and the Persian Gulf Crisis," *Current History* 87(526) (1988): 61–64; Anthony Cordesman, "Lessons of the Iran-Iraq War: The First Round," *Armed Forces Journal International* 119(8) (1982): 32–46.

45. Joost R. Hitlermann, *A Poisonous Affair: America, Iraq, and the Gassing of Halabja* (New York: Cambridge University Press, 2007), 30–32.

46. Ibid, 37.

47. Ramazani, *Revolutionary Iran,* 70–86.

48. Hitlermann, *Poisonous Affair,* 75.

49. Joost Hitlermann, "Outsiders as Enablers: Consequences and Lessons from International Silence on Iraq's Use of Chemical Weapons during the Iran-Iraq War," in *Iran, Iraq, and the Legacies of War*, ed. Lawrence G. Potter and Gary G. Sick, 151–167 (New York: Palgrave Macmillan, 2004).

50. Bruce Jentleson, *With Friends like These: Reagan, Bush, and Saddam, 1982–1990* (New York: Norton, 1994), 46.

51. Lawrence Freedman, *A Choice of Enemies: America Confronts the Middle East* (New York: Public Affairs, 2008), 165.

52. George Shultz, *Turmoil and Triumph: My Years as Secretary of State* (New York: Scribner, 1993), 237.

53. Hitlermann, *Poisonous Affair*, 52.

54. Efraim Karsh, "From Ideological Zeal to Geopolitical Realism: The Islamic Republic and the Gulf," in *The Iran-Iraq War*, ed. Efrahim Karsh (New York: St. Martin's, 1989), 33; Geiling, *Religion and War in Revolutionary Iran*, 28; Ramazani, *Revolutionary Iran*, 233.

55. Rafsanjani, *Karnamah va khatirat-i 1361*, 317.

56. IRNA (May 31, 1986).

57. Ibid. (Nov. 10, 1986).

58. Eric Hooglund, "Reagan's Iran: Factions behind U.S. Policy in the Gulf," MERIP Middle East Report (March/April 1988): 31; Gary G. Sick, "Trial by Error: Reflections on the Iran-Iraq War," *Middle East Journal* (Spring 1989): 240.

59. *New York Times* (July 22, 1987). See also Shahram Chubin, "The Last Phase of the Iran-Iraq War: From Stalemate to Ceasefire," *Third World Quarterly* (April 1989); Nader Entessar, "Superpowers and Persian Gulf Security," *Third World Quarterly* (October 1988); Thomas McNaugher, "U.S. Policy and the Gulf War: A Question of Means," and Maxwell More Johnson, "The Role of U.S. Military Force in the Gulf War," in *The Persian Gulf War: Lessons for Strategy, Law, and Diplomacy*, ed. Christopher Joyner (New York: Greenwood, 1990).

60. Freedman, *Choice of Enemies*, 197.

61. Chubin and Tripp, *Iran and Iraq at War*, 177.

62. *Kayhan* (July 9, 1987).

63. *Tehran Times* (Oct, 15, 1987).

64. S. Taheri Shemirani, "The War of Cities," in Rajaee, ed., *Iran-Iraq War*, 32–41.

65. *Iran Times* (Sept. 25, 1987).

66. *Kayhan* (Oct. 28, 1987).

67. Ibid. (June 8, 1988).

68. Ibid. (July 19, 1988).

69. *Jumhuri-i Islami* (July 19, 1988).

70. Http://www.Aftabnews.ir (July 17, 2008).

71. Iranian Labor News Agency (Sept. 29, 2006).

72. In his recollection of the encounter between Khomeini and Rezai, Nateq-Nuri recounts the following: "When asked what he needed for victory after eight years of war, the commander of the guards answered 300 airplanes, 3,000 tanks, and seven more years are necessary. Also, the size of the army must be doubled while the size of the guards has to

increase by fivefold. The imam asked Prime Minister Mussavi what is the possibility of providing that budget. The answer was negative. Still, the commander of the guards expressed his readiness to continue the war. Imam declared these are mere slogans. For [the] sake of protecting Islam and the revolution, we have to drink the poison chalice." Ali Akbar Natiq-Nuri, *Khatirat-i Hujjat al-Islam va al-Muslimin Ali Akbar Natiq Nuri,* vol. 2 (Tehran, 2005), 68.

73. Http://www.rajanews.com/ (Mar. 10, 2008).

74. Iranian Labor News Agency (Sept. 29, 2006).

75. Kenneth Pollack, *The Persian Puzzle: The Conflict between Iran and America* (New York: Random House, 2004), 232.

76. *Ittila'at* (Sept. 7, 1988).

CHAPTER 5

1. For valuable studies on this period see Bahman Baktiari, *Parliamentary Politics in Revolutionary Iran: The Institutionalization of Factional Politics* (Gainesville: University of Florida Press, 1996), 53–145; Ali Ansari, *Iran, Islam, and Democracy: The Politics of Managing Change* (London: Chatham House, 2000), 52–110; Anoushiravan Ehteshami, *After Khomeini: The Iranian Second Republic* (London: Routledge, 1995), 100–119; David Menashri, *Post-revolutionary Politics in Iran: Religion, Society, and Power* (London: Frank Cass, 2001), 13–78; Asef Bayat, *Street Politics: Poor People's Movements in Iran* (New York: Columbia University Press, 1997); Mansoor Moaddel, *Class, Politics, and Ideology in the Iranian Revolution* (New York: Columbia University Press, 1993), 199–255; Mehdi Moslem, *Factional Politics in Post-Khomeini Iran* (Syracuse, N.Y.: Syracuse University Press, 2002), 82–252.

2. Cyrus Valili-Zad, "Conflict among the Ruling Revolutionary Elite in Iran," *Middle Eastern Studies* (July 1994): 618–631; Susan Siavoshi, "Factionalism and Iranian Politics: The Post-Khomeini Experience," *Iranian Studies* 25(3/4) (1992): 27–49.

3. *Kayhan* (Dec. 5, 1990).

4. Anoushiravan Ehteshami, "After Khomeini: The Structure of Power in the Iranian Second Republic," *Political Studies* 39(1) (1990): 148–157.

5. M. Hashem Pesaran and Massoud Karshenas, "Economic Reform and the Reconstruction of the Iranian Economy," *Middle East Journal* (Winter 1995): 89–111.

6. Ansari, *Iran, Islam, and Democracy,* 84–85.

7. Ali Gheissari and Vali Nasr, *Democracy in Iran: History and the Quest for Liberty* (New York: Oxford University Press, 2006), 105–127; Mehdi Mozaffari, "Changes in the Iranian Political System after Khomeini's Death," *Political Studies* 4(4) (1993): 611–617.

8. Jahangir Amuzegar, *Iran's Economy under the Islamic Republic* (London: Tauris, 1993), 300–350.

9. *Ittila'at* (Sept. 18, 1991).

10. *Salam* (Mar. 17, 1991).

11. Ibid. (Nov. 4, 1992).

12. Ruhollah Ramazani, "Iran's Foreign Policy: Both North and South," *Middle East Journal* (Summer 1992): 393–412; Shireen Hunter, *Iran after Khomeini* (New York: Prager,

1992), 101–126; Hooshang Amirahmadi, "A Vision for the Place of Iran in the New World," *Journal of Iranian Research and Analysis* (April 2004).

13. *Ittila'at* (Aug. 10, 1991).

14. Baktiari, *Parliamentary Politics in Revolutionary Iran*, 207.

15. *Jumhuri-i Islami* (Dec. 2, 1988).

16. IRNA (Mar. 28, 1989).

17. Ervand Abrahamian, *A History of Modern Iran* (New York: Cambridge University Press, 2008), 182–183.

18. *Kayhan* (June 11, 1989).

19. Roy Mottahedeh, "The Islamic Movement: The Case of Democratic Inclusion," *Contention* (Spring 1995): 107–127; Shireen Hunter, "Post-Khomeini Iran," *Foreign Affairs* (Winter 1989/1990): 134.

20. Saskia Gieling, "The Marja'iya in Iran and the Nomination of Khamenei in December 1994," *Middle Eastern Studies* (October 1997): 775–787; Ahmad Kazemi Moussavi, "A New Interpretation of the Theory of Vilayat-i Faqih," *Middle Eastern Studies* (January 1992): 101–107.

21. Menashri, *Post-revolutionary Politics in Iran*, 13–32; Mohsen Milani, "The Transformation of the Velayat-e Faqih Institution: From Khomeini to Khamenei," *Muslim World* (July–October 1992): 175–190.

22. *Jumhuri-i Islami* (Feb. 8, 1989).

23. Moslem, *Factional Politics in Post-Khomeini Iran*, 84.

24. *Jahan-i Islam* (May 24, 1993).

25. Ali Banuazizi, "Iran's Revolutionary Impasse: Political Factionalism and Societal Resistance," *Middle East Report* (November/December 1994): 5.

26. Ibid.

27. Farzin Sarabi, "The Post-Khomeini Era in Iran: The Elections of the Fourth Majlis," *Middle East Journal* (Winter 1994): 89–107.

28. Moslem, *Factional Politics in Post-Khomeini Iran*, 120.

29. *Salam* (Feb. 18, 1992).

30. Ibid. (July 30, 1993).

31. *Asr-i ma* (Aug. 18, 1994).

32. Moslem, *Factional Politics in Post-Khomeini Iran*, 84.

33. *Salam* (Feb. 18, 1992).

34. *Ittila'at* (Mar. 28, 1992).

35. *Arbar* (Apr. 11, 1992).

36. Sarabi, "Post-Khomeini Era in Iran"; Baktiari, *Parliamentary Politics in Post-Revolutionary Iran*, 217–235.

37. Ehteshami, *After Khomeini*, 101.

38. *Ittila'at* (Nov. 6, 1991).

39. Farhang Rajaee, *Islamism and Modernism: The Changing Discourse in Iran* (Austin: University of Texas, 2006), 163.

40. *Ittila'at* (Oct. 22, 1992).

41. *Iran* (Mar. 31, 1996).

42. *Iran Times* (July 25, 1992).

43. *Risalat* (June 9, 1992).

44. Ansari, *Iran, Islam, and Democracy,* 52–79.

45. H. E. Chehabi, "Religion and Politics in Iran: How Theocratic Is the Islamic Republic?" *Daedalus* (Summer 1991): 69–92.

CHAPTER 6

1. *IRNA* (Nov. 19, 1988).

2. Ibid. (Nov. 21, 1989).

3. Ahmed Hashim, *The Crisis of the Iranian State: Domestic, Foreign, and Security Policies in Post-Khomeini Iran* (New York: Oxford University Press, 1995), 33–36.

4. Anoushiravan Ehteshami, *After Khomeini: The Iranian Second Republic* (London: Routledge, 1995), 151.

5. Ali Akbar Vilayati, "The Persian Gulf: Problems of Security," *Iranian Journal of International Affairs* (Spring 1991): 1–3.

6. *Kayhan* (Sept. 27, 1989).

7. Christin Marschall, *Iran's Persian Gulf Policy: From Khomeini to Khatami* (London: Curzon, 2003), 149–179; David Menashri, *Post-revolutionary Politics in Iran: Religion, Society, and Power* (London: Frank Cass, 2001), 227–261.

8. Menashri, *Post-revolutionary Politics in Iran,* 239–242; Henner Furtig, *Iran's Rivalry with Saudi Arabia between the Gulf Wars* (London: Garnet and Ithaca, 2002), 23–91.

9. *Jumhuri-i Islami* (Nov. 15, 1990).

10. *Risalat* (May 16, 1991).

11. *Kayhan* (June 28, 1990).

12. Ibid. (July 6, 1989).

13. Marschall, *Iran's Persian Gulf Policy,* 121–142.

14. Shireen Hunter, *Iran after Khomeini* (New York: Praeger, 1992), 126–137; Shireen Hunter, "Post-Khomeini Iran," *Foreign Affairs* 68(5) (Winter 1989/1990): 133–149.

15. Marschall, *Iran's Persian Gulf Policy,* 106.

16. Bahman Baktiari, *Parliamentary Politics in Revolutionary Iran: The Institutionalization of Factional Politics* (Gainesville: University of Florida Press, 1996), 204–214.

17. *International Herald Tribune* (Jan. 21, 1991).

18. John Calabrese, *Revolutionary Horizons: Regional Foreign Policy in Post-Khomeini Iran* (London: Macmillan, 1994), 68.

19. Shaul Bakhash, "Iran: War Ended, Hostility Continued," in *Iraq's Road to War,* ed. Amatzia Baram and Barry Rubin, 220–221 (New York: St. Martin's, 1993).

20. Hooman Peimani, *Iran and the United States: The Rise of the West Asian Regional Grouping* (Westport, Conn.: Praeger, 1999), 72.

21. Marschall, *Iran's Persian Gulf Policy,* 107.

22. Bakhash, "Iran: War Ended, Hostility Continued," 214.

23. Menashri, *Post-revolutionary Politics in Iran,* 242.

24. *Jumhuri-i Islami* (Mar. 16, 1991).

25. This point has been emphasized by Louis J. Freeh in *My FBI: Bringing Down the Mafia, Investigating Bill Clinton, and Fighting the War on Terror,* with Howard Means (New York: St. Martin's, 2006). For an alternative view on the complexity of the Khobar Towers bombing as an operation conducted by al-Qaeda and its affiliates rather than Iran, see Yitzak Nakash, *Reaching for Power: The Shi'a in the Modern Arab World* (Princeton, N.J.: Princeton University Press, 2006), 131; Olivier Roy, *Globalized Islam: The Search for a New Ummah* (New York: Columbia University Press, 2004), 52.

26. In his enterprising reporting, Akbar Ganji has demonstrated that Rafsanjani was intimately linked to state terrorism in Iran; see Tarik-Khaneh-ye ashbah (Tehran, 1999).

27. For an incisive assessment of European-Iranian relations see Shireen Hunter, *Iran and the World: Continuity in a Revolutionary Decade* (Bloomington: Indiana University Press, 1990), 139–157; Adam Tarock, "Iran's Foreign Policy since 1990: Pragmatism Supersedes Islamic Ideology" (New York: Nova Science, 1999), 77–96; Fred Halliday, "An Elusive Normalization: Western Europe and the Iranian Revolution," *Middle East Journal* (Spring 1994): 309–326.

28. *The Cambridge History of Iran,* vol. 7, *From Nader Shah to the Islamic Republic,* ed. P. Avery, G. R. G. Hambly, and C. Melville, 219–220 (New York: Cambridge University Press, 1991).

29. For important accounts of the coup see Stephen Kinzer, *All the Shah's Men: An American Coup and the Roots of Middle East Terror* (Hoboken, N.J.: John Wiley and Sons, 2003); Mark Gasiorowski, "The 1953 Coup d'état in Iran," *International Journal of Middle Eastern Studies* (August 1987): 261–286; Mavin Zonis, *Majestic Failure: The Fall of the Shah* (Chicago: University of Chicago Press, 1991), 100–114.

30. Anthony Parson, "Iran and Western Europe," *Middle East Journal* (Spring 1989): 220.

31. Hunter, *Iran and the World,* 148.

32. Eric Rouleau, "European Union and French Views of the Islamic Republic," in *Twenty Years of Islamic Revolution: Political and Social Transitions in Iran since 1979,* ed. Eric Hooglund, 143–147 (Syracuse, N.Y.: Syracuse University Press, 2002).

33. Adam Tarock, "Iran–Western Europe Relations on the Mend," *British Journal of Middle Eastern Studies* (Winter 1999): 47–48; Halliday, "Elusive Normalization," 313.

34. *Kayhan* (July 24, 1983).

35. For an insider's account of Iran's approach to Europe see Muhammad Javad Larijani, *Mozakerah dar Landon* (Tehran, 1997).

36. Muhammad Saidabadi, "Iran's European Relations since 1979," in *Iran and Eurasia,* ed. Ali Mohammadi and Anoushiravan Ehteshami, 64–76 (Reading, UK: Ithaca, 2000), 59–80.

37. *Reuters* (June 1, 1995).

38. Halliday, "Elusive Normalization," 322.

39. Rouleau, "European Union and French Views of the Islamic Republic," 149.

40. *Independent* (Oct. 13, 1993).

41. Charles Lane, "Germany's New Ostpolitik," *Foreign Affairs* (November/December 1995): 79–82.

42. *Financial Times* (Feb. 8, 1993); *Middle East Economic Digest* (Feb. 19, 1993).

43. Hunter, *Iran and the World,* 79–98; Martin Sicker, *The Bear and the Lion: Soviet Imperialism in Iran* (New York: Praeger, 1988), 45–60; Tarock, *Iran's Foreign Policy since 1990,* 57–77.

44. Shahroguh Akhavi, "Soviet Perceptions of the Iranian Revolution," *Iranian Studies* (Winter 1989): 3–29; Aryeh Y. Yodfat, *The Soviet Union and Revolutionary Iran* (New York: St. Martin's, 1984), 45–70; Hunter, *Iran and the World,* 83–86.

45. Yodfat, *Soviet Union and Revolutionary Iran,* 65–66.

46. Alvin Rubinstein, "The Soviet Union and Iran under Khomeini," *International Affairs* (Fall 1980): 606.

47. Ibid., 610–611; Robert O. Freedman, "Moscow and the Iraqi Invasion of Kuwait," in *The Middle East after Iraq's Invasion of Kuwait,* ed. Robert O. Freedman (Gainesville: University of Florida Press, 1993), 74–136.

48. Robert O. Freedman, "Gorbachev, Iran, and the Iran-Iraq War," in *Neither East nor West: Iran, the Soviet Union, and the United States,* ed. Nikki R. Keddie and Mark Gasiorowski (New Haven, Conn.: Yale University Press, 1990), 115–144.

49. Ervand Abrahamian, *Tortured Confessions: Prisons and Public Recantations in Modern Iran* (Berkeley: University of California Press, 1999), 177–290; Maziar Behrooz, *Rebels With a Cause: The Failure of the Left in Iran* (London: Tauris, 2000), 124–135.

50. Yodfat, *Soviet Union and Revolutionary Iran,* 143.

51. *Kayhan* (Jan. 9, 1989).

52. Richard Hermann, "The Role of Iran in Soviet Perceptions and Policy," in Keddie and Gasiorowski, eds., *Neither East nor West,* 70–74; Shireen Hunter, "Iran from the August 1988 Cease-fire to the April 1992 Majlis Elections," in Freedman, ed., *Middle East after Iraq's Invasion of Kuwait,* 186.

53. Eugene Rumer, *Dangerous Drift: Russia's Middle East Policy* (Washington, D.C.: Washington Institute for Near East Policy, 2000), 15–31; Robert O. Freedman, "Russia and Iran: A Tactical Alliance," *SAIS Review* (Summer/Fall 1997): 3–5, and "Russian Policy toward the Middle East: The Yeltsin Legacy and the Putin Challenge," *Middle East Journal* (Winter 2001): 63–71.

54. *Kayhan* (Mar. 9, 1996).

55. Ali Jalali, "The Strategic Partnership of Russia and Iran," *Parameters* (Winter 2000/2001): 103–107; Robert Einhorn and Gary Samore, "Ending Russian Assistance to Iran's Nuclear Bomb," *Survival* (Summer 2002): 51–70.

56. Lrszek Buszynski, "Russia and the West: Toward Renewed Geopolitical Rivalry," *Survival* (Summer 1995): 104–125; Adam Tarock, "Iran and Russia in Strategic Alliance," *Third World Quarterly* 18(2) (1997): 209–212.

57. Hanna Yousif Freij, "State Interests vs. the Umma: Iranian Policy in Central Asia," *Middle East Journal* (Winter 1996): 71–83; Jalali, "Strategic Partnership of Russia and Iran," 101–103.

58. Calabrese, *Revolutionary Horizons,* 80.

59. *Tehran Times* (Aug. 18, 1992); *Hamshahri* (Jan. 28, 1993); *Ittila'at* (Feb. 18, 1992).

60. A. William Samii, "Iran and Chechnya: Realpolitik at Work," *Middle East Policy* (March 2001): 48–57; Freedman, "Russian Policy toward the Middle East," 71–72.

61. Richard Hermann, "Russian Policy in the Middle East: Strategic Change and Tactical Contradictions," *Middle East Journal* (Summer 1994): 455–474; Vitaly Naumkin, "The Russian-Iranian Relations: Present Status and Prospects for the Future," *Perceptions* (March/May 1998): 67–85.

62. Ayatollah Ruhollah Khomeini, *On Issues Related to the Struggle of the Muslim People of Iran, Speeches of January 1978–January 1980* (San Francisco, 1980).

63. For the best account of Iran's relations with China see John Garver, *China and Iran: Ancient Partners in a Post-imperial World* (Seattle: University of Washington Press, 2006).

64. Ibid., 64.

65. Ibid., 65.

66. Bates Gill, *Chinese Arms Transfers: Purposes, Patterns, and Prospects in the New World Order* (London: Praeger, 1992), 96–99; Steve Yetiv and Chunlong Lu, "China, Global Energy, and the Middle East," *Middle East Journal* (Spring 2007): 210–215.

67. *Strategic Survey, 1982–1983* (London: International Institute for Strategic Studies, 1983), 70–82; *Facts on File,* 1987, 420; *Middle East Economic Digest* (Aug. 22, 1987): 11.

68. *Christian Science Monitor* (Aug. 16, 1990).

69. *Kayhan* (July 5, 1985).

70. Garver, *China and Iran,* 79.

71. *Kayhan* (Aug. 20, 1988).

72. IRNA (May 10, 1990).

73. Ibid. (May 11, 1989).

CHAPTER 7

1. Agence France-Presse (AFP) (Nov. 2, 1994).

2. Ibid.

3. Ali Khamenei, *Farhang va tahajum-i farhangi, bargiriftah az sukhanan-i maqam-i mu'azzam-i rahbari, Hazrat-i Ayatollah Khamenei* (Tehran, 1996), 4.

4. IRNA (May 19, 1997).

5. Ibid. (Dec. 20, 1996).

6. *Ittila'at* (Nov. 23, 1990).

7. Ali Akbar Hashemi Rafsanjani, *Isra'il va Quds-i Aziz* (Qum, 1986), 43.

8. An example of such language can be found in Khamenei's sermon; *Ittila'at* (May 20, 1979).

9. *Arzishha* (Jan. 18, 1999).

10. David Menashri, *Post-revolutionary Politics in Iran: Religion, Society, and Power* (London: Frank Cass, 2001), 261–301; Shaul Bakhash, "Iran's Relations with Israel, Syria, and Lebanon," in *Iran at Crossroads: Global Relations in a Turbulent Decade,* ed. Miron Rezun, 117–123 (Boulder, Colo.: Westview, 1990); Eric Hooglund, "Iranian Views of the Arab-Israeli Conflict," *Journal of Palestine Studies* 25, 1 (Autumn 1995): 86–95; Nader Entessar, "Israel and Iran's National Security," *Journal of South Asian and Middle Eastern Studies* (Summer 2004), 4–13.

11. *Ittila'at* (Apr. 26, 1990).

12. *Kayhan* (Feb. 1, 1993).

13. *Salam* (July 27 1994).

14. Muhammad Faksh, "The Shi'a Community of Lebanon: A New Assertive Political Force," *Journal of South Asian and Middle Eastern Studies* 14, 3 (Spring 1991): 33–56.

15. A. Nizar Hamzeh and R. Hrair Dekmejian, "The Islamic Spectrum of Lebanese Politics," *Journal of South Asian and Middle Eastern Studies* (Spring 1993): 38–39; Augustus Richard Norton, *Hezbollah: A Short History* (Princeton, N.J.: Princeton University Press, 2007), 98.

16. *New York Times* (Aug. 15, 1989).

17. Giandomenico Picco, *Man without a Gun: One Diplomat's Secret Struggle to Free the Hostages, Fight Terrorism, and End a War* (New York: Times Books, 1999), 12–123.

18. *Washington Post* (Dec. 6, 1991).

19. H. E. Chehabi, "Iran and Lebanon after Khomeini," in *Distant Relations: Iran and Lebanon in the Last 500 Years,* ed. H. E. Chehabi, 289–293 (London: Tauris, 2006).

20. *Iran Times* (Sept. 21, 1990).

21. Dennis Ross, *The Missing Peace: The Inside Story of the Fight for Middle East Peace* (New York: Farrar, Straus, and Giroux, 2004), 79–88.

22. Kenneth Pollack, *The Persian Puzzle: The Conflict between Iran and America* (New York: Random House, 2004), 265–270; Ahmed Hashim, *The Crisis of the Iranian State: Domestic, Foreign, and Security Policies in Post-Khomeini Iran* (New York: Oxford University Press, 1995), 45–49.

23. *Columbus Dispatch* (Nov. 10, 1992).

24. *Ittila'at* (Oct. 31, 1991).

25. Daniel Byman, *Deadly Connections: States That Sponsor Terrorism* (New York: Cambridge University Press, 2006), 85; Richard Clarke, *Against All Enemies: Inside America's War on Terror* (New York: Free Press, 2004), 103; U.S. Department of State, *Patterns of Global Terrorism 1993,* U.S. Department of State, 1994.

26. *Kayhan International* (Dec. 14, 1993).

27. *New York Times* (Feb. 1, 1993).

28. *Kayhan* (Feb. 1, 1993).

29. *Risalat* (Nov. 4, 1992).

30. Anthony Lake, "Confronting Backlash States," *Foreign Affairs* (March/April 1994): 45–55.

31. Menashri, *Post-revolutionary Politics in Iran,* 199.

32. Warren Christopher, "America's Leadership, America's Opportunity," *Foreign Policy* (Spring 1995), 5–27.

33. Martin Indyk, "The Clinton Administration's Approach to the Middle East," Soref Symposium, Washington Institute for Near East Policy, May 18, 1993.

34. F. Gregory Gause, "The Illogic of Dual Containment," *Foreign Affairs* (March/April 1994); Zbigniew Brezezinski, Brent Scowcroft, and Richard Murphy, "Differentiated Containment," *Foreign Affairs* (May/June 1997): 20–30.

35. *New York Times* (July 5, 1994); *Risalat* (Sept. 14, 1993).

36. Trita Parsi, *Treacherous Alliance: The Secret Dealings of Israel, Iran, and the United States* (New Haven, Conn.: Yale University Press, 2007), 175.

37. Elie Rekhess, "The Iranian Impact on the Islamic Jihad Movement in the Gaza Strip," in *The Iranian Revolution and the Muslim World,* ed. David Menashri (Boulder, Colo.: Westview, 1991), 189–206.

38. *Jumhuri-i Islami* (Apr. 4, 1999).

39. Ibid. (Nov. 5, 1996).

40. Parsi, *Treacherous Alliance*, 192.

41. Mehrad Valibeigi, "U.S.-Iranian Trade Relations after the Revolution," in *Post-revolutionary Iran*, ed. Hooshang Amirahmadi and Manoucher Parvin (Boulder, Colo.: Westview, 1988), 210–224; Robert Snyder, "Explaining the Iranian Revolution's Hostility toward the United States," *Journal of South Asian and Middle Eastern Studies* (Spring 1994): 19–31.

42. Ali Ansari, *Confronting Iran: The Failure of American Foreign Policy and the Next Great Crisis in the Middle East* (New York: Basic Books, 2006), 140–141; Parsi, *Treacherous Alliance*, 186–187.

43. *New York Times* (May 10, 1995).

44. Menashri, *Post-revolutionary Politics in Iran*, 199.

45. Ibid.

46. *New York Times* (Jan. 26, 1996).

CHAPTER 8

1. For valuable studies on this period see Bahman Baktiari, *Parliamentary Politics in Revolutionary Iran: The Institutionalization of Factional Politics* (Gainesville: University Press of Florida, 1996); Ali Ansari, *Iran, Islam, and Democracy: The Politics of Managing Change* (London: Chatham House, 2000), 52–110; Anoushiravan Ehteshami, *After Khomeini: The Iranian Second Republic* (London: Routledge, 1995); David Menashri, *Post-revolutionary Politics in Iran: Religion, Society, and Power* (London: Frank Cass, 2001), 13–78; Asef Bayat, *Street Politics: Poor People's Movements in Iran* (New York: Columbia University Press, 1993); Mansoor Moaddel, *Politics, Class, and Ideology in the Iranian Revolution* (New York: Columbia University Press, 1993), 199–255; Asef Bayat, *Making Islam Democratic: Social Movements and the Post-Islamist Turn* (Stanford: Stanford University Press, 2007), 106–136; Farhang Rajaee, *Islamism and Modernism: The Changing Discourse in Iran* (Austin: University of Texas Press, 2007), 193–237.

2. Abdul Karim Soroush, *Idiuluzhi-i Shaytani* (Tehran, 1996), 39.

3. Rajaee, *Islamism and Modernism*, 227.

4. Geneive Abdo, "Rethinking the Islamic Republic: A Conversation with Ayatollah Husayn Ali Montazeri," *Middle East Journal* 55 (Winter 2001): 9–24; Rajaee, *Islamism and Modernism*, 208–214.

5. Mohsen Kadivar, *Hukumat-i valayi* (Tehran, 1999), 237.

6. Rajaee, *Islamism and Modernism*, 219.

7. Ali Gheissari and Vali Nasr, *Democracy in Iran: History and the Quest for Liberty* (New York: Oxford University Press, 2006), 133–137.

8. Menashri, *Post-revolutionary Politics in Iran*, 83.

9. *Salam* (Apr. 28, 1997).

10. *Risalat* (May 21, 1997).

11. *Hamshahri* (Mar. 13, 1997).

12. *Salam* (Apr. 8, 1997).

13. Akbar Ganji, "The Leadership, Direct Elections with Limited Terms, and Continued Supervision," *Rah-e No* (September 1999).

14. Hasan Yousefi Ashkevari, "Seminary and the State: Twenty Years after the Merger," *Nishat* (May 1999): 6; Ziba Mir-Hosseini and Richard Tapper, *Islam and Democracy in Iran: Eshkevari and the Quest for Reform* (London: Tauris, 2006), 101–136.

15. Ansari, *Iran, Islam, and Democracy*, 131.

16. Menashri, *Post-revolutionary Politics in Iran*, 95.

17. *Risalat* (July 24, 1998).

18. *Khurdad* (Sept. 27, 1999).

19. *Quds* (Nov. 17, 1997).

20. *Hambastegi* (Mar. 17, 2001).

21. Bayat, *Making Islam Democratic*, 115–122; Mehdi Moslem, *Factional Politics in Post-Khomeini Iran* (Syracuse, N.Y.: Syracuse University Press, 2002), 257–266; Gheissari and Nasr, *Democracy in Iran*, 136–142.

22. Said Amir Arjomand, "The Rise and Fall of President Khatami and the Reform Movement in Iran," *Constellations* (Winter 2005): 510.

23. Gholam Khibany, "The Iranian Press, State, and Civil Society," in *Media, Culture, and Society in Iran: Living with Globalization and the Islamic State*, ed. Mehdi Semati (London: Routledge, 2008), 17–36.

24. Bayat, *Making Islam Democratic*, 109.

25. Ibid.

26. Ansari, *Iran, Islam, and Democracy*, 141.

27. Islamic Republic News Agency (IRNA) (May 12, 2000).

28. *Jame'eh* (Apr. 30, 1998).

29. Abullah Nuri, *Shawkaran-i islah: difa'iyat-i Abdullah Nuri dar dadagh-i vizhah-i ruhaniyat* (Tehran 2000), 72.

30. Wilfried Buchta, *Who Rules Iran? The Structure of Power in the Islamic Republic* (Washington, D.C.: Washington Institute for Near East Policy, 2000), 131.

31. For an important investigative account of the serial killings see Akbar Ganji, *Alijanab-i surkhpush va alijanaban-i khakistari: asib shina'i guzAar bih dawtai dimukratik-i tawsi'ah-gara* (Tehran 2000), as well as *Tarikkane-ye Asbah* (Tehran, 2002).

32. Akbar Ganji, *Dimukratisian dar barabar-i Sultanistan*, a web-based publication.

33. *Jumhuri-yi Islami* (July 9, 1999).

34. Ali Akbar Natiq-Nuri, *Khatirat-i Hujjat al-Islam Ali Natiq-Nuri*, vol. 2 (Tehran, 2005), 262, 371.

35. Said Amir Arjomand, "The Rise and Fall of President Khatami and the Reform Movement in Iran," *Constellations* (Fall 2005): 502–520; A. William Samii, "Iran's Guardians Council as an Obstacle to Democracy," *Middle East Journal* (Autumn 2001): 643–662.

36. Ruhollah Ramazani, "The Shifting Premise of Iran's Foreign Policy: Towards a Democratic Peace?" *Middle East Journal* (Spring 1998): 4.

37. Muhammad Khatami, *Az Dunya-yi Shahr* (Tehran 1997), 14–15.

38. IRNA (Dec. 11, 1997).

39. Menashri, *Post-revolutionary Politics in Iran*, 130.

40. *Tehran Times* (Aug. 15, 1998).

41. Menashri, *Post-revolutionary Politics in Iran*, 244.

42. Gawdat Bahgat, "Iranian-Saudi Rapprochement: Prospects and Implications," *World Affairs* (Winter 2000): 112.

43. Gwen Okruhlik, "Saudi Arabian–Iranian Relations: External Rapprochement and Internal Consolidation," *Middle East Policy* (Summer 2003): 113–125.

44. IRNA (May 20, 1999).

45. Adam Tarock, "Iran–Western Europe Relations on the Mend," *British Journal of Middle Eastern Studies* (May 1999): 51.

46. Trita Parsi, *Treacherous Alliance: The Secret Dealings of Israel, Iran, and the United States* (New Haven, Conn.: Yale University Press, 2007), 204.

47. Interview with Muhammad Khatami, CNN (Jan. 8, 1998).

48. Ibid.

49. *Iran News* (Aug. 5, 1997).

50. *New York Times* (Jan. 3, 1998).

51. *Jumhuri-yi Islami* (Jan. 17, 1998).

52. *Kayhan* (Jan. 23, 1998).

53. Associated Press (June 8, 1998).

54. *New York Times* (June 18, 1998).

55. For an assessment of the Clinton administration's Iran policy see Ali Ansari, *Confronting Iran: The Failure of American Foreign Policy and the Next Great Crisis in the Middle East* (New York: Basic Books, 2006), 147–163; Kenneth Pollack, *The Persian Puzzle: The Conflict between Iran and America* (New York: Random House, 2004), 312–342.

56. Pollack, *Persian Puzzle*, xxv.

57. IRNA (Mar. 5, 2000).

58. Ibid. (Mar. 25, 2000).

59. Fakhreddin Azimi, *The Quest for Democracy in Iran: A Century of Struggle against Authoritarian Rule* (Cambridge, Mass.: Harvard University Press, 2008), 396.

CHAPTER 9

1. Islamic Republic News Agency (IRNA) (Sept. 28, 2001).

2. Ali Ansari, *Confronting Iran: The Failure of American Foreign Policy and the Next Great Crisis in the Middle East* (New York: Basic Books, 2006), 181.

3. Associated Press (Nov. 3, 2001).

4. Agence France-Presse (AFP) (Oct. 14, 2001).

5. Bruce Cummings, Ervand Abrahamian, and Moshe Ma'oz, *Inventing the Axis of Evil: The Truth about North Korea, Iran, and Syria* (New York: New Press, 2004), 196.

6. Condoleezza Rice, "Promoting the National Interest," *Foreign Affairs* (January/ February 2000): 45–62.

7. For contrasting views of the Bush foreign policy see Michael Oren, *Power, Faith, and Fantasy: America in the Middle East, 1776 to the Present* (New York: Norton, 2007), 580–

604; Lawrence Freedman, *A Choice of Enemies: America Confronts the Middle East* (New York: Public Affairs, 2008), 373–504.

8. *Washington Post* (Dec. 10, 2005).

9. Robert Jervis, "Understanding the Bush Doctrine," *Political Science Quarterly* (Fall 2003): 368.

10. Jack Snyder, "Imperial Temptations," *National Interest* (Spring 2003): 29–40; Barry Posen, "The Struggle against Terrorism: Grand Strategy, Strategy, and Tactics," *International Security* (Winter 2001–2002): 39–55; Jonathan Monten, "The Roots of the Bush Doctrine: Power, Nationalism, and Democracy Promotion in U.S. Strategy," *International Security* (Spring 2005): 112–156.

11. John Gaddis, "A Grand Strategy of Transformation," *Foreign Policy* (November/December 2002): 50–57; James Chace, "Imperial America and the Common Interest," *World Policy Journal* (Spring 2002): 1–9; Charles Krauthammer, "The Unipolar Moment Revisited," *National Interest* (Winter 2002–2003): 5–17; Walter Lafeber, "The Bush Doctrine," *Diplomatic History* (Fall 2002): 543–558; Colin Dueck, *Reluctant Crusaders: Power, Culture, and Change in American Grand Strategy* (Princeton, N.J.: Princeton University Press, 2006), 147–171.

12. Ivo Daalder and James Lindsay, *America Unbound: The Bush Revolution in Foreign Policy* (Washington, D.C.: Brookings Institution, 2003), 123.

13. Ibid.

14. Robert Litwak, "The New Calculus of Pre-emption," *Survival* (Winter 2002): 53–79; David Hendrickson, "Toward Universal Empire," *World Policy Journal* (Fall 2002): 1–10.

15. Peter Steinfels, *The Neoconservatives: The Men Who Are Changing America's Politics* (New York: Simon and Schuster, 1979); Andrew Bacevich, *The New American Militarism: How Americans Are Seduced by War* (New York: Oxford University Press, 2005); Julie Kosterlitz, "The Neoconservative Moment," *National Journal* (May 2003): 1540–1546.

16. Bernard Lewis, "Time for Toppling," *Wall Street Journal* (Sept. 28, 2002).

17. Robert Jervis, "Why the Bush Doctrine Cannot Be Sustained," *Political Science Quarterly* (Fall 2005): 351–377; G. John Ikenberrry, "America's Imperial Ambitions: The Lure of Preemption," *Foreign Affairs* (September/October 2002): 44–60.

18. Robert Litwak, *Regime Change: U.S. Strategy through the Prism of 9/11* (Baltimore: Johns Hopkins University Press, 2007), 217–244.

19. *Al-Sharq al-Awsat* (Oct. 29, 2001).

20. IRNA (Dec. 7, 2001).

21. BBC (Feb. 5, 2002).

22. IRNA (Feb. 18, 2002).

23. President Bush, State of the Union address, Jan. 29, 2002 (www.whitehouse.gov/news/release/2002).

24. Bob Woodward, *Plan of Attack* (New York: Simon and Schuster, 2004), 86–88.

25. Kenneth Pollack, *The Persian Puzzle: The Conflict between Iran and America* (New York: Random House, 2004), 351.

26. Associated Press (Feb. 16, 2002).

27. U.S. Department of State press release, Aug. 2, 2002.

28. AFP (Feb. 1, 2002).

29. Ibid. (Feb. 3, 2002).

30. Reuters (Feb. 14, 2002).

31. Iranian Student News Agency (ISNA) (May 11, 2002).

32. AFP (Mar. 14, 2002).

33. Ibid. (Feb. 23, 2002).

34. *Financial Times* (Nov. 2, 2002).

35. Reuters (Apr. 19, 2003).

36. IRNA (Apr. 16, 2003).

37. Reuters (May 14, 2003).

38. *New York Times* (Apr. 14, 2003).

39. AFP (Apr. 14, 2003).

40. *Financial Times* (May 2, 2003).

41. Trita Parsi, *Treacherous Alliance: The Secret Dealings of Israel, Iran, and the United States* (New Haven, Conn.: Yale University Press, 2007), 341–346.

42. *New York Times* (May 14 and 23, 2003).

CHAPTER 10

1. Farhang Rajaee, *Islamism and Modernism: The Changing Discourse of Iran* (Austin: University of Texas Press, 2007), 191–202.

2. *Financial Times* (July 10, 2001).

3. Rajaee, *Islamism and Modernism*, 239.

4. Mebah-Yazdi's revolutionary credentials have come under question by some politicians, most notably Ali Akbar Mohtashamipur, who even criticized him for his "Taliban" ideology (http://www.Fardanews.com, June 5, 2008).

5. BBC Monitoring Service (Oct. 25, 2002).

6. *Risalat* (Mar. 29, 2001).

7. A. W. Samii, "Haqqani: Theology and Thought," RFE/RL, Iran Report 4, no. 17 (Apr. 30, 2001).

8. Anoushiravan Ehteshami and Mahjoob Zweiri, *Iran and the Rise of Its Neo-Conservatives: The Politics of Tehran's Silent Revolution* (London: Tauris, 2007), 36.

9. Http://www.isna.ir (Mar. 3, 2003).

10. *Christian Science Monitor* (Aug. 13, 2003).

11. Agence France-Presse (AFP) (May 7, 2002).

12. IRNA (February 5, 2004).

13. Reuters (May 15, 2003).

14. *Jumhuri-yi Islami* (Feb. 25, 2004).

15. *Financial Times* (Feb. 3, 2004).

16. For useful studies on Ahmadinejad see Ali Ansari, *Iran under Ahmadinejad: The Politics of Confrontation* (London: Routledge, 2007); Kasra Naji, *Ahmadinejad: The Secret*

History of Iran's Radical Leader (London: Tauris, 2008); Ehteshami and Zweiri, *Iran and the Rise of Its Neoconservatives.*

17. Ansari, *Iran under Ahmadinejad,* 29.

18. Fars New Agency (June 21, 2005).

19. Vali Nasr, "The Conservative Wave Rolls On," *Journal of Democracy* (2005): 9–22; Ali Gheissari and Vali Nasr, "Conservative Consolidation in Iran," *Survival* (Summer 2005): 175–190.

20. *Sharq* (Feb. 26, 2005).

21. *Sharif News* (May 8, 2005).

22. *Sharq* (July 14, 2005).

23. *Aftab-i Yazd* (June 22, 2005); *Iran* (Dec. 22, 2005).

24. Naji, *Ahmadinejad,* 68–72.

25. Kaveh Ehsani, "Iran's Presidential Run-off: The Long View," *Middle East Report* (June 24, 2005); *Sharq* (June 26, 2005).

26. IRNA (Aug. 20, 2005).

CHAPTER 11

1. *Kayhan* (Nov. 25, 2007).

2. IRNA (Aug. 8, 2008).

3. *Farhang-i Ashti* (Feb. 28, 2006).

4. *New York Times* (June 26, 2005).

5. Ray Takeyh, "Time for Détente," *Foreign Affairs* (March/April 2007): 26.

6. Islamic Student News Agency (Jan. 4, 2008).

7. For important studies on Iran's nuclear designs see Shaharam Chubin, *Iran's Nuclear Ambitions* (Washington, D.C.: Carnegie Endowment for International Peace, 2006); Kasra Naji, *Ahmadinejad: The Secret History of Iran's Radical Leader* (London: Tauris, 2008), 111–139; Jahangir Amuzegar, "Nuclear Iran: Perils and Prospects," *Middle East Policy* (Summer 2006): 90–112.

8. Mustafa Kibaroglu, "Iran's Nuclear Ambitions from a Historical Perspective and the Attitude of the West," *Middle Eastern Studies* 43(2) (March 2007): 225.

9. Asadollah Alam, *The Shah and I: The Confidential Diary of Iran's Royal Court, 1968–1977* (London: Tauris, 2008), 453.

10. *Wall Street Journal* (June 25, 2004).

11. *News Statesman* (Sept. 11, 2008).

12. *I'timad* (Apr. 8, 2008).

13. Gordon Corera, *Shopping for Bombs: Nuclear Proliferation, Global Insecurity, and the Rise and Fall of the A. Q. Khan Network* (New York: Oxford University Press, 2006), 59–86.

14. For a technical assessment of Iran's nuclear program see Mark Fitzpatrick, "Assessing Iran's Nuclear Programme," *Survival* (Autumn 2006): 5–26.

15. Etel Solingen, *Nuclear Logics: Contrasting Paths in East Asia and the Middle East* (Princeton, N.J.: Princeton University Press, 2007), 165–166.

16. Etel Solingen, *Nuclear Logics: Contrasting Paths in East Asia and the Middle East* (Princeton, N.J.: Princeton University Press, 2007), 175.

17. Mehr News Agency (Mar. 12, 2005).

18. Sean Smeland, "Countering Iranian Nukes: A European Strategy," *Nonproliferation Review* (Spring 2004): 40–72.

19. IRNA (June 20, 2005).

20. Islamic Republic Student New Agency (Feb. 6, 2006); *Keyhan* (Feb. 12, 2006).

21. *Farhang-i Ashti* (Nov. 30, 2005).

22. Ray Takeyh, "A Profile in Defiance: Being Mahmoud Ahmadinejad," *National Interest* (Spring 2006): 16.

23. IRNA (Aug. 23, 2008).

24. Http://www.baztab.com (Feb. 18, 2007).

25. *Jumhuri-yi Islami* (Sept. 29, 2005).

26. Yitzhak Nakash, *Reaching for Power: The Shi'a in the Modern Arab World* (Princeton, N.J.: Princeton University Press, 2006), 72–99; Vali Nasr, *The Shia Revival: How Conflicts within Islam Will Shape the Future* (New York: Norton, 2006), 185–211; Ali Allawi, *The Occupation of Iraq: Winning the War, Losing the Peace* (New Haven, Conn.: Yale University Press, 2007); Fouad Ajami, *The Foreigner's Gift: The Americans, the Arabs, and the Iraqis in Iraq* (New York: Free Press, 2006).

27. Ahmad al-Rahim, "The Sistani Factor," *Journal of Democracy* (July 2005): 50–53; Rod Nordland and Babak Dehghnapisheh, "What Sistani Wants," *Newsweek* (Feb. 14, 2005); Allawi, *Occupation of Iraq*, 204–219.

28. *New York Times* (Oct. 2, 2003); *Washington Post* (June 30, 2003); George Packer, "Testing Ground: In Shiite South, Islamists and Secularists Struggle over Iraq's Future," *New Yorker* (Feb. 28, 2005); *New York Times* (Jan. 31, 2005); Larry Diamond, "What Went Wrong in Iraq," *Foreign Affairs* (September/October 2004): 34–56.

29. Nir Rosen, "Anatomy of a Civil War: Iraq's Descent into Chaos," *Boston Review* (November/December 2006); Ahmed Hashim, "Iraq's Chaos: Why the Insurgency Won't Go Away," *Boston Review* (October/November 2004); also *Insurgency and Counter-insurgency in Iraq* (Ithaca, N.Y.: Cornell University Press, 2006).

30. International Crisis Group, *Iran in Iraq: How Much Influence?* Middle East Report no. 38 (March 21, 2005); Kayhan Barzegar, "Understanding the Roots of Iranian Foreign Policy in the New Iraq," *Middle East Policy* (Summer 2005): 49–57; Anoushiravan Ehteshami, "Iran's International Posture after the Fall of Baghdad," *Middle East Journal* (Spring 2004): 179–194, and "Iran-Iraq Relations after Saddam," *Washington Quarterly* (Autumn 2003): 115–129.

31. For instance, see Prince Saud al-Faisal, "The Fight against Extremism and the Search for Peace," *Council on Foreign Relations* (Sept. 7, 2005).

32. *Kayhan* (July 29, 2007).

33. Reuters (April 28, 2003).

34. IRNA (Feb. 5, 2005).

35. Reuters (July 10, 2006).

36. Http://www.baztab.com (Dec. 26, 2006).

37. IRNA (Aug. 28, 2007).

38. *Financial Times* (May 10, 2007).

39. Ali Ansari, *Iran under Ahmadinejad: The Politics of Confrontation* (London: International Institute for Strategic Studies, 2008), 51–53; Naji, *Ahmadinejad,* 139–149.

40. IRNA (Dec. 8, 2005).

41. Ibid. (Jan. 3, 2002).

42. Agence France-Presse (AFP) (Mar. 11, 2006).

43. Http://www.roozonline.com (Feb. 22, 2005).

44. Menachem Klein, "Hamas in Power," *Middle East Journal* (Summer 2007): 442–459.

45. *Jumhuri-yi Islami* (July 7, 2006).

46. Lara Deeb, "Deconstructing a 'Hizbullah Stronghold,'" and Reinoud Leenders, "How the Rebel Regained His Cause: Hizbullah and the Sixth Arab-Israeli War," and Robert Blecher, "Will We Win?: Convergence and Israel's Latest Lebanon War," all available at http://web.mit.edu/.

47. Http://www.farsnews.com (Aug. 16, 2006).

48. *I'timad* (Oct. 28, 2005).

49. *Jumhuri-yi Islami* (Oct. 12, 2007).

AFTERWORD

1. Whitehouse. gov, March 21, 2009.

2. IRNA, June 13, 2009.

Index